Sanctity and Female Authorship

I0593010

Birgitta of Sweden (Birgitta Birgersdotter, 1302/03–1373) and her younger contemporary Catherine of Siena (Caterina Benincasa, 1347–1380) form the most powerful and influential female duo in European history. Both enjoyed saintly reputations in life while acting as the charismatic leaders of a considerable group of followers consisting of clergy as well as mighty secular men and women. They are also among the very few women of the Trecento to leave a substantial body of written work, which was widely disseminated in their original languages and in translations. Copies of Birgitta's *Liber celestis revelacionum* (The Heavenly Book of Revelations) and compilations of Catherine's letters (*Le lettere*) and prayers (*Le orazioni*) and her theological work *Il Dialogo della Divina Provvidenza* (The Dialogue) found their way into monastic, royal, and humanist libraries all over Europe. After their deaths, Birgitta's and Catherine's respective groups of supporters sought to have them formally canonized. In both cases, however, their political and theological outspokenness, orally and in text, and their public authority represented obstacles.

In this comparative study, leading scholars from different disciplinary backgrounds offer, for the very first time, a comprehensive exploration of the lives and activities of Birgitta and Catherine in tandem. Particular attention is given to their literary works and the complex process of negotiating their sanctity and authorial roles. Above all, what the chapters reveal is the many points of connections between two of the most influential women of the Trecento and how they were related to one another by their peers and successors.

Maria H. Oen is Associate Professor of Art History and Deputy Director of the Swedish Institute of Classical Studies in Rome. She is also the editor of *A Companion to Birgitta of Sweden and Her Legacy in the Later Middle Ages* (Brill, 2019).

Unn Falkeid is Professor of the History of Ideas at the University of Oslo. She is the author of *The Avignon Papacy Contested: An Intellectual History from Dante to Catherine of Siena* (Harvard University Press, 2017) and co-editor, with Albert Russel Ascoli, of *The Cambridge Companion to Petrarch* (Cambridge University Press, 2015) and, with Aileen A. Feng, of *Rethinking Gaspara Stampa in the Canon of Renaissance Poetry* (Ashgate, 2015).

Routledge Studies in Medieval Literature and Culture

For more information about this series, please visit: https://www.routledge.com

Sanctity and Female Authorship

Birgitta of Sweden & Catherine of Siena

Edited by
Maria H. Oen and Unn Falkeid

Routledge
Taylor & Francis Group

NEW YORK AND LONDON

First published 2020
by Routledge
605 Third Avenue, New York, NY 10017

and by Routledge
2 Park Square, Milton Park, Abingdon, Oxon, OX14 4RN

First issued in paperback 2021

Routledge is an imprint of the Taylor & Francis Group, an informa business

Library of Congress Cataloging-in-Publication Data
A catalog record for this title has been requested

ISBN 13: 978-1-03-208798-6 (pbk)
ISBN 13: 978-0-367-36855-5 (hbk)

Typeset in Sabon
by codeMantra

Contents

Illustrations

Abbreviations

AASS	*Acta sanctorum*, eds. Johannes Bollandus, Godefridus Henschenius, et al., 68 vols (Antwerp: 1643–1940)
AP	*Acta et processus canonizacionis b. Birgitte*, ed. Isak Collijn. SFSS, Ser. 2, Latinska skrifter 1 (Uppsala: 1924–31)
ES	Alfonso of Jaén, *Epistola solitarii ad reges*, ed. Arne Jönsson, in Birgitta of Sweden, *Revelaciones Book VIII*, ed. Hans Aili (Stockholm: 2002), 47–81
Extrav.	Birgitta of Sweden, *Reuelaciones Extrauagantes*, ed. Lennart Hollmann. SFSS, Ser. 2, Latinska skrifter 5 (Uppsala: 1956)
KVHAA	Kungliga Vitterhets Historie och Antikvitets Akademien. The Royal Academy of Letters, History and Antiquities
LM	Raymond of Capua, *Legenda maior sive Legenda admirabilis virginis Catherine de Senis*, ed. Silvia Nocentini (Florence: 2013)
PC	Marie-Hyacinthe Laurent (ed.), *Il Processo Castellano. Con appendice di documenti sul culto e la canonizzazione di S. Caterina*. Fontes Vitae S. Catharinae Senensis Historici 9 (Milan: 1942)
Prol. M.	*Prologus Magistri Mathie*, in Birgitta of Sweden, *Reuelaciones Book I*, ed. Carl-Gustaf Undhagen (Stockholm: 1977), 229–40
Rev. I–VIII	Birgitta of Sweden, *Reuelaciones Books I–VIII*, eds. Hans Aili, Birger Bergh, Ann-Mari Jönsson, and Carl-Gustaf Undhagen, 8 vols (Stockholm: 1967–2002)
RS	Birgitta of Sweden, *Opera minora I: Regvla salvatoris*, ed. Sten Eklund (Stockholm: 1975)
SA	Birgitta of Sweden, *Opera minora 2: Sermo angelicus*, ed. Sten Eklund (Uppsala: 1972)
SFSS	Samlingar utgivna av Svenska fornskrift-sällskapet. Swedish Medieval Texts Society

Notes on Editions and Translations

All references to Birgitta of Sweden's *Revelations* are to the critical edition (Rev. I–VIII; ES; Extrav.; RS; SA) published by Kungliga Vitterhets Historie och Antikvitets Akademien (KVHAA), together with Samlingar utgivna av Svenska fornskrift-sällskapet (SFSS). The complete critical edition of the *Revelations* is available as downloadable pdf files on https://riksarkivet.se/digital-resources. English translations have been taken from *The Revelations of St. Birgitta of Sweden*, trans. Denis Searby, with Introductions and Notes by Bridget Morris, 4 vols (Oxford University Press, 2006–15), unless otherwise indicated. The English translations of the individual books in the corpus correspond to the Oxford translation.

References to Catherine of Siena's *Letters* give the numbering from the Tommaseo edition, with quotations taken from Antonio Volpato's edition (same numbering) unless otherwise stated in the notes. English translations of this work are by Suzanne Noffke in Catherine of Siena, *The Letters of Catherine of Siena*, ed. Suzanne Noffke, 4 vols [Arizona Center for Medieval and Renaissance Studies. 2000–08]), unless otherwise noted. Volpato's edition of Catherine of Siena's *Lettere*, together with Giuliana Cavallini's editions of *Il Dialogo della Divina Provvidenza* and *Le Orazioni*, are available as downloadable pdf files on the website of Centro Internazionale di Studi Cateriniani: http://www.centrostudicateriniani.it/it/santa-caterina-da-siena/scritti

Contributors

Roger Andersson is Professor of Scandinavian Languages and a researcher at the Centre for Medieval Studies at Stockholm University. His interests include medieval Swedish literature, philology and manuscript studies, medieval sermons, and preaching. Andersson previously served as the editor of medieval charters at the *Diplomatarium Suecanum* (Swedish National Archives) and has worked and published extensively on the preserved sermons from Vadstena Abbey. He is currently the main editor of a new critical edition of the Old Swedish version of the *Revelations* of Birgitta of Sweden (*Heliga Birgittas texter på fornsvenska*), four volumes of which have been published to date (Runica et Mediævalia, 2014–).

Renate Blumenfeld-Kosinski is Distinguished Professor of French at the University of Pittsburgh. She is the author of numerous books and articles, including *Poets, Saints, and Visionaries of the Great Schism, 1378–1417* (Penn State University Press, 2006) and *The Strange Case of Ermine de Reims: A Medieval Woman between Demons and Saints* (University of Pennsylvania Press, 2015). She has also translated and co-edited many volumes, including three collections on Philippe de Mézières, co-edited with Kiril Petkov and Joël Blanchard. She is currently working on a translation of the *Vies de Sainte Colette de Corbie* and a monograph on Philippe de Mézières.

Unn Falkeid is Professor of the History of Ideas at the University of Oslo. She has published extensively on late medieval and early modern Italian literature and history. Her publications include *The Avignon Papacy Contested: An Intellectual History from Dante to Catherine of Siena* (Harvard University Press, 2017), for which she was awarded the Helen and Howard R. Marraro Prize in Italian History; *The Cambridge Companion to Petrarch* (Cambridge University Press, 2015), co-edited with Albert Russell Ascoli; and *Rethinking Gaspara Stampa in the Canon of Renaissance Poetry* (Ashgate, 2015), co-edited with Aileen A- Feng. Falkeid is currently the Principal Investigator of the interdisciplinary research project *The Legacy of Birgitta of Sweden: Women, Politics and Reform in Renaissance Italy*, funded by the Research Council of Norway (2018–21).

Gábor Klaniczay is Professor at Central European University, Budapest. His principal field of expertise is the historical anthropology of Christianity (sainthood, miracle beliefs, stigmata, visions, healing, magic, and witchcraft). His books include *The Uses of Supernatural Power* (Princeton University Press, 1990); *Holy Rulers and Blessed Princesses* (Cambridge University Press, 2002); *Manufacturing the Middle Ages*, co-edited with Patrick Geary (Brill, 2013); *Discorsi sulle stimmate dal Medioevo all'età contemporanea – Discours sur les stigmates du Moyen Âge à l'époque contemporaine*; the monographic issue of *Archivio italiano per la storia della pietà* 26 (2013) (ed.); and *Witchcraft and Demonology in Hungary and Transylvania*, co-edited with Éva Pócs (Palgrave Macmillan, 2017).

F. Thomas Luongo is Associate Professor of History at Tulane University in New Orleans, Louisiana. He received his graduate education at the Centre for Medieval Studies of the University of Toronto and at the Medieval Institute of the University of Notre Dame, from which he received his PhD in 1998. His publications include *The Saintly Politics of Catherine of Siena* (Cornell University Press, 2006) and "Inspiration and Imagination: Visionary Authorship in the Early Manuscripts of the Revelations of Birgitta of Sweden," *Speculum* 93 (2018): 1102–50.

Silvia Nocentini (PhD, 2000) is Assistant Professor (tenure track) in Latin Medieval and Humanistic literature at the University of Rome "Tor Vergata" (Roma 2). A philologist of medieval Latin hagiography, she has published several articles on Dominican literary production and women's mystic literature. She is the editor of the Latin *Life* of Catherine of Siena, written by Raymond of Capua (*Legenda maior*, SISMEL, Edizioni del Galluzzo, 2013). Recent publications include the edition of the complete medieval Latin hagiographical *corpus* on St. Minias (SISMEL, Edizioni del Galluzzo, 2018) and a study on Birgitta of Sweden's earliest Latin *Lives* (in *Hagiographica* 2019).

Maria H. Oen (PhD, University of Oslo, 2015) is Associate Professor of Art History and Deputy Director of the Swedish Institute of Classical Studies in Rome. She has been a Marie Curie Fellow at the Centre for Medieval Studies, Stockholm University, and a Postdoctoral Fellow at the Department of Linguistics and Scandinavian Studies, University of Oslo. Oen's research focuses on late medieval and early modern visual culture. She has published extensively on Birgitta of Sweden: most recently, *A Companion to Birgitta of Sweden and Her Legacy in the Later Middle Ages* (Brill, 2019)

Camille Rouxpetel (PhD, Paris-Sorbonne University, 2012) is a historian specializing in the transcultural and interreligious relationships between the Latin, Greek, and Eastern Christian communities in the Mediterranean. She has held a postdoctoral fellowship at the École Française de Rome (2014–2017), and she has been a Florence Gould Fellow at the Villa I Tatti, the Harvard University Center for Italian Renaissance Studies (2017–2018). Rouxpetel is currently Associate Professor at the University of Angers. Her publications include *L'Occident au miroir de l'Orient chrétien. Cilicie, Syrie, Palestine, Égypte (XIIe-XIVe siècle) (Rome, BEFAR 369, 2015)*.

Jane Tylus is Andrew Downey Orrick Professor of Italian and Professor of Comparative Literature at Yale University, where she also has a teaching appointment in the Divinity School. Recent books include *Siena, City of Secrets* (2015); the co-edited *Cultures of Early Modern Translation* (with Karen Newman, 2015); *The Poetics of Masculinity in Early Modern Italy and Spain* (with Gerry Mulligan, 2011); a translation and edition of the complete poetry of Gaspara Stampa (2010); and *Reclaiming Catherine of Siena: Literature, Literacy, and the Signs of Others* (2009), which received the Howard Marraro Prize for Outstanding Work in Italian Studies from the Modern Language Association. She has been General Editor for the journal *I Tatti Studies in the Italian Renaissance* since 2013. Tylus is currently at work on a monograph, "Saying Good-bye in the Renaissance: Meditations on Leave-taking," and a collection of essays on music and translation. She is a socio corrispondente (honorary member) of the Accademia degli Intronati, Siena.

André Vauchez is Professor Emeritus of Medieval History at the University of Paris-Ouest-Nanterre and former Director of École Française de Rome (1995–2003). His specialized areas of research include Western medieval history, history of Christianity, medieval conceptions of holiness and sacralization of space and time, Francis of Assisi and Franciscan history, and dissent and orthodoxy in the West (10th to the 15th centuries). Vauchez is a member of Académie des inscriptions et belles-lettres, Institut de France (Paris), and in 2013, he was awarded the Balzan price for Medieval History. His numerous publications include *Catherine de Sienne. Vie et passions* (Cerf, 2015, trans. *Catherine of Siena: A Life of Passion and Purpose*, Paulist Press, 2018); *François d'Assisi. Entre histoire et mémoire* (Fayard, 2009, trans. *Francis of Assisi: The Life and Afterlife of a Medieval Saint*, Yale University Press, 2012); *Saints, prophètes et visionnaires. Le pouvoir surnaturel au Moyen Age* (Albin Michel, 1999); and *La Sainteté en occident aux derniers siècles du Moyen Age, d'après les procès de canonisation et les documents hagiographiques* (École française de Rome, 1981, trans. *Sainthood in the later Middle Ages*, Cambridge University Press, 1997).

Acknowledgements

The inspiration for this volume lies with two workshops held at the Norwegian Institute in Rome in 2015 and in the former monastery of the *Ordo Sanctissimi Salvatoris* in Vadstena, Sweden, in 2017, where scholars from various disciplinary and geographical backgrounds met to discuss the connections between the two trecento authors, Birgitta of Sweden and Catherine of Siena. The meetings, which resulted in this collection of essays, were made possible thanks to generous financial support from Riksbankens Jubileumsfond (The Swedish Foundation for Humanities and Social Sciences); the Norwegian Institute in Rome; and the Department of Philosophy, Classics, History of Art and Ideas, University of Oslo. The administrative staff of the Norwegian Institute in Rome and of the Department of Culture and Aesthetics, Stockholm University, provided invaluable assistance with the organization of the two workshops. We are deeply grateful to all of the participants in our fruitful and inspiring meetings in Rome and Vadstena, and to the contributors to this volume.

With regard to the use of images, we would like to thank Biblioteca comunale degli Intronati, Siena, and The Pierpont Morgan Library, New York.

Maria H. Oen's work on this volume was made possible through grants from the Sven och Dagmar Saléns Stiftelse, Stiftelsen Torsten och Ingrid Gihls fond, the Research Council of Norway, and the European Research Council (European Union's Seventh Framework Programme for research, technological development, and demonstration under Marie Curie grant agreement no. 608695). For their invaluable assistance, she is particularly grateful to the staff of The Swedish Institute of Classical Studies in Rome; Biblioteca comunale degli Intronati in Siena, Biblioteca Nazionale Centrale, Biblioteca Medicea Laurenziana, Biblioteca Riccardiana in Florence, Biblioteca Apostolica Vaticana, and The Warburg Institute Library; and Manuela Michelloni at the Norwegian Institute in Rome. Oen also wishes to extend her personal thanks to her friend, colleague, and great source of inspiration Unn Falkeid (with whom it is always a great pleasure to work, discuss, and laugh!). She is also thankful to Kurt Villads Jensen, Gustav Zamore, and Roger

Andersson at the Centre for Medieval Studies, Stockholm University; Halfdan Martin Baadsvik at the Department of Philosophy, Classics, History of Art and Ideas, University of Oslo; and Kathryn Boyer for her careful proofreading of the Editors' Introduction and Chapter 6. Above all, she is grateful to Stefano Fogelberg Rota, whose love, support, and friendship mean everything.

Unn Falkeid expresses her gratitude to the Royal Swedish Academy of Letters, History and Antiquities in Stockholm and to the Research Council of Norway for generous fellowships. The work on this book started when she was still a fellow at the Royal Academy of Letters, and it continued after she received funding from the Research Council of Norway for the international research project *The Legacy of Birgitta of Sweden: Women, Politics, and Reform in Renaissance Italy* (2018–21), of which she is the Principal Investigator. Falkeid is most grateful to her colleagues at the Department of Philosophy, Classics, History of Art and Ideas, University of Oslo. She especially wishes to thank the core group of the research project: the PhD student Francesca Canepuccia, the postdoctoral fellow Eleonora Cappuccilli, the research assistant Victor Frans, and the dear friend and co-manager Anna Wainwright. Finally, Falkeid wishes to extend her heartfelt thanks to Maria H. Oen for the friendship and joyful collaboration, both on this present book and on several other projects, including those belonging to the future!

Introduction

Maria H. Oen and Unn Falkeid

When Tommaso di Antonio da Siena (d. *c*.1434), known in scholarly literature as Caffarini, instigated a hearing in Venice in 1411 as a part of his efforts to see Catherine of Siena (1347–80) canonized, one of his principal strategies for promoting her holiness involved connecting Catherine's saintly image to that of her contemporary Birgitta of Sweden (1302/03–73).[1] Birgitta, a noblewoman who had left her native country for Rome in 1349, had been solemnly proclaimed a saint in 1391. The many comparisons between the two women found in Caffarini's own deposition was highly pertinent.[2] Birgitta, like Catherine, was a laywoman who had become known in her lifetime for her particular relationship with God, who she claimed spoke to her—or, rather, through her—about redemption for the Church and for humankind. And Birgitta, again like her younger contemporary, had been the charismatic leader of a group of followers comprising both women and men. By the time Caffarini's testimony was recorded in Venice, Birgitta's name embellished a broadly circulating literary corpus known as the *Liber celestis revelacionum* ("The Heavenly Book of Revelations"), which contained the accounts of more than 700 visions, including a rule for a new monastic order.[3] The contents of these revelations frequently touch directly on pressing political issues of the time. Some of the principal causes that Birgitta worked for, and which Catherine would take up shortly after Birgitta's death, included the papacy's return from Avignon to Rome as well as ecclesiastical and spiritual reform.[4]

There are several parallels between Birgitta's and Catherine's strategies to promote their common causes. At a time when women were strongly dissuaded from taking on public roles, not least when it came to instructing men in spiritual and political matters, the two stand out precisely because of their public personas. Both traveled extensively as a part of their political interventions, and each was responsible for a substantial literary corpus containing explicit instructions for reform, addressing an audience consisting of popes, bishops, cardinals, royalties, monastics of all orders, and laypeople of all social strata.

Ever since Caffarini sought to link Catherine to Birgitta in his testimony from the canonization hearing in Venice, the two women have frequently been mentioned in conjunction with each other, historically and in more recent scholarship. Nonetheless, and with the exception of a few pioneering articles, there exist no attempts in modern research to investigate the two women and their literary legacies together in a comprehensive manner.[5] This collection of essays offers a set of comparative studies, from different disciplinary perspectives, of Birgitta's and Catherine's writings and their reception, as well as of the construction of their saintly images, which, as the proceedings from their canonization processes reveal, were inextricably tied to their literary works.

The Prophetic Widow from Sweden

Although these two trecento authors were united in their political battles in adult life, their social backgrounds differed significantly. Birgitta Birgersdotter was born into the rural aristocracy of Sweden and was married to a nobleman at the age of 13.[6] During her life with her husband, Ulf Gudmarsson, Birgitta gave birth to eight children while also having an active role at the Swedish court; for instance, she was appointed *magistra* to the queen, Blanche of Namur, consort of King Magnus Eriksson.[7] In the 1340s, however, a series of events led to a complete transformation of Birgitta's life. Early in the decade, she and her husband went on a pilgrimage to Santiago de Compostela. After their return, the couple took a vow of chastity and decided to convert to a religious life, but shortly afterwards, Ulf died (1344 or 1346),[8] and Birgitta was left a widow. She did not remarry or enter a monastery (though, for a period, she kept close contact with the Cistercian house of Alvastra, and she may have lived in a house on the property of the monastery). Instead, Birgitta assumed a public role and engaged herself in the current political debate, both in Sweden and abroad. Claiming that she was a visionary, instructed directly by God to be his medium on earth, Birgitta became the center of a group of followers that included theologians and religious men. Some of these men acted as her envoys, bringing her prophetic messages to the pope in Avignon and to the warring kings of France and England.[9] Among Birgitta's loyal supporters were Hemming, bishop of Åbo; Master Mathias, canon of Linköping and prominent theologian; and the sub prior and later prior of the Cistercian house of Alvastra, Peter Olofsson.

During the latter half of the 1340s, Birgitta began working on what would subsequently be collected and disseminated under the title *Liber celestis revelacionum* (hereafter, *Revelations*) in collaboration with Peter and probably also Master Mathias. Although it is difficult to give exact dates for the composition of the various texts in the corpus, it seems that many of the chapters that concern the Avignon Papacy, the Baltic crusades, and a plan for a peace treaty between France and England date from this period.[10] Furthermore, the many revelations criticizing the

Swedish clergy and nobility most likely also stem from the late 1340s, as well as Birgitta's monastic rule, *Regula sanctissimi Salvatoris*.[11]

In 1349, Birgitta, who was now a wealthy and independent widow, moved permanently to Rome, where she quickly found influential friends among the noble families. She was soon followed by her daughter Katarina and the prior of Alvastra monastery, Peter, who left his post to join her group. The three of them, together with another Swedish *magister*, also known as Peter Olofsson, stayed in the palace of Cardinal Hugues Roger de Beaufort, close to the church of San Lorenzo in Damaso (Campo de' Fiori), and in due course moved into a house offered to Birgitta by her new friend, the noblewoman Francesca Papazzura, on today's Piazza Farnese. The visionary and her Swedish entourage continued to work for the same causes as earlier: advocating the papacy's return to Rome, promoting spiritual reform, and seeking to establish a new religious order that would follow Birgitta's rule. Together with her collaborators, Birgitta also traveled widely: she visited virtually all of the major shrines in Italy as well as the Holy Land, where she went on a pilgrimage in the last year of her life.

In the late 1360s, Birgitta's group added one more prominent member—Alfonso Pecha—the former bishop of Jaén. Alfonso had left his position in Spain to live as a hermit in Italy, where he was engaged in the Observant Reform movement and in the struggle against the so-called "Avignon Captivity."[12] Alfonso and Birgitta traveled together to Montefiascone in 1370, where they met with Pope Urban V and sought to persuade him to permanently return to Rome. Later, upon Birgitta's death, on 23 July 1373, the collection of her recorded revelations were given to Alfonso as per her request, and he was charged with the task of editing the texts and publishing them. Alfonso organized the revelations into books and chapters, a structure that the corpus still retains in succeeding printings as well as in the modern critical edition, and he ordered numerous copies from a scriptorium in Naples.[13] His final edition consists of seven books of revelations, introduced by an apologia defending the authenticity of Birgitta's visions, written in the late 1340s by Master Mathias of Linköping. It also includes an eighth book of Alfonso's own collection of Birgitta's revelations that concern secular politics, compiled in a separate book under the title *Liber celestis imperatoris ad reges* ("The Heavenly Emperor's Book to Kings."Book VIII in the critical edition). This collection is preceded by a prologue Alfonso wrote, *Epistola solitarii ad reges* ("The Hermit's Letter to Kings"), which takes the form of an apologetic treatise on Birgitta's visions. Within a few years, other visionary texts were added to the corpus as it was disseminated in manuscripts, including *Sermo angelicus* ("The Angel's Sermon"), *Quattuor oraciones* ("The Four Prayers"), the *Regula Sanctissimi Salvatori* (Birgitta's rule, "The Rule of the Most Holy Savior"), and *Revelaciones extravagantes* (also dubbed "Extravagant Revelations" in the modern translation). The last is a collection of revelations that Alfonso initially excluded from the corpus but which Prior Peter Olofsson later introduced into the manuscripts.

Alfonso of Jaén came to play a key role in the promotion of Birgitta's cult and canonization process, which was initiated immediately after her death. The diffusion of illuminated deluxe copies of the *Revelations* to prominent addressees, including the pope and many royalties, was a part of his strategy to ensure the proclamation of Birgitta's sanctity. At the end of her life and after overcoming much opposition, Birgitta succeeded in establishing a monastic order. The first house was founded in Vadstena, Sweden (establishment approved by the pope in 1370), but the order soon spread all over Europe, beginning with Santa Maria del Paradiso outside of Florence (1394).[14] And in 1391, the visionary was canonized by an Italian pope (Boniface IX), again in the face of significant opposition, in the middle of the Great Schism.[15]

Intertwined Lives and Networks

At the time Birgitta was establishing a prophetic career for herself in Sweden, Caterina Benincasa was born in Siena, in 1347.[16] Although not of noble birth, she came from a prosperous family characteristic of the urban society in which she grew up: her father was a wool dyer, and among her relatives were other masters, notaries, and merchants, including a poet.[17] According to Catherine's principal *vita*, the *Legenda maior* by her confessor Raymond of Capua (d. 1399), she converted to a religious life already as a child living in her parents' home. At the age of seven, her hagiographer claims, she made a vow of chastity to Christ, and by the time she was a young adult, she was living an ascetic life in her home, practicing rigorous fasting and self-mortification.[18]

In the latter half of the 1360s, Catherine became connected to the *mantellate*, a group of laywomen, most of whom were financially independent widows like Birgitta. The *mantellate* in Siena were affiliated with the local Dominicans and did charity work in the city. Around 1370, Catherine formally joined the group, thus taking her religious life into the public realm.[19] Her spiritual reputation spread quickly, and she soon attracted a group of followers that included laypeople of both sexes, as well as monastics and priests. Several of her supporters and disciples— the group that she referred to as her *famiglia*—were connected to the Dominican Order, among them Catherine's first confessor, Tommaso della Fonte, Tommaso Caffarini, and Raymond of Capua (Catherine's confessor from 1374).

By 1373, when Birgitta died, Catherine already had a reputation that reached beyond the walls of Siena, and she had begun articulating in letters her desire for spiritual reform. Not long after, in 1374, Catherine's political and literary career took a new turn. As she describes in a letter dated to March that year (T127), Catherine had been contacted by

Alfonso of Jaén.[20] The letter implies that Alfonso was acting on behalf of Pope Gregory XI, who sought to persuade the young Sienese woman to campaign for the Church in a manner similar to that of Birgitta.[21] Later, in the same year, Catherine attended the general chapter of the Dominicans in Florence. While many scholars have assumed that she appeared there as a result of accusations of heresy, F. Thomas Luongo has suggested that, on the contrary, Catherine was summoned to Florence "to be vetted for a role that had already been conceived for her, as a political visionary—a second Birgitta."[22] It was also here that, he proposes, Raymond of Capua was assigned as her new confessor; by then a prominent Dominican, he would assume the role of Master General of the order (Italian obedience), following her death.[23]

After the events of 1374, Catherine became an active figure on the political scene beyond Siena, benefiting from the introduction into a larger network via the aegis of Alfonso and Raymond. She traveled in Tuscany as a peace negotiator, representing the papacy in the clash between the pope and the coalition of Italian city states of the area, known as the "War of Eight Saints."[24] In 1376, she went to Avignon, where she was received by Pope Gregory XI. During this period, Catherine also became an even more ardent letter writer, addressing both church and civic leaders.[25] Her epistles became Catherine's principal weapon in the struggle for peace and reform.

Birgitta's and Catherine's political networks on the Italian peninsula are connected by another key figure beyond Alfonso of Jaén: Queen Johanna I of Naples and Sicily (Giovanna d'Angiò, d. 1382). Birgitta and the Anjou queen became acquainted during the period 1365–67, when the Swedish visionary stayed in Naples.[26] According to Elizabeth Casteen, the queen was eager to befriend Birgitta, who already then had a saintly reputation, as part of her attempt to restore her own *fama*, tainted after the assassination of her husband, Andrew of Hungary, of which she had been accused.[27] Birgitta probably resided with Johanna again in the last year of her life, when she visited Naples on her way to and from the Holy Land in 1372/73. After the visionary's death, the queen took part in the campaign advocating Birgitta's sanctity. She petitioned the pope, and possibly also provided Alfonso with an artist and a scriptorium.[28] The first panel paintings, which show Birgitta made to promote her cult, were executed by the Florentine artist Niccolò di Tommaso, then in the service of Johanna, and the three oldest extant manuscripts containing the *Revelations* all stem from the same Neapolitan scriptorium that was responsible for several sumptuous codices connected to the House of Anjou.[29]

A few years after Birgitta's death, in late June and in early July 1375, Catherine wrote to Johanna, urging her to support the crusade being promulgated by Pope Gregory XI in a bull on 1 July.[30] Catherine addressed the queen warmly as a sister and a mother, and, as is evident from another letter to Johanna on 4 August, Catherine, "jubilantly happy," had received a positive answer to her advice.[31] The contact between the two women changed three years later, immediately after the outbreak of the Schism, when Johanna declared her support for the French pope, Clement VII, elected in opposition to the Roman pope, Urban VI, in the months following the death of Gregory XI in Rome. In a series of letters, Catherine sought to persuade the queen to return to Roman obedience.[32] She referred to Johanna as an innocent who has been misguided and deceived by others: "Open, open your mind's eye, and sleep no longer in such blindness! You shouldn't be so ignorant or so cut off from the true light that you don't know about the villainous lives of these men who have led you into such heresy."[33]According to Suzanne Noffke, this particular letter was written in the aftermath of a failed plan to send Catherine and Katarina, Birgitta's daughter, who knew Johanna personally, to the queen in an attempt to change her mind.[34] Proposed by Urban VI, the plan was canceled owing to worries that Katarina and Raymond of Capua had for their safety.[35]

In 1377, Catherine had embarked on a project to write a book, which would later be known as *Libro della divina dottrina* or *Dialogo della divina provvidenza* (hereafter, the *Dialogue*).[36] In the work, she lays out her spiritual and political views in the form of a dialogue between the Creator and the soul (Catherine). As has already been suggested by scholars, it is possible that the inspiration for Catherine to compose a work of her own came from Birgitta's *Revelations*, which had just started to circulate in manuscripts commissioned by Alfonso.[37] Indeed, three years earlier, when Catherine had met with Alfonso, he was probably in the middle of his editing, gathering the revelations into a book.

Catherine of Siena died in Rome on 29 April 1380, seven years after Birgitta's passing in the same city. She was 33 years old then, whereas Birgitta had died at the age of 70. Just as the supporters of so many other holy women, including Birgitta of Sweden, the *famiglia* of the Sienese author immediately began to campaign for her canonization. Both Raymond of Capua and Tommaso Caffarini composed hagiographical texts; however, they offered quite different images of Catherine, particularly in terms of her writing.[38]

Significantly, as in the case of Birgitta, the promotion of Catherine's sanctity included the dissemination of her writings. Although several of Catherine's followers cum scribes had collected her texts, Caffarini took on the task of establishing a scriptorium from which numerous illuminated manuscripts were publicized, emulating in many ways Alfonso's efforts to widely promote Birgitta's *Revelations*. Catherine's canonization, however, took much longer than Birgitta's and was not proclaimed until 1461.

Birgitta's and Catherine's writings spread swiftly across Italy and Europe, and were soon translated into other languages. The *Revelations*, which originally circulated in Latin, were immediately rendered into Swedish and shortly thereafter into Italian and other central European vernaculars. One of Catherine's followers translated her *Libro* (the *Dialogue*) into Latin, a version that was also disseminated by Caffarini's workshop in Venice. As several chapters in the present book demonstrate, when it came to the diffusion and translation of the two women's writings, those working with the manuscripts crossed paths frequently: followers of Birgitta read, copied, and translated Catherine's works and vice versa. The texts of the two authors quickly found their ways into very different contexts, from private humanist libraries to monastic libraries; they were anthologized and placed side by side, sometimes with classical and contemporary political authors, and other times with devotional or theological texts. The *Revelations*, the *Letters*, and the *Dialogue* also appeared in illustrated incunables shortly after the printing press came into use, and they have continuously been in print since.

Presentation of the Chapters

The inspiration for this current volume stems from the absence of a broad comparative study of two of the pre-modern era's most towering and fascinating women. To a certain degree, Birgitta and Catherine may be regarded as fountainheads for the extraordinary increase in both the number and status of female writers in early modern Europe; and the many commonalities between them invite investigations into the parallels. The range of scholars represented in this anthology offers an examination and comparison of the lives, networks, authorship, and the reception of these two women and their works. Case studies from the fields of history, literature, philology, and art history provide the readers with critical and nuanced approaches to the issues of how Birgitta and Catherine, either alone or through the help of powerful people, established their authority and sanctity in the fourteenth century and beyond.

For the production of their texts, both Birgitta and Catherine depended on their confessors and followers, who acted as their scribes and editors. Furthermore, in both cases, the saintly authors and their collaborators who were responsible for writing their *vitae* emphasized the passivity of the two women before God—presented as the true author of their words—thereby reducing Birgitta and Catherine to (mere) conduits of divine inspiration. The volume opens with a chapter by F. Thomas Luongo, in which he explores the question of what it means to think of Birgitta and Catherine as authors. Through an examination of the saints' respective textual communities, Luongo challenges certain received notions of the authorial agency of female religious writers in the later Middle Ages.

In Chapter 2, Jane Tylus focuses on pilgrimage, a major theme in the writings of both Birgitta and Catherine. At first glance, it seems that the two embraced radically opposed views on that hallmark of medieval spirituality, the pilgrim's journey. Birgitta appears as the paragon, the over-achiever of the late medieval *pellegrina*. Catherine, on the other hand, often violently advocated against embarking on pilgrimages, viewing them as a distraction from the lives people should be leading. At the same time, even if pilgrimage as practice is strikingly absent in Catherine's works, pilgrimage as metaphor fills her prose. How, then, might these two concepts of pilgrimage be both recognized and addressed? Perhaps they are in conflict yet related, with one arguably dependent on the other. Tylus tackles this question by examining the vital role of pilgrimages—as lived experiences and as symbolic registers—for both Birgitta and Catherine.

In Chapter 3, Unn Falkeid explores the roles of two of the biblical Marys as models for Birgitta and Catherine in the construction of their images as powerful public agents. Using intertextual and comparative analyses, Falkeid demonstrates the manner in which Birgitta and Catherine contested the contemporary politics of the Avignon papacy, grounding their authority in the Virgin Mary and Mary Magdalene, respectively. Scholars have long acknowledged the central role of the Virgin in Birgitta's self-promotion as a holy woman. The Virgin Mary offered Birgitta, and other medieval religious women, a role model as both mother and bride of Christ. But Birgitta adopted the persona of the Virgin in a particular manner: in several of her revelations, Birgitta casts Mary as the foundation of her own *auctoritas*, in political as well as in religious matters. In the case of Catherine of Siena, another Mary assumes a pivotal role, namely, Mary Magdalene, Christ's notable female disciple. In Catherine's *Letters*, Magdalene's status as the repentant prostitute is significantly downplayed; instead, she is presented as the woman who dared to raise her voice and challenge the authorities of her time.

Crusading, a principal theme in the writings of both Birgitta and Catherine, is the subject of Chapter 4, by Renate Blumenfeld-Kosinski. While Birgitta engaged in the specific Swedish case of King Magnus Eriksson's military campaign against Novgorod (1348–51) and the conversion of the Baltic pagans as well as the Orthodox Christians, Catherine, like many of her contemporary theorists, was concerned with a pan-European crusade to the Holy Land. Proceeding from an exploration of the theoretical and political contexts in which the two women wrote, Blumenfeld-Kosinski carefully analyzes their respective ideas, aims, and concrete strategies regarding the topic of holy war.

In Chapter 5, Silvia Nocentini turns to the reception of Birgitta's and Catherine's writings and demonstrates to what extent their works and the transmission of these were intertwined in the late fourteenth century and throughout the fifteenth. Nocentini argues that in the context of late medieval mystical spirituality, the broad transmission of Birgitta's and Catherine's literary output—in terms of geography, languages, and religious affiliations—must be understood to be remarkable. She focuses on two figures who connect the two textual traditions—Birgitta's editor and confessor, Alfonso of Jaén, and Catherine's follower and favorite scribe, Cristoforo di Gano Guidini—both of whom played a key role in the transmission of the writings of both women in Italy. Based on an examination of preserved manuscripts Nocentini demonstrates the central role of Birgitta's writings in Catherinian circles and vice versa.

In Chapter 6, Maria H. Oen returns to the question of Birgitta's and Catherine's status as authors, but with an emphasis now on the visual representations of the two women, notably in the context of the manuscripts containing their texts. Images found in the earliest extant codices portray Birgitta in the act of writing—an extremely uncommon visual rendering of a female author in the medieval period—whereas Catherine is never depicted with a pen in her hand. This difference emerges as a paradox when contrasted with representations of the two women in their respective texts, where Birgitta is often put forward as a passive medium while Catherine explicitly is delineated as a writer with agency. The tension between texts and images serves as the point of departure for scrutinizing the role of the visual in shaping the authority of their works as well as notions of Birgitta and Catherine as authors in a time when female literary authority was still controversial.

Using the concepts of sanctity and authority as analytical tools, in Chapter 7 Roger Andersson compares the similarities and differences between Catherine and Birgitta and their literary legacy in late medieval sermons. The two visionary women—both responsible for books claimed to be the product of divine dictation and supernatural mediation—quickly attracted the attention of a number of preachers. A comparison of the presentation of Birgitta and Catherine and their respective works in surviving sermons reveals that the clerical reception and use of these writings served diverging purposes; preachers promoted the canonization of Catherine, but not that of Birgitta. Instead, Birgitta's presence in this material is not in homiletical campaigns for her sanctity, but in quotations taken from her *Revelations*. Interestingly, these quotations serve the function of theological *auctoritas* on par with Scripture.

In Chapter 8, Gábor Klaniczay turns to the saintly portrayals of Birgitta and Catherine and investigates the roles of supernatural bodily tokens in the construction of their holiness. Klaniczay demonstrates that the respective hagiographical sources offer two very different attitudes toward corporeal expressions of sanctity. Contrary to most holy women of the time, including Catherine, whose stigmatization is a common theme in her legends, the hagiographical image of Birgitta relies little on bodily attributes of holiness and *imitatio Christi*, and when such phenomena are encountered, it is more fitting to describe them as acts of *imitatio Mariae*. Concentrating on the saints' *vitae* and their own writings, Klaniczay discusses the different types of physical signs of sanctity that emerge in the sources, and he compares the roles played by supernatural bodily behavior in the women's lives and in the attempts to demonstrate their merit of sainthood.

The topic of reform—spiritual as well as directed toward organized religious structures in society—was a critical issue for the two fourteenth-century authors. In the book's final chapter, Camille Roux-petel looks at the later impact of Birgitta and Catherine on the Observant Reform movement in the Italian peninsula at the time of the Great Schism, focusing in particular on the eager reformist and collaborator of Birgitta, Alfonso of Jaén, who served as a point of contact between Birgitta and Catherine. Based on an assiduous study of unpublished sources, Rouxpetel maps the wider Observant network within which Alfonso played a key role and, through him, the influence of the two female reformers on the movement.

The book concludes with an epilogue by André Vauchez, in which he summarizes the significance of, and the results from, the volume's comparative approach to Birgitta of Sweden and Catherine of Siena as well as their impact on their contemporaries and their politics.

Notes

1 For Tommaso Caffarini, see Jeffrey F. Hamburger and Gabriela Signori, "The Making of a Saint: Catherine of Siena, Tommaso Caffarini, and the Others," in *Catherine of Siena: The Creation of a Cult*, eds. Jeffrey F. Hamburger and Gabriela Signori (Turnhout: Brepols, 2013), 1–22. For the documents from the hearing in Venice, known as "Processo Castellano," see PC.

2 An example can be found in PC, 93–94, where, after having listed "the young maiden" Catherine's extraordinary signs of sanctity, Caffarini notes:

> Dixi autem notanter feminam virginem ad differentiam venerande beate et sancte Brigide de Suetia, que temporibus huius virginis licet etiam per-antea floruit et ut dicitur per septennium ante virginem istam, et in Urbe ad Dominum quemadmodum ista virgo migravit, ac etiam scripturas plurimas revelationum celestium ecclesie dereliquit.
>
> (However, I have markedly said 'young maiden' to distinguish her from the venerable blessed saint Birgitta of Sweden, who flourished in the time of this virgin and even earlier, and who, they say, seven years before this virgin, died in Rome in the same way as her, and also left to the church several writings on heavenly revelations).

3 For a critical edition of the complete corpus, see Rev. I–VIII; SA; QO; RS; Extrav.

4 On Birgitta's and Catherine's campaigns against the Avignon papacy, see Unn Falkeid, *The Avignon Papacy Contested: An Intellectual History from Dante to Catherine of Siena* (Cambridge, MA: Harvard University Press, 2017).

5 André Vauchez, "Sainte Brigitte de Suède et Sainte Catherine de Sienne. La mystique et l'église aux dernier siècles du Moyen Age," in *Temi e problemi nella mistica trecentesca* (Todi: Accademia Tudertina, 1983); "The Reaction

of the Church to Late Medieval Mysticism and Prophecy," in André Vauchez, *The Laity in the Middle Ages: Religious Beliefs and Devotional Practices*, ed. Daniel E. Bornstein, trans. Margery J. Schneider (Notre Dame, IN: University of Notre Dame Press, 1993); Julia Bolton Holloway, "Saint Birgitta of Sweden, Saint Catherine of Siena: Saints, Secretaries, Scribes, Supporters," *Birgittiana* 1 (1996): 29–45; and Joan Isobel Friedman, "Politics and the Rhetoric of Reform in the Letters of Saints Bridget of Sweden and Catherine of Siena," in *Livres et lectures de femmes en Europe entre Moyen Âge et Renaissance*, ed. Anne-Marie Legaré (Turnhout: Brepols, 2007).

6 For Birgitta's biography, see Bridget Morris, *St Birgitta of Sweden* (Woodbridge: Boydell Press, 1999); Claire L. Sahlin, *Birgitta of Sweden and the Voice of Prophecy* (Woodbridge: Boydell Press, 2001); and *A Companion to Birgitta of Sweden and Her Legacy in the Later Middle Ages*, ed. Maria H. Oen (Leiden: Brill, 2019). Studies devoted to Birgitta of Sweden are too numerous to be listed here. The reader is instead referred to the Bibliography of the Brill Companion.

7 AP, 528.

8 The correct year of Ulf's death, which marks the beginning of Birgitta's prophetic career, has been subject to much debate; for a summary, see Birgitta of Sweden, *Birgitta of Sweden: Life and Selected Revelations*, ed. Marguerite Tjader Harris, trans. Albert Ryle Kezel (New York: Paulist Press, 1990), 240, n. 32.

9 For Birgitta's Swedish years as a prophetess, see Päivi Salmesvuori, *Power and Sainthood: The Case of Birgitta of Sweden* (New York: Palgrave Macmillan, 2014).

10 The recent English translation of the KVHAA critical edition offers suggestions for dating the various chapters. See Birgitta of Sweden, *The Revelations of St. Birgitta of Sweden*, trans. Denis Searby, with Introductions and Notes by Bridget Morris (Oxford: Oxford University Press, 2006–15).

11 On the textual history of Birgitta's rule, and edition, see the editor's introduction in RS.

12 For an introduction to Alfonso, see Arne Jönsson, *Alfonso of Jaén: His Life and Works with Critical Editions of the Epistola Solitarii, the Informaciones and the Epistola Serui Christi* (Lund: Lund University Press, 1989).

13 In a letter from Alfonso to the archbishop in Uppsala, Sweden, on 15 January 1378 (see SDHK 11166 in the database of the National Archives in Sweden, https://sok.riksarkivet.se/SDHK), Alfonso informs about the ongoing dissemination of the *Revelations*, which had by then spread in Spain and Italy; he explains that more copies were "continuously being produced in the Kingdom of Naples and in Italy." There is a general consensus that the oldest three extant manuscripts containing the *Revelations* (Warszawa, Biblioteka Narodowa, 3310; New York, Pierpont Morgan Library, M. 498; and Palermo, Biblioteca Centrale della Regione Siciliana, IV.G.2) can all be attributed to a scriptorium in Naples connected to the Angevin royal family. See Hans Aili and Jan Svanberg, *Imagines Sanctae Birgittae: The Earliest Illuminated Manuscripts and Panel Paintings Related to the Revelations of St. Birgitta of Sweden*, 2 vols (Stockholm: The Royal Academy of Letters, History and Antiquities, 2003); Andreas Bräm, *Neapolitanische Bilderbibeln des Trecento. Anjou-Buchmalerei von Robert dem Weisen bis zu Johanna I* (Wiesbaden: Reichert, 2007), vol. 1, 154–68; Anette Creutzburg, *Die heilige Birgitta von Schweden. Bildliche Darstellungen und theologische Kontroversen im Vorfeld ihrer Kanonisation (1373–91)* (Kiel: Verlag Ludwig, 2011).

14 For an introduction to Birgitta's monastic order and its abbeys, see Tore Nyberg, *Birgittinische Klostergründungen des Mittelalters* (Leiden: CWK Gleerup, 1965); Ulla Sander-Olsen, Tore Nyberg, and Per Sloth Carlsen (eds.), *Birgitta Atlas: Saint Birgitta's Monasteries. Die Klöster der Heiligen Birgitta* (Uden: Societas Birgitta Europa, 2013).

15 On the negative responses to Birgitta's prophetic claims and her canonization, see Sahlin, *Birgitta of Sweden*, 136–68.

16 For a biographical introduction to Catherine, see Eugenio Dupré Theseider, "Caterina da Siena," in *Dizionario biografico degli Italiani* 22 (Rome: Istituto della Enciclopedia Italiana, 1979), 361–79. See also Carolyn Muessig, George Ferzoco, and Beverly Mayne Kienzle (eds.), *A Companion to Catherine of Siena* (Leiden: Brill, 2012); and André Vauchez, *Catherine de Sienne. Vie et passions* (Paris: Cerf, 2015). Scholarship on Catherine is continuously collected in bibliographies published by Edizioni Cateriniani and more recently by Centro Internazionale di Studi Cateriniani. The bibliographies cover, thus far, publications from the period 1905–2010, see www.centrostudicateriniani. it/it/attivita/pubblicazioni (accessed 15 November 2018).

17 On Catherine's family background, see F. Thomas Luongo, *The Saintly Politics of Catherine of Siena* (Ithaca, NY: Cornell University Press, 2006), 29–32.

18 LM, I.3, pp. 140–45. Catherine's ascetic practices as presented in Raymond's *Legenda maior* have been the subject of numerous studies, most famously Rudolph Bell's, *Holy Anorexia* (Chicago, IL: The University of Chicago Press, 1985), and Caroline Walker Bynum's, *Holy Feast and Holy Fast: The Religious Significance of Food to Medieval Women* (Berkley: The University of California Press, 1987).

19 On the dating of her formal entry in the group, see Luongo, *The Saintly Politics*, 34.

20 For Catherine's letters, see Antonio Volpato's edition available on the website of Centro Internazionale di Studi Cateriniani: www.centrostudicateriniani. it/it/santa-caterina-da-siena/scritti. For an English translation, see Catherine of Siena, *The Letters of Catherine of Siena*, ed. and trans. Suzanne Noffke, 4 vols (Tempe: Arizona Center for Medieval and Renaissance Studies, 2000–08).

21 That Gregory XI was "looking to Catherine as a possible continuing source of wisdom" after Birgitta was first suggested by Suzanne Noffke in *Letters*, 1: 40, n. 13. Birgitta had herself met Gregory XI in Montefiascone when he was still a cardinal, and she had, for a time, been living in a residence in Rome, provided to her by Cardinal Hugues Roger de Beaufort, a nephew of the pontiff.

22 Luongo, *The Saintly Politics*, 58.

23 On the assignment of Raymond as Catherine's confessor, see Luongo, *The Saintly Politics*, 69–71.

24 For Catherine's role in this conflict, and her political activity in general, see Luongo, *The Saintly Politics*.

25 On Catherine as a writer, see Jane Tylus, *Reclaiming Catherine of Siena: Literacy, Literature, and the Signs of Others* (Chicago, IL: The University of Chicago Press, 2009).

26 One of Birgitta's most colorful visions addresses Queen Johanna, see Rev. VII: 11. On the relationship between Johanna and Birgitta, see Elizabeth Casteen, *From She-Wolf to Martyr: The Reign and Disputed Reputation of Johanna I of Naples* (Ithaca, NY: Cornell University Press, 2015), especially 156–95; and Bridget Morris, "Birgitta of Sweden and Giovanna of Naples: An Unlikely Friendship?" in *Santa Brigida, Napoli, l'Italia*, eds. Olle Ferm,

Alessandra Perriccioli Saggese, and Marcello Rotili (Naples: Arte Tipografica Editrice, 2009), 22–33.

27 Casteen, *From She-Wolf to Martyr*, 156–95.
28 For the petitions, see AP, 54–55.
29 See n. 13 above.
30 Letters T138 and T133.
31 Letter 143 (4 August), quoted from Noffke, *Letters*, 1: 148.
32 The letters are T312, T317, T348, and T362. Letter T348 implies that there were several more letters, which are now lost.
33 Letter T317, English translation from Noffke, *Letters*, 4: 8.
34 Noffke, *Letters*, 4: 5 and 166.
35 See LM, III.1, p. 364. See also Blake Beattie, "Catherine of Siena and the Papacy," in Muessig, Ferzoco, and Kienzle, *A Companion to Catherine of Siena*, 90.
36 Catherine of Siena, *Il Dialogo della Divina Provvidenza: ovvero Libro della divina dottrina*, ed. Giuliana Cavallini (Rome: Edizioni Cateriniane, 1968).
37 Jane Tylus, "Mystical Literacy: Writing and Religious Women in Late Medieval Italy," in Muessig, Ferzoco, and Kienzle, *A Companion to Catherine of Siena*, 178–79; F. Thomas Luongo, "Catherine of Siena, *Auctor*," in *Women Leaders and Intellectuals of the Medieval World*, eds. Katie Bugyis, Kathryn Kerby-Fulton, and John Van Engen (Woodbridge: Boydell & Brewer, [forthcoming]).
38 On this subject, see Jane Tylus, "Writing versus Voice: Tommaso Caffarini and the Production of a Literate Catherine" and Catherine M. Mooney, "Wondrous Words: Catherine of Siena's Miraculous Reading and Writing According to the Early Sources," both in Hamburger and Signori, *Catherine of Siena*.

1 Birgitta and Catherine and Their Textual Communities

F. Thomas Luongo

The writings we possess of Birgitta of Sweden and Catherine of Siena—like the writings of virtually all female spiritual authors from the Middle Ages—come to use through the mediation of the communities of confessors, advisors, and followers who served as their scribes and editors, and on whom both women depended for the production of their texts.[1] The extent of mediation is more obvious and dramatic in the case of Birgitta's *Liber celestis revelacionum* (*The Heavenly Book of Revelations*), whose text in Latin is a product of immediate or simultaneous translation by her confessors/scribes of what Birgitta either wrote or dictated to them in Swedish. Even more important, the *Liber celestis revelacionum* consists (at least for the most part) of collections made by her confessors and followers of individual visions issued on separate occasions, rather than a work composed as such by Birgitta; Birgitta did not set out to author her books of *Revelations*. The extent and nature of the mediation of Catherine of Siena's letters and book, her *Libro di divina dottrina* (known these days more often as the *Dialogue*), is in some ways more complicated—as we will see. Catherine's self-awareness as a writer is far more evident than Birgitta's, and there is no question that Catherine in composing her *Libro* did so with the intention of producing a book. At the same time, Catherine, too, depended on the followers who served as her scribes for production of her letters and book, which to a very large extent were composed in collaboration with them.

There remain many questions of what this mediation might mean to our understanding of Birgitta and Catherine as writers. For example, the role played by Birgitta's confessors in the collecting and editing of her revelations in the *Liber celestis revelacionum* is central to discussions of the manuscript history of her texts, but there has been less attention to the possible role of Birgitta's confessors as collaborators in the composition of her revelations. Catherine's dependence on scribes led to her marginalization in Italian literary history; her dictation to scribes has often been taken, anachronistically, to make her a figure of "oral" rather than literary culture.[2] Discussion of Catherine's literary status has tended to revolve around the question of her literacy and the status of a key letter—discussed below—in which she announced to her confessor,

Raymond of Capua, that she had learned to write. But as we will see, tying Catherine's status as a writer to her ability to write independently of her scribes runs the risk of oversimplifying the process of composition of her texts and is, in its own way, as anachronistic as denying her the status of writer because she depended on scribes.

It is important to recall that the use of scribes in literary composition had a range of symbolic associations in the Middle Ages. For instance, far from suggesting illiteracy, it could be considered a more authoritative form of writing than taking the pen into one's own hand. A more complicated understanding of the possible meanings of scribal mediation and agency is evident, for instance, in the authorial iconography of Birgitta and Catherine examined in Maria H. Oen's essay in this volume. Oen has shown that, while Birgitta is represented in the act of writing and Catherine is never similarly shown with a pen (or, for that matter, in the act of reading), both iconographic choices represent complicated arguments for their authority as authors that depend on other aspects of their personae as saints and religious figures. For example, the Sienese manuscript of the Latin translation of Catherine's *Libro di divina dottrina* (or the *Dialogue*) produced by the workshop of her follower and the chief promoter of Catherine's cult, Tommaso Caffarini, uses as author portraits an iconographic image of Catherine as a virgin saint (see Figure 6.2, Chapter 6)—essentially the same image used in the hagiographic manuscripts about Catherine produced by that workshop—and an image of Catherine engaged in inspired dictation to several scribes, a gesture (as Oen has pointed out) to the hagiographic trope of simultaneous dictation to multiple scribes (see Figure 6.3, Chapter 6). This image is very specific: the scribe with the notary's *capello* is presumably meant to be the Florentine notary Barduccio Canigiani, Catherine's most important scribe in the last two years of her life and one who we know worked most assiduously with her on the *Libro*, whose identification here as a notary perhaps adds to the authorization of the text contained in the manuscript.[3]

In the Birgittine manuscripts, on the other hand, what Oen calls an audacious choice to show Birgitta pen in hand, in imitation of the iconography of scriptural authors (Figure 1.1), also serves the purpose of eliding what we know of the participation of Alfonso of Jaén and others of her clerical circle in the construction of the *Liber celestis revelacionum*. Indeed, especially telling are the images that illustrate the sections of the *Revelations* where Alfonso's contributions were most prominent. For example, in the historiated initial for his treatise, the *Epistola solitarii ad reges*, Alfonso is pictured not as the author of the text but as a mere connection in the chain between Christ and Birgitta, and the public to which the treatise is addressed (Figure 1.2). And in the full-page miniature for the *Liber celestis imperatoris ad reges* (Book VIII in the critical edition), of which Alfonso was a very active editor—about half of the contents of the *Liber celestis imperatoris ad reges* have been shown to be reworked

Figure 1.1 Birgitta of Sweden receiving a vision (Frontispiece to the *Liber ce-lestis revelacionum*). New York, Pierpont Morgan Library, MS M.498, fol. 4v. Date: Last quarter of 14th century. Photo: The Pier-pont Morgan Library & Museum. MS M.498, fol. 4v. Purchased by J. Pierpont Morgan (1837–1913) in 1912.

versions of texts that appear in earlier books of the *Liber celestis reve-lacionum*[4]—Birgitta receives a book, already composed and complete, from Christ and passes it to Alfonso and another one of Birgitta's confes-sors, Peter Olofsson (Petrus Olavi), who deliver it to the seated monarchs

Figure 1.2 Birgitta of Sweden writing down her Revelations and Alfonso of Jaén communicating these to their royal addressees (historiated initial opening *Epistola solitarii ad reges*). New York, Pierpont Morgan Library, MS M.498, fol. 328r. Date: Last quarter of 14th century. Photo: The Pierpont Morgan Library & Museum. MS M.498, fol. 4v. Purchased by J. Pierpont Morgan (1837–1913) in 1912.

(Figure 1.3). Both images minimize Alfonso's roles as author of the *Epistola solitarii ad reges* and something like co-author of the *Liber celestis imperatoris ad reges*, as if to insist that only Christ and Birgitta—whose authorship is signified by the repeated presence of her writing desk—are

Figure 1.3 Birgitta of Sweden receiving the heavenly emperor's book to kings from Christ (Frontispiece to *Liber celestis imperatoris ad regem*). New York, Pierpont Morgan Library, MS M.498, fol. 343v. Date: Last quarter of fourteenth century. Photo: The Pierpont Morgan Library & Museum. MS M.498, fol. 343v. Purchased by J. Pierpont Morgan (1837–1913) in 1912.

responsible for the texts before us. While for Catherine the presence of scribes is authorizing, Birgitta's authorial standing is enhanced here—for reasons that will be discussed below—by eliding what was, in fact, an even greater mediation in her texts of her textual community. In other words, the illustrations of Birgitta's manuscripts in their own way also pay special attention to her scribes and editors in order to occlude *their* roles in the production of the texts and emphasize Birgitta's.

These images should alert us to how inadequate our assumptions might be to the situations of Birgitta and Catherine as writers. For instance, while the images address scribal mediation in very different ways, they are all meant to present Birgitta and Catherine as authors of the texts they illustrate—a reminder of how complicated medieval ideas of authorship and authority were. And they serve as author portraits of Birgitta and Catherine at the same time as they seem to point away from the women, toward God's authorship and the authorization of scribes—a reminder of the differences between our ideas and medieval conceptions of authorship and authority. What remains of this chapter will examine some of the key issues to be taken into account in Birgitta's and Catherine's collaboration with their scribes and editors, and then conclude with some thoughts about the implications of these collaborations for how we think about Birgitta and Catherine as writers.

Birgitta

Neither the form nor the content of the *Liber celestis revelacionum* was produced solely by Birgitta or entirely under her control. What we know as Birgitta's *Revelations* is the product of at least two main stages of editorial intervention by her scribes and editors.[5] The first is in the creation of the original text or texts. It is not clear how much mastery Birgitta had of Latin and whether it was sufficient for her to have contributed to the translations, but at the very least, one can assume that her more Latinate confessors must have played a dominant role in the generation of the Latin text, whether they did so by simultaneous translation of Birgitta's dictation in Swedish or by translating texts that she had written out in Swedish.[6] The second obvious stage was the conversion of the individual revelations into books. As mentioned already, the texts contained in the books of the *Liber celestis revelacionum* were not composed as part of a coherent work but as individual revelations, sometimes in the form of letters, directed to their intended recipients.[7] Birgitta's confessors were responsible for collecting the individual revelations into books, a process that probably began during Birgitta's lifetime. Book I may consist of a collection made by her Swedish confessor Master Mathias of Linköping in the 1340s, and Book V, the so-called *Liber questionum*, narrates a vision Birgitta received in the 1340s and may have been composed at that time (see below).[8] But the major work of turning the individual revelations into a work of spiritual literature was done after Birgitta's death by Alfonso of Jaén and others of her clerical circle, who organized the selected revelations into books and made corrections and changes.[9] Roger Ellis has shown how difficult, if not impossible, it is in the *Revelations* to distinguish Birgitta's voice from the voices of her editors, and Bridget Morris and others have concluded that we cannot assume that the text of the *Revelations* as we have it is in every instance Birgitta's words rather than those of her confessors.[10]

As the illustrations in the early manuscripts suggest, the Birgittine hagiography displays a marked defensiveness over the role of her editors in the production of her *Revelations*. Whereas it seems likely (as Morris has concluded)[11] that Birgitta dictated her revelations to scribes more often than she put pen to paper, the *Vita* produced by several of her clerical circle shortly after her death, perhaps to minimize the interventions of her scribes and editors, insists that her normal practice was to serve as her own scribe. A similar interest might explain the *Vita's* account of Birgitta reviewing the Latin translation to make sure that it accorded with her vision—thus providing a kind of *concordat cum originali*.[12] The way her command of Latin is cited in the testimonies for her canonization process suggests that her Latinity had become a hagiographic trope, meant to establish her control over the text.[13] At the very least, the interest taken in her command of the language is itself interesting. One might take in the same vein her hagiographers' attention to the process of composition, whether they say that Birgitta wrote out her revelations herself or refer to her dictating her revelations to them immediately after having received them. On the one hand, for Birgitta's hagiographers, her words were not hers at all but God's. On the other hand, her words had to be hers, at least so that they would not seem to be the creation of her scribes and clerical supporters.[14] While it might be true that male mediators of medieval women's spiritual writings tended "to accentuate the importance of their own roles, or to occlude female involvement," Birgitta's hagiographers accentuated and possibly exaggerated Birgitta's role in the composition of her texts in order to occlude their own roles as collaborators in the creation of the *Liber celestis revelacionum*.[15]

Scholars have previously stressed Birgitta's creative autonomy as an interpreter of divine inspiration, against hagiographic accounts of her passivity and against the tendency in the *Revelations* themselves to direct attention toward her heavenly interlocutors away from Birgitta; that is, they have treated her as fully an author. But many aspects of her authorial process and the nature of her collaboration with her confessors remain obscure.[16] That collaboration was certainly more complex than the hagiographic accounts given by Birgitta's confessors, in which the only collaboration amounts to the influence of Birgitta's divine knowledge on their (merely) human learning. For example, in his prologue to the *Revelations*, Mathias of Linköping stresses that Birgitta's revelations were the words "Not of her who is empty of power but of him who is full of the power of truth" (Prol. M.: 30) and pointed to her complete ignorance—"She would not have been able to make it up even had she wanted to, since she was a simple and gentle soul" (Prol. M.: 41)—as evidence of the marvelous nature of the wisdom contained in her texts. And so Mathias, an influential scriptural scholar, sought Birgitta's help when working on his commentary on the *Book of Apocalypse*, by having Birgitta ask God directly for answer to questions he was having trouble answering. In this sense, Birgitta—or divine inspiration working through her—influenced her confessor; as Claire Sahlin has noted, Birgitta became in effect co-author of Mathias's scriptural commentary.[17] But it is not difficult to find evidence of Mathias's influence on Birgitta, as Anders Piltz and Mats Malm, among others, have suggested.[18] This influence is most dramatically evident in Book V of the *Liber celestis revelacionum*, known as the *Liber questionum*, a book that is unique in the *Revelations* corpus in that it is a coherent work rather than a compilation of individual revelations; it is also the most theologically speculative of Birgitta's texts. Based on a vision Birgitta experienced in the 1340s, while she was still in Sweden, of a monk standing on a ladder extending to the heavens and asking questions of Christ, the book is structured around the questions posed by the monk, and Christ's responses, interspersed with revelations from Christ and the Virgin Mary. The overall theme of the book is the nature of revelation itself, how and why God communicates to humans through images and metaphors—a feature of revelation to which the monk objects strenuously.[19] Christ's answers to the monk serve not only as a defense of Birgitta's revelations and their image-laden content but also as a kind of actualization of Mathias's theories, in his theological and literary writings, concerning divine signification and the relationship between divine truth and human imagination in literary representation.[20] Mathias's influence on Birgitta's vision in the *Liber questionum* suggests a kind of influence that goes beyond editing or emending revelations already composed or even experienced by Birgitta. It suggests that Birgitta's understanding of revelation—indeed, her very experience of revelation—was shaped to a considerable extent by what she learned from Mathias and that he was a very crucial collaborator indeed in the formation of her career as a visionary. But it is impossible to define this kind of contribution by Mathias or others of Birgitta's confessors with any level of precision.

It is also not clear whether or to what extent Birgitta herself played a role, in collaboration with her confessors, in the creation of the eventual books of *Revelations*. To what extent or at what point did Birgitta—or her confessors, for that matter—conceive of her *Revelations* as an eventual collected work? On this question, the example of the *Liber questionum* is again central. Because it is a coherent text rather than a compilation of individual revelations, it might have been expected to have circulated independent of the rest of Birgitta's revelations if it is, as it purports to be, the product of Birgitta's immediate dictation/composition at the time of the vision—that is, in the 1340s, before she left

Sweden for Rome. The fact that no manuscripts of this book exist that predate the version issued by Alfonso's scriptorium after Birgitta's death suggests that the *Liber questionum* as we know it might have been composed or completed later in Birgitta's life, the result of a longer process of reconsideration and revision by Birgitta and/or by her confessors and editors. A later date of composition or completion would change dramatically the way the book reads, making it a retrospective justification and explanation of her career after Sweden. And regardless of when it was composed, what explains this book's distinctive form, so radically different from the rest of Birgitta's revelations? That these questions have not been sufficiently raised in the Birgittine scholarship is perhaps evidence of the success of Alfonso and others in representing the texts as the result of spontaneous inspiration rather than authorial deliberation and revision, and their success in linking Birgitta as author of the *Revelations* in the form they gave it in the 1370s.[21]

The text of the *Revelations* itself generally makes only oblique references to the role of Birgitta's scribes and editors in its creation, but the issue of collaboration is addressed directly in a revelation often cited in that connection. This is Revelation 49 in the *Revelaciones extravagantes*, a series of revelations apparently collected (and preserved) by Alfonso but not included by him in the canonical *Liber celestis revelacionum*.[22] In this revelation, Christ explains to Birgitta that divine inspiration is compatible with two kinds of collaboration: between God and the imagination of the inspired human author, and between the inspired author and her editors and readers. Christ compares himself to a carpenter who takes wood and makes a beautiful image from it, but then "his friends see that the image can be adorned with still more beautiful colors, and so they paint it with their own colors." The metaphor here—coloring the image carved by Christ the carpenter—seems mainly to mean verbal adornment (by elaboration or gloss), but Christ's words also refer clearly and specifically to books, and seem to gesture to the work of manuscript decoration: "I, God, cut words from the forest of my divinity and placed them in your heart. My friends edited and arranged them in books, coloring and adorning them according to the grace given them."[23] He then commands Birgitta, "In order to adapt them to several languages, give all these books containing revelations of my words to my bishop hermit"—a reference to Alfonso of Jaén—"so that he might compile [*conscribat*—literally, 'co-write'] them and clarify obscure passages, capturing the catholic sense of my spirit."[24] As with the image Christ crafted from the wood, his inspiration is not given fully formed or complete. Christ explains that, like the Evangelists and Doctors of the Church, Birgitta must think over what has been revealed to her from God, work out its meaning, and devise the best ways to express it:

> Your own heart is not always capable and enough on fire to express in writing the things you experience [*sentis*]. Often instead you

consider and reconsider them in your mind, and then you write and rewrite them, until you arrive at the true meaning of my words. In a similar way my Spirit used to ascend and descend on the evangelists and doctors of the Church. At certain times they would set down some things that had to be corrected, at other times things that had to be revised later, at still other times they were examined and reprimanded by others. Yet others came later who pondered their words more thoroughly and explained them more clearly.[25]

Christ here emphasizes the provisional, imperfect nature of any text purporting to be God's words. But he also stresses that the necessary process of interpretation and reinterpretation of revelation does not make the writings that result any less divinely inspired: "And yet all my evangelists received the words of my Spirit through inspiration and declared them and wrote them down." And he commands Alfonso to be such an evangelist: "Tell the hermit that he should carry out and fulfill the office of an evangelist."[26]

This revelation seems to reflect Birgitta's awareness late in her career of the circulation of her *Revelations* as a work of literature independent of the particular moments in which the individual revelations were issued, and acknowledges an aspiration to be an author—or rather coauthor with Christ—by having her revelations "published" as illuminated manuscript books. But what is perhaps even more striking than the reference to Birgitta's agency as author is the way in which this revelation diverges from the hagiographic accounts and the representation of Birgitta's inspired authorship in the early manuscript illustrations by adding Birgitta's editors, and Alfonso in particular, as agents in the process whereby Birgitta's experience of revelation becomes text and book. (It seems likely that the attention drawn here to Alfonso is what led him to omit the revelation from the *Liber celestis revelacionum*.) Indeed, Christ in this revelation might even seem to be suggesting a kind of indeterminacy to revelation, opening up a role for Birgitta's readers in the interpretation (and perhaps revision) of her texts. In any case, the revelation also emphasizes that such mediation or collaboration does not diminish Birgitta's authority or authorship but puts her on a level with the evangelists and Doctors of the Church.

Catherine

A number of questions remain to be answered about Catherine's process of composition and the history of her texts—especially the history of the compilation of her letters. Scholarship on these issues has lagged for many years, in part due to the lack of a complete critical edition of her writings.[27] The lack of a critical edition has created a void in which untested assumptions have been repeated, but the last decade has seen a revival of interest in linguistic and other issues connected to Catherine's texts.[28] Discussion of Catherine's compositional process and its relationship to her scribes inevitably revolves around interpretations of the dramatic letter to Raymond of Capua in October 1377 (Letter T272). In this particularly long letter, Catherine recounts how she turned to God from an experience of great bitterness (*amaritudine*), obviously connected to her frustrations with Italian and ecclesiastical politics, to an experience of union with God in which she received from Him responses to four petitions she had made. As has long been understood, this experience, and these petitions, formed the basis for her book, her *Libro*, which it is clear she began at this time: the letter is, in effect, a first draft or prolegomena of the book. In a breathless postscript—the translation here maintains the somewhat scattered syntax of the original—Catherine announces to Raymond that God has given her the ability to write and that she has written this letter, and another she sent him, in her own hand:

> This letter, and another I have sent you, I wrote in my own hand in the Isola della Rocca, with many sighs and an abundance of tears, so much so that the eye, seeing, could not see. But I was full of amazement at myself, and in the goodness of God, considering his mercy towards his creatures who possess reason, and his Providence, which overflowed [*abondava*] over me, in that for refreshment— having been deprived of this consolation, which on account of my ignorance I did not know—he had given me, and provided for me by giving me the ability of writing [*l'attitudine dello scrivere*], so that having descended from the heights, I might have some small way in which to vent the heart [*sfogare 'l cuore*], so that it not burst. Not wishing to take me yet from this shadowy life, in a marvelous way he fixed it in my mind, just as the master does to the pupil, when he gives him an exemplar. Whence, immediately he parted from me, with the glorious Evangelist and Thomas Aquinas, thus sleeping I began to learn. Pardon me for writing too much, for the hands and the tongue are in accordance with the heart.[29]

I have discussed this letter elsewhere, and it has been a focus of discussion in analysis of Catherine's status and self-awareness as a writer by Jane Tylus and Marina Zancan, among others.[30] When Catherine writes that she acquired "l'attitudine dello scrivere," it seems obvious that she means more than the "ability" to write; as other scholars have noted, "attitudine" here seems to mean something more like "disposition" or even "vocation."

Catherine's announcement is at least in part symbolic, intended to signal a departure from the writing she had done before and a new kind of authorial identity connected to her embarking on the project of her book. As to the character of this new identity and how her postscript works to create it, there is much more to be said. For the purposes of this essay, it is enough to note that Tylus is surely right that Catherine in her announcement intended, in her new identity as a writer, to liberate herself in some sense from her scribes.[31] But it seems likely that what Catherine is really liberating herself from by shifting from letter-writing to the writing of a book is engagement with the worldly politics that was increasingly a source of the *amaritudine* that she mentions at the start of her letter to Raymond. As I have argued at greater length elsewhere, it is very likely that the writing of letters, a kind of labor closely associated with that bitterness, was by this point in her career closely associated with her scribes and the formal and efficient semi-chancery that had developed to produce her letters. In composing her book, on the other hand, Catherine was in a sense alone with God, and this form of writing was, as she makes clear, a source of refreshment and spiritual consolation.[32]

But what might Catherine's announcement mean in more practical terms, and what bearing did it have on her actual collaboration with her scribes in the creation, as well as the production, of her texts? First of all, on the question of Catherine's literacy, it would not be surprising if Catherine had learned to write—indeed, it would perhaps be more surprising if she had not learned to write. But no autograph document of hers survives, and neither Raymond of Capua in his authoritative *Legenda maior* of Catherine nor any of her other followers—including some, like Stefano di Corrado Maconi, who served frequently as her scribes—mention that she could write. Tommaso Caffarini, on the other hand, who was not among Catherine's more intimate followers in the 1370s, reports her learning to write as a miracle in his *Legenda minor* and other writings on Catherine. Catherine Mooney has argued persuasively that Caffarini's promotion of Catherine's miraculous ability is tied to a preoccupation with miraculous reading and writing in his works on other female saints.[33] And Mooney has also observed, astutely, that Catherine does not, in fact, say that she learned to write miraculously, but only that God assisted her in her learning. What she describes as waking up with newfound understanding or competence after intense study is not an experience all that unfamiliar to anyone who has struggled to learn something new or difficult.

It is also very clear that, whatever Catherine meant by reporting that she had acquired "l'attitudine dello scrivere," it did not mean that she henceforth did her writing herself, without the use of scribes. If anything, in the final two years of her life, the participation of Catherine's scribes became more prominent—as well as more organized and professional—perhaps under the influence of the Florentine notary Barduccio Canigiani, who joined her circle in 1378. Catherine became more dependent on them and on the dictation minutes and registers of her letters that they apparently kept. For example, from this period, we have a number of letters sent to different recipients that are almost identical in content, save for the opening and closing protocols, a sign that Catherine and her scribes were working with and from base texts that existed in registers of some kind. And, of course, we know that many, perhaps most, of her letters survived because copies were kept by her scribes and not because they were copied from gatherings of the fair copies sent to recipients. And while the participation of scribes was essential to the production of Catherine's letters, it is also hard to imagine the composition of the *Libro* without them. Her followers almost never mention the *Libro* without stating that it was dictated in a state of ecstasy, but even if we set those comments aside as hagiographical exaggeration, it seems very unlikely that Catherine wrote out, rather than dictated, a lengthy work like the *Libro*.[34]

It is necessary to think clearly about what Catherine might have meant when she told Raymond that she "wrote this letter with my own hand"— indeed, what it meant to write a letter. One presumes that there were at least two stages in the production of any letter by Catherine. All of her followers describe her dictating the contents of her letters to one or more of her scribes. The scribes who recorded her dictation did so probably in the form of minutes or notes. (It is very unlikely that any scribe took dictation directly into the fair copy—the final copy—of the letter.) Those minutes or notes were probably then checked—very possibly by Catherine herself; as Lino Leonardi has noted recently, the fact that Catherine could read in the vernacular means that she could, and very likely did, participate in the reviewing and correcting of her letters.[35] Then one of the scribes wrote a fair copy of the letter, on a square or rectangular sheet of paper, to be sent to the intended recipient.

Catherine could have meant here that she wrote out the fair copy of the letter sent to Raymond and added the postscript—as indeed her scribes sometimes added postscripts to her letters in order to salute other members of her *famiglia*. But this is perhaps the least likely meaning. After all, it is Caffarini—and not Catherine—who claims that her learning to write was a miracle, thereby implying she was transformed miraculously from an illiterate to an accomplished scribe who could write out a presentable fair copy of a letter. A more likely possibility is either that she wrote only the postscript, on the back of the fair copy of the letter, or that she wrote some version of the letter in the form of notes, on a wax tablet or a piece of scrap paper or in one of the registers kept by her scribes for that purpose, and one of her scribes wrote the final, fair copy.

While the eight of Catherine's letters that survived as sent are usually referred to as "originals," the true original text—in one sense—was the text in the registers from which fair copies were made to send to the recipients. That Catherine read and worked with the registers of her letters is implied very strongly by the repetition of content between one letter and another. In addition to re-reading, it is not much of a stretch to imagine Catherine editing by *writing* in the registers of her letters and book. So, when Catherine says that she wrote this letter in her own hand, she could have meant that she wrote out some version of the text in a rough copy, probably in one of the registers in which her scribes recorded her dictation. If this is the case, then the absence of autographs of Catherine's letters is no more surprising than the absence of the original registers of dictation minutes. And as for the fact that her close followers and scribes—those who, unlike Caffarini, were with her on a daily basis and present as she composed her texts—do not mention her writing, the simple explanation might be that they did not think this activity worth mentioning, compared, for instance, to her dictation while in ecstasy. That she had the ability to write in this way was neither miraculous nor even surprising.

It is very likely that something like this scenario was also involved in Catherine's composition of her *Libro*: that she revised the text by working with—or perhaps correcting, editing—the register in which she wrote and in which her scribes took dictation. Her direct engagement with the scribal register is strongly implied in a couple of references in her letters, where she requested that her followers send her book, "il libro" or "il mio libro," because she wanted to write in it; the book had been left behind first at the Salimbeni Castle at Rocca d'Orcia when she went to Florence in Spring 1378, and then left in Florence when she returned to Siena after the Florentine Ciompi uprising that summer.[36] Catherine was not (only) dictating or otherwise composing her *Libro* spontaneously or in ecstasy but (also) working with and revising the text, contained in what was apparently a single register. That the "libro" in question was a scribal register and not a book in which Catherine alone wrote is strongly implied by the fact that it did not accompany her person as she travelled, but rather remained with her followers/scribes.[37]

It seems entirely reasonable to take Catherine's announcement that she had learned to write as meaning that she had found new skills and confidence as a writer of a sort that brought her more directly into the process of composition and editing of her letters and *Libro*. And as has already been suggested, the announcement also involved identifying herself as a writer subjectively distinct from her scribes and signifying a change in her vocation as an author. But her announcement did not mean that she had become a solitary agent in the composition of her texts. For one thing, Catherine's liberation from her scribes was gained not by greater independence as a writer but by writing in dependence on God.[38] And more important for the theme of this essay, her newfound *attitudine dello scrivere* did not in practice mean independence from her circle of followers. Indeed, that Catherine saw her new identity as compatible with her continued dependence on and collaboration with her scribes and other followers is strongly implied in her final, valedictory letter to Raymond of Capua, in which she asks that Raymond and others of her followers "take in hand the book and any writings of mine, and do with them what seems to you best for the honor of God."[39] Giovanna Frosini has pointed out that the phrase Catherine uses here to instruct Raymond to take collect her writings, "ve le rechiate per le mani," had the specific meaning during Catherine's lifetime of putting someone else in charge of a text, with agency to make changes as needed.[40] Indeed, while Catherine's reference to "el libro" here is usually taken to mean her *Libro della divina dottrina* as a finished work, it is perhaps more likely that the book here is like the other references to a book in her letters we have already seen: it is a material object, the actual register containing her scribes' dictation as well as her own additions and editing. In other words, she was not bequeathing a completely finished work but a work-in-progress, which she wanted Raymond and the others to "take in hand," in the sense of forming it or, at least, giving it its final form. Catherine was not so much making Raymond and the others her literary executors as she was authorizing them to continue in their roles as collaborators with her by serving as her editors, responsible for making her writings into a complete and final work.

Conclusion

It is clear that in order to assess the texts of Birgitta and Catherine, we have to abandon the idea of univocal authorial agency. For instance, while they make the claim in different ways and perhaps mean different things by it, both Birgitta and Catherine insist that God spoke through them, and so any account of their writing has to accommodate the co-authorship of God—or else risk trying to recover their agency as writers by disregarding the claims they made about their own experiences of writing.[41] Similarly, the participation of scribes and editors was a condition of both Birgitta's and Catherine's writing, and both women express awareness of this fact, albeit in different ways. But divine inspiration and the contributions of scribes and editors should be seen not as problems to be overcome or explained but, instead, as key elements of their practice and identities as writers. Any evaluation of their identities of writers has to take account of their relationships with their scribes and editors, who along with God constituted their textual communities.[42]

And this emphasis on the multiple agents responsible for their texts is also an argument for special attention to the manuscript tradition of Birgitta's and Catherine's texts. It seems that Birgitta and Catherine were both leaving their scribes and editors texts that were to some extent unfinished. (Indeed, as Christ suggests to Birgitta in *Extravagantes* 49, any writing about God is by its nature unfinished.) This is more obvious in the case of Birgitta, since the *Liber celestis revelacionum* took form mostly after her death and as part of the creation of the first manuscripts, but the manuscript tradition of Catherine's *Libro* also shows that her most intimate scribes and editors (Barduccio Canigiani, Stefano di Corrado Maconi, Cristofano di Gano Guidini, and Raymond of Capua himself) might have struggled to understand what she had left them as they sought to clarify the structure of her magnum opus in the first generation of manuscripts.[43]

At the same time, the emphasis here on Birgitta and Catherine as writers in collaboration with their communities is not meant to suggest that we should not think of them as individual authors or that the very idea of the individual author is not relevant. While it is "often a mistake to speak about Christian texts, particularly those from medieval manuscript culture, in terms of individual authorship," authorial identity did mean something in the fourteenth century, whether we are referring to the identity of scriptural authors, ancient *auctores* (Christian or pagan), or contemporaries like Petrarch or Christine de Pizan.[44] Indeed, while the communal nature of the production of their texts is something Birgitta and Catherine have in common with virtually all medieval women authors of spiritual texts, what is much more unusual—perhaps unique—is the prominence of Birgitta's and Catherine's personae as authors.

Birgitta and Catherine's hagiographers were preoccupied, in a way that seems to be without parallel among medieval female saints, with the question of what it meant to call them authors and, indeed, what it meant to call them "writers." Hence the extraordinary attention (in text and image) to exactly how they composed their texts: dictation to scribes or taking the pen into their own hands could mean different things in difference circumstances. And in an unprecedented way, their followers made publication of manuscripts of their writings central to the campaigns for their canonizations: Birgitta and Catherine were promoted as authors at the same time as they were promoted as saints. That Birgitta and Catherine were authors clearly mattered to the communities that participated in both the creation and the dissemination of their writings. As we have seen, both women were aware not only of their literary posterity but also of themselves as writing subjects in dialogue with God and in cooperation—and sometimes tension—with their scribes and editors.

And perhaps also in dialogue with each other: when Catherine announced in October 1377 that she had taken the pen into her own hand in order to write a book, she was probably aware (directly or through her clerical circle) of the manuscripts of Birgitta's *Revelations* produced in Naples, which we know had started to circulate by May 1377. While Birgitta's *Revelations* and Catherine's *Libro* are very different works, it is hard to resist the thought that in authoring a book, Catherine was in some sense imitating Birgitta or that her book project was to some degree authorized by Birgitta's model. This confluence of Birgitta's *Liber* and Catherine's *Libro* is a reminder of why, in spite of the many obvious differences between them, it makes sense to discuss these two writers together.

Notes

1 As Amy Hollywood has noted, "Virtually all the medieval women's spiritual texts available to us are mediated in some way, either by scribes, editors, translators, or compilers." Amy Hollywood, "On Gender, Agency, and the Divine in Religious Historiography," in *Acute Melancholia and Other Essays: Mysticism, History, and the Study of Religion* (New York: Columbia University Press, 2016), 107–08.

2 Jane Tylus, *Reclaiming Catherine of Siena: Literacy, Literature, and the Signs of Others* (Chicago, IL: University of Chicago Press, 2009), especially 18–23. It seems that the question of literary status is more a feature of scholarship on Catherine than scholarship on Birgitta. Perhaps this is because there is no Swedish parallel to the robust Italian fourteenth-century literary tradition—dominated by the *tre corone* Dante, Petrarch, and Boccaccio—from which Catherine can be excluded.

3 At the same time, one might ask whether any scribes took dictation onto scrolls of the type represented in the image or whether the scrolls here are iconographic in meaning rather than realistic.

4 Hans Aili has determined that of the 58 chapters in Book VIII, 25 have been taken entirely from chapters of Books II–VII, while an additional 3 chapters have been quoted at length. Alfonso adapted the borrowings from earlier books by changing words and phrases to suit the theme of the new book. Aili notes that scribes of some of the early manuscripts—but not New York, Pierpont Morgan Library, M. 498—recognized the repetitions and declined to include the repeated passages. See Aili's Introduction in Rev. VIII, pp. 21–22.

5 On the textual history of the *Revelations*, see the editors' introductions in Rev. I and Rev. IV; Hans Aili, "St. Birgitta and the Text of the *Revelationes*. A Survey of Some Influences Traceable to Translators and Editors," in *The Editing of Theological and Philosophical Texts from the Middle Ages*, ed. Monika Asztalos (Stockholm: Almqvist and Wiksell, 1986), 75–91; Hans Aili and Jan Svanberg, *Imagines Sanctae Birgittae: The Earliest Illuminated Manuscripts and Panel Paintings Related to the Revelations of St. Birgitta of Sweden*, 2 vols (Stockholm: Royal Academy of Letters, History and Antiquities, 2003); and Roger Ellis, "The Divine Message and Its Human Agents: St. Birgitta and Her Editors," *Studies in St. Birgitta and the Brigittine Order* 35 (1993): 209–33.

6 On Birgitta's Latinity and her confessors' assessment of it, see Undhagen's Introduction in Rev. I, p. 7, and Morris's "Introduction" in Birgitta of Sweden, *The Revelations of St. Birgitta of Sweden*, trans. Denis Searby, with Introductions and Notes by Bridget Morris, 4 vols (Oxford: Oxford University Press, 2006–15), 1: 12. Roger Ellis reasons that after Birgitta's scribes had translated her revelations from Swedish into Latin, they read it back to her retranslated into Swedish so she could check it against her memory of the original—in other words, she did not have sufficient Latin to check the translation itself (Ellis, "Divine Message and Its Human Agents," 210).

7 The *Vita* written for Birgitta's canonization process, known usually as the "Process Vita," notes how she wrote and sent *epistolas* to both ecclesiastical and secular world leaders. See AP, 86.

8 This is not to mention the preservation of some early revelations in Old Swedish versions that predated the translations by Mathias of Linköping. See Undhagen's Introduction in Rev I, p. 10.

9 For a summary of the evidence for this process, which includes several revelations in Birgitta's own hand and fragments of what seem to be earlier collections, see Morris's Introduction in Birgitta of Sweden, *The Revelations*, I: 15–17.

10 Ellis, "Divine Message and its Human Agents." As Bridget Morris notes, the text of the *Revelations* cannot be taken to be purely Birgitta's voice, isolated from her clerical circle, but is rather an interpretation and wording "imposed upon" her visions "in collaboration with her confessors" (Morris, "Introduction," in Birgitta of Sweden, *The Revelations*, 1: 8). And for Claire L. Sahlin: "One cannot presume that the extant writings are Birgitta's precise words or exact reflections of her visions and thoughts," in *Birgitta of Sweden and the Voice of Prophecy* (Woodbridge: Boydell Press, 2001), 32.

11 See Bridget Morris, *St Birgitta of Sweden* (Woodbridge: Boydell Press, 1999), 74; and Aili and Svanberg, *Imagines Sanctae Birgittae*, 1: 11–12.

12 AP, 84:

> Et tunc dabat ei verba, que habuerat a Christo uel a beata virgine Maria, responsura ad illam materiam; vel illa verba diuinitus ei data scribebat in lingua sua materna manu sua propria, quando erat sana, et faciebat illa translatari in lingua latina fidelissime a nobis confessoribus suis et postea ascultabat illa cum scriptura sua, quam ipsa scripserat, ne vnum verbum ibi plus adderetur uel deficeret, nisi que ipsa in visione diuinitus audierat et viderat. Si vero erat infirma, vocabat confessorem et scriptorem suum secretarium ad hoc specialiter deputatum, et tunc ipsa cum magna deuocione et timore Dei et aliquando cum lacrimis referebat ei verba illa in uulgari suo cum quadam attenta eleuacione mentali, quasi si legeret in libro, et tunc confessor dicebat illa verba in lingua latina illi scriptori, et ille scribebat illa ibidem in sua presencia, et postea cum erant verba conscripta, ipsa volebat illa ascultare et ascultabat valde diligenter et attente.

13 See AP, 254, 276, and 393.

14 These comments of Birgitta's followers, by limiting control of the text to Birgitta and thereby eliding their contributions, accomplish in a particular way aspects of what Michel Foucault described as the "author-function." See Foucault "What Is an Author," in *The Foucault Reader*, ed. Paul Rabinow (New York: Pantheon Books, 1984), 101–20.

15 Carolyn Dinshaw and David Wallace, "Introduction," in *The Cambridge Companion to Medieval Women's Writing* eds. Dinshaw and Wallace (Cambridge: Cambridge University Press, 2003), 5.

16 On Birgitta's role as an engaged interpreter of divine revelation, see Morris, "Introduction," Birgitta of Sweden, *The Revelations*, 1: 8; Ellis, "The Divine Message and its Human Agents," 209; Anders Piltz, "Revelation and the Human Agent: St. Birgitta and the Process of Inspiration," in *Tongues and Texts Unlimited. Studies in Honour of Tore Janson on the Occasion of His Sixtieth Anniversary*, eds. Hans Aili and Peter af Trampe (Stockholm: Stockholms Universitet, Institutionen för klassiska språk, 2000), 181–88; and Anders Piltz, "Birgitta and the Bible," in *A Companion to Birgitta of Sweden and Her Legacy in the Later Middle Ages*, ed. Maria H. Oen (Leiden: Brill, 2019), 53–79.

17 Sahlin, *Birgitta of Sweden*, 124.

18 See, for example, Anders Piltz, "Magister Mathias of Sweden in His Theological Context: A Preliminary Survey," in Asztalos, *The Editing of Theological and Philosophical Texts*; Mats Malm, *The Soul of Poetry Redefined: Vacillations of Mimesis from Aristotle to Romanticism* (Copenhagen: Museum Tusculanum Press, University of Copenhagen, 2012), 61–74.

19 See Bridget Morris, "The Monk-on-the-Ladder in Book V of St. Birgitta's *Revelaciones*," *Kyrkohistorisk Årsskrift* (1982): 95–107; and F. Thomas Luongo, "God's Words or Birgitta's? Birgitta of Sweden as Author," in Oen, *A Companion to Birgitta of Sweden*.

20 Malm, *The Soul of Poetry Redefined*. Mathias's influence on the *Liber questionum* has been noted by Morris, among others; see Birgitta of Sweden, *The Revelations*, 2: 264.

21 Birger Bergh has pointed out that there are inconsistencies between Alfonso's description of the book in the prologue he wrote for it and the book's actual contents, evidence that Alfonso was not involved in its compilation—and perhaps had not read it carefully; see Bergh's Introduction in Rev. V, pp. 17–18. Arne Jönsson comes to the same conclusion in *Alfonso of Jaén. His Life and Works with Critical Editions of the Epistola Solitarii, the Informaciones and the Epistola Serui Christi* (Lund: Lund University Press, 1989), 55–56. But while this evidence suggests that the book was complete before Alfonso began his work on the *Liber celestis*, there is apparently no evidence of what form it existed before it reached Alfonso or, indeed, of when it was completed.

22 On the textual history of these revelations, see Lennart Hollman's analysis in the modern edition: Extrav., pp. 28–45; and Morris's Introduction in Birgitta of Sweden, *The Revelations*, 4: 219–27.

23 Extrav., 49.3: "Sic ego Deus prescidi de silua deitatis mee verba mea, que posui in cor tuum. Amici vero mei redegerunt ea in libros secundum graciam eis datam et colorauerunt et ornauerunt illa."

24 Extrav., 49.4: "Nunc igitur uvt ipsa pluribus linguis conueniant, trade omnes libros reuelacionum eorundem verborum meorum episcopo meo hermite, qui conscribat et obscura elucident et catholicum sensum spiritus mei teneat."

25 Extrav., 49.6–7: "Nam sicut cor tuum non semper est capax et feruidum ad proferendum et scribendum illa, que sentis, sed nunc voluis et reuoluis ea in animo tuo, nunc scribis et rescribis illa, donec venis ad proprium sensum verborum meorum, sic spiritus meus cum euangelistis et doctoribus ascendebat et descendebat, qui nunc ponebant aliqua emendanda, nunc aliqua retractanda, nunc iudicabantur et reprehendebantur ab aliis." Et tamen alii postea venerunt, qui subtilius discusserunt et lucidius explanauerunt verba eorum.

26 Extrav., 49.7–8: "Attamen omnes euangeliste mei a spiritu meo per infusionem habuerunt verba, que loquebantur et scripserunt. Item dic eidem heremite, quod faciat et impleat officium euangeliste."

27 The lack of a critical edition is both a symptom and a cause of Catherine's lack of literary standing in modern Italian scholarship. Antonio Volpato has issued, as part of a CD-ROM collection of Catherine's writings, a newly edited text of the letters, but without any annotations or reference to textual variants. See *Santa Caterina da Siena: Opera Omnia. Testi e concordanze*, ed. Fausto Sbaffoni (Pistoia, 2002) (CD-ROM edition). We are in better shape with the *Libro* (or *Dialogo*), for which we have Guiliana Cavallini's edition based on several early and authoritative manuscripts, in which she made important observations about the overall structure of the work: *Il Dialogo della Divina Provvidenza: ovvero Libro della divina dottrina*, ed. Giuliana Cavallini, (Rome: Edizioni Cateriniane, 1968; 2nd edn., Siena: Cantagalli, 1995). But her edition is not a true critical edition in that it does not take into account the full range of manuscripts and includes minimal textual commentary. On this point see Silvia Nocentini, "Il problema testuale del *Libro di divina dottrina* di Caterina da Siena: questioni aperte," *Revue d'histoire des Textes* 11 (2016): 255–94.

28 For example, the assumption that in the collections of the letters Catherine's followers or subsequent readers translated her Sienese vernacular into more acceptable forms (alternately more "Florentine," or more "northern") and that they excised informational postscripts from the original letters. But it is not clear that either of these claims is precisely correct. On these issues, see most recently Lino Leonardi, "Il problema testuale dell'espistolario

cateriniano," and Giovanna Frosini, "Lingua e testo nel manoscritto viennese delle lettere di Caterina," in *Dire l'ineffabile. Caterina da Siena e il
linguaggio della mistica. Atti del Convegno (Siena, 13–14 novembre 2003)*,
eds. Lino Leonardi and Pietro Trifone (Florence: SISMEL, Edizioni del Galluzzo, 2006), 71–90 and 91–126 respectively.

29 Letter T272:

> Questa lettera, e un' altra che io ve ne mandai, ò scritte di mia mano
> in su l'Isola della Rocca, con molti sospiri e abondanzia di lagrime; in
> tanto che l'occhio, vedendo, non vedeva; ma piena d'amirazione ero di
> me medesima,e de la bontà di Dio—considerando la sua misericordia
> verso le sue creature che ànno in loro ragione—, e de la sua providenzia,
> la quale abondava verso di me, che per refrigerio, essendo privata de la
> consolazione—la quale per mia ignoranzia io non cognobbi— m'aveva
> dato e proveduto col darmi l'attitudine dello scrivere, a ciò che, discen-
> dendo da l'altezza, avessi un poco con che sfogare el cuore perché non
> scoppiasse. Non volendomi trare ancora di questa tenebrosa vita, per
> amirabile modo me la formò nella mente mia, sì come fa el maestro al
> fanciullo, che gli dà l'essemplo. Unde, subbito che fuste partito da me,
> col glorioso evangelista e Tomaso d'Aquino, così dormendo cominciai a
> imparare. Perdonatemi del troppo scrivere, però che le mani e la lingua
> s'accordano col cuore.

Author's translation.

30 F. Thomas Luongo, *The Saintly Politics of Catherine of Siena* (Ithaca, NY:
Cornell University Press, 2006), Ch. 5, "Prophetic Politics;" Tylus, *Reclaiming Catherine of Siena*; Marina Zancan, "Lettere di Caterina da Siena,"
in *Letteratura italiana. Le opere*, vol. 1, *Dalle origini al Cinquecento*, ed.
Alberto Asor Rosa (Turin: Einaudi, 1992), 593–633; and Marina Zancan,
"Lettere di Caterina da Siena. Il testo, la tradizione, l'interpretazione," *Annali d'italianistica, Women Mystic Writers* 13 (1995): 151–61.

31 Tylus, *Reclaiming Catherine of Siena*, 213–14: "And in charge of her life,
too, in a way that did not require the presence of scribes who, assiduous as
they may have been, nonetheless took from her a measure of independence."

32 "Catherine of Siena, *Auctor*," in *Women Leaders and Intellectuals of the
Medieval World*, eds. Katie Bugyis, Kathryn Kerby-Fulton, and John Van
Engen (Woodbridge: Boydell & Brewer, [forthcoming]).

33 Catherine M. Mooney, "Wondrous Words: Catherine of Siena's Miraculous
Reading and Writing According to the Early Sources," in *Catherine of Si-
ena: The Creation of a Cult*, eds. Jeffrey F. Hamburger and Gabriella Signori
(Turnhout: Brepols, 2013), 277–78.

34 On the other hand, as Silvia Nocentini has pointed out ("Il problema
testuale," 260), it is not impossible that Catherine dictated the entire book
over the course of several days, as Raymond of Capua recounts.

35 Leonardi, "Il problema testuale dell'espistolario cateriniano."

36 Letter T365, from Florence to Stefano di Corrado Maconi, probably in May
or June 1378: "Mandai a chiedere alla Contessa il libro mio; e hallo aspettato
parecchi dì: e non viene"; and Letter T179, from Siena to the Francesco di
Pipino in Florence, August 1378: "Date a Francesco el libro e li privilegii, perché vi voglio scrivere alcuna cosa, e 'l privilegio voglio per fare dire la messa
si che dareteglili." The privileges she mentions here are the papal documents
giving her permission to receive the Eucharist. Siena, along with Florence,
was under interdict at this time. Suzanne Noffke, among others, argues for
Catherine's direct involvement in the editing of the text; see "The Writings
of Catherine of Siena," in *A Companion to Catherine of Siena*, eds. Carolyn

Muessig, George Ferzoco, and Beverly Mayne Kienzle (Leiden: Brill, 2012), especially 324–29. See also Nocentini, "Il Problema testuale," 260.

37 The image of Catherine working alongside her scribes with the registers and other drafts of her texts actually brings her more deeply into the writing process than does an image of Catherine writing solo. Indeed, it makes her a participant not only in the generation of the texts but also in their publication.

38 And while in Catherine's letters—the writing she apparently associated with her scribes—the voice is unambiguously and forcefully hers (*Io Caterina, scrivo a voi*), her new voice in the *Libro* is blended with the voice of God the Father. Indeed, most of the words of this text that made her fully a writer are spoken by God and not by Catherine.

39 Letter T373: "Anco vi prego che el Libro e ogni scrittura la quale trovaste di me, voi e frate Bartolomeo e frate Tommaso e il Maestro ve le rechiate per le mani; e fatene quello che vedete che sia più onore di Dio, con missere Tommaso insieme." Catherine refers here to the Sienese Dominican friars Bartolomeo Dominici and Tommaso della Fonte; the Augustinian Hermit Giovanni Tantucci ("il Maestro"); and Tommaso Petra, papal protonotary. See Catherine of Siena, *The Letters of Catherine of Siena*, ed. and trans. Suzanne Noffke, 4 vols (Tempe: Arizona Center for Medieval and Renaissance Studies, 2000–08), 4: 369 n. 26.

40 Frosini, "Lingua e testo nel manoscritto viennese delle lettere di Caterina," 94–95. And after all, Catherine's scribes *did* translate her *Libro* into Latin.

41 I am aware of opening up a larger question than I can address here, one whose terms of which have been set very nicely by Amy Hollywood ("On Gender," 117–27).

42 I am using the concept of "textual community" in a simpler sense than that given it by its coiner, Brian Stock, in his influential book, *The Implications of Literacy: Written Language and Models of Interpretation in the Eleventh and Twelfth Centuries* (Princeton, NJ: Princeton University Press, 1983).

43 Not only was the *Libro* translated into Latin, but the manuscripts (both the Italian and Latin ones, as Nocentini has emphasized in "Il problema testuale") witness the development of a chapter structure and eventually the division of the work into "treatises." Indeed, the work of reception continued in the insights of Cavallini into the internal logic of the structure of the *Libro,* insights that are represented in her editions of the work.

44 Hollywood, "Feminist Studies in Christian Spirituality," in *Acute Melancholia*, 107.

2   "Su dunque, peregrino!"

Pilgrimage and Female Spirituality in the Writings of Birgitta and Catherine

Jane Tylus

Birgitta of Sweden was the paragon, the over-achiever of late medieval pilgrims.[1] She traveled to local shrines in Scandinavia in the 1330s, to Santiago de Compostela with her husband Ulf in the 1340s, to Rome for the Jubilee of 1350, and to the Holy Land in 1371–72. She was so obsessed with pilgrimage, as we learn from Book VI of the *Revelations*, that one day, tired of studying Latin, she asks Mary's permission to visit the pilgrim sites of Rome. Mary grants her leave to see "these lovely places" but insists that Birgitta not "neglect your grammar lessons or the holy obedience you owe to your spiritual father."[2] Going off to see local relics and shrines, that is, should not trump learning Latin! Birgitta also established and ran a home for pilgrims from northern Europe like herself in her lovely palazzo on today's Piazza Farnese. So central was pilgrimage to her life that Prayer 14, from the "Fifteen Oos," closes: "I beg of thee at the hour of my death to receive my spirit, a pilgrim and exile returning to you"[3]—a prayer written by members of the Birgittine Order in England a century after her death, who recognized the importance of her peregrinations.[4]

And she was a pilgrim in more than one sense. For one thing, Birgitta was a pilgrim in its original Latin meaning: a stranger or foreign resident who did not have Roman citizenship. Birgitta was indeed a foreigner in Rome, where she lived for over two decades. But the word has other resonances for the history of Christianity, beginning with the Church Fathers. As Matthew Kraus has shown, Jerome used *peregrinus* to translate the Hebrew word for "sojourner," and in such a way does he refer to Abraham, Isaac, and Jacob.[5] The first letter of Peter extends this term to the Christian community as a whole, as Peter enjoins his audience to behave "as though you were aliens and exiles" with respect to the passions of the flesh (*advenas et peregrinos*; Ep.I, 2:11). The plight of foreignness faced by the original Hebrew tribes will come to characterize Christian life itself on an alien earth, with resonances in not only Jerome but John of Chrysostom, the Epistle to Diognetus, and, most famously, Augustine, who, in the *Confessions*, writes, "Our hearts are restless until they rest in you, O Lord."[6] These would seem to be the contexts on which Birgitta's followers were drawing a century after her death—while they were no doubt also fully cognizant of Birgitta's own peregrinations.

These rituals of medieval pilgrimage had little resonance for the other major figure in this volume whose citation provides the title for this essay. Catherine too tended to pilgrims, at the Spedale di Santa Maria della Scala in Siena as well as at the Casa di Misericordia, to whose rector she addressed a number of letters. And like Birgitta, she lived in Rome, spending the last 18 months of her life there, when undoubtedly it would have been hard to ignore the many pilgrims crowding into the city. But Catherine's Rome was that of a besieged Urban VI, newly crowned pope and hotly contested by the French cardinals, who promptly elected their own pope and returned to Avignon. Given that the immediate crisis demanded all of her attention, Catherine was not tempted to go out to visit the pilgrim sites nearby. Nor would she hear of others going to Jerusalem, actively discouraging one Monna Agnesa da Toscanella: "it seems to me that it would be more in keeping with God's sweet will for you to stay put."[7] But long before Urban became pope and Catherine moved to Rome, she had revealed herself as no fan of pilgrimages, actively dissuading a Carthusian monk named Giovanni from going to the Purgatorio di San Patrizio in Ireland. He should remain in his cell, "hugging the tree of the most holy cross" and seeking good "only in God, rather than in transitory things, in which there is no perfection."[8] Pilgrimage is symptomatic of man's fragility, as he seeks only "his own mental consolation."[9] In fact, she says, "I think your wish to go [to St. Patrick's Purgatorio] may be a trick of the devil, who wants to catch you on the hook of what is good. I'm certain that in this light you will come to know the truth, and knowing it you will thank the supreme eternal Father who through holy obedience has rescued you from this danger"[10] (Letter 201; Noffke, *Letters*, 2: 257).

It seems unlikely that we will thus find any common ground between the fourteenth century's two most famous women when it comes to pilgrimage. Indeed, one can hardly ignore even more fundamental differences between Birgitta and Catherine: the one a mother of eight children, the other a virgin (nonetheless called "Mamma" by her circle of disciples); the one from the highest ranks of the Swedish nobility, the other the daughter of a middle-class dyer; the one a visionary and prophetess whose writings are dominated by voices not her own, the other an energetic writer of letters that all open with the voice of "Io Catarina"; the one strongly influenced by the Franciscans, the other a *mantellata* or third-order Dominican. Still, the extent to which the complex and multiple meanings of *peregrinatio* dominated their lives makes for an arguably powerful way for understanding the dynamics of female mysticism and action in the Trecento. Moreover, in putting Birgitta's and Catherine's conceptions of pilgrimage in dialogue, we can grasp ways in which this dialogue manifested itself elsewhere, such as in writings by two of Italy's *tre corone*, Dante and Francesco Petrarca, as I will discuss briefly in closing.[11] And finally, we may also come to realize why understanding medieval pilgrimage demands more than the simple elucidation of two opposing sides.

A pair of biblical passages can illuminate how Birgitta and Catherine conceptualized the role of pilgrimage in their lives. In Birgitta's case, the biblical text is closely tied to a defining moment late in her life: a dramatic scene from Book VII of the *Revelations* when Christ instructs her to leave Rome for Jerusalem. It is not the first time he has told her to travel to the Holy Land, but here he is especially urgent: she must go *now*: "I shall lead you there, and bring you back to Rome, and I shall procure for you what you need, more sufficiently than you ever had before" (Rev. VII: 9.2). The phrase "ego ducam et reducam vos ad Romam" closely echoes a passage from the Book of Tobias.[12] The angel Raphael, disguised as a young man, promises the blind, impoverished Tobias that he will lead his son safely away from home in order to collect a debt, and then back again: "I will lead him there and bring him back to you" (*Et dixitei angelus: Ego ducam et reducam eum ad te*; Tobias 5:15).[13] And he does: with not only the money, but much more, including the liver of a fish that heals Tobias's blindness, and a wealthy wife for his son.

From the Old Testament apocrypha, Tobias offered a reassuring prototype for medieval pilgrimage. It accords quite well with the description of pilgrimage provided by Gábor Klaniczay: "Pilgrimage was itself a complex religious manifestation: beyond its culminating moment—the miraculous healing at the shrine—the pilgrim's liminal way of life and the vicissitudes of the whole process of pilgrimage contributed to its sacral benefits."[14] The elderly Tobias who has spent his life serving others suffers blindness and abjection, to be miraculously healed when his son undertakes the dangerous voyage he cannot. The "sacral benefits" accrue with the son's return, facilitated by the angel—a return that allowed medieval pilgrims to testify to others about their faith and their journey, and to be reintegrated into the community, as is Tobias's son.

What does Birgitta gain on her journey to Jerusalem, and what does she bring back? And perhaps most urgently, why does she go at all? Birgitta's revelations tend to be triggered by place, by a particular setting. The increasing focus on pilgrimage in the final third of the *Revelations,* beginning with the close of Book V, connects the holy places to which Birgitta would travel as a *peregrina*—Assisi, Naples, Gargano, Jerusalem, and Bethlehem—and the status of revelation itself. The end of Book V, with its list of five "sacred places in Jerusalem and Bethlehem" (Rev. V: rev. 13), [15] catapults us directly into the language of pilgrimage to the Holy Land, which will be fulfilled in the course of Book VII. This book also marks the sanctity of time as well as place, as Birgitta's visits to holy sites are aligned with the calendrical/liturgical year. Before leaving for Jerusalem, Birgitta has a vision at Santa Maria Maggiore in Rome on the feast day of Mary's purification; she encounters St. Francis at his church in nearby Trastevere on 4 October, Francis's feast day. At the shrine of Thomas the Apostle in Ortona, Jesus solemnly tells her, "When people visit the shrines of my saints and show reverence to the relics of those who have been glorified by miracles and canonized by popes, it is my heart's great delight to grant them eternal rewards after the measure of the will and faith and struggles of those pilgrims" (Rev. VII: 4.6). The reward here will not only be that of indulgence, but a much more tangible one—as is implicit in the wording of Christ's rebuke to princes who "have eyes and will not see. They have ears and will not hear. They have hands and will not touch" (Rev. VII: 4.10). Unlike those princes, Birgitta has traveled to the very places where she can see, hear, and touch sanctity itself, as Jesus ensures that a "piece of one of the bones of Blessed Thomas" arrives in Birgitta's hand through Thomas's intervention: "I shall give you a treasure that you have long desired" (Rev. VII: 4.21).

As scholars have commented, there is narrative justice in the fact that prior to her trip to Jerusalem, Birgitta sees—and touches—St. Thomas, "who doubted the resurrection and was invited to touch the wounds of the risen Christ. In Jerusalem and Bethlehem, Birgitta will personally see and hear the birth and death scenes of Christ at the original locations...The Holy Land experiences will be for Birgitta comparable to St. Thomas's palpable experience of the risen Lord."[16] While *peregrinatio* for Catherine should foster estrangement from daily life,[17] these moments in Birgitta's text point rather to the intensity and immediacy of the pilgrim's visits. They culminate in the reliving of a climactic moment in Christian history in a way that acknowledges that like Thomas, we are weak and need to see in order to believe. When she arrives in Bethlehem, Birgitta not only hears but also witnesses the protagonists of Christ's Nativity, as is clear from the repetition of "vidit" ("she saw") in chapters 21 and 23 (Rev. VII). The suddenness, moreover, with which Birgitta arrives at the holy sites—she omits all pedestrian information regarding the journey itself—only enhances the immediacy of their visual aspects. Thus, the abrupt opening of Birgitta's vision of the Crucifixion in Chapter 15, as she says without preamble, "As I was weeping in sorrow at Mount Calvary, I saw my Lord, naked and scourged, led out to be crucified..." (Rev. VII: 15.1).[18] Jerome's Paula had merely seen the traces of events from the life of Christ, throwing herself down in adoration "before the Cross...as though she beheld the Lord hanging upon it."[19] Birgitta actually *sees* her Lord, and her writings thus argue for the physical travels of pilgrimage as a *sine qua non* of mysticism. Christ, Mary, and the saints speak to her only in locations that are spiritually significant because they were already *there*.

For all this, Birgitta was hardly unaware of the dangers of pilgrimage, or of its many critics who challenged the veracity of pilgrims' accounts or questioned whether women should undertake arduous voyages. In *Revelations* Book IV, Chapter 4, the perhaps genuinely conflicted Birgitta is trying to decide whether to stay in Sweden—where she might be overcome by pride—or travel on pilgrimage to Rome, which would involve "coming down from my proud throne and humbling my body" (Rev. IV: 4.22). The bad spirit within her says, "Going on a pilgrimage is characteristic of an inconstant mind" and suggests she might be raped and kidnapped on her travels by "greedy men, having heard of your reputation." Further, "what will happen if you should be unworthy of divine consolation and impatient about poverty and humility? Then you will regret having taken such rigorous discipline upon yourself. Then you will have a staff in your hand instead of a ring, a cloth on your head instead of a crown, and lowly sackcloth instead of a crimson gown." The good spirit invokes Holy Elizabeth of Hungary and other women who have made pilgrimages, while the bad inspiration continues to raise fears of scandal and loss. But the conflict is resolved when Birgitta agrees that she will "leave her bodily friends for God's sake and come to a place where there is a shortcut between heaven and death in order to avoid the pains of purgatory, because indulgences are obtained there that offer souls advancement and redemption, which have been granted by the holy pontiffs and earned by the blood of God's saints" (Rev. IV: 4.42–43).[20] What wins the day is the good spirit's observation that one of the very points of pilgrimage is self-mortification, as clarified in a later exchange that Birgitta will have with her husband Ulf after his death. In one of the "Extravagant Revelations," Ulf visits Birgitta in the midst of his purgatorial sufferings to ask for her help, so he may arrive more quickly in paradise, asking that votive masses be offered to "Holy Mary our savior-ess" for an entire year and urging Birgitta to be mindful of the poor. Ulf also mentions the mortification he suffered during their pilgrimage to Santiago de Compostela—precisely those mortifications which the "bad spirit" argues against (Extrav., 56).[21] But the "good spirit" also wins be-cause he can hold out to Birgitta one of the gains accrued through going to Rome for the jubilee—a "shortcut" out of purgatory.

Or as we learn in Book VII (14.1) from Christ himself, when Birgitta arrives at the Holy Sepulcher, "When you came together into my temple, which was dedicated through my blood, you were cleansed from all your sins as though you had just been lifted from the baptismal font."[22] Heal-ing and timely release from purgatory are precisely the gains that Christ promises Birgitta, her version of the tangible earthly gifts Tobias's son brings home with him. Birgitta will discuss this purgatorial process in a much more compressed fashion in three crucial chapters from Rev. IV: 7–9, expanding on the scene of Ulf's request. Pilgrimage reduces one's stay in purgatory because one receives indulgences upon arriving at the Holy Sepulcher or other shrines; in turn, the very existence of purgatory enables links between the living and the dead. The gain that Birgitta brings back is this: the more time she spends as a pilgrim on earth, the less time she will spend as a pilgrim in purgatory.

Pilgrimage thus inhabits a bounded, alternate time and space, a tem-porary heightening of the Christian sensibility to the necessity of living life as a stranger that for the layperson could be too easily obscured in the course of the everyday. Yet it is not solitary: it is connected to a larger community, and there is gain not only for herself but also for her future readers. What is striking about Birgitta's intensely visual reactions to the places of her pilgrimage is the way she enables them to become the reader's own, following, for example, her witnessing of Christ's birth (in Rev. VII: 21) with Mary's personal commentary to Birgitta in the following chapter. The detailed engagement in an almost theatrical setting would be employed by Ignatius of Loyola as well as by writers of pilgrimage guides, but rarely to Birgitta's dramatic effect. Her particular skill consists in personalizing and even possessing the sacred through her words as her *Revelations* become the textual version of souvenirs procured by pilgrims, such as the shell from Santiago or the pilgrim's staff wreathed with palm. Birgitta returns not with relics but with the *Revelations,* a more valuable testimony to her journey than a palm or a shell, insofar as it will awaken in its audience their own desire for such travels.

Some of these souvenirs appear on a small panel painted several decades before Catherine of Siena was born, by the great Sienese painter Duccio. One of the many panels from the reverse of his *Maestà*, placed in Siena's Duomo in 1311, depicts Jesus himself dressed as a pilgrim, bearing the shell from Santiago de Compostela on his hat, the seal of Veronica's veil on his purse. And so to our second biblical passage. As described in the final chapter of Luke's gospel, the scene is the road just outside the gates of Emmaus, the city to which Jesus's disciples are heading several days after the Crucifixion, and unbeknownst to them, Jesus himself joins them. As they walk together, they ask if he has heard of the recent death of Jesus, and when he feigns ignorance, the disciple Cleopas says, "Are you the only stranger (*peregrinus*) to Jerusalem who has not heard of the things that have happened here in recent days?"[23] Night begins to fall, and "when they draw near the village, [Jesus] appeared to be going further, but they constrained him, saying 'Stay with us, for it is toward evening and the day is now far spent'" (Luke 24:13–20).

This is the moment Duccio decided to paint: one of the disciples extending his hand toward the gate in invitation even as Jesus seems to be going further. In other representations from the *Maestà* of events after the Resurrection—Jesus's triumphant rising up from the tomb, his meeting with Mary Magdalene, his ascension into heaven—Duccio depicts Jesus wearing a fine, blue cloak lined with golden thread, new symbols of his divinity. But in the panel featuring the road to Emmaus, Duccio gives him the recognizable garb of the medieval pilgrim, with the souvenirs proclaiming that he has been to sacred sites. Duccio has drawn on the resonant word *peregrinus*, chosen by Jerome to translate the original Greek *paroikos*—literally, someone who is outside of his own home—in order to bring us into a scene of contemporary pilgrimage. As night draws near, the disciples extend hospitality to a pilgrim returning from his travels; and indeed, the bricks within the gateway evoke the recently-paved streets of Siena.

Transporting the reader to the sites of pilgrimage to convey the immediacy and significance of the Christian experience, rendering it tangible: this could be said to embody Birgitta's sense of the pilgrim. And yet Duccio's fellow Sienese, Catherine, would have her own characteristically independent thoughts on this biblical scene in one of her late prayers, written while she was in Rome. Composed during Easter week of 1379, the prayer dwells on events after the resurrection, first invoking Jesus standing at heaven's gate, replacing the angel with his flaming sword: [24] "You, sweet gatekeeper, humble lamb, that gardener who having opened the doors of the heavenly garden—thus, paradise itself—you bring us the flowers and fruits of the eternal God"(Orazione 13).[25] And Catherine continues, "And now I clearly see that you spoke the truth when, appearing to your two disciples on the road in the dress of a pilgrim, you said that Christ had to suffer and come into glory through the way of the cross...and you revealed to them the Scriptures, although they didn't understand you because their intellects were darkened. But you were referring to your very self with those words."[26] In this prayer dense with biblical allusions, Catherine moves from one resurrection narrative— that of John, whose Mary Magdalen confuses the Christ who tells her not to touch him with the "ortolano" or gardener—to Luke's, who tells of the disciples en route to Emmaus, whose minds were too darkened to recognize either Jesus or the truth of the words that he spoke. Unlike the doubting Thomas, Mary Magdalene is forbidden the act of touch, while unlike both Thomas and the men outside Emmaus, she instantly recognizes and believes her Savior. Catherine goes on to close this section of the prayer with "And now I truly know that you have spoken the truth"[27]—making it unclear as to whether she aligns herself with the perspicacious Mary Magdalene or with the two disciples who recognize Christ only when they are later at the table with Jesus: "and he took the bread and blessed and broke it, and gave it to them. And their eyes were opened and they recognized him, and he vanished out of their sight" (Luke 24:30–31).

But perhaps of most interest here is Catherine's phrase "in forma di pellegrino" to describe Christ's appearance on the road—in the manner or the dress of a pilgrim, as though she had Duccio's panels before her. Duccio, of course, knew he was dressing Jesus up as someone he was not. On the most literal level, Jesus has not been to Santiago or Rome. The biblical text may have urged Duccio toward this fictional image; Jerome's Latin notes that Jesus is said to have "appeared"—*se finxit*, literally, pretended—to be going further."[28] Does Catherine likewise call attention to a false move on Jesus's part, one that she is capable of seeing through? "Ora io certamente conosco le verità": now I—Catherine— clearly know. The two disciples, whose "intellects were darkened," are unable to recognize Jesus, perhaps out of human weakness; similarly, the other disciples earlier in Luke 24 refused to believe the women, among them Mary Magdalene, witnesses of Jesus's resurrection from the dead. How is Catherine positioning herself at this scene of unknowing, as Jesus purposefully estranges himself from these men by pretending to be a stranger?

The phrase from one of Peter's letters, cited earlier, can be said to do something similar with the word *peregrinus*: "I beseech you as though you were aliens and exiles to abstain from passions of the flesh" (*tamquam advenas et peregrinos*; Ep.I, 2:11). The interesting word here is *tamquam*—as *though* you were aliens and exiles, as Peter frames the status of being a "paroikos"—a stranger—in the hypothetical mode.[29] That is, Peter wants to make us strangers to our own flesh, facilitating such an abstraction through an act of the imagination. But Catherine, it might be said, is impatient with such imaginative games, as is seen in her editing *out* of the biblical "tamquam"—"as though."[30] We are not *like* pilgrims and strangers, we *are* pilgrims and strangers—as she says on some forty-one occasions, as opposed to five instances, all of them from early letters, where she retained the qualifying simile ("siamo *come* peregrini e viandanti"). Jesus *is* a stranger, in the original Latin sense, in his very estrangement from sin. And he *is* a pilgrim, in the medieval sense, insofar as he has been to the holiest place that there is, heaven itself, returning to tell of his journey. As a result, he is a genuine *peregrinus* to all that exists on earth. Such estrangement is fundamental to Catherine, for whom the true Christian is never at home.

For Catherine, Jesus's disguise arguably tests the disciples' hospitality even as he encourages them to be pilgrims in a different sense from Duccio's, asking them to embrace the fundamentally disorienting effects of estrangement from life on earth.[31] Catherine's impatience with pilgrimage's fictionality and its temporary realization in practice does not mean she was unaware of what could be called the occasional instrumentality of the practice of pilgrimage. Thus, annoyed that Raymond refuses to travel overseas to Avignon on an important mission to the pope because of the dangers of the current political crises, she tells him, "if you can't go as a friar, go as a pilgrim...put on a costume so you can slip by the guards."[32] (One is reminded of what worried friends tell Birgitta when she is deciding whether to travel to Jerusalem: masquerade as a Saracen and paint your face black, so you don't get into trouble among the Muslims on your pilgrimage. Christ tells her not to [Rev. VII: 16]). What is *not* a fiction is that we are all, every day, "peregrini e viandanti." We must go, Catherine says to Regina della Scala in an early letter, "virilmente": manfully, leaving behind the "troubles and anxieties of the world," and, "inebriated with the blood of Christ crucified," head toward a single thing, on a road "neither dark nor gloomy nor overgrown with thorns, but lighted with the true light, Jesus Christ" (Letter 29; Noffke, *Letters*, 1: 208–9, rev.).

And a road, moreover, "cemented with Christ's own blood" (Noffke, *Letters*, 1: 208). References such as these suggest that Catherine is thinking of pilgrimage as linked to martyrdom and death, as is starkly clear from the one letter in which she favorably mentions the possibility of her own travel to the Holy Land, to the "santo sepolcro" in Jerusalem. Strikingly, it is in the only letter of Catherine's where she mentions Birgitta—the "contessa who has died in Rome."[33] It is 1374, and Alfonso Pecha of Jaén, Birgitta's confessor, has just traveled to Siena at the request of Gregory XI to confer with Catherine.[34] In this relatively early letter (127) to Frate Bartolomeo Dominici and Frate Tommaso d'Antonio,[35] both in Pisa at the time, Catherine writes that Alfonso asked her "in the holy father's name to...offer special prayers for him and for holy Church." Toward the end, she adds,

> A young man will come to give you this letter. Trust what he tells you. He has a holy desire to go to the Holy Sepulcher and is on his way to the holy father to get that permission for himself and a few others, religious and layfolk. I have written a letter to the holy father asking him, for love of that most sweet blood, to give us permission to offer our bodies for every sort of torment. Beg supreme eternal Truth...to grant this mercy to us and to you: for all of us as a splendid company to give our lives for him.[36]

This is the same Holy Sepulcher that God tells Birgitta to travel to in Book V of the *Revelations*. But Catherine's reference to "every sort of torment" suggests that her intentions for traveling to Jerusalem are quite different from Birgitta's. As Suzanne Noffke has observed, Catherine uses the phrase "bella brigata"—"splendid company"—whenever "she is speaking of active participation in that (to her) great enterprise of faith, the crusade."[37] In that same spirit, shortly thereafter, she encourages several local men to make themselves martyrs (Letter 134) and asks the mercenary Bartolomeo Smeducci da Sanseverino to "take back what was taken from us—that is, the holy place of Christ's sepulcher" (Letter 374).[38] "Let's not waste any more time, dearest father: go follow the footsteps of Christ"[39]: the footsteps, in other words, of the martyr. In a letter cited earlier, she urges Regina della Scala, "So run, mother! And let all true faithful Christians run to this blood, attracted by its fragrance"[40] (Letter 29; Noffke, *Letters*, 1: 209). In these early letters, the terminus of this journey is the Jerusalem of the Muslims, while in later years, it becomes Rome, where all must come fight and die for the true pope, Urban VI. Or as she pointedly says to tailor Francesco di Pipino and his wife Agnesa, the Crusade "is right here"—in Rome.[41]

With this invocation of martyrdom, however, the Crusade is not so much about reclaiming a sacred place as finding the place of one's death, and hence one's real life. Catherine ultimately seeks the Augustinian city of God, not the city of man,[42] and the endpoint of pilgrimage is death. "We are pilgrim travelers in this life, running on toward our ending in death," she writes to Monna Stricca, widow of Giovanni d'Agnolino Salimbeni, from the famous house of Sienese bankers. "We have no permanence in time" (Noffke, *Letters*, 2: 399).[43] Or in the Italian, we have no "stanza di tempo"—no space, no resting place *within* time. This was that very "stanza" within which Birgitta would make her real and imaginary pilgrimages, to then come home again. But the one-way journey, the pilgrimage without return, was a constant in Catherine's letters. We see it in one of her earliest epistles, of 1375, to her faithful disciple Sano di Maco in Siena, where she suggests that "we pilgrim travelers need this holy wood for support until we have reached our destination, where our soul is at rest in our final home" (Letter 142: Noffke, *Letters*, 1: 77), and we see it in one of her last, to Piero Canigiani, and the letter from which the title of this essay, "Su dunque, peregrino," is taken: "The pilgrim waits for nothing other than arriving at his goal."[44] And she continues: "For my sake, be a true pilgrim, for we are all pilgrims and travelers in this life. Pilgrims pay attention to nothing but getting to their goal. They take with them their life and nothing more" ("Pigliasi la vita e niente più," Letter 378; Noffke, *Letters*, 4: 277–78).

Or in some copies of the letter, "Pigliasi la *via*": they take themselves to the *road*, and nothing more. The true pilgrim suffers constant mortification and has no home, and is thus a permanent *paroikos*: a Mary who after Christ's death and resurrection, is brought into the house of John, "as a guest and a pilgrim," "come ospita, e perregrina," as Catherine writes her mother Lapa (Letter 117; Noffke, *Letters*, 2: 442). But since the Christian's only true home is heaven, every place on earth must be equally far from heaven—including Jerusalem or Rome where Catherine ended her life, and from which she writes to the hermit Antonio da Nizza to urge him to leave the woods of Lecceto to join the fight to establish Urban VI as the true pope. After reminding him that his namesake, St. Anthony, did not hesitate to leave the desert when he was needed elsewhere, she elaborates, painstakingly. "One's spirit is rooted pretty shallowly, if it would be lost simply by going to another place! It would seem that God is partial to locality and can be found only in the woods and not somewhere else in times of need."[45] And elsewhere: "Who is so foolish as to believe that God is found in one place but not another? To God's true servant, every place is to him the right place, every time is to him the right time" (Letter 328, Noffke, *Letters*,4: 79–80, rev.).[46] In another letter to Antonio and William Flete, she writes, "there are woods here [in Rome] too, and forests. Get up, dearest sons, and don't sleep any longer, because now is the time to be watchful" (Letter 326; Noffke, *Letters*, 4: 30, rev.).[47] Antonio considers the forest to be holy, insofar as that is where his monastery is. But Catherine insists that "ogni luogo" can be made holy by God's presence.[48] And so the urban Rome becomes, paradoxically, a forest—no less, no more holy than Antonio's woods.

Such musings militate against Birgitta's insistence on the particularity of place, on pilgrimage's role in procuring rewards. This is not to say that Birgitta did not see pilgrimage in metaphorical terms, nor that she overlooked the importance of the condition of estrangement. Her Mary speaks of Christ as "a pilgrim on earth wandering from place to place... like a wayfarer seeking welcome" (*peregrinos fuit in terra, vadens de loco in locum et quasi viator...suscipi mereretur*, Rev. II: 3.1). Several chapters later, Christ will say, "I came to the wilderness like a pilgrim" (Rev. II: 15.9). But as we have seen, Birgitta valued the practice of pilgrimage for its capacity to transform a hypothetical condition of estrangement into something tangible, conferring a reward on those who enacted it and exacting from them the promise to tell others about it—as Birgitta would faithfully do.

Catherine's studied omission of references to purgatory—a place which for Birgitta can be mitigated by pilgrimage—also reflects her impatience with what she might have considered a concession to human fallibility. Catherine mentions purgatory only four times in the *Dialogue,* and once in her letters. Her dismissal of its occupants as poor souls who foolishly wasted their time[49] on earth is consonant with her view of her life as an ongoing march toward heaven in which one must never look back. In refusing to sanction an earthly narrative that might lead toward purification or healing, she holds instead to a conception of time as immediate and compressed. Increasingly in her late letters, she dwells on what she calls the "casa" or the "cella" (and in several instances, the "sepolcro") of self-knowledge, insisting on the superiority of the interior life over residing in holy places—much as Jerome would say to Paulinus that "nothing is lacking to your faith although you have not seen Jerusalem and I am none the better for living where I do. Be assured that, whether you dwell here or elsewhere, a like recompense is in store for your good works with our Lord."[50] Speaking to Monna Montagna of Narni about the fire of "divine goodness" and where to find it, Catherine rhetorically asks, "Where do we find it? In the house of self-knowledge, within ourselves. We find it in ourselves, that sweet and loving flame"[51] (Letter 263). Only through self-knowledge, not travel or physical contact with the divine, does one learn to be a true Christian. The only movement that engages Catherine is that constant forward movement toward death—a death that increasingly becomes the "terminus" of her own pilgrimage in her late letters.

There are two interesting, though perhaps only apparent contradictions to this assessment. First, Catherine often dedicates detailed attention in her letters to *this* world, to the concerns and affairs of others that in the grand scheme of things—warring cities, plague, the schism— might seem insignificant, although not to those who are suffering from them: a husband's infidelity, a son's sickness, a mother's death, a question about whom to marry. When moving from Birgitta's revelations to Catherine's epistles, one notes the emphatic individual speaking voice: "Io, Catarina"—often asking forgiveness for her Eve-like presumption. Her responses, that is, are initiated in her body and in the day-to-day, even as many of the no-doubt mundane details are now sadly gone, excised by her followers as they copied her hundreds of letters readying them for the canonization process. Who knows what these details might have covered? Surely, more of what we see in the passages that do survive: goings-on in Siena, logistics for taking care of a sick relative or friend, requests to send messages to other disciples, and political jockeying of a kind to which we are accustomed in Birgitta. Recurring ellipses and the formulaic "altro non dico"—I say no more—stand in for omitted details about the everyday that we shall never know, teasing us to speculate on the quotidian events that rooted Catherine to the earth and to a community of living, human beings. As Unn Falkeid has put it, such responsiveness "does not necessarily contradict the understanding that the aim of the earthly life is the hereafter. Perhaps such care could even be regarded as the very sign of such understanding." Indeed, as Falkeid goes on to point out, the act of offering hospitality to a Christ who has nowhere else to go in the evening makes him and his hosts at Emmaus equals and co-sufferers. For the experience of being the host "is the other side of the coin, closely bound to the radical experience of *peregrinus*"—a radicality that seems to be the only thing that Catherine embodies. Yet, in fact, it is also grounded in the daily gestures of charity and *cura* that she so scrupulously observed in her life and, we can conjecture, in her letters.[52]

Second, there is Catherine's last, astonishing, even heartbreaking letter, in a Rome on the verge of revolt. Sick, near death, she claims on the one hand that she seeks to "renounce things down here below,[53] but as I converse with the true citizens, my soul neither can nor wishes to delight in their joy. No, I want to delight in the hunger they had while they were pilgrim travelers in this life,[54] a hunger they still have." This hunger translates into her desire, against all odds, that the schism be quickly revolved.

> I am begging Divine Goodness to let me see soon the redemption of his people. At the hour of Tierce I get up from Mass and you would see a dead woman walking to Saint Peter's, and I enter once more to work on board the little ship of Holy Church. There I stay until close to the hour of Vespers. I don't want to leave that place, day or night, until I see this people a bit stabilized and settled with their father. This body of mine is living without food—not even a drop of water—with such sweet physical torment as I've never endured. So my life is hanging by a hair! Well, I don't know what divine Goodness wants to do with me.[55]

This is an odd, almost unprecedented moment of self-doubt in the letters. It seems not to be a modesty trope—Catherine was never modest—but an expression of genuine uncertainty. Catherine is left clinging to St. Peter's, possessed by the desire to stay in "quello luogo" until some *stabilità* has been granted, some progress made, in acknowledgment of her own penitence and obedience unto death. Her bitter words,[56] as she calls them, make for a painful contrast with what would seem to be Birgitta's joyous acceptance of her death—even allowing for the intervention of another hand in composing the end of *Revelations* as well as Birgitta's comparatively advanced age. Yet Birgitta understood the importance of pilgrimage as an experience that could offer a pale foreshadowing of heaven and hence what one might expect in the afterlife: the immediacy of seeing Christ born in a stable and hearing him cry. Pilgrimage provided a necessary encouragement in a world populated by Christians not at all like the inimitable Catherine. Birgitta's story provided a sense of hope. Like the tale of Tobias, it had a happy ending, and like the tale of Tobias, it recognizes that humans are weak, needing the guidance of an angel or the reassurance of the risen Christ. Or as the souls in Birgitta's purgatory cry out in Book IV, "May God reward those who send us help in our weakness!" (Rev. IV: 7.73). In this light, pilgrimage and the purgatorial journey alike are concessions to the radical imperfection of the human condition—as Catherine seems to have been aware. But Birgitta was willing to engage in the narrative that moved forward and backward as a way of recalling and repairing earlier points in one's own and others' lives.

As, of course, was Dante. Indeed, he too combines penitential and experiential practices in the *Commedia*, and specifically in *Purgatorio*, which depicts the voyage through this section of the afterlife as a pilgrimage through the use of similes in which he is compared to a pilgrim heading toward Jerusalem. Thus in the final canto Beatrice asks Dante to carry within himself the pilgrim's staff wreathed with palm,[57] symbol of having reached the Holy Sepulcher. The journey through Purgatory, that is, acquires the same purposefulness as the pilgrimage of a medieval *peregrino*: with various resting spots; changes and transformations; the mortification and education of the self; and the cleansing of the seven sins, or *peccati*, which one by one are erased from Dante's forehead until he is literally ready for Paradise.[58] The opening lines to *Purgatorio* 8 are particularly evocative, as the pilgrim's heart is struck with love as he remembers the home that he has left behind recalled to that home by the bells of his now distant city. He is like and yet unlike Christ on the threshold of Emmaus at dusk: "It was the hour that turns seafarers' longings/ homeward—the hour that makes their hearts grow tender/ upon the day they bid sweet friends farewell;/ the hour that pierces the new traveler/ with love when he has heard, far off, the bell/ that seems to mourn the dying of the day...."[59] This remembrance occurs for Birgitta and Dante alike not only within the mind alone, but through one's body and one's contacts with the material world, just as the reincarnation of the Nativity is played out before Birgitta's very eyes.[60]

These productive examples of medieval pilgrimage in turn were contested not only by Catherine but by her contemporary Francesco Petrarca, who was dubious of pilgrimage's good graces, whose pilgrimage to Rome in 1350 was derailed because of a minor injury to his foot, and who notoriously wrote a guide to the Holy Land without ever going there in person, fancying himself capable of imagining Jerusalem in the abstract, unlike Birgitta or Jerome's Paula.[61] Physical presence in a place, that is, conferred no epistemological advantages—or, by extension, any particular spiritual advantage. Both Petrarch and Catherine also problematize what might be seen as their age's typical narratives: Catherine with her insistence on immediacy, Petrarch with his far more complex questioning of the meaning of notions of progress and conversion, as in his famous letter on climbing Mt. Ventoux, *Familiares* 4.1. Just as Petrarch is skeptical as to what he might learn by traveling elsewhere, so does Catherine demonstrate considerable skepticism regarding changes of place for spiritual reasons, particularly those that interfered with her most important work and the work she wanted slackers like Antonio da Nizza to take on. (Despite—perhaps because of—Catherine's fierce reproaches, Antonio never came to Rome.) Like future proponents of the Reformation, Catherine and Petrarch questioned the traces of the holy in the everyday world, and saw travel as a distraction: you must find within yourself the place of self-knowledge, or the "casa del cognoscimento di sè." Both would have sided with Birgitta's Mary when she insisted that Birgitta should stay home working on her Latin rather than running off to visit Rome's holy sites. Even as they did travel, extensively, their letters became the real "travelers," radiating outward not from centers of holiness but simply from themselves.

And yet, Caterina and Birgitta are alike in at least one thing: their dying requests that their survivors gather their words together and do with them what they would. "I ask that my book and any writing that you find of mine.... be gathered up in your hands, and do with it what you think will bring most honor to God" (Letter 373),[62] Catherine writes to Raymond of Capua in that sad final letter. Book VII of Birgitta's *Revelations* ends with Jesus asking his bride to "tell the prior to hand over all these words of mine, in all the revelations, to the brothers and to my bishop, to whom I shall give the fervor of my Spirit and whom I shall fill with my grace" (Rev. VII: 31.6). Of course, it is the "bishop," Alfonso of Jaén, who links the two women most tangibly, working with Birgitta on her text and perhaps even encouraging Catherine to preserve her own words, and thus enabling the works of both to find their places in the world. Seven centuries later, their writings still encourage us to puzzle out their varying interpretations of the importance of their journeys, and to reflect on the many resonances of peregrination in late medieval Europe, as well as on the contemporary figures with whom their attitudes and thoughts intersected.

Notes

1 From Catherine of Siena's letter 378, to Piero Canigiani: "Su dunque, peregrino, destatevi dal sonno, ché non è oradormire, ma è tempo di vigilia": "Get up then, pilgrim, rise from your sleep, since this is no time for bed, but for staying awake." All references to the *Lettere* of Catherine are from the CD-ROM, *Santa Caterina da Siena: Opera omnia. Testi e concordanze*, ed. Fausto Sbaffoni (Pistoia: Provincia Romana dei Frati Predicatori, 2002).

2 Rev. VI: 105. The episode is inserted into other chapters such as "St. Nicholas Appears to Birgitta in Bari" (Rev. VI: 103), "Birgitta Receives some Relics of St. Anne" at San Paolo fuori le mura (Rev. VI: 104), and Birgitta's travels to Amalfi to the Relics of St. Andrew in obedience to Christ's command (Rev. VI: 107). In the episode with the Virgin, Mary reaches out to an obviously unhappy Birgitta, asking, "What is disturbing you, my daughter?" and Birgitta's response is "My Lady, it is because I am not visiting the holy places in Rome." Mary is not hostile per se to pilgrimage; she opens Book VII of the *Revelations* by telling Birgitta, "I announce to you that you will go on pilgrimage to the holy city of Jerusalem, where it so pleases my Son" (Rev. VII: 1.5). Birgitta of Sweden, *The Revelations of St. Birgitta of Sweden*, trans. Denis Searby, Introductions and Notes by Bridget Morris, 4 vols (Oxford: Oxford University Press, 2006–15); future citations will be from this edition unless otherwise noted.

3 In Latin, "et in novissima hora exitus mei suscipe ad te revertentem spiritum meum exulem et peregrinum." Latin text from the online edition of the *Revelaciones* edited by Birger Bergh; www.umilta.net/bk7.html.

4 *The Prayers of Saint Bridget: The Fifteen Oos*, online in Latin and English at www.preces-latinae.org/thesaurus/Filius/StBrigid.html

5 Matthew A. Kraus, *Jewish, Christian, and Classical Exegetical Traditions in Jerome's Translation of the Book of Exodus* (Leiden: Brill, 2017), 118 (with reference to Exodus 12:48). In his translation of the pseudo-Pauline letter to the Hebrews, Jerome uses *peregrini* to refer to Abraham and his followers, who become *alienas* as well in Hebrews 11:13.

6 For references to attitudes about pilgrimage prior to Birgitta's and Catherine's time, see Jack Finegan, *The Archaeology of the New Testament: The Life of Jesus and the Beginning of the Early Church* (Princeton, NJ: Princeton University Press, 1992) and the excellent chapter dedicated to figurative meanings of pilgrimage in Peter Brown, *Augustine of Hippo: A Biography*, 2nd edn. (Berkeley: University of California Press, 2000), ch. 22.

7 In Italian, "credo che sia più la dolce volontà di Dio che vi stiate ferma." For a brief discussion of Catherine's insistence that all stay in Rome to work for Urban VI, see Alfonso Capecelatro, *Storia di Santa Caterina e del papato del suo tempo* (Florence, 1858), 401. Suzanne Noffke notes that almost nothing is known about Toscanella, save for the fact that she lived in Viterbo and was referred to in the rubric of Catherine's letter (340) as a "very penitential servant of God." See Noffke, in Catherine of Siena, *The Letters of Saint Catherine of Siena*, ed. and trans. Suzanne Noffke, 4 vols (Tempe: Arizona Center for Medieval and Renaissance Studies, 2000–08), 4: 371.

8 "...abbracciando l'arbore della santissima Croce"; "cose transitorie, nelle quali non è perfezione di bene."

9 "...le proprie consolazioni mentali."

10 This and remaining English translations of Catherine's letters where noted are taken from Noffke, *Letters*, here at 2: 257. Catherine was hardly alone in discouraging a monk from traveling to a pilgrimage site. Sylvia Schein notes that Elizabeth of Schönau told a monk who communicated to her his desire to go to Jerusalem that he was falling prey to the devil and that his vocation demanded that he remain within his monastery; see "Bridget of Sweden, Margery Kempe, and Women's Jerusalem Pilgrimages in the Middle Ages," *Mediterranean Historical Review* 14, no. 1 (1999): 44–58, at 48.

11 For women's involvement in pilgrimages in Europe, which became especially numerous in the fourteenth century, see Schein, "Bridget of Sweden, Margery Kempe, and Women's Jerusalem Pilgrimages." She suggests that the rise of ascetic movements gave women the independence and opportunity for the "freedom of movement" that allowed them to experience the places of Christ's birth and passion (p. 55).

12 The entire Latin phrase is "Ego ero vobiscum, ego dirigam viam vestram, ego ducam et reducam vos ad Romam et procurabo vobis necessaria sufficiencius quam vmquam habuistis prius."

13 Birgitta of Sweden, *Life and Selected Revelations*, ed. Marguerite Tjader Harris, trans. Albert Ryle Kezel (New York: Paulist Press, 1990), 247n. The editor notes that the same phrase is quoted in *The Life of Blessed Birgitta,* from the same edition, 101.

14 Gábor Klaniczay, "Using Saints: Intercession, Healing, Sanctity," in *The Oxford Handbook of Medieval Christianity*, ed. John Arnold (Oxford: Oxford University Press, 2014), 221.

15 The five places are "where Mary was born and reared", Bethlehem, Calvary, the garden of Christ's grave, and the Mount of Olives. The Father promises Birgitta that "whoever comes clean and with a good and perfect intention to these places will see and taste the sweetness and goodness of me, God. And when you come to these places I will show you more" (Rev. V: rev. 13.23). Bridget Morris suggests that in this final revelation, as Birgitta "expresses her impatience for a new order to be founded, she is told that the kingdom is not yet ready and that she will first go to the Holy Land," in Birgitta of Sweden, *The Revelations*, 2: 267. Thus, the pilgrimage also fills in a period of waiting, becoming a "holding space."

16 Birgitta of Sweden, *Life and Selected Revelations*, 283n. Also see Morris, in Birgitta of Sweden, *The Revelations*, 3: 192: "St. Thomas, the doubter of the risen Christ, wanted to be given tangible evidence, just as St. Birgitta received a true relic in her own hands. In doing so, she become part of a miraculous chain of evidence, which strengthens her case for sainthood"; this revelation is the only one referred to in Boniface IX's bull of 1391.

17 See the classic article of Gerhart B. Ladner, "Homo Viator: Mediaeval Ideas about Alienation and Order," *Speculum* 42, no. 2 (1967): 233–59.

18 This would not have been unique to Birgitta. Nicole Chareyron, in *Pilgrims to Jerusalem in the Middle Ages,* trans. Donald W. Wilson (New York: Columbia University Press, 2005 [2000]), maintains that the visit to Jerusalem involved a ritual led by Franciscans in which the pilgrims were urged to envision the scenes from the Passion, adding that "The pilgrim certainly needs a great deal of imagination to mentally rediscover the sites mentioned in the Gospels that are buried under the buildings," 87.

19 Jerome, *Select Letters of St. Jerome,* trans. F.A. Wright (Cambridge, MA: Harvard University Press, 1933), Letter 108.

20 "... dimittere amicos carnales ad tempus propter Deum, et venire ad locum ubi compendium est inter celum et mortem ad fugiendam penam purgatorii,

quia ibi sunt indulgencie, que sunt eleuaciones et redempciones animarum, quas sancti pontifices dederunt et sancti Dei sanguine suo promeruerunt."

21 On Birgitta's understanding of purgatory, and her attentiveness to it as a space that allows for continuity between the living and the dead—with a special role for women—see Päivi Salmesvuori's chapter, "Holiness in Action," in *Power and Sainthood: The Case of Birgitta of Sweden* (New York: Palgrave MacMillan, 2014), especially 133–45. Birgitta herself served as a special vehicle to purgatory: "she gained fame as a mediator between the living and the dead" (p. 137). Most of the comments in these pages are based on Rev. VI: 10, which informs the living how to get their loved ones out of purgatory more quickly.

22 See Morris in Birgitta of Sweden, *The Revelations*, 3: 234, n. 3: "pilgrimage shrines were always endowed with indulgences that had been granted by bishops, cardinals, and popes. The indulgence was technically a relaxation of a certain amount of the penance that a person had incurred by sinning, and was granted on specified condition. Here, however, Christ grants Birgitta and her party a full, or plenary, indulgence as potent as the sacrament of baptism."

23 "Tu solus peregrinus es in Jerusalem et non cognovisti quae facta sunt in illa his diebus?" *Biblia Sacra: Vulgatae Editionis* (Rome: Edizioni San Paolo, 2003).

24 As Giuliana Cavallini, the editor of Catherine's *Orazioni*, notes, "nel clima pasquale che pervade questa Orazione, sulla porta del giardino già non sta più l'angelo con la spada fiammeggiante a interdirne l'ingresso ma il Redentore"; *Le orazioni*, ed. Giuliana Cavallini (Siena: Cantagalli, 1993), 118n.

25 "O dolce portinaio, o umile agnello, tu sei quell'ortolano il quale, avendo aperte le porte del giardino celeste, cioè del paradiso, porgi a noi i fiori e i frutti della Deità eterna."

26 "E ora certamente conosco che tu hai detto la verità quando, in forma di pellegrino apparendo nella via due tuoi discepoli, dicesti che così bisognava che patisse Cristo e che per la via della croce entrasse nella sua gloria .... E gli dischiarivi le scritture, ma essi non t'intendevano perché era offuscato l'intelletto loro, ma tu medesimo t'intendevi."

27 "E ora io certamente conosco che tu hai detto la verità."

28 The full Latin text is "et ipse se finxit longius ire," Luke 24:28.

29 "Carissimi, obsecro *tamquam advenas et peregrinos* abstinere vos a carnalibus desideriis quae militant adversus animam."

30 In the Vulgate, "est in terra repromissionis tanquam in aliena."

31 For this understanding of the scene from Emmaus and the following paragraph, see my essay "Parole pellegrine. L'ospitalità linguistica nel Rinascimento," in *L'ospite del libro: Sguardi sull'ospitalità*, eds. Nicola Catelli and Giovanna Rizzarelli (Lucca: Facci Editore, 2015), 13–26.

32 See the *Legenda maior*, translated as *The Life of Saint Catherine of Siena by Raymond of Capua*, trans. Conleth Kearns (Wilmington, DE: Michael Glazier, 1980), par. 231.

33 Catherine mentions that "the pope sent his representative here, the one who was spiritual father to that countess who died in Rome," Letter 127 (trans. Noffke, *Letters*, 1: 40.).

34 Noffke, *Letters*, 1: 295. Noffke is referring to the (incomplete) edition by Eugenio Dupré Theseider of Catherine's letters, *Epistolario di Santa Caterina* (Rome: Istituto storico italiano per il medioevo, 1940), I, 14.

35 Otherwise known as Tommaso Caffarini, who would become crucial in the first efforts to promote Catherine's canonization.

36 Noffke, *Letters*, 1: 40.

37 Noffke observes that the letter Catherine sent to the pope is lost, one in which "Catherine apparently asked his permission to go with her disciples ... to the Holy Sepulcher ... Perhaps she even wanted to take part in the crusade herself, which she believed was imminent." *Letters,* 1: 295. On Catherine's early attitudes about a crusade, see Renate Blumenfeld-Kosinski, *Poets, Saints, and Visionaries of the Great Schism, 1378–1417* (University Park, PA: Pennsylvania State University Press, 2006), 71–73. See also Chapter 4 by Blumenfeld-Kosinski in the present volume.

38 "... racquistare quello che ci è tolto, cioé, 'l luogo santo del sepolcro di Cristo."

39 "Non indugiamo più tempo, padre carissimo, seguitate le vestigie di Cristo."

40 "... adunque correte, madre, e corriamo tutti fedeli cristiani, all'obietto di questo sangue, dietro all'odore suo."

41 "We have the unbelievers and the persecutors of God's Church at our door, so we don't have to go anywhere else for a crusade!" (Letter 274; Noffke, *Letters,* 4: 188).

42 Once she arrived in Rome to protest the schism, Catherine would abandon all rhetoric of a crusade to Jerusalem and argue instead that "the crusade is right here"—as she puts it in a letter to a Florentine couple to whom she addressed a number of letters, Francesco di Pipino and his wife Agnese; Letter 274.

43 "... senza alcuna stanza di tempo corriamo verso il termine della morte."

44 "Il peregrino non attende ad altro se non di giungere al termine suo."

45 "Pare che Dio sia accettatore di luogo, e chi si trovi solamente nel bosco."

46 "Al vero servo di Dio, ogni luogo gli è luogo, e ogni tempo gli è tempo."

47 "... ché qui ha de' boschi e delle selve. Su, carissimi figliuoli! E non dormite più: ché tempo è di vigilia."

48 Catherine seems to anticipate what Thomas à Kempis would protest in his *De imitatione Christi* of 1413: "quod potes alibi videre, quod hic non videas?"—what can you see elsewhere that you can't find at home?—even as she rephrases it in order to make Antonio *leave* his home.

49 "... perderono il tempo"; *Dialogo* 148.

50 F.A. Wright Letter, 58.

51 "Dove 'l troviamo? Nella casa del cognoscimento di noi. In noi troviamo questo dolce e amoroso fuoco."

52 From the comments Unn Falkeid provided to a draft version of this paper, August 2017, in Vadstena. I am grateful for her thoughtful reflections and have learned a great deal from our conversations about this work.

53 "... le cose di qua giù."

54 "... peregrini e viandanti," her final use of this phrase.

55 Letter 373 (Noffke, *Letters,* 4: 368):

> Prego la divina bontà che tosto mi lassi vedere la redenzione del popolo suo. Quando egli è l'ora de la Terza, io mi levo da la messa, e voi vedreste andare una morta a San Pietro; e entro di nuovo a lavorare ne la navicella de la santa Chiesa. Ine mi sto così infine presso all'ora del Vespro; e di quello luogo non vorrei uscire né dì né notte, infino che io non veggo un poco fermato e stabilito questo popolo col padre loro. Questo corpo sta senza veruno cibo, eziandio senza la gocciola dell'acqua, con tanti dolci tormenti corporali quanti io portasse mai per veruno tempo, in tanto che per uno pelo ci sta la vita mia. Ora non so quello che la divina bontà si vorrà fare di me.

56 "... parole d'amaritudine."

57 "... il bordon di palma cinta," Dante, *Purgatorio* 33:78, trans. Allen Mandelbaum (New York: Bantam, 1984).

58 While studies linking purgatory to pilgrimage are legion, Giuseppe Mazzotta, *Dante, Poet of the Desert: History and Allegory in the Divine Comedy* (Princeton, NJ: Princeton University Press, 1979) remains fundamental, as does Jacques Le Goff's, *The Birth of Purgatory*, trans. Arthur Goldhammer (Chicago, IL: The University of Chicago Press, 1984).

59 Dante, *Purgatorio*, 8:1–6; trans. Allen Mandelbaum."Era già l'ora che volge il disio/ ai navicanti e 'ntenerisce il core/ lo dì c' han detto ai dolci amici addio;// e che lo novo peregrin d'amore/ punge, se ode squilla di lontano/ che paia il giorno pianger che si more."

60 See the fascinating work of Shayne Legassie, *The Medieval Invention of Travel* (Chicago, IL: The University of Chicago Press, 2017).

61 See Theodore Cachey's edition and translation of *Itinerarium*, trans. as *Petrarch's Guide to the Holy Land: Itinerary to the Sepulcher of Our Lord Jesus Christ* (Notre Dame: University of Notre Dame Press, 2002) as well as his essay "'Peregrinus (quasi) ubique': Petrarca e la storia del viaggio," *Intersezioni* 17, no. 3 (1997): 369–84.

62 "... vi prego che il libro e ogni scrittura la quale trovaste di me ... ve le rechiate per le mani; e fatene quello che vedete che sia più onore di Dio."

3 Constructing Female Authority

Birgitta of Sweden, Catherine of Siena, and the Two Marys

Unn Falkeid

In a revelation dated 1350, Birgitta of Sweden delivers a sharp rebuke to the Catholic Church, charging church leaders with misgovernment, immorality, and the neglect of many holy shrines and monuments (Rev. IV: 78).[1] Rather than being an ordinary revelation, the text is written as a formal letter. It is addressed to an anonymous prelate, probably Pope Clement VI, or to a person of high rank close to him, and its apparent basis was Birgitta's vision in Santa Maria Maggiore, one of the major basilicas in the city and the only one dedicated to the Virgin Mary. The year 1350 had been proclaimed a Holy Jubilee, a year of special grace for the pilgrims who visited Rome and its basilicas, and the Swedish *principessa* and her companions had joined the pilgrims flocking to the city. Then, one day during her visit to Santa Maria Maggiore, she received a vision in which the Virgin Mary appeared to her, complained that the basilica was about to collapse, and commanded Birgitta to inform the prelate about the terrible state of not only the structure in which they stood but also the whole of the Catholic Church:

> I would have him [the prelate] know that the foundation of the Holy Church is so heavily deteriorated on its right side that its vaulted roof has many cracks at the top, and that this causes the stones to fall so dangerously that many of those who pass beneath it lose their lives. Several of the columns that should be standing erect are almost level with the ground, and even the floor is so full of holes that blind people entering there take dangerous falls. Sometimes it even happens that, along with the blind, people with good eyesight have bad falls because of dangerous holes in the floor. Because of all this, the church of God is tottering dangerously. The result of this will shortly be seen. I assure you that she will suffer a downfall if she does not receive the help of repairs. And her downfall will be so great that it will be heard throughout all of Christendom. All this is to be taken in a spiritual sense.[2]

Perhaps the most striking aspect of this vision is Mary's august authority, which she transfers to Birgitta by entrusting her with the role of divine messenger. Indeed, Mary's authority was the very subject on which the

Basilica di Santa Maria Maggiore was based. Erected under Pope Sixtus III (432–40), it was built in celebration of the Council of Ephesus (431), which proclaimed the doctrine of *Theotokos* (Bearer of God). The church is adorned with mosaics depicting the idea of Rome as the center of the Christian world and Mary as the savior of the Roman people (*Salus Populi Romani*). The mosaics of the triumphal arch and the nave configure Mary as goddess, empress, and Mother of God combined. As Miri Rubin has described it, "Mary is less maternal than matriarchal here: seated on high, dressed in rich and multi-layered garments, her hair is carefully set as befitted a Roman matron and her bearing majestic."[3] In other words, in the Mary of Santa Maria Maggiore, Classical and Christian Rome converge. It is this *domina*, the mighty Queen sitting on her throne, who addresses Birgitta, commanding her to be the Virgin's mouthpiece.

Let us move a few decades ahead to the year after Birgitta's death. In a letter dated 1374, Catherine of Siena writes the following to one of her *mantellate*, Monna Agnese Malavolti, who was a widow belonging to one of the prominent families of Siena:

> Oh sweetest virgin, how well you imitated that devoted disciple Magdalen! See, dearest daughters, how Magdalen knew herself, and humbled herself. With what great love she sat at our gentle Savior's feet! And speaking of showing him love, we surely see it at the holy cross. She wasn't afraid of the Jews, nor did she fear for herself. No, like a passionate lover she ran and embraced the cross. Indeed, in order to see her Master she was bathed in blood. Surely you were drunk in blood, oh Magdalen! As a sign that she was drunk with love for her Master, she showed it in her actions toward his creatures, when after his holy resurrection she preached in the city of Marseilles.[4]

What this quotation conveys is a picture of Mary Magdalen as the woman who stood closest to Jesus, who freely and fearlessly moved around in a world of men, and who after Christ's death preached in public and even traveled to foreign lands to bring the Gospel to the Gentiles. Catherine's Magdalen is, in other words, not the composite sinner in the tradition of Gregory the Great, but the preacher—indeed, the *apostola apostolorum* (the apostle of the apostles)—whom Catherine now encourages her group of women to imitate.[5] As she explains in another epistle (Letter T165), Mary Magdalen should be regarded as their spiritual *Maestra*.

Reformist Women

Perhaps the gravest watershed within the Church's history before the Reformation was the crisis created by the papacy's residence in Southern France in the fourteenth century. From 1309 to 1377, the pope and his curia resided in the city of Avignon, in Provence. What happened during this period was an extraordinary centralization of the Church, a process underpinned by the pope's new claim to political and juridical primacy over secular rulers. As the papacy consolidated its power, the institutional bureaucracy became bloated. Moreover, the papal court enriched itself through taxation and a broad reorganization of the financial system. The city of Rome quickly declined, politically and economically. Avignon, on the other hand, developed into a cosmopolitan center, with the papal curia as the richest, most lavish and powerful court in Europe.[6]

The sojourn in Avignon was in many ways successful for the papacy as well as for the French city, but in the long run, it created deep divisions within the church. The escalating secular power of the papacy, as well as the papal curia's long exile from Rome, met with increasing resistance. The opposition was manifold, and it came from every corner of Europe, including political theorists, early humanists, and the growing groups of educated people in European cities who often supported their secular rulers. Other sources of opposition were the Spiritual Franciscans, who upheld their founder's ideal of apostolic poverty; the Italian city states that were fighting for sovereignty; and the many defenders of Rome as the holy institutional center of Europe. Two of the most remarkable voices in this expansive choir of critics were those of Birgitta and Catherine. Both were deeply engaged in the contemporary reform movements and managed to make their voices heard despite strong opposition.[7]

An important question is how Birgitta and Catherine built their authority. How did they manage to raise their voices against mighty institutions and powerful figures at a period in time when women were excluded not only from the universities and church hierarchies but also from the very act of preaching in public? The impressive networks of powerful contacts they created extended to Italy and other parts of Europe. At the heart of Birgitta's and Catherine's circles of supporters, we find not only two laywomen but also women who skillfully intervened in political and ecclesiastic affairs, preached in public, and addressed pointed letters to popes, queens, kings, and cardinals. So strong was the impact of these two figures that their opponents portrayed them as the main provocateurs of the Great Western Schism, which occurred upon the pope's return to Rome in 1377. At the Council of Constance (1414–18), Birgitta's *Revelations* were criticized by Jean Gerson, Chancellor of the University of Paris and one of the most prominent theologians of his time. Indeed, he strongly condemned the authority of female writers, a judgment which damaged the political and intellectual reputations of both Birgitta and Catherine.[8]

There are no simple answers to the question of why Birgitta and Catherine achieved such exalted positions. What the present chapter aims to explore, however, is how they both vigorously constructed their authority by referring to two of the most powerful female figures in Christian history—namely, the Virgin Mary and Mary Magdalen. The two Marys enjoyed widespread popularity throughout the late Middle Ages but became particular objects of interest within the context of fourteenth-century popular piety. This intensified focus on the Virgin Mary and Mary Magdalen was something that Birgitta and Catherine knew how to exploit.[9] By means of subtle genealogies that configured the two Marys as examples of female authority, Birgitta and Catherine used these biblical women as shields, enabling them to criticize the Avignon papacy.

The Virgin Mary in Birgitta's *Oeuvre*

The Virgin Mary plays a crucial role in Birgitta's theology. In her *Revelations*, no figure other than Christ appears as often as the Virgin, who is given a prominent position as Birgitta's interlocutor in one-third of the revelations. In addition to the *Revelations*, we have the prayers in praise of Mary attributed to Birgitta and, above all, the liturgical readings *Sermo angelicus de Virginis excellentia*, which locate Mary at the heart of the Birgittine Order (Order of the Most Holy Savior), to which I will soon return.

The Virgin figures prominently in the story of Birgitta's life starting with her early childhood. According to Birgitta's *Vita*, she received her first vision when she was in her seventh year, which probably was around the age of her first communion. In the vision, a lady in shining garments came to the *puella*, the little girl, while she was in her bed. When the young Birgitta rises from her bed, the lady places a crown on her head.[10] Even though the vision is highly conventional within the context of medieval hagiographies, it gives us a glimpse of the intense Marian devotion in Birgitta's spirituality, and as the *Revelations* make clear, this devotion continued for the rest of her life.

Birgitta is said to have received other revelations in the early part of her life, but the beginning of her true visionary career coincided with her husband's death in the middle of the 1340s. In this period, she received two revelations of great significance. In the first of these, often dubbed "the calling vision," Christ appears to Birgitta, refers to her as his bride, and prepares her for the many spiritual things she will hear and see in the future.[11] The other revelation is the well-known vision she received one Christmas Eve in Alvastra, the Cistercian monastery in Östergötland (Sweden), where she and her husband, Ulf Gudmarsson, may have lived periodically and where he was buried along with one of their sons. In the revelation from Alvastra (Rev. VI: 88), Birgitta relates that on Christmas Eve she experienced "such a great and wonderful feeling of exultation ... in [her] heart that she could scarcely contain herself for joy." This tremendous joy was accompanied by "a wonderful sensible movement in her heart like that of a living child turning and turning around."[12] Soon after, the Virgin Mary came to her and explained that the motion, which resembled the conception of the child Jesus in her own womb, was a sign of Birgitta's calling as an instrument for divine revelation. Declaring Birgitta her "daughter-in-law," Mary entrusted her with the mission of proclaiming God's will throughout the world.

As Claire L. Sahlin has argued in her compelling reading of this vision, similar moments of identification with Mary run like a thread throughout the *Revelations*, conveying in different ways the idea that God's mother offered Birgitta the authority of a prophet, supporting her power to teach, write, and speak on behalf of God.[13] In other words, the text portrays Birgitta's vision as a mystical pregnancy in which her heart, like Mary's womb, becomes a vessel filled with the Word of God. Just as Francis of Assisi's and later Catherine of Siena's profound acts of *imitatio Christi* resulted in stigmata—in physical signs on their bodies, which lent their words and deeds revelatory significance—so Birgitta's *imitatio Mariae* authorized her pneumatic, prophetic speech.[14] Mary, thus, functions for Birgitta as a paradigm of her own role as God's spokesperson, and in the years following the revelation in Alvastra, Birgitta offered herself as a spiritual guide who obediently transmitted the will of God to the world.

A cluster of eight visions gathered in the sixth book of the *Revelations* (Rev. VI: 55–62), all dating from the 1350s, reiterates the biography of the Virgin, from her conception to her assumption. Together with the revelations from Birgitta's last pilgrimage to Jerusalem, in which she received two of her most poetically elaborated visions— of the Passion (Rev. VII: 15) and of the Nativity (Rev. VII: 21)—the revelations from Book VI uncover different aspects of Birgitta's Marian piety. Here, we meet the idea of the immaculate conception (Rev. VI: 55), which she shared with the contemporary Franciscans. Another central notion is that the birth of Mary inaugurated a new era in the history of salvation, "the beginning of joys" (Rev. VI: 56). A vision of Mary's six sorrows follows (Rev. VI: 57): The first is the sorrow of knowledge, which refers to Mary's foreknowledge of the Passion. As Mary quite movingly explains to Birgitta, "[a]s often as I looked at my Son, as often as I wrapped him in linen-cloth, as often as I saw his hands and feet, my spirit was as though engulfed in fresh grief with the thought of how he would be crucified."[15] Next comes the sorrow of hearing (when she heard the insults, lies, and plots directed at her Son); of sight (when she saw her Son being bound, scourged, and crucified); of touch (when she took the Son down from the cross and wrapped him before laying the body in the tomb); of yearning (when she wanted to accompany him to the heaven); and finally, of compassion in the face of the suffering of the apostles and the friends of God.

Another aspect of the Birgittine Mariology exposed in this small hagiography centers on the assumption of the Virgin. In a highly interesting vision, Mary denies that St. Jerome ever doubted the assumption of her body into heaven (Rev. VI: 60). Even though the assumption of Mary was not proclaimed as a dogma until 1950, there had been a long tradition of celebrating the Virgin's corporeal ascension to heaven, a tradition coinciding in many ways with the adoration of Mary as *Theotokos*, to which the basilica of Santa Maria Maggiore in Rome also testifies. As Birgitta makes clear, the theory of Mary's assumption was contested in her time: referring to a certain schoolmaster whom she ironically dubs "that winnower of words" ("ille ventilator verborum"), Birgitta argues that if, as the schoolmaster claimed, St. Jerome had expressed doubts about the assumption of the Virgin in his work, that should be taken as a sign of his humble belief rather than denial of a revealed truth. As Birgitta explains in the next vision, the truth was not fully revealed in Jerome's time or in early Christianity because the people were not yet prepared for it (Rev. VI: 61). According to Birgitta, history is a process of continuous revelation in which the truth slowly unfolds. Offering herself as a tool in this process, she lays claim to the truth that was still hidden in the time of St. Jerome.

The identity of the schoolmaster to whom she refers is unclear. Nevertheless, there can be no doubt that the idea of Mary's assumption was strongly disputed both in fourteenth-century Italy and in the violent decades of the Reformation.[16] Just as women were often the ones presenting the strongest defense of Mary's assumption in the Cinquecento, so Birgitta served as the Trecento's supreme advocate of the doctrine.[17]

The Angel's Discourse

Probably no Birgittine text was more influential in the coming centuries after her death than the *Sermo angelicus de Virginis excellentia*. It was widely read every day in the divine offices of every Birgittine monastery throughout Europe. In this way, it encouraged the sisters, in a rhythmical and insisting manner, to locate Mary at the center of their worship. For that reason, it is important to look closely at how Mary is configured in the text.

As Anders Piltz has described it, *Sermo angelicus* is the most remarkable contribution to the Mariology ever made by a Scandinavian.[18] It is also, as Bridget Morris has noticed, "the most resonant and eloquent expression of Birgitta's Mariology."[19] It was written for the sisters of the Birgittine Order to sing after the ordinary divine office. The text consists of 21 lessons, 3 for each day of the week. Each of these lessons contemplates, as the full title makes clear, the worth or excellence of the Virgin Mary. The lessons were composed by Birgitta in the 1350s and later translated from Swedish into partly metrical Latin by her friend from Alvastra Master Peter Olofsson of Skänninge, who had followed her to Rome. Master Peter wrote the hymns, antiphons, and responses to accompany the lessons, with content that follows the structure of the

Sermo angelicus. He composed the accompanying musical arrangements as well. The entire work, which came to constitute the content of the Birgittine office, was given the title *Cantus sororum* (The Song of the Sisters). However, our focus here will be the lessons, the *Sermo angelicus*, authored by Birgitta herself.

As already noted, the lessons are spread out over the week—three for each day—and what they reflect is the history of salvation, with Mary as the true stepping stone between transitory and eternal life. Stylistically, they can be described as solemn and far more elevated than the *Revelations*. In them, we read about how Mary was eternally present in Divine thought and how she received the matter of her blessed body from the four elements of the world (Sunday, first reading). Mary brought joy to a world of tears (Sunday, second reading). She is the most excellent of all creatures closer to God than the angels (Monday, first reading). She is the microcosmos (*minor mundus*) who will remain while the rest of the world will perish (Monday, second reading). Adam grieved about his sin but still rejoiced because he had foreknowledge of the Virgin's coming (Tuesday, first reading). In the Wednesday readings, the Virgin's conception and birth are described, as is God's eternal love for her. The readings of the Thursday and Friday lessons focus upon Mary's beauty, the birth of Christ, and the mother's profound suffering and pain upon his death.

The *Sermo angelicus* concludes with the Saturday readings, which amount to fireworks celebrating the unreserved sublimity of Mary. Indeed, Saturday is Mary's day, according to a longstanding Christian tradition—the day when the creation was completed and, as such, the day of fulfillment of the plan of salvation. And as Birgitta demonstrates, Mary is the final realization—indeed, the aim of this plan. In the Saturday lessons, she is depicted in all her majesty: she is "the instructor of the apostles, the comforter of the martyrs, the teacher of confessors, the bright mirror of virgins, the consoler of widows, the counselor of the married and the perfect strengthener of everyone in the Catholic faith."[20] Above all, Mary is the mother of wisdom (*logos*), which requires special knowledge or insight superior to that of learned men.

It is striking how Birgitta draws the reader's attention towards Mary's intellectual abilities. As we soon shall see, in contrast to Catherine, Birgitta claimed that it was the Virgin Mary and not Mary Magdalen who was the first to discover Christ's resurrection. In fact, Birgitta explicitly corrects Scripture at this point: "Although the bible also says that Mary Magdalen and the apostles were the first witnesses of the resurrection, there can be no doubt that his worthy mother had certain knowledge of it before they did and that she had seen him alive and risen from the dead before they did."[21] Because of her profound wisdom, according to Birgitta, Mary remained in this world after her son's ascension in order to instruct the apostles and the confessors "who learned perfectly well from her teaching and example." On this occasion, she gives Mary the remarkable nickname *magistra apostolorum* (the master of the apostles), which to a certain degree competes with Mary Magdalen's *apostola apostolorum*.

Memento Mariae!

In the two last readings of the Saturday lesson, the Queen of Heaven is celebrated in a manner similar to how the empress is configured in the mosaics of Santa Maria Maggiore. There we can read: "Because she was humblest among angels and men, she has been raised up highest over all creation, the most beautiful creature of all and the one most like to God himself."[22] In the heavenly court, a throne awaited her at God's side: "This glorious soul's glorified throne was placed for all eternity closest to the Trinity itself."[23] After describing the royal ceremony in which Mary is crowned while seated on this throne, Birgitta returns once again to the notion that Mary was lifted up both in her body and her soul: "Only the body of Christ and the body of his Mother were worthy to receive their merited rewards together with their souls long before the bodies of others."[24] Only Christ and Mary have, in other words, been bodily assumed into heaven, and they will not be joined by other human bodies before the general resurrection at the end of time. Finally, Mary is called "the tree of life" who will bend or incline herself towards those who pray so that they can receive her precious fruit, the body of Christ.

Of great interest here are the circumstances connected to the composition of the *Sermo angelicus*. As the prologue by Alfonso of Jaén narrates, Birgitta wrote the treatise after some years in Rome, when she was living in the house of Cardinal Beaufort, adjacent to the church of San Lorenzo in Damaso. Alfonso describes it as follows:

> Now Blessed Birgitta had a room with a window facing the high altar from which she could see the body of Christ every day. Every day in that room, as soon as she had read her hours and her prayers, she made herself ready with a notebook and pen in hand, ready and waiting for the angel of the Lord. When he came, he would place himself at her side with an upright, courteous stance, reverently facing the altar where the body of Christ lay concealed. Standing in this way, he dictated clearly and in order, in Blessed Birgitta's own language, the following readings to be used at matins in the abbey, which describe the supreme and eternal excellence of the Blessed Virgin Mary.[25]

The quotation depicts Birgitta facing the altar through the window of her room, indeed through the window of a house belonging to the same pope whom she had so harshly criticized in the letter from Santa Maria Maggiore (Cardinal Beaufort was the brother of Pope Clement VI). Sitting in this posture, and with the Eucharist in mind, she is visited by an angel of the Lord, whose arrival recalls the visitation of Mary by the angel Gabriel. The message that the angel whispers in Birgitta's ear, then, is to a certain degree a new "Ave." The divine wisdom which Birgitta, the new bride and the new vessel, receives—or the spectacle that is unfolding before her inner eye—is the very truth about the role of Mary in the history of salvation. In Mary, God's original plan for the entirety of creation is fulfilled. She is the hub around which the universe rotates. She is the tree of life in the middle of the Garden of Eden, the powerful and indomitable plant that grows out of the old and perishable world, offering her life-saving fruit, the body of Christ, to humanity. Mary is, in other words, *redemptrix*, the co-redeemer, and must be remembered and celebrated as such.

Birgitta draws heavily, of course, from theological and popular traditions. Here, we have the legacy of Bernard of Clairvaux, conveyed by the Cistercian brothers from Alvastra, who surrounded her also in Rome. We also have the *Speculum virginum* (Mirror of Virgins), an important text which is mentioned in Birgitta's sources. Moreover, she knew the pseudo-Bonaventurian *Meditationes vite Christi*, in which Mary plays a crucial role. Above all, we can recognize the influence of the *Legenda aurea* (Golden Legend), by Jacobus de Voragine (1230–98). This work achieved enormous popularity in the fourteenth century, and it was translated into several European vernaculars. Birgitta herself is said to have read from it to her servants from the Swedish translation (*Old Swedish Legendary*) every day after breakfast.[26] Without a doubt, the popularity of Marian devotion gave weight to Birgitta's voice. However, no one had previously placed herself so prominently in direct dialogue with Mary as Birgitta did, and the effect was remarkable. Indeed, Birgitta could not find a better ally than the Queen of Heaven in conveying her political ideas. No matter how tough her messages may have been, it would have amounted to a profound sacrilege to reject them as they were received directly from her divine mother-in-law.

Mary the Preacher

The Virgin Mary also plays a major role in Catherine of Siena's spiritual universe. Mary is the optimal model who "with the sound of her word" ("col suono della parola") made the incarnation possible (Letter T38). Only after uttering the words "Ecce ancilla Domini" the conception could happen. As such, Catherine replaces Mary's traditional humility with her unique will and authority. Moreover, she usually opens her letters with a salutation that includes both Mary and her son, reflecting the centrality of Mary in the Dominican tradition: "In the name of Jesus Christ crucified and of gentle Mary" ("Al nome di Gesù Cristo crocifisso e di Maria dolce"). Of equal importance, and as Jane Tylus has discussed intriguingly, Siena was a city especially associated with the Virgin, thus creating a suitable surrounding for Catherine's embodiment of a modern *domina* or *donna*.[27]

However, another recurring figure also plays a key role in Catherine's literary corpus, despite her elusiveness compared to the Virgin: Mary Magdalen. Indeed, the hagiographic sources emphasize the close connection between Catherine and the Magdalen. In his *Libellus de Supplemento*, Tommaso Caffarini depicted Catherine as a friend of Mary Magdalen and indicated that the two often had intimate conversations. Likewise, Raymond of Capua claimed in his *Legenda maior* that in one of Catherine's visions, Christ and the Virgin assigned the Magdalen to Catherine as her teacher and mother.[28] As the discussion below will show, Catherine's relationship to Mary Magdalen reveals some of the fundamental aspects of Catherine's authorial role.

Mary Magdalen appears in a variety of Catherine's letters, and as in the already quoted letter to Monna Agnese (Letter T61), Catherine frequently refers to the Magdalen as a model, or a figure worthy of imitation. Moreover, the texts in which she is mentioned are usually letters addressed to females in Catherine's group of *mantellate* or to women whom she encourages to recover their special powers. In letter T276, probably composed in May 1376, she writes to a prostitute in Perugia, reminding her that like all other human beings, she is created in God's image and likeness. Catherine's message is that her addressee can and should retrieve her dignity: "Get up from such wretchedness and filth. Run back to your Creator, who will receive you if you only are willing to abandon deadly sin and return to the state of grace."[29] Mary Magdalen is the inspirational model Catherine invokes: "Take along as your companion and learn from that dear Magdalen, so in love."[30] In another letter, probably written a month before (Letter T165) and addressed to Monna Bartolomea di Salvatico, a member of her circle of pious women, Catherine encourages Bartolomea to take up her apostolic mission without fear: Rise from your sleep, she writes, and embrace the sweet venerable cross. With reference to Magdalen taking up her shield of hatred, love, and patience in her fight, Catherine exhorts Monna Bartolomea to protect herself with these "three sturdy pillars that free the soul from weakness and keep it strong."[31] With this protection, Magdalen was able to move through a man's world, among the soldiers of Pilate, without fear of damaging her reputation. Concluding the letter, Catherine writes as follows: "She [Magdalen], then, is the companion I am giving you. I want you to follow her because she knew the way so well that she has been made our teacher. Run, my daughter and my daughters! Don't fall asleep on me any more, for time is racing on and won't wait even a moment for you. I don't want to say any more."[32]

"From Strength to Strength"

Catherine's Magdalen is obviously a conflation of three biblical figures—
Mary Magdalen, Mary of Bethany, and the anonymous sinner from Luke
7:38–50.[33] This fusion, which Katherine Ludwig Jansen has dubbed "the
composite saint," goes back to Pope Gregory the Great (590–604).[34] In
591, he quite scandalously declared that these clearly distinct persons
were in fact the same woman, with the result that the transgressive Mary
Magdalen was turned into a penitent prostitute. Gregory's decision set
the standard for the worship of the saint for several centuries. In fact,
Magdalen as the penitent sinner remained the official Magdalen of the
Roman Church until the last general revision of the liturgical calendar
in 1969. However, as Jansen stresses, other traditions existed within
the Christian world: the Greek Church, for instance, never accepted the
Gregorian composite Saint Magdalen.[35]

In the late Middle Ages, the cult of the *apostola apostolorum* emerged.
The story is based on John 20:1–18, which describes how Magdalen
went to the tomb while it still was dark. When she discovered its empti-
ness, she was filled with sorrow. But at the moment she realized that the
gardener behind her was really the risen Christ, she cried out in Aramaic
(Jesus's own spoken language): "Rabboni!" ("Teacher!"). According to
John, Christ then gave her the apostolic mission of instructing the apostles about the profound mystery that was about to unfold before her
eyes: the ascension of Christ. As Jansen describes it, Magdalen's title
of *apostola* originated in the early twelfth century, the period of Pierre
Abelard and Bernard of Clairvaux, both of whom used this title for
Magdalen.[36] In the same period, the first pictorial representations of the
apostola apostolorum appeared, such as the richly illuminated English
manuscript known as the St. Albans Psalter (1120–30).

In Catherine's time, the veneration of the Magdalen as *apostola* had
become widespread, despite the strong resistance to female preachers
among many learned men. In fact, canon law prohibited women from
preaching or teaching, even if they were *docta et sancta*. It also for-
bade them to perform baptisms; to handle sacred objects, vestments,
and incense; and to carry the consecrated host to the sick.[37] Supporting
this law were the *quodlibetal* tracts, preaching manuals, and powerful
theologians such as Thomas Aquinas, who repeatedly, and quite notoriously, asserted women's inferiority due to their physical and intellectual
weakness. Still, despite these persistent and long-lived misogynist ideas,
the motive of the active Magdalen *apostola* grew in popularity, through
sermons, legends, and artistic representations.[38]

The tradition of Magdalen *apostola* is clearly central to Catherine's
self-fashioning as a new *apostola*, as Karen Scott has pointed out in a
ground-breaking article.[39] Undermining misogynistic arguments, Catherine uses the example of the Magdalen to recast the supposed weaknesses

of women as unique strengths. In a letter to Monna Franceschina, one of her female disciples in Lucca, Catherine writes: "So I want you to follow the Magdalen, that lovely woman in love, who never let go of the tree of the most holy cross."[40] Stressing the virtue of perseverance, she urges her interlocutor: "This is what I want you to do right up to the end of your life, growing from strength to strength."[41] Catherine's advice repeats the words of Psalm 84: "Blessed are those whose strength is in you,/ whose hearts are set on pilgrimage .... They go from strength to strength,/ till each appears before God in Zion." The word Catherine uses on this occasion is *virtù*, and the Italian expression *virtù* (and the Latin *virtus*) maintains the double sense of "virtue" and "strength."[42] To this, one might add that Catherine must have been conscious of the noun's gender implications since, as she was certainly aware, the Latin root *vir* denotes "man." In other words, Catherine encourages her disciple to let a masculine force arise from her supposed feminine weakness.

Similar advice appears in another letter (T173), which, in contrast to those discussed above, is addressed to a man. In this case, she advises her addressee to step down from his superior position. The man is a friar who has left his order, and Catherine rebukes him for his pride and lack of perseverance (recalling that perseverance is one of Magdalen's three pillars). As we know, pride in the medieval system of deadly sins is the most serious of them all and the sin of Lucifer himself, as Dante illustrated in his *Commedia*. The only way for humans to foster their persistence is to acknowledge their own lowliness, Catherine argues. Only through acknowledgement of their own profound weakness and nothingness can humans withstand the sufferings of life. As an ultimate example of this self-knowledge, and indeed, a climax moment in her devotion to Magdalen, Catherine holds Magdalen up to the friar as an example:

> Go into the tomb of self-knowledge, and with Magdalen ask, "Who will roll back the stone from the tomb for me? For the stone (that is, the guilt of sin) is so heavy that I can't budge it." And as soon as you have acknowledged and confessed how imperfect and heavy you are, you will see two angels, who will roll this stone away .... Persevere in staying there until you find Christ risen in your soul by grace. Once you have found him, go and proclaim it to your brothers—and your brothers are the true, solid, lovely virtues with whom you want to and do take up your residence. Then, Christ lets you touch him in continual humble prayer by appearing to your soul in a way you can feel. This is the way; there is no other.[43]

As this passage makes clear, Mary Magdalen's significance for Catherine is not only her role as the *apostola apostolorum*. Catherine uses her exemplar as the repository of the deepest insight and wisdom a human being can achieve and a means of attaining salvation for all of humanity.

Mary in Provence

There were certainly many reasons for Catherine's invocation of the Magdalen. One aspect of her appropriation had to do with the traditions of Mary Magdalen as the *apostola apostolorum*. Catherine was able to create and defend her own and her female disciples' public roles and authorial voices by holding up the Magdalen as an example. As an itinerant preacher, Magdalen was an especially fitting object of veneration by the Dominican Order, or the Order of Preachers (Ordo Praedicatorum), as their formal name was. Other factors informing this fourteenth-century appropriation of Mary Magdalen are the legends about her life, two of which appeared in the Middle Ages—one in the Carolingian period and the other in the eleventh century.[44] The first is the legend about St. Mary of Egypt, in which Magdalen withdrew to the desert and lived as a naked hermit in a cave after her apostolic mission was completed. The other originated in Southern France and was disseminated in particular through the *vita* that Jacobus de Voragine constructed in his *Legenda aurea*. According to this legend, which revisited the story of St. Mary in Egypt, Mary Magdalen travelled to Marseille and evangelized Gaul. As we have already seen, Catherine clearly refers to the latter Magdalen cult, grounded in the tradition of St. Mary of Egypt that emerged in Provence.

When studied in the context of contemporary political events, the legend of Mary Magdalen in Provence seems even more remarkable.[45] Beatrice, the mother of King Charles II of Naples (1254–1309), was born in Provence and was the daughter of Ramon Berenguer IV, Count of Provence, whom Dante mentions in his enigmatic story of the exiled Romeo (*Par.* VI). Beatrice and her family were the descendants of the same ruler of Provence whom, according to the legend, Magdalen had converted. She brought with her a dowry that included sovereignty over Provence, with the consequence that when Pope Clement V decided to move to Avignon, the city was already a vassal of King Charles of Naples, who, for his part, held his Italian lands from the pope. There were, in other words, close and multilayered bonds between the House of Anjou and the Avignon papacy. This was true both in King Charles's time and during the reign of his successors, King Robert of Naples and Robert's granddaughter Queen Johanna.

The myth of Mary's apostolic mission in Provence became increasingly influential during the Avignon papacy, thanks in part to the efforts of the Dominican friars, with whom King Charles was particularly close. Thus, at the same time that the popular cult of Magdalen as the *apostola apostolorum* exploded, the authorities were actively cultivating the myth. Even erudite humanists such as Francesco Petrarch, who often expressed a certain disdain for common superstitions, showed considerable enthusiasm for the Magdalen. In a letter to his friend Philippe de Cabassoles, written around 1370, Petrarch recalls an episode from his youth: More than three decades earlier, in 1337, he had followed Humbert II of Viennois to the cave of Sainte-Baume near Marseille, where Magdalen was said to have lived the last 30 years of her life in penitence. Humbert was the great-grandson of King Charles II and a son of Beatrice, who was named after their Angevine ancestress. Visiting the cave was not only a devotional act but also a way to demonstrate secular power by alluding to the proud and holy lineage of the Angevines. Petrarch stayed in the cave for three days and nights. Imagining that he was visiting the cave in the presence of the absent Philippe, who had inspired him to compose a poem to Magdalen, he wrote: "when we set down on one side of the cave; I fancied you urging me to say something brief in honor of that most holy lady. I obeyed you all the more readily because, just as the minds of pious men are inclined toward every devotion but more so to a particular one, I had already realized that you had picked her out among the sainted women, like Martin among the sainted men. I did it extemporaneously and rapidly .... Upon my return I read to you these unrevised verses."[46]

When Petrarch wrote the letter, he knew very well of Philippe de Cabassole's special devotion to Mary Magdalen. In 1355 Philippe, who as the bishop of Cavaillon was, like Petrarch, closely connected to the Avignon papacy, had in fact published a *vita* of Magdalen, the *Libellus hystorialis Marie beatissime Magdalene*. In 1368, when Pope Urban V and Emperor Charles IV entered Rome, an event witnessed by Birgitta of Sweden, Philippe was appointed the leadership of Avignon but left to help the pope in Rome only a year after Urban's transfer. However, as we know the story today, the pope's stay in Rome was short-lived. Doubtless to the great pleasure of the disloyal French cardinals, the pope's Italian journey was a fiasco, and in 1370, after just three years, he returned to Avignon and died soon thereafter. Coinciding with the pope's return was a period of fervent political engagement on the part of Catherine. As F. Thomas Luongo has noted in his important study on Catherine's political activity, her attempts to establish peace in the war-ridden Italian peninsula and her persistent efforts to lobby the papacy to return to Rome reached a fever pitch in the 1370s.[47]

Contra papam

In her portrayal of Magdalen, Catherine refers to the *apostola apostolorum* while also invoking the legend of Marseille. The second reference point may be less obvious, but in fact it gives Catherine's advice to her disciples a burning actuality. Catherine made clear allusions to the myth of the Magdalen cultivated by the authorities of her day as a way of lending authority to her instructions to her female disciples. As she writes to Monna Agnese: "As a sign that she [Magdalen] was drunk with love for her Master, she showed it in her actions toward his creatures, when after his holy resurrection she preached in the city of

Marseilles."[48] Thus adopting not only the popular devotional language of the time but also the discourse of contemporary kings, princes, bishops, and poets, Catherine frankly encourages her friend—and indirectly her female disciples—to let their voices be heard. Just as Magdalen's profound love once gave the saint the strength to convert hostile gentiles in foreign lands, so her descendants—Catherine and her *mantellate*—must fearlessly continue their apostolic mission, even if it entails trying to tame the will of a stubborn pope.

Some of the most important letters in which Catherine speaks of Magdalen are dated from spring 1376 (Letters T163, T165, and T276). After this period, she vanishes from Catherine's letters, reappearing only in the abovementioned letter to the friar who had left his order (Letter T173, dated to October 1377 by Suzanne Noffke). The reason for Catherine's sudden shift in focus away from Magdalen after 1376 is unclear, but it is tempting to speculate that it had something to do with Catherine's visit to Avignon in the same year. In May 1376, she was sent to Avignon by the Florentines to intervene on behalf of the city with Pope Gregory XI, who had placed it under interdict after a series of antipapal revolts. We do not know whether during this trip, she visited the cave of Magdalen in Marseille where Petrarch wrote his poem. One thing is clear, though: she followed the example of Magdalen the *apostola apostolorum* in that she preached to the pope, the successor of Apostle Peter, and to his curia. According to Raymond of Capua's *Legenda maior*, she had several encounters with the pope, and a number of her letters addressed to Gregory were also written in Avignon.

Catherine's Florentine mission failed, but she apparently managed to convince the pope to return to Rome. He did so in September 1376, while Catherine stayed in Avignon until November. Thereafter she returned to Siena, where she wrote her *Dialogue*, in which she authoritatively outlines the issues that threatened to tear the Church apart: the increasing secular power of the Church, the corruption of the priesthood, and the need for reform. Like her model, the fearless Magdalen who once cried out her "Rabboni," Catherine's weapon was the vernacular speech that forcefully contested, as Tylus has noted, the Latin discourse of the ecclesiastic authorities.[49] Her writings and dictations were always in her Sienese dialect, which served her constant expressions of humility particularly well, as, for instance, when she depicted herself as "serva e schiava de'servi di Gesù Cristo" ("a servant and slave of Jesus Christ").[50] Thus, one can say that under the shield of Mary Magdalen, Catherine turned the lack of appropriate language and the perceived weaknesses of her gender into a formidable strength.

Conclusion

The aim of this chapter has been to explore how Birgitta of Sweden and Catherine of Siena fashioned their authority and their political and theological discourses using two of the most central female figures from the New Testament. There is no doubt that the fourteenth century represents a historical peak in the veneration of the Virgin Mary and Mary Magdalen, and this development influenced the paths of Birgitta and Catherine. They both emphasized the quality that most of all prompted the praise and popular celebrations of the two female saints in the late Middle Ages: their profound humility. However, in Birgitta's universe and Catherine's as well, this meekness becomes a source of wisdom and power that could be exploited. While Birgitta transformed the passive *ancilla* (maidservant) into the forceful *magistra apostolorum* (the master of the apostles) and the Queen of Heaven, Catherine accentuated Magdalen's undertaking as the *apostola apostolorum* (the apostle of the apostles) rather than her role as a subservient and penitent sinner. Birgitta and Catherine placed the two respective Marys at the center of their piety, and perhaps even more important, they presented themselves as their spokespersons and imitators. In the company of the two biblical women, Birgitta and Catherine could enter the political-historical stage and influence public and religious discourse through their writings, sermons, revelations, and letters. Over subsequent decades and centuries, their texts were circulated, invoked, imitated, copied, and printed in numerous volumes and editions. Of equal importance, the legacy of Birgitta and Catherine was to inspire many ensuing generations of women writers to raise their voices in public more persistently than ever before.[51]

Notes

1 I am most grateful to Maria H. Oen for our friendship and our close and joyful collaboration on this book. In addition to Maria, I owe a warm thank to Jane Tylus and Renate Blumenfeld-Kosinski for their valuable comments and thorough reading of this chapter.

2 Rev. IV: 78.10–12:

> Ego quidem illi notum facio, quod in parte dextera sancte ecclesie fundamentum vehementer dilapsum est in tantum, quod summa testudo plures in se rupturas habet dans ex se casus tam periculosos, quod multi de subeuntibus perdunt vitam. Plereque eius columpne, que in altum tendere deberent, usque ad terram se iam inclinant, totumque pauimentum ipsius tam fossum est, quod ceci introeuntes periculose cadunt, et adhuc interdum contingit clare videntes una cum cecis grauiter cadere causa periculosarum fossarum eiusdem pauimenti. Et propter has causas stat nimis periculose ecclesia Dei. Et quid sibi ex hoc eueniet, statim propinquius esse dinoscitur. Nam ruinam certissime pacietur, nisi reparacionis iuuamen habuerit. Et ipsius ruina tam grandis erit, quod per totam Christianitatem audietur; et hec debent spiritualiter intelligi.

3 Miri Rubin, *Mother of God: A History of the Virgin Mary* (New Haven, CT: Yale University Press, 2009), 95.

4 Letter T61:

> O dilettissime figliuole mie, imparate da questa vergine santa Agnesa, cioè della santa vera umilità, ché sempre volse avilire sé medesima, sommettendosi a ogni creatura, retribuendo ogni grazia e virtù avere da Dio:

così conservava in sé la virtù de l'umilità. Dico ch'ella arse de la virtù de la carità, sempre cercando l'onore di Dio e la salute de le creature, dando sempre sé medesima nell'orazione con una carità liberale, larga ad ogni creatura, e così dimostrava l'amore che aveva al suo creatore. L'altra fu la continua sollecitudine e perseveranzia che ella ebbe, che mai non lassò né per dimonia né per creature.

Trans. by Noffke, *Letters*, 1: 4.

5 For a rich examination of the history of Mary Magdalen, see Katherine Ludwig Jansen, *The Making of the Magdalen: Preaching and Popular Devotion in the Later Middle Ages* (Princeton, NJ: Princeton University Press, 2001).

6 See Guillaume Mollat, *The Popes at Avignon (1305–1378)* (London: Thomas Nelson, 1963) and Yves Renouard, *The Avignon Papacy: The Popes in Exile 1305–1403* (New York: Barnes & Noble Books, 1994 [1954]). A more recent historical study on the Avignon papacy is Joëlle Rollo-Koster, *Avignon and its Papacy, 1309–1417: Popes, Institutions, and Society* (New York: Rowman & Littlefield, 2015).

7 The political debates in the fourteenth century are the subject of my book *The Avignon Papacy Contested: An Intellectual History from Dante to Catherine of Siena* (Cambridge, MA: Harvard University Press, 2017).

8 See Anna Fredriksson, "The Council of Constance, Jean Gerson, and St. Birgitta's *Revelaciones*," *Mediaeval Studies* 76 (2014): 217–39. For a good discussion of how Gerson's condemnation impacted female authors, see Jane Tylus, "Mystical Literacy: Writing and Religious Women in Late Medieval Italy," in *A Companion to Catherine of Siena*, eds. Carolyn Muessig, George Ferzoco, and Beverly Mayne Keinzle (Leiden: Brill, 2012), 155–84, especially 177–79.

9 For a classical study of medieval piety, see André Vauchez, *The Laity in the Middle Ages: Religious Beliefs and Devotional Practices*, ed. Daniel E. Bornstein, trans. Margery J. Schneider (Notre Dame, IN: University of Notre Dame Press, 1993).

10 AP, 75; Bridget Morris, *St Birgitta of Sweden* (Woodbridge: Boydell Press, 1999), 37–39.

11 AP, 80–81.

12 Rev. VI: 88.1: "Nocte natalis Domini tam mirabilis et magna aduenit sponse Christi exultacio cordis, vt vix se pre leticia tenere posset, et in eodem momento sensit in corde motum sensibilem admirabilem, quasi si in corde esset puer viuus et voluens se et reuoluens."

13 Claire L. Sahlin, *Birgitta of Sweden and the Voice of Prophecy* (Woodbridge: Boydell Press, 2001), 78–109.

14 The comparison between Birgitta's mystical pregnancy and stigmata has already been suggested by Aron Andersson, *Guds moder och den heliga Birgitta: En antologi* (Vadstena: Vadstena Affärstryck, 1978), 46. On this subject, see also Chapter 8 by Gábor Klaniczay in the present volume. In her thought-provoking reading of Birgitta's "mystical pregnancy," Maria H. Oen has emphasized how this passage connects Birgitta's task as a visionary to Mary's role in giving flesh to Christ. Birgitta's mission was to be a vessel to make Christ present in the world. See Oen, *The Visions of St. Birgitta: A Study of the Making and Reception of Images in the Later Middle Ages* (PhD diss., University of Oslo, 2015), 223–4.

15 Rev. VI: 57.7: "Nam quociens aspiciebam filium meum, quociens inuoluebam eum pannis, quociens videbam eius manus et pedes, tociens animus meus quasi nouo dolore absortus est, quia cogitabam, quomodo crucifigeretur."

16 See Rubin, *Mother of God*, 355–79. An important study on the negotiations of Mary in the Italian reform movement of the sixteenth century is Abigail

Brundin, *Vittoria Colonna and the Spiritual Poetics of the Italian Reformation* (Aldershot: Ashgate, 2008).

17 Although the doctrines of Mary's Assumption and the Immaculate Conception were not made dogma until much later, they were popular subjects for lyrics by sixteenth-century Italian women. See Virginia Cox, *Lyric Poetry by Women of the Italian Renaissance* (Baltimore, MD: The Johns Hopkins University Press, 2013), 9–10.

18 Anders Piltz, "Nostram naturam sublimaverat. Den liturgiska och teologiska bakgrunden till det birgittinska mariaofficiet," in *Maria i Sverige under tusen år. Föredrag vid symposiet i Vadstena 6–10 oktober 1994*, eds. Sven-Erik Brodd and Alf Härdelin (Skellefteå: Artos, 1996), 261.

19 Bridget Morris, "Introduction," in Birgitta of Sweden *The Revelations of St. Birgitta of Sweden*, trans. Denis Searby, Introductions and Notes by Bridget Morris, 4 vols (Oxford: Oxford University Press, 2006–15), 4: 53.

20 *Sermo angelicus* (SA), XIX: 12: "magistra apostolorum, confortatrix martyrum, doctrix confessorum, clarissimum speculum virginum, consolatrix viduarum, in coniugio viuencium saluberrima monitrix atque omnium in fide catholica perfectissima roboratrix."

21 SA, XIX: 10: "Item quamuis eciam Scriptura dicat, quod Christi resurreccionem Magdalena et apostoli prius viderunt, sine dubio tamen credendum est, quod sua mater dignissima antequam illi veraciter hoc sciebat et priusquam illi eum viuum resurrexisse a mortuis vidit."

22 SA, XX: 9: "Et quia inter omnes angelos et homines ipsa inuenta est humillima, ideo super omnia, que creata sunt, facta est sublimissima omniumque pulcherrima atque ipsi Deo super omnes simillima."

23 SA, XX: 16: "Huic igitur gloriose anime sedes glorifica ipsi Trinitati propinquissima ab eterno constituta erat."

24 SA, XXI: 12; "ita eciam solo excepto Christi corpore sue matris corpus fuit dignissimum longiori tempore quam aliorum corpora cum sua anima meritorum premia recipere ...."

25 SA, prol.: 4–6:

> Igitur beata Birgitta habens cameram, cuius fenestra ad altare maius respondebat, vnde corpus Christi cotidie videre poterat, preparabat se cotidie in eadem camera ad scribendum cum pugillari et carta et penna in manibus, postquam horas et oraciones suas legebat, et sic parata angelum Domini expectabat. Qui veniens ponebat se prope eam a latere eius et stabat erectus honestissime, habens semper faciem cum reuerenti gestu respicientem versus altare, ubi corpus Christi reconditum erat. Et sic stans dictam lecturam, idest infrascriptas lecciones legendas in matutinis in dicto monasterio, que tractant de excellentissima excellencia ab eterno beate Marie Virginis, ipse dictabat distincte et ordinate in lingua materna beate Birgitte.

26 AP, 66. For Birgitta's literary sources, see Birgit Klockars, *Birgitta och böckerna. En undersökning av den heliga Birgittas källor* (Stockholm: KVHAA, 1966). Piltz, "Nostram naturam sublimaverat," 261–74; Päivi Salmesvuori, *Power and Sainthood: The Case of Birgitta of Sweden* (New York: Palgrave Macmillan, 2014), 41–61.

27 Jane Tylus, *Reclaiming Catherine of Siena: Literacy, Literature, and the Signs of Others* (Chicago, IL: The University of Chicago Press, 2009), 143–61.

28 See LM, II. 6.13–15, p. 252.

29 Letter T276: "levati di tanta miseria e fracidume, ricorre al tuo Creatore, che ti riceverà, pure che tu voglia lassare el peccato mortale e tornare a lo stato della grazia." Trans. Noffke, *Letters*, 1: 292.

30 Letter T276: "Acompagnati e impara da quella dolce e inamorata Madalena." Trans. Noffke, *Letters*, 3: 293.
31 Letter T165: "quelle tre colonne forti che conservano e tolgono la debilezza dell'anima." Trans. Noffke, *Letters*, 4: 42.
32 Letter T165: "Or questa è quella compagna la quale io ti do, e che io voglio che tu seguiti, però che ella seppe sì bene la via che ella è fatta a noi maestra. Corre, figliuola e figliuole mie, non mi state più a dormire, che 'l tempo corre e non v'aspetta punto. Non voglio dire di più." Trans. Noffke, *Letters*, 2: 42.
33 This is also noted by Suzanne Noffke, *Letters*, 1: 5, n. 8.
34 Jansen, *The Making of the Magdalen*, 32–35.
35 Jansen, *The Making of the Magdalen*, 35, n. 54.
36 Jansen, *The Making of the Magdalen*, 62–82, 63.
37 Jansen, *The Making of the Magdalen*, 54–55.
38 However, as Carolyn Muessig, among others, has argued, despite the widespread notion among medieval theologians that women were biologically inferior and intellectually weak, women did, in fact, teach and preach in and outside of cloisters. See Carolyn Muessig, "Prophecy and Song. Teaching and Preaching by Medieval Women," in *Women Preachers and Prophets through Two Millennia of Christianity*, eds. Beverly Mayne Kienzle and Pamela J. Walker (Berkeley: University of California Press, 1998).
39 Karen Scott, "St. Catherine of Siena, 'Apostola,'" *Church History* 61, no. 1 (Mar., 1992): 34–46, at 42.
40 Letter T163. Also this is probably written in spring 1376. "Unde io voglio che seguitiate questa dolce e inamorata di Magdalena, la quale non si staccò mai dall'arbore della santissima croce, ma con perseveranzia ella si bagnava e inebriava del sangue del Figliuolo di Dio." Trans. Noffke, *Letters*, 2: 48.
41 Letter T163: "Così voglio che facciate voi infine all'ultimo de la vita vostra, crescendo di virtù in virtù." Trans. Noffke, *Letters*, 2: 48.
42 This is also discussed by Noffke, *Letters*, 4: 48, n. 4.
43 Letter T173:

> E entrarete nel sepolcro del cognoscimento di voi con Magdalena e dimandarete: 'Chi mi rivollarebbe la pietra del monimento? però che la gravezza della pietra, cioè la colpa del peccato, è sì grave che io per me non la posso muovere.' E subbito allora, confessata e veduta la vostra imperfezione e gravezza, vedrete due angeli che rivoltaranno questa pietra ... con perseveranzia sta, infine che truova Cristo resuscitato nell'anima sua per grazia. E poi che l'à trovato, ella el va ad anunziare a' fratelli suoi; e suoi fratelli sono le vere reali e dolci virtù, con le quali vuole fare e fa mansione insieme con loro. Allora Cristo, apparendo nell'anima per sentimento, si lassa toccare con l'umile e continua orazione. Or questa è la via; e altra via non c'è.

Trans. Noffke, *Letters*, 2: 512–13.
44 Katherine Ludwig Jansen, "Maria Magdalen: Apostolorum Apostola," in Kienzle and Walker, *Women Preachers and Prophets*, 65.
45 See Jansen, *The Making of the Magdalen*, 307–32.
46 Francesco Petrarca, *Sen.* XV, 15. Translated in *Letters of Old Age: Rerum Senilium Libri I–XVIII*, eds. and trans. Aldo S. Bernardo, Saul Levin, and Reta A. Bernardo (Baltimore, MD: Johns Hopkins University Press, 1992), vol. II, 596. The verses involving Mary Magdalen to which Petrarch refers are the 36 hexameters in Poëmata, III, 22–4 (Appendix).
47 F. Thomas Luongo, *The Saintly Politics of Catherine of Siena* (Ithaca, NY: Cornell University Press, 2006).

48 Letter T61: "In segno che ella è inebriata del maestro suo, ella el dimostra ne le creature sue, e questo fece dipo' la santa resurrezione, quando ella predicò ne la città di Marsilia." Trans. Noffke, *Letters*, 1: 4. A central point in Jane Tylus's compelling reading of the letters is, however, that Catherine admonishes Monna Agnese and her disciples to temper Magdalen's fearlessness with Agnes's humility. The perfect *donna santa*, Tylus argues, should according to Catherine search for a balance or a compromise between engagement and withdrawal (i.e. between Magdalen's zeal to find Christ when arriving at the empty tomb and Saint Agnes's contemplation, which led her to the Lord). See Tylus, *Reclaiming Catherine of Siena*, 197–99.

49 Tylus, *Reclaiming Catherine of Siena*, 153–54.

50 This humble presentation, however, must be read with care, as Blake Beattie has noted. To a certain degree it only reflects the usual beginnings of papal bulls, where the pope is entitled *servus servorum Dei* ("servant of the servants of God"). See Beattie, "Catherine of Siena and the Papacy," in Muessig, Ferzoco, and Keinzle, *A Companion to Catherine of Siena*, 84.

51 The influence of Birgitta on Renaissance women writers is the topic of the international research project which I currently direct: *The Legacy of Birgitta of Sweden: Women, Politics and Reform in Renaissance Italy* (funded by The Research Council of Norway, 2018–2021): https://www.hf.uio.no/ifikk/english/research/projects/the-legacy-of-birgitta-of-sweden/. The project involves a series of distinguished researchers from Scandinavia, Europe and USA, including some of the contributors to this volume.

4   Saint Birgitta's and Saint Catherine's Visions of Crusading

Renate Blumenfeld-Kosinski

In the Middle Ages, many holy personages felt compelled to speak truth to power. Among them were women visionaries like Hildegard of Bingen (1098–79) and later on Birgitta of Sweden and Catherine of Siena who, in revelations and letters, spoke to the secular and ecclesiastical leaders of their time. They admonished them, praised them occasionally, predicted great calamities, and eventually turned against some of them. The problems they were concerned with included not only general issues like the reform of the Church, the moral behavior of the faithful, and the way to salvation but also very specific political problems like the papacy's return to Rome, the Great Schism, peace in Western Christendom during the Hundred Years War, reconciling the Italian city states with the papacy (for Catherine), and the crusade. Birgitta and Catherine— one coming from the high Swedish aristocracy, the other from an Italian artisan milieu—were the only female visionaries to make the crusade a central concern of their spiritual lives, and they did so in an age when the "classical" crusades were long over. This fact did not prevent many theorists of the crusades as well as popes and secular rulers to keep on planning for and dreaming about the crusade.

But which kind of crusades were Birgitta and Catherine thinking about? Birgitta's revelations related to the crusade were both general— in the ways she thought about converting the remaining Baltic pagans as well as the "schismatic" Orthodox Christians—and quite specific: she was involved in King Magnus IV Eriksson of Sweden's (r. 1316–64) ill-fated "crusades" against Novgorod in 1348–51.[1] Catherine, by contrast, agitated for the *passagium generale*, the pan-European crusade to the Holy Land that was championed by many thinkers, from early-fourteenth-century theorists like Pierre Dubois or Marino Sanudo Torsello to the late fourteenth-century writer and diplomat Philippe de Mézières.[2] In order to understand the ideas and strategies our two saints espoused I will first briefly describe the political situation with regard to the crusades from the 1340s to the 1360s. Then we will explore what the two women's goals were and how they tried to achieve them.

Realpolitik: Birgitta and Catherine's "Crusading Moments"

The crusades had a "classic age" that lasted from the First Crusade in 1095 to the late thirteenth century: in May 1291 the last Christian stronghold in the Holy Land, the town of Acre, fell to the Mamluk Sultan al-Ashraf Halil, marking the end point of the two-hundred-year Christian presence in Syria and Palestine. This calamitous event prompted Pope Nicholas IV (1288–92) to issue the encyclical *Dirum amaritudinis [calicem]* on 13 August 1291, which "included a call for advice on the recovery of the Holy Land."[3] Thus, starting in the early fourteenth century a number of crusade theorists began to imagine a concerted European effort at retaking the Holy Land.[4] The crusades of the later Middle Ages on the whole did not correspond to the pan-European *passagium generale* envisioned by the many theorists of this time as well as by Catherine of Siena later in the century.[5] The military campaigns of the fourteenth century were fragmented, not necessarily directed at the Holy Land (they included Spain and the Baltic lands), and for the most part unsuccessful.

In this climate a strange mix of nostalgia for the "classic" international crusades of earlier centuries and innovative ideas on correcting past crusaders' mistakes flourished. Significantly, the idea of conversion that had become more pronounced as the crusades progressed, does not figure prominently in these treatises. William of Adam, Ramon Lull, Pierre Dubois, and Marino Sanudo Torsello, to name just a few of these theorists active in the late thirteenth and early fourteenth centuries, all, though with different emphases, treated the same themes: the financial and strategic preparation of crusading armies; identifying the most important targets (Egypt, Palestine, North Africa) and the best routes to get there; plans for an economic blockade of Mamluk Egypt; the unification of the chivalric orders to save money and increase their military power; the conquest of Constantinople as a precondition for a successful crusade; and the cooperation with the Mongols in order to stop the Muslim advance to the North.[6]

At the same time, various rulers did in fact try to organize a *passagium generale*. In Birgitta and Catherine's era it was above all Pierre I de Lusignan, king of Cyprus, who, together with his chancellor Philippe de Mézières and the papal legate Pierre de Thomas, championed the crusade and traveled throughout Europe in the early 1360s to drum up support and raise funds.[7] Both our saints came into their orbit at some point and may well have drawn energy from their enthusiasm.

This brief sketch of the crusading situation shows that very detailed proposals for the recovery of the Holy Land circulated in Europe, that continuous attempts at organizing crusades by secular rulers were made, and that papal bulls calling for a crusade were issued just as continuously, all of this to little actual effect. It is in this climate of "aspirational crusading" that we have to situate Catherine of Siena.[8] Birgitta existed in a different climate, for no theorists expounded on the Baltic crusades and no pan-European calls were issued, though there was plenty of crusading activity in the Baltic, some of it supported by papal bulls.

Birgitta, King Magnus, and the Baltic Crusades

Let us step back for a moment to 1147 to Bernard of Clairvaux, a pivotal figure in crusading ideology, who will form a bridge between Birgitta and Catherine long before their lifetime. Benjamin Z. Kedar, in his magisterial study *Crusade and Mission*, shows how the idea of conversion, including forced conversion, took hold in the European *imaginaire*. Anyone who has read the late eleventh-century *La Chanson de Roland* will recall that when Charlemagne takes Saragossa "many pagans" (i.e. Muslims) are led to baptism and that anyone who refuses to be baptized will be "hanged, burned, or killed."[9] In that spirit, Bernard of Clairvaux "held the view that the aims of a projected military expedition should be the extermination or Christianization of the enemy." Or, as Peter the Venerable put it, first the "word," and, if that does not work, the "sword."[10] In 1147 Bernard issued a letter supporting the German expedition "against the Wends—the Northeastern counterpart of Louis VII's and Conrad III's expedition to the Levant—calling on Christians to "utterly annihilate or surely convert' the pagan enemy." Kedar speculates that this violent exhortation was then applied to the Saracens and so "by 1147 Saracen conversion had become the major objective of the Oriental crusade."[11]

At the same time, Bernard, while preaching the crusade in Germany, found that "recruitment amongst the Saxon nobility was disappointing." An "influential group" of northern German rulers persuaded Bernard to approach Pope Eugene III "to allow the north Germans to attack the pagan Slavs in lieu of joining the general crusade." Eugene complied with the bull *Divina dispensatione* which extended "the same crusading privileges to those who wished to fight against the Wends in the defense of northern Christendom as those proceeding on the second crusade were given."[12] Thus the Baltic Crusades were born.[13] They, as Peter Lock observes, "combined conversion and conquest in a blend that was not found in any other crusading endeavor."[14]

Eugene III's crusading directives targeted Livonia, Estonia, Finland, and Prussia, thus buttressing the "growing jurisdiction of the papacy."[15] Iben Fonnesberg-Schmidt analyzes how the "Baltic wars" became crusades through the granting of indulgences by Pope Innocent III in 1198 and by an extension of the Augustinian "just war theory" to the Baltic lands. Wars for conversion were not permitted but fighting apostates and heretics was acceptable, and because the Baltic missions had predated the crusades these military forays could be interpreted as responses to requests for support of endangered missions. Thus, the elements that justified crusades to the Holy Land came to legitimize the Baltic crusades. From Eugene III's first authorization to Honorius III (1216–27) an "upgrading" of the Baltic crusades occurred that put them on a par with the Holy Land crusades. They were supposed to "support missionary bishops in their work," and they were authorized in "defense of converts and missionaries."[16] A new phase in Baltic crusading began with the involvement of the Teutonic Order and the pious rationale of conversion did not hold up for long. Raids for booty, settling of border disputes, and other worldly issues became the reality of crusading in the Baltic.

It is against this background that we can explore Birgitta's ideas on crusading and her involvement in King Magnus's ill-fated crusading endeavors.[17] Many historians agree that Birgitta had a role in Magnus's launching of a crusade against Novgorod;[18] indeed, for some scholars "the direct connection with Birgitta and her revelations made this the strangest crusading enterprise to originate in Scandinavia."[19]

Hostilities between Sweden and Novgorod had simmered for a long time, and Norman Housley speculates that Magnus chose the moment to attack the Novgorodians in 1347 because conditions in his own kingdom were favorable, and Novgorod was isolated between Lithuania and Moscow.[20] However, the Russian sources make clear that Magnus's first action was to send an embassy to the Novgorodians, apparently to discuss the relative merits of the Catholic and Orthodox faiths but most probably to "dispute existing frontiers."[21] What was the balance, then, between conversion and conquest in this enterprise? Where did Birgitta stand on these issues?

In several revelations, Birgitta envisioned the salvation of the heathen or pagans also referred to as infidels. But who were they? John Lind notes that "in the Old Swedish version of the *Revelations* the term pagans [hedhninge] is used exclusively to describe the adversaries." The Latin version, from which the extant Swedish version was translated, however alternates between "infidels (*infideles*) ...and pagans (*paganos*)." But in the revelations that more specifically refer to King Magnus's crusade (Rev. VIII: 39, 43, 45) *infideles* refers to the schismatic Novgorodians, while *paganos* "denotes heathen Ingrians and Karelians."[22] Interestingly, Birgitta never uses the term "Saracens" which, however strange it may seem to us, was commonly used to designate the pagan Lithuanians in Birgitta's era.[23]

What is known about the actual practices of these non-Christian "pagans" comes mostly from the accounts of Western travelers since they themselves left no written sources. Travelers, both secular and clerical, in the thirteenth century saw "the Balts as victims of superstition induced by demons" but for the most part did not condemn them for idolatry. The practices most often remarked upon were their un-Christian funeral rites (that is, the burning of corpses), and sacrifices to "their gods" in "sacred woods," a practice mentioned for example by Thomas of Cant-impré in *De apibus*.[24]

In Revelation I: 57 Birgitta seems to speak of actual pagans (*paganos*) whose conversion is desired by Christ because, according to him, he had become "like rotten and stinking meat" (*quasi caro putrida et fetens*) in Christians' mouths; he will therefore turn to the pagans in whose mouths he will turn from bitterness to sweet honey (Rev. I: 57.3, trans. 1: 157).[25] Continuing the honey metaphor, Christ sees himself as a bee, turning away from bitter herbs, that is, the Christians who have disappointed him and abandoned him, and turn to other bitter herbs, that is, the pagans with debased morals (*idest paganos moribus satis auersos*), some of which would be willing to convert, if only they had some help (Rev. VI: 44.7, trans. 3: 96). Here Birgitta espouses the traditional ecclesiastical tenet that as long as the pagans do not attack Christians one should not blame but rather help them. But the "beekeepers" (= prelates and princes; Rev. II: 19.62; trans. 1: 224) in charge of this conversion often do a bad job, for instead of instructing them in the faith they deny them the sacraments and send them to hell, a worse punishment than the one for "their traditional paganism" (*in suo assueto paganismo*; Rev. II: 19.100, trans. 1: 226). Birgitta is probably thinking here of the apostates, a continuous problem in the newly converted lands. Pagan Lithuania was a perpetual target of crusaders of the Teutonic Order, who, even after the country's official conversion to Christianity in 1387, continued their raids.[26] Indeed, even at the Council of Constance in 1415 a Polish delegation protested the constant raids by Teutonic Knights who were not interested in converting and baptizing the infidels but rather in grabbing as much booty as they could.[27]

Crusade and mission, the two strategies that often were at loggerheads in the crusades in the Levant, thus also collided in the Baltic and surface in Birgitta's revelations: first offer the latter, then embark on the former, that is the message of revelations VIII: 40 (where the term is *pagani*) and VIII: 43 (where the term is *infideles*).[28] First, the pagans should be offered peace, faith, and freedom by their adversaries, Christ determines, but if they refuse to accept their admonitions, then the crusaders should attack them (Rev. VIII: 40.2; trans. 4: 67). In any case, this kind of swift extermination would be good for the pagans because it would give them less time to sin! In VIII: 43.1, Christ puts the same kind of advice—or threat—into figurative language by evoking two banners that the king should have, one symbolizing mercy by depicting Christ's suffering, the second "the sword of my justice" (*gladius iustitiae*). The second banner should be raised up only if the first one is refused (trans. 4: 68).

Things get more specific in a revelation on the king's counselors where Christ says "The third thing [the king should do] is that he should send his vassals and his own people to those lands of the infidels (*ad illa loca infidelium*) where Catholic faith and charity can spread and grow" (Rev. VIII: 2.9, trans. 4: 46). Christ adds that Magnus's vassals were killed because he had set his sights on another Christian kingdom, that is, Denmark, a country that Magnus had fought for the possession of Scania. Christian Oertel believes in a direct cause and effect sequence when he states that "Magnus reacted to this reproach by promising a crusade in his and his wife's joint testament of 1346."[29] Pavlína Rychterová adopts a much more skeptical view of Birgitta's influence. She sees our saint as just a small cog in a political machinery consisting of important leaders that may have used her but would not have been motivated to action by her. Still, she argues, King Magnus found support and justification for his crusade—in reality a military campaign for economic gain—through Birgitta.[30]

Rychterová makes this observation in relation to Birgitta's attempted intervention in the Hundred Years War through a revelation that floated the idea of a marriage alliance between England and France (Rev. VI: 34),[31] and through a letter sent to Pope Clement VI (Rev. VI: 63) in 1348, that is, just as King Magnus was about to embark on the crusade.[32] Two years before that date, a commission of three Swedish bishops together with Birgitta's mentors Mathias of Linköping and Peter Olofsson, prior of Alvastra, had examined Birgitta's revelations. Their approval resulted in a text that now forms the Prologue to Book I of the *Revelations*. Thus, before Birgitta's advice could be used for any kind of intervention in European politics she had to be vetted as a bona fide political visionary.[33]

We cannot know for certain that King Magnus was pushed to his attack on Novgorod primarily by Birgitta. As Bridget Morris shows, the king's decision also formed part of Swedish foreign policy in the 1340s. Early in his reign that began in 1319 when he was a mere three years old—his mother and her second husband acted as regents—Pope John XXII (1316–34) had called for a crusade against the "enemies of Christianity," the Orthodox Russians, and there were continuous border skirmishes. In 1347 the "Novgorodians attacked Swedish territory" and Swedish merchants wanted protection for their trade routes. Morris concludes that "when Magnus planned his enterprise to the eastern Baltic in the 1340s, to settle border differences once and for all, he was pursuing an aspect of longstanding national foreign policy."[34]

But what about the embassy he sent from the island of Björkö outside of Viborg that invited the Novgorodians to a discussion of the relative merits of the Catholic and Orthodox faiths? John Lind points to Birgitta's influence for this unusual strategy, stating that an "invitation to a theological debate as a preliminary to a military campaign is unique in Russo-Swedish relations and can only be seen as an attempt to conform with Birgittine demands."[35] The issue is more complex, however, for another possible source of influence exists in the shape of a saintly Swedish ancestor, the twelfth-century St. Erik.

Beyond a doubt, the invitation to a debate about the two faiths "baf-fled the Novgorodians," as John Lind shows in his analysis of King Mag-nus's "Testament," a curious document chronicling the king's (fictitious) last days as a monk converted to the Orthodox faith. At first, despite their bafflement, the Novgorodians welcomed the idea, expecting a real debate that could even end in their side winning it. "When the king, however, actually received the Novgorodian delegation, which for a dis-cussion of the faith referred him to the Patriarch in Constantinople, the demand was that the Novgorodians should convert to his faith or he would attack them."[36] While precedents for this kind of choice can be found in a number of epics (such as the *Chanson de Roland*, mentioned above) and chronicles in reference to the Muslim enemy, it has only one precedent in the Scandinavian tradition, namely in the fourteenth-century *Life of Saint Erik*. King Erik IX Jedvardsson was said to have led a crusade against Finland from 1155 to 1159 that converted the Suomi in south-western Finland. This "crusading" expedition may just have been a "small-scale raid exaggerated into great deeds for the purposes of mis-sionary propaganda by the author" of the *Life*.[37] As it is presented there, this episode directly parallels Magnus's carrot-and-stick strategy toward the Novgorodians and also corresponds to the choice represented by the "two banners" in Birgitta's Revelation II: 43. Was Birgitta perhaps in-spired by saint Erik? As the Virgin Mary states at the end of revelation VI: 66 (trans. 3: 139), St. Erik was a patron saint for Birgitta, but she also condemned him in other revelations.[38] For Magnus, it is important to remember, St. Erik was a holy ancestor and Birgitta as well "descended from a family that had a close relationship to St. Erik."[39] While Oertel does not go as far as John H. Lind, who describes Magnus as a "Birgit-tine king," he does ascribe a large dose of influence to Birgitta as far as Magnus's crusade is concerned. In my view, although the choice between conversion and violence had a long tradition, it seems possible that St. Erik served as a model for Birgitta and Magnus. In the Russian sources Magnus is certainly seen as a proselytizer, a king bent on conversion. But as soon as the talks between Magnus's delegation and the Novgorodians broke down Magnus embraced the military option, designed to advance his political goals.[40]

These goals—such as settling border disputes and protecting endan-gered trade routes—are missing from or disguised so as to be barely discernible in Birgitta's most dramatic vision concerning the crusade. In Revelation IV: 2.2–3 (trans. 2: 25) "About a Fantastic Beast and Fish" Birgitta tries to present various choices as to launching a crusade. She sees a balance with two scales of which the first contains a fish with razor-sharp scales, spouting venom like a unicorn, with sharp steel-like ears. Hot flames emerge from the mouth of the animal in the second scale; its eyelids seem like swords and sharp arrows fly from its ears. Then three groups of people appear and strategies are proposed to subdue these animals. In Revelation IV: 129 an exegesis of this complicated vision is offered and we learn that the animals and the humans represent different approaches to the crusade. As Morris concludes, "the revelation looks like a deliberation on the usefulness and expediency of the northern crusades." Birgitta was "never wholly convinced by the need for a crusade" but supported one that is "properly carried out."[41] In Revelation VI: 41.7 (identical to Rev. VIII: 44) Christ explains that the king is like a child choosing between two apples, of which one is gilded on the outside but actually empty and rotten, while the other, less attractive one, is fresh and beautiful. Magnus chose the gilded apple, that is, worldly appearances and gain over the spiritual truth, and thus his army returned, tired, hungry, and miserable (trans. 3: 91–92).

Indeed, Magnus's crusade was not carried out properly. The initial victory, the taking of the fortress of Orechov that controlled the Neva basin at the entrance to Lake Ladoga in August 1348, was reversed by its loss in February 1349, when almost all the Swedish defenders were killed or captured after Magnus had returned to Sweden. While the expedition of 1348–49 was not sanctioned by the pope as a crusade, in 1351 a "papal crusading bull was issued, which stated that the purpose of the royal crusade was to help and rescue the recently converted Karelians and Izhorians" threatened by the Russians.[42] This crusade also failed, resulting in uprisings against the king who had levied heavy taxes for his failed campaigns.

Birgitta had left Sweden for Rome in 1349; the *Visby Chronicle* suggests that it was the bloody ending of Magnus's crusade that may have caused her departure.[43] Later her anger at Magnus erupted in a number of revelations, of which the strongest is Revelation VIII: 47, the "last letter" that Birgitta would send Magnus. Instead of bringing the "holy Catholic faith to pagan countries (*ad paganism um*)" Magnus listened to counselors worse than the devil's servants who cared more about grabbing land than saving souls (trans. 4: 72–73). This judgment sums up how the balance between crusade and mission was tilted in favor of the former, and that the crusade was in fact an attempted, finally unsuccessful, Swedish land grab. But it is not enough for Birgitta to reprimand Magnus. In her famous "insurrection revelation" (Extrav.: 80), one of two autograph revelations, Birgitta calls for Magnus's deposition, accuses him of sodomy (a sin punishable by death),[44] betraying his subjects, receiving Mass while excommunicated, robbing lands from the crown, and abandoning Scania.[45] She calls on four noblemen to overthrow the king. Olle Ferm has shown that Birgitta's "accusations and plea for Magnus's removal correspond closely to regulations laid down in the "Konungabalker" in the national law code promulgated by the king himself about 1350."[46] The same accusations—and more—appear in the anonymous anti-Magnus tract the *Libellus de magno Erici rege* (1365–71) that purports to show "*Qualiter regnavit rex Magnus.*"[47]

The accusation of sodomy reappears (Magnus is said to feign cohabitation with his wife, but many know the truth ...), and the queen is accused of poisoning her son.[48]

Magnus's reign after the failed crusades was indeed marked by continuous crises, revolts of his sons, and loss of territory. In 1364, he was deposed, imprisoned, and finally liberated, only to drown in 1371 in a shipwreck. By that time, Birgitta had lived in Rome for decades and had other concerns.

Catherine and the Crusade to the Holy Land

Was Catherine in some ways the successor of Birgitta when it comes to thinking about the crusade? Noële Denis-Boulet emphasizes the great differences between the two visionaries. Without mentioning that Birgitta's revelations actually concerned the Baltic crusades rather than the *passagium generale* desired by Catherine, Denis-Boulet heaves a sigh of relief: with Catherine's letters we no longer have to suffer through Birgittine pseudo-biblical Joachimite discourse—that Denis-Boulet dismisses as convoluted "prophétisme franciscanisant"—but now we encounter a refreshingly direct polemic.[49] But how informed was that polemic? Franco Cardini believes that when it came to the crusade, "Catherine had no properly political perception of the problems in their complex vastness or of the political means to solve them."[50] Indeed, Catherine arrived on the scene when about all possible crusading ideas had been put forward by many theorists, as we saw above. Crusades had been attempted repeatedly—in vain or with disastrous results. In many ways, Catherine was a latecomer to the debates on and plans for the fourteenth-century crusades.

But, undeterred, Catherine addressed the question of the crusade in a large number of letters to a variety of recipients in both a religious/symbolic context and in a very pragmatic one, thinking, for example, about the numbers of troops that certain individuals could supply, or about redeploying the marauding troops of the commander John Hawkwood in the crusading enterprise. In disagreement with Cardini, Jörg Jungmayr believes that Catherine pursued "eine höchst realpolitische Absicht."[51] She was a fighter for the crusade, using much of the militant language—but calibrated to each recipient of her letters—that characterized much of Dominican crusade preaching.[52] What then was Catherine's understanding of the crusade in the late fourteenth century? How did she see the Muslim enemy? What were her goals and how did she hope to achieve them?

Before Catherine wrote any of her divinely inspired crusade letters, she was, at the Dominican Chapter of 1374 in Florence, "vetted for a role that had already been conceived for her, as a political visionary—a second Birgitta."[53] Certain elements in her crusade thinking were brought to her by Alfonso Pecha of Jaén who indeed saw in her a successor to Birgitta and approached her about the crusade.[54] Thus, unlike Birgitta, whose crusade polemic was not sanctioned by the pope, Catherine was from the very beginning part of a prestigious team that labored for the common goal of the crusade.

Pope Gregory XI, not discouraged by over eighty years of failures to bring about a *passagium generale*, continued to pursue the dream of taking back the Holy Land. On 1 July 1375 (a date that also marked the end for the time being of the conflict with the Visconti),[55] Gregory issued a crusade bull (Catherine mentions it in her letter to Monna Pavola (Letter T144), immediately asking for written commitments to a crusade. Raymond of Capua was designated as collector of these engagements. Thus, when a bull of 17 August 1376, confirmed Raymond as spiritual director of Catherine he became part of the team campaigning for the crusade. The Dominican General Elias of Toulouse, successor of Simon de Langres who had long been agitating for a crusade, chose Raymond over other, Tuscan, possibilities. The bull mentions that Catherine occupied herself with the salvation of souls as well as the holy *passagium,* and that Raymond aided Catherine in this endeavor. Denis-Boulet argues that Raymond's Neapolitan family origin predisposed him to shore up even more crusade enthusiasm in Catherine who thus became a kind of "papal agent in Italy" (while the pope was still in Avignon).[56] Catherine wrote a few letters on the crusade before Gregory's crusade bull (notably to John Hawkwood in June 1375), but the pace of the letters concerning the crusade picks up after that date and continues in a steady stream until the Great Schism, beginning in the fall of 1378, eclipses the crusade as a central problem for Catherine.[57] Her letter to Queen Johanna of Naples in early December 1378 seems to be the last one explicitly focusing on the crusade.

Birgitta's revelations on the crusade had essentially one major intended recipient and one defined goal: King Magnus should move against the "infidels" (both pagan and Russian Orthodox) and try to convert them. Catherine did not have just one idea, one strategy, or even just one view of the enemy—who for her was Muslim—although the principal ideas of taking back the Holy Sepulcher and securing peace in Europe in order to enable a joint crusade pervade most letters.[58] She very effectively adjusted each letter, each definition of the "infidels" for maximum effect on a given recipient. A few examples will have to suffice to illustrate her multi-pronged approach.

The pope, already on board for the crusade, needed nothing more than frequent reminders. In Letter T185, (January 1376), her first letter to Gregory XI, Catherine laid out her principal ideas: that the crusade should be delayed no longer and that the rebellious Italian cities should be pacified so that any fighting can be diverted toward the unbelievers (Noffke, *Letters*, 1: 249). A few months later Catherine traveled to

Avignon, her main business (*principalis causa*) being the crusade, as Raymond of Capua later states in the *Legenda maior.*[59] Throughout 1375, Catherine had been agitating for the crusade in letters to John Hawkwood (Letter T140), Queen Johanna of Naples (Letters T138, T133, and T143), Bernabò Visconti (T28), and others. She was au courant as to various preparations, as when she joyfully conveys to her friend William Flete[60] (T65, Aug./Sept. 1375) that Mariano IV, ruler of Arborea, Sardinia, has promised for two years ten galleys (*galee*),[61] 1,000 knights, 3,000 foot soldiers, and 600 crossbowmen (Noffke, *Letters*, 1: 158). And just a few months later (T132) she excitedly writes to Cecca di Clemente Gori and other *mantellate* that she had spoken with the ambassador from Cyprus who was on his way to the pope to get news about the holy crusade (Noffke, *Letters*, 1: 202).

The letter to Hawkwood was carried by Raymond himself;[62] it is short and to the point: stop the fighting in Italy, and instead fight "the unbelieving dogs" (*cani infideles*), and be ready to die for Christ in this holy crusade (T140, Noffke, *Letters*, 1: 80–81). Catherine used the same derogatory term to designate Muslims in her letter to Queen Elizabeth of Hungary, mother of Louis the Great (T145, Noffke, *Letters*, 1: 170, late October 1375). This most insulting term seems tailored to what Catherine saw as extremely urgent situations: Hawkwood's troops destabilized the situation in Italy and Elizabeth's son had abandoned the crusade.[63] For Bernabò Visconti she chose a somewhat milder term: the worst unbelievers (*pessimi infedeli*; T28, Noffke, *Letters*, 1: 137, summer 1375). Here she appealed to his leadership ambitions: he should stop fighting the pope and instead help get back what she considers rightfully belonging to Christians, that is, Jerusalem.

Catherine also envisioned the possibility of converting and saving the Muslim enemy but only in certain letters.[64] Writing in the second half of 1375 to the condottiere Bartolomeo Smeducci she stated that the unbelievers are not "dogs" but "our brothers," also saved by Christ's blood.[65] Still, she argued, we have to retake what is ours, namely the Holy Sepulcher. But here Catherine offers a kind of exchange that admirably combines crusade and mission: we must wrest the holy place from their hands and at the same time wrest their souls away from demons and from those without faith. Another possibility is that the Muslims are God's bastard or natural children ready to be converted. In a letter to the pope in early September 1376 (T239, Noffke, *Letters*, 2: 246) she calls the Muslims "bastard children ... who have not yet been legitimized through holy baptism."[66] Note that Catherine says "not yet," so conversion is on the horizon. How will it be achieved? "With the divine power of the sword of the holy word, and with human power and force" (Noffke, *Letters*, 2: 246).[67] The image of the sword undermines (or completes?) the prospect of conversion by "parola santa" and thus brings together the two aspects of the holy passage: crusade and mission.

The Holy Land thus is in the hands of unbelievers who may be open to conversion. But Catherine knows that another threat looms. Let us remember that 1376 is only twenty years before the disastrous battle of Nicopolis (in today's Bulgaria) designed to stop the Turkish advance north. It was called by Sigismund of Hungary and involved also French troops commanded by the Jean de Nevers, son of the duke of Burgundy. Thousands of the Western coalition were killed or taken prisoner. At least twice Catherine evokes the Turkish threat and implies that the Turks are on the move: in her letter to Queen Elizabeth of Hungary (T145) she accuses the Turks (Turchi) of "seizing the land of the Holy Church" (Noffke, *Letters*, 1: 170),[68] and in another letter to the pope (T218) in July 1376 she warns that the aggressive unbelievers are coming closer and closer (Noffke, *Letters*, 2: 200).[69]

For Johanna of Naples Catherine uses a slightly different approach. In her first letter to Johanna (T138), Catherine works with a horticultural metaphor of brambles versus sweet fruit to urge Johanna to come to the aid of Christ's bride (Noffke, *Letters*, 1: 102), a theme she pursues throughout her other letters to Johanna. But Catherine also has the brilliant idea to remind Johanna that she is in fact queen of Jerusalem (T143, 4 August 1375), which makes her the natural "leader and patroness of this holy crusade" (Noffke, *Letters*, 1: 148).[70] Catherine also identified another potential leader, Louis of Anjou, brother of the French king Charles V, whom she had met in Avignon in 1376. She first writes to Charles V (T235) in August 1376, and, just as Birgitta had implored his predecessor, urges him to stop the war with his neighbor and instead concentrate on the "recuperatio" of the Holy Land.[71] With this term, Catherine inscribes herself in the long lineage of treatises on recovery (*recuperatio*) of the Holy Land. This letter, as are so many of her crusade letters, is both a "mystical exhortation and a program" that includes the important message that Charles brother, Louis of Anjou, is "willing to dedicate himself to this holy work for the love of Christ" (Noffke, *Letters*, 2: 222).[72]

Around the same time Catherine writes to Louis of Anjou himself (T237, late summer 1376), urging him to take the cross (Noffke, *Letters*, 2: 226), and soon after she assures the pope that Louis is on board, willing to lead the crusade, waiting only for Gregory to give him the signal for departure (T238, Noffke, *Letters*, 2: 233–34). With these three letters, Catherine skillfully juggles the mutual promises and commitments of this powerful threesome.

In the beautifully constructed letter (T191) to condottiere Tommaso d'Alviano in early 1377 Catherine advances again a theological argument, namely that of washing away sins through a plenary indulgence, promised all those who fight in a papal army.[73] She ends the letter with the joyful exhortation "let's all go together, as a lovely troop, against the unbelievers" (Noffke, *Letters*, 2: 231).[74] Catherine had indeed envisioned her own participation in the crusade as "pilgrim" and hopefully as "martyr."[75] Catherine did try to recruit other women, but not successfully. In her letter to Monna Pavola (T144, summer 1375) she invites the women to the "wedding feast" (*nozze*) of spilling their blood for Christ at the Holy Sepulcher. But a nun named Domitilla was dissuaded in the strongest terms by Giovanni delle Celle from going on the dangerous pilgrimage to Jerusalem, even though "the saintly woman Catherine preaches the crusade outre-mer."[76] Two years later, in October 1378, right after the beginning of the Great Schism, Catherine herself counsels her recipient, Monna Agnesa da Toscanella, not to go to the Holy Sepulcher at this moment. She should stay put and rather cry out against the "the heresy being created by wicked folk to contaminate our faith by saying that Pope Urban VI is not the true pope" (Noffke, *Letters*, 3: 310).[77] The enemy is now within, not anymore outre-mer;[78] the crusade has now migrated to "here" (quì) as she states in a letter (T274) to Francesco di Pippino and his wife Agnesa in late May 1379. These letters mark a crucial turning point for Catherine's preoccupation with the crusade. It is as if the admonishment to Monna Agnesa applies to Catherine herself: her main goal from now on will be the termination of the Schism.

Conclusion

For Birgitta and Catherine the crusade was a means to add a spiritual dimension to political life. They were not crusade theorists but rather political visionaries, sanctioned as such by their superiors. Unlike Catherine's letters, Birgitta's revelations regarding the crusade were directed at one person, King Magnus, and limited to the goal of converting the remaining Baltic pagans as well as the Russian Orthodox Christians. Catherine, by contrast, targeted a wide spectrum of possible supporters of a *passagium generale,* tapping into the themes of the fourteenth-century "recovery" treatises, and often made her exhortations to the crusade part of her general spiritual messages. When the crusade did not come to pass, she did not send out letters evoking divine vengeance for this failure but turned her attention to the most pressing domestic problem: the Great Schism. In Birgitta's world, on the other hand, the desired crusade was realized, albeit with disastrous results. She then reveled in vengeful thoughts—expressed in dramatic revelations—that culminated in the call to depose King Magnus. His deposition and death, occurring after Birgitta's move to Italy, provided a kind of closure to the "crusading chapter" in her life, at least for the Baltic crusades. Was she gripped by crusading fever while in Italy or on her eventful visit to Cyprus, this hotbed of crusade ambitions? This is a question I cannot yet answer. In any case, both Birgitta and Catherine, although pursuing different specific goals, made the crusade against unbelievers central parts of their spiritual messages. Indeed, they were the only female thinkers to reflect on, plan, and seek support for the crusade, this essentially Christian enterprise that for centuries occupied such a crucial place in the Western *imaginaire*.

Notes

1 For a brief summary of her attitudes, see Bridget Morris, *St Birgitta of Sweden* (Woodbridge: Boydell Press, 1999), 83–87.
2 On the theorists see Antony Leopold, *How to Recover the Holy Land: The Crusade Proposals of the Late Thirteenth and Early Fourteenth Centuries* (Aldershot: Ashgate, 2000); on the later crusades see Norman Housley, *The Later Crusades, 1274–1580. From Lyons to Alcazar* (Oxford: Oxford University Press, 1992). For a selection of primary texts see Jacques Paviot, *Projets de croisade, v. 1290–1330* (Paris: Académie des inscriptions et Belles-Lettres, 2008).
3 Leopold, *How to Recover*, 9.
4 On the political situation, see Robert Irwin, *The Middle East in the Middle Ages: The Early Mamluk Sultanate, 1250–1382* (London: Croom and Helm, 1986), Ch. 4.
5 See Aziz Suryal Atiya, *The Crusade in the Later Middle Ages* (London: Methuen, 1938); Kenneth M. Setton, *The Papacy and the Levant (1204–1571)* (Philadelphia: American Philosophical Society, 1976); Housley, *Later Crusades*; Christopher Tyerman, *God's War: A New History of the Crusades* (Cambridge, MA: Harvard University Press, 2006), Ch. 25.
6 I paraphrase here the list Otto Gerhard Oexle gives in his "Utopisches Denken im Mittelalter: Pierre Dubois," *Historische Zeitschrift* 224 (1977): 293–339, at 324. See also the introduction to Paviot, *Projets*. Most recently on Dubois see Renate Blumenfeld-Kosinski, "Roles for Women in Colonial Fantasies in Fourteenth-Century France: Pierre Dubois and Philippe de Mézières," in *The French of Outre-mer: Communities and Communications in the Crusading Mediterranean*, eds. Laura Morreale and Nicholas Paul (New York: Fordham University Press, 2018).
7 His "crusade," the sack of Alexandria in October 1365, was a complete failure (though it yielded some booty), costing Peter his treasure and eventually his life when he was brutally assassinated in 1369. See Peter W. Edbury, "The Crusading Policy of King Peter I of Cyprus, 1359–1369," in *The Eastern Mediterranean Lands in the Period of the Crusades*, ed. P. M. Holt (Warminster: Aris and Phillips, 1977). For the roles of Mézières and Pierre de Thomas in this doomed enterprise see Renate Blumenfeld-Kosinski, "Philippe de Mézières's *Life of Saint Pierre de Thomas* at the Crossroads of Late Medieval Hagiography and Crusading Ideology," *Viator* 40 (2009): 223–48.
8 See Franco Cardini, "L'idea di crociata in Santa Catarina da Siena," in *Atti del Simposio Internazionale Cateriniano–Bernardiniano, Siena 17–20 aprile 1980*, eds. Domenico Maffei and Paolo Nardi (Siena: Accademia Senese degli Intronati, 1982). He surveys different crusading options in Catherine's era and calls the idea of taking back the Holy Sepulcher "grotesque" (81).
9 Note the triple threat of total extermination: "Il le fait pendre o ardeir ou ocire" (laisse 266, line, 3670). *La Chanson de Roland*, ed. Joseph Bédier (Paris: H. Piazza, 1921).
10 For background on the tension between conquest and conversion in the Baltic see Kurt Villads Jensen, "Martyrs, Total War, and Heavenly Horses," in *Medieval Christianity in the North: New Studies*, eds. Kirsi Salonen, Kurt Villads Jensen, and Torstein Jørgensen (Turnhout: Brepols, 2013).

11 Benjamin Z. Kedar, *Crusade and Mission: European Approaches Towards the Muslims* (Princeton, NJ: Princeton University Press, 1984), 99 and 70–71. The term "Saracen" also became associated with Baltic "pagans." See Alan V. Murray, "The Saracens of the Baltic: Pagan and Christian Lithuanians in the Perception of English and French Crusaders to Late Medieval Prussia," *Journal of Baltic Studies* 41, no. 4 (2010): 413–29.

12 Peter Lock, *The Routledge Companion to the Crusades* (New York and London: Routledge, 2006), 217.

13 For background see *Jerusalem in the North: Denmark and the Baltic Crusades, 1100–1522*, eds. Ann Bysted, Carsten Selch Jensen, Kurt Villads Jensen, and John H. Lind (Turnhout: Brepols 2012); Eric Christiansen, *The Northern Crusades: The Baltic and the Catholic Frontier 1100–1525* (Minneapolis: University of Minnesota Press, 1980); Housley, *Later Crusades*, Ch. 11–12; *Crusade and Conversion on the Baltic Frontier 1150–1500*, ed. Alan V. Murray (Aldershot: Ashgate, 2001); William L. Urban, *The Baltic Crusades*, 2nd edn. (Chicago, IL: Lithuanian Research and Studies Center, 1994). See also *Medieval History Writing and Crusading Ideology*, eds. Tuomas M. S. Lehtonen, Kurt Villads Jensen, with Janne Malkki and Katja Ritari (Helsinki: Finnish Literature Society, 2005), part III.

14 Lock, *Routledge Companion*, 214.

15 Iben Fonnesberg-Schmidt, *The Popes and the Baltic Crusades 1147–1254* (Leiden: Brill, 2007), 2.

16 I summarize here the intricate and well-documented conclusions of Fonnesberg-Schmidt, *The Popes*. For the quotes see 9–12 and 252–53.

17 For details of the political situation in Sweden at this time, see Hans Torben Gilkær, *The Political Ideas of St. Birgitta and her Spanish Confessor, Alfonso Pecha. Liber Celestis Imperatoris ad Reges: A Mirror of Princes*, trans. Michael Cain (Odense: Odense University Press, 1993), Ch. 3.

18 For example Housley, *Later Crusades*, 336; Bysted et al., *Jerusalem in the North*, 329–30; Christiansen, *Northern Crusades*, 185–86 (he characterizes Birgitta's intervention as "a war-cry from the boudoir" [85]!).

19 Bysted et al., *Jerusalem in the North*, 329. Christiansen downplays Birgitta's influence, stating that "the decision to declare war on Novgorod was the king's own, and since he was not such a fool as Bridget pretended, he was moved by political calculation, rather than by religious zeal" (*Northern Crusades*, 185). Päivi Salmesvuori concludes that "the king also used Birgitta and her revelations to legitimate his actions." For Novgorod, "the king listened to Birgitta carefully as long as it suited him." (*Power and Sainthood: The Case of Birgitta of Sweden* [New York: Palgrave Macmillan, 2014]), 171. Erich Hoffmann gives more credit to Birgitta's influence by presenting her as a "counselor" to the king who, if she did not suggest it, nonetheless was in agreement with him on the need for a crusade against the Orthodox "heretics"("Politische Heilige in Skandinavien und die Entwicklung der drei nordischen Reiche und Völker" in *Politik und Heiligenverehrung im Hochmittelalter*, ed. Jürgen Petersohn [Sigmaringen: Thorbecke, 1994], 277–324.)

20 Housley, *Later Crusades*, 336.

21 See John L. I. Fennell, "The Campaign of King Magnus Eriksson against Novgorod in 1348: An Examination of the Sources," *Jahrbücher für Geschichte Osteuropas*. Neue Folge, Bd. 14, H. 1 (March 1966): 1–9; 3. Fennell's main focus is on how the Pskovs gained independence through their assistance to Novgorod.

22 John Lind, "Magnus Eriksson som Birgittinsk Konge I Lyset af Russiske Kilder," in *Birgitta, hendes værk og hendes klostre i Norden* [Birgitta, her works, and her Five Abbeys in the Nordic Countries], ed. Tore Nyberg

(Odense: Universitetsforlag, 1991), 103–28, 104. Hatred of the Orthodox was often greater than that of the Muslims or pagans because the Orthodox were considered heretics. See Kiril Petkov, "The Rotten Apple and the Good Apples: Orthodox, Catholics, and Turks in Philippe de Mézières' Crusading Propaganda," *Journal of Medieval History* 23, no. 3 (1997): 255–70 and Camille Rouxpetel, "D'or ou de pourriture, les pommes de Philippe de Mézières," in *Philippe de Mézières et l'Europe. Nouvelle Histoire, nouveaux espaces, nouveaux langages,* eds. Joël Blanchard and Renate Blumenfeld-Kosinski (Geneva: Droz, 2017).

23 For an analysis of this terminology see Murray, "Saracens of the Baltic."

24 Rasa Mazeika and Loïc Chollet, "Familiar Marvels? French and German Crusaders and Chroniclers Confront Baltic Pagan Religions," *Francia* 43 (2016): 42–3.

25 The first number refers to the Latin edition, the second to the English translation by volume and page number.

26 Sven Ekdahl, "Crusade and Colonisation in the Baltic: A Historiographical Analysis," in *The North-Eastern Frontiers of Medieval Europe*, ed. Alan V. Murray (Farnham: Ashgate, 2014) estimates that about 300 raids took place between 1305 and 1409 (6).

27 On these events at the Council of Constance, see Loïc Chollet, "Croisade ou évangélisation? La polémique contre les chevaliers teutoniques à l'aune des témoignages des voyageurs français de la fin du moyen âge," *Ordines militares* 20 (2015): 175–203.

28 But we should remember that the distinction between *pagani* and *infideles* is proper to the Latin text and may not have been made by Birgitta herself.

29 Christian Oertel, *The Cult of St Erik in Medieval Sweden: Veneration of a Royal Saint, Twelfth–Sixteenth Centuries* (Turnhout: Brepols, 2016), 164.

30 Pavlína Rychterová, *Die Offenbarungen der heiligen Birgitta von Schweden. Eine Untersuchung zur alttschechischen Übersetzung des Thomas von Štítné* (Cologne: Böhlau, 2004), 37 and n. 123.

31 This idea was also put forward by Philippe de Mézières several decades later in his *Letter to King Richard II* of 1395. The alliance came to pass when Richard II married Isabella of France in 1396, but Richard's deposition and subsequent death in 1400 precluded ending the war through this marriage.

32 In Rev. IV: 103–105 we also find various proposals for ending the Anglo-French conflict.

33 Rychterová, *Offenbarungen*, 34.

34 I simplify here the complicated situation Bridget Morris lays out in "Swedish Foreign Policy of the 1340s in the Balance: An Interpretation of Book IV Chapter 2 of St. Bridget's *Revelations*," *Studies in St. Birgitta and the Brigittine Order* 1 (1993): 180–91, quote on p. 182.

35 Lind, "Magnus Eriksson som Birgittinsk Konge i Lyset af Russiske Kilder," 103.

36 John H. Lind, "The Russian Testament of King Magnus Eriksson – A Hagiographic Text?" in *Medieval Spirituality in Scandinavia and Europe. A Collection of Essays in Honour of Tore Nyberg,* eds. Lars Bisgaard et al. (Odense: Odense University Press, 2001), 206. Lind refers to the accounts of the *Novgorodian Chronicles* here. Fennell sees the embassy as a pretext for a discussion of borders ("Campaign," 3).

37 Lock, *Routledge Companion*, 223.

38 Though I cannot agree with Cordelia Heß here, who says that Birgitta sees Erik "in der Hölle schmoren." (*Heilige machen im spätmittelalterlichen Ostseeraum. Die Kanonisierungsprozesse von Birgitta von Schweden, Nikolaus von Linköping und Dorothea von Montau* [Berlin: Akademieverlag],

2008), 77. According to Birgitta he could be either in hell or purgatory (*in inferno vel in purgatorio*. II: 30.23). See also André Vauchez, *La Sainteté en occident aux derniers siècles du Moyen Age, d'après les procès de canonisation et les documents hagiographiques* (Rome: École française de Rome, 1981), 202 and n. 51.

39 Oertel, *St. Erik*, 167.

40 Fennell, "Campaign," 3. The Russian sources state that in fact "many were baptised and 'had their beards shaved'" (Christiansen, *Northern Crusades*, 186).

41 Morris offers a close reading of this vision and its interpretation in "Swedish Foreign Policy" to which I refer the reader. Quotes on 187 and 188. As for the "proper" execution of the crusade, Christiansen comments, "Bridget expected such high moral standards from her crusaders that no actual expedition against the Russians could ever have satisfied her. If only the pure of heart were allowed to fight for Christ, the Orthodox of Novgorod were safe" (*Northern Crusades*, 191).

42 Thomas Lindkvist, "Crusades and Crusading Ideology in the Political History of Sweden," in *Crusade and Conversion on the Baltic Frontier, 1150–1500*, ed. Alan V. Murray (Aldershot, Burlington: Ashgate, 2001) 119–30; 126.

43 Immediately after the sentence stating that those who were left in the fortress *a Rutensis trucidati sunt* the text continues, *Tunc enim beata Birgitta Sweciam reliquit et ad Romam iuit* (Göte Paulsson, ed., *Chronica Visbycensis, 815–1444* in *Annales Suecici Medii Aevi*. [Lund: Gleerup, 1974], 321).

44 "... dicentem vos habere et exercere naturalem commixtionem et turpitudinem cum masculis contra naturalem disposicionem" ("it is said that you carry on sexual intercourse and perversion with other men against nature.") Extrav.: 80.6. On this grave accusation and its possible punishment see James A. Brundage, *Law, Sex, and Christian Society in Medieval Europe* (Chicago, IL: The University of Chicago Press, 1987), 533–34. In fourteenth-century Europe exile and forfeiture of all possessions as well as public burnings were common penalties.

45 Morris, *St Birgitta*, 86.

46 Olle Ferm, "Heliga Birgittas program för uppror mot Magnus Eriksson: En studie i politisk argumentationskonst," in *Heliga Birgitta – budskapet och förebilden. Föredrag vid jubileumssymposiet i Vadstena 3–7 oktober 1991*, eds. Alf Härdelin and Mereth Lindgren (Stockholm: KVHAA, 1993), 141.

47 *Scriptores rerum svecicarum medii aevi*, ed. Claudius Annerstedt, vol. 3 (Uppsala: E. Berling, 1871 and 1876), 12–16, followed by a commentary on some of Birgitta's anti-Magnus revelations (16–20). For an analysis of the *Libellus* see Ferm, "Heliga" and Bernd-Ulrich Hergemöller, *Magnus versus Birgitta. Der Kampf der heiligen Birgitta von Schweden gegen König Magnus Eriksson* (Hamburg: HHL Verlag, 2003), 110–34 and Kevin Scott Echart, "Birgitta of Sweden and Medieval Prophecy," (PhD diss., Yale University, 1993), 229–38.

48 The rumor was that the king had an unhealthy interest in his protégé Bengt Algotsson (*c*.1330–60).

49 Noële Denis-Boulet, *La carrière politique de Sainte Cathérine de Sienne: Étude historique* (Paris: Desclée et Brouwer, 1939), 36. On Birgitta's "Joachimite slant," see Echart, "Birgitta of Sweden," 248–51.

50 Cardini, "L'idea," 62.

51 Raymond of Capua, *Die Legenda Maior (Vita Catharinae Senensis) des Raimund von Capua*, ed. Jörg Jungmayr, 2 vols (Berlin: Weidler Buchverlag, 2004), vol. 2: *Kommentar*, 799. André Vauchez agrees more with Cardini:

"Catherine n'évoque jamais les opérations militaires qui seront nécessaires pour arriver à ce but et ne propose pas de plan de reconquête" (*Catherine de Sienne. Vie et passions* [Paris: Cerf, 2015], 67).

52 Christoph T. Maier, *Preaching the Crusades: Mendicant Friars and the Cross in the Thirteenth Century* (Cambridge: Cambridge University Press, 1995). For the Baltic areas see esp. 43, 78, 87–93.

53 F. Thomas Luongo, *The Saintly Politics of Catherine of Siena* (Ithaca, NY: Cornell University Press, 2006), 58.

54 Denis-Boulet, *La carrière*, 82.

55 Luongo, *Saintly Politics*,88.

56 Denis-Boulet, *La carrière*,87.

57 On her letters concerning the pope's return to Rome and the Great Schism, see Renate Blumenfeld-Kosinski, *Poets, Saints, and Visionaries of the Great Schism, 1378–1417* (University Park: Pennsylvania State University Press, 2006), Ch. 2.

58 See Paul Rousset, "Cathérine de Sienne et le problème de la croisade," *Revue Suisse d'histoire* 25 (1975): 499–513. This idea pervades crusade thinking from Dubois to Mézières.

59 Jungmayr, ed. 2: 398.

60 Flete came all the way from England. "No member of the English province had ever embarked on such a venture," comments Benedict Hackett, O.S.A., in *William Flete, O.S.A., and Catherine of Siena* (Villanova: Augustinian Press, 1992), 82. The date of their first meeting is controversial. Hackett is certain that it was around 1368. For his evidence, see *William Flete*, 101 n. 10. For another view see Luongo, *Saintly Politics*, 67 and n. 35.

61 Noffke translates *galee* as galleons but these large ships, as Kiril Petkov pointed out to me, were not built before the sixteenth century.

62 Before 27 June, according to Noffke (*Letters*, 1: 79). See Luongo, *Saintly Politics*, 82, 135, 157.

63 See Noffke, *Letters*, 1: 165–6 for a brief analysis of this complicated situation.

64 Cardini, "L'idea," 83.

65 "... gl'infideli che sono nostri fratelli, ricomperati del sangue di Christi, come noi." Edited in Edmund G. Gardener, *Saint Catherine of Siena: A Study in the Religion, Literature and History of the Fourteenth Century in Italy* (London: J. M. Dent, 1907), 410.

66 "... quelli che vi sono figliuoli naturali, che si pascono alle mammelle della sposa di Cristo, per li figliuoli bastardi, che non sono anco legittimati col santo battesimo." See Noffke, *Letters*, 2: 246 n. 16 for an explication of this terminology.

67 "Con la virtù divina del coltello della parola santa, e con la virtù e forza umana." See the analysis by Joan Patterson Del Pozzo, "Speaking in Imagery, Speaking in Ecstasy: A Discussion of Saint Catherine of Siena's Language and Style" (PhD Diss., The Johns Hopkins University, 1991), 233.

68 "... tollendo le terre della santa Chiesa." See Luongo, *Saintly Politics*, 162.

69 In 1461, when the Turkish threat has come even closer, Pope Pius II connects Catherine (and Bernardino of Siena) to his projected crusade in his *exordium* for Catherine's canonization. Ottfried Krafft, "Many Strategies and One Goal: The Difficult Road to the Canonization of Catherine of Siena," in *Catherine of Siena: The Creation of Cult*, eds. Jeffrey F. Hamburger and Gabriela Signori (Turnhout: Brepols, 2013), 36. And centuries later Catherine's crusade thinking was evoked when Italy fought the Turks in Libya in 1909 using the crusade vocabulary (Gerald Parsons, *The Cult of Catherine of Siena. A Study in Civil Religion* [Aldershot: Ashgate, 2008]), 49–50.

70 "… intitolata reina di Ierusalem, per quì siete capo e cagione di questo santo passaggio." On Joanna's claims to this title see Elizabeth Casteen, *From She-Wolf to Martyr: The Reign and Disputed Reputation of Johanna I of Naples* (Ithaca: Cornell University Press, 2016), 145–46.

71 T235, trans. Noffke, *Letters*, 2: 221.

72 "'l vostro fratello … per l'amore di Cristo vuole prendare a faticarsi in questa santa operazione." See Paul Ourliac, "Les Lettres à Charles V," in Maffei and Nardi, *Atti del Simposio Internazionale Cateriniano-Bernardiniano*, 173–80; 173. He dates it to October 1376 while Noffke dates it to August.

73 For a rhetorical analysis of this letter's crescendo structure see Del Pozzo, "Speaking," 43–5; Jungmayr, ed., vol. 2, *Kommentar*, 800; and Noffke, *Letters*, 2: 231 n. 14.

74 "… andiamo tutti di bella brigata sopra gl'Infedeli."

75 Hanno Helbling, *Katharina von Siena. Mystik und Politik* (Munich: Beck, 2000), 114.

76 Denis-Boulet, *La carrière*, 80. She dates this letter 1372 but Luongo correctly dates it 1376 (Giovanni delle Celle, *Lettere* 2: 305–10; *Saintly Politics*, 25). He refers to Catherine's invitation to "an imminent crusade." Denis-Boulet believes that Birgitta's pilgrimage to Jerusalem may have been inspired by pope Gregory's 1370–71 call for a crusade. In 1372 Birgitta, on her return, stopped on Cyprus, still suffering from the repercussions of the disastrous crusade to Alexandria seven years earlier. Her revelations on the fate of Cyprus are all doom-laden.

77 "… eresia che è levata dagl'iniqui uomini per contaminare nostra fede, dicendo que papa Urbano VI non è vero papa" (T340).

78 Both the Muslim faith and the opposing side in the Great Schism were often erroneously referred to as "heresies."

5 The Transmission of Birgittine and Catherinian Works within the Mystical Tradition

Exchanges, Cross-Readings, Connections

Silvia Nocentini

In the context of the general interest in mystical spirituality in fifteenth-century Europe, the diffusion of the writings of Catherine of Siena and Birgitta of Sweden is remarkable for two reasons: their widespread circulation and their ability to cross borders of religious affiliations and linguistic affinities. This chapter aims to trace the role of Catherine and Birgitta within the Observant Reform.[1] I will focus on some significant manuscripts from the Italian peninsula, the contexts in which they appeared, as well as the people who read them. I will take into account the mystical writings of the two women, that is, Birgitta of Sweden's *Revelations* and Catherine of Siena's *Libro di divina dottrina* (better known as the *Dialogue*). Both works were published posthumously, respectively in 1377 and 1380, thanks to the promoters of their cults: the hermit Alfonso of Jaén, Birgitta's former confessor, who established a scriptorium *ad hoc* in Naples;[2] and the Dominican Tommaso da Siena, dubbed Caffarini, who worked in his scriptorium at SS. Giovanni e Paolo in Venice.[3] While the *Dialogue* was written directly in Italian and had a remarkable diffusion in its restricted linguistic environment (at least 26 manuscripts),[4] the *Revelations* were collected and published in Latin and achieved a great success (at least 180 manuscripts, of which 80 are complete).[5]

The Manuscript Transmission

The transmission of the works of the two saints developed almost in parallel from a well-structured strategic plan: first, a collection of material, followed by the organization of the text into chapters (as in the case of the *Dialogue* of Catherine), books (the *Revelations* of Birgitta), or other homogeneous blocks (Catherine's letters are divided by addressees, for example); then the copying of the work(s) and finally, sending the completed text to other conservation or copying centers. This, of course, was not a static process since reading methods and modes of dissemination also varied according to the different contexts. For example, the procedures might have differed if the manuscripts were copied for male religious communities, which were recipients of works in Latin, or female ones, who preferred the vernacular and the anthologized form. Moreover, in the first phase of expansion of Catherinian and Birgittine thought, it is more common to find sumptuously designed manuscripts, richly decorated, and, generally, complete texts, as they were conceived by the groups (still male) who also were in charge of the promotion of the cults.[6] However, as the demand for content began to correspond to this promotion, the form and substance of the manuscripts changed until they became, in large part, sizable collections of spiritual works, sometimes focused on a specific theme or sometimes just chosen for their synthesis of several topics. An example of this is the situation in the German linguistic area, as described by Werner Williams-Krapp, who identifies a directly proportional relationship between popularity and selective transmission of texts.[7]

Nuns needed to be educated by the texts that their confessors preached. The texts had to be in vernacular, and generally, they were prepared in excerpted or anthologized form, which allowed for easier reading by sparing the nuns the most slippery passages. The same process is found in England, where, in the late Middle Ages, Catherine of Siena was known through two sources: the Latin translation of the *Dialogue*, and the *Legenda maior*, which was mostly transmitted in *excerpta*.[8] In the Middle-English translations, the figure of Catherine is transformed: abandoning the traits of mysticism, she adopts the role of the saint and a model of virtue for the virgins.[9] Thus, at the beginning of the fifteenth century, on the wave of the Observant Reform, many nuns were engaged in copying and illustrating the Catherinian and Birgittine works intended for the libraries of the new monasteries. At the same time, their requests for personal reading material became more pressing. The nuns became recipients of *ad hoc* collections, in which the saints were somehow reshaped from mystics, who provided revelations (and the related interpretations) for their audience, to women who were role models for holy living. Birgitta and Catherine were, in other words, transformed from prophetesses to imitable saints.[10]

In a certain sense, both for Catherine's and Birgitta's works, their transmission through extracts was facilitated by a certain structure. Their texts were typically arranged in blocks, and only later were they assembled in the two hagiographic workshops—Alfonso of Jaén's scriptorium in Naples and Tommaso Caffarini's in Venice. Their writings had, however, previously circulated in the form of letters or single revelations, which lent themselves to a partial reading. Therefore, upon closer inspection, the purpose of the Latin diffusion of the works in their entirety was only in part a question of spirituality. Rather, the need to create a single corpus of the many visions or revelations—to limit ourselves to the *Revelations* and the *Dialogue*—was dictated by the men

(Alfonso, Caffarini, and their successors) who controlled the image of the two women, and not by specific requests of an engaged audience. This is true in particular for Catherine, as the transmission of the epistolary collection and of the *Dialogue* clearly demonstrate.[11] In the case of Catherine's letters, this kind of "partial reading" is even more evident as each letter contained a distinct message which could stand on its own. The author herself would have been the first to have no specific collection project in mind. Moreover, the physical documents that contained the letters, circulated autonomously and independently, as witnessed by the history of transmission, which traces, in addition to the ordered collections, the emergence of sparse letters, small personal collections, or single epistles copied alongside the most diverse works of various literary genres. On the other hand, it is plausible that the *Dialogue* circulated among Catherine's devotees while she was still alive, and that she herself had gathered, around an original nucleus, the materials arranged later by her scribes.[12] Moreover, some parts of the *Dialogue* had one, albeit brief, independent tradition.[13] The same is true for Birgitta. In order to demonstrate this point, I will limit myself to a couple of examples taken from the Italian context, because they are also paradigmatic of the two-way contamination between the Dominican and Birgittine spiritual traditions.

In a letter dated 13 October 1395, the Dominican Antonio Cancellieri sent a prayer written by Birgitta, perhaps in a fly sheet, to Margherita Datini, with the instructions that she should teach it to other women.[14] This letter is an early testimony of the independent circulation of the prayers of Birgitta, a text which was certainly suited to potential extraction and dissemination, allowing single prayers to be separated from the entire corpus, as it was collected by Alfonso of Jaén. The second example is offered by the manuscript in the Florentine Biblioteca Riccardiana, MS 1345, dated 26 December 1406.[15] This codex comes from the Paradiso monastery of the Birgittine Order.[16] It is a typical spiritual miscellany, in which diverse texts are collected—from Isaac the Syrian to Giordano of Pisa, from Augustine to Bernard of Clairvaux, from the *vitae* of some female saints to the Virgin's Miracles—including Birgitta's *Sermo angelicus* in Italian translation.[17] In addition, it contains a single letter from Catherine to the hermit Antonio of Lecceto (Letter T17).[18] This manuscript also indicates a very early Birgittine interest in Catherine's doctrine, since it is not until the second half of the fifteenth century that two other volumes are produced in the Birgittine monastery of Paradiso, which also concern the works of the Sienese saint.[19]

Even in the Dominican context, we find nuns determining the success of the hagiography of non-Dominican saints, like Birgitta, who was very popular throughout the fifteenth century. The case of the Dominican observant female monastery in Schönensteinbach (1397) is exemplary in this sense: it was named after Birgitta by decision of the Dominican sisters, whose devotion to the Swedish saint was clearly so prominent that it overcame even the Dominican saints. On the other hand, Dominican nuns were also the recipients of hagiographic collections of Dominican saints; these collections were not largely widespread, as they were limited inside the convent walls and the Dominican Order itself.[20] The only exception was made for Catherine of Siena.

The *Legenda maior* became a reference reading for different historical, linguistic, religious, and spiritual milieus. The same thing happened to Birgitta, who, as Caffarini reminds us, preceded Catherine of seven years and benefited from an enormous favor among the reformed religious circles, in which both the *vita* and works of the Swedish saint circulated.[21] The Dominicans extensively read and cited Birgittine materials, as we shall see, since they viewed Birgitta as close to Catherine in terms of their shared prophetic charisma. In this climate of continuous religious exchanges and intersections, of search for spiritual alliances to strengthen the reform, a few figures, in light of the extant source material, were decisive for the development of history as we know it.

Alfonso Pecha of Jaén

The first key figure is Alfonso Pecha of Jaén, whose presence in Italy was crucial for many events concerning the penitential life and political management of the Great Schism, since he, at the end of the fourteenth century, was at the center of many religious reforms.[22] Alfonso left his post as bishop of Jaén in 1367 and joined the Italian hermit movement. He became, in fact, its uncontested leader. Similarly, his brother Pedro was recognized as the head of the Spanish hermits, later known as Hieronymites. In 1368, Alfonso was in Umbria, where he intervened in defense of a group of poor friars[23], interrogated by the Church for their strict observance. Alfonso obtained a *consilium* that sheltered them from further canonical investigations.[24] He was, in this period, in contact with various hermitical groups and with their supporters, all of whom lived in the Umbrian area. In fact, despite having taken up residence in Rome in 1369, in the *Transtiberim* region, Alfonso continued to live in hermitages between his diplomatic journeys: first in Umbria, then around Genzano, nearer to Rome.

In the late 1360s, Alfonso joined the entourage of Birgitta of Sweden as one of her confessors, and together they went to Montefiascone to meet Pope Urban V. Alfonso also met the nobleman Orsini, who would introduce him to the Curia of Avignon, where he eventually managed to intercede for the Italian and Spanish spirituals and held prestigious positions. In July 1373, he went to Avignon to deliver a revelation of Birgitta to Pope Gregory XI. In the following years, the same pope entrusted several missions to Alfonso, to be brought back to Italy, including the famous bull *Provenit ex affectu*, which officially approved the Franciscan

Observance. In October 1373, when Alfonso received the news of Birgitta's death, he was prevented to go directly to Rome because of his brother Pedro's arrival in Avignon, in order to deliver his solemn profession in the hands of the pope. After having attended to curial business, Alfonso left for Montefalco, in Umbria, where he met the caravan that was bringing the relics of Birgitta back to Sweden. From here, the Swedish brigade left for Vadstena, while Alfonso continued with his mission on behalf of the pope. Gregory had sent him to the *Patrimonium Sancti Petri* and the Reign of the Two Sicilies, with the specific task of founding other hermitic-cenobite families on the model of the Florentine community of S. Maria del Santo Sepolcro alle Campora, with whom Alfonso had maintained a close relationship for some years.[25] During his journey on behalf of the pope, Alfonso stopped in Siena (1374), where, at the pope's request, he was required to leave an indulgence in the hands of Catherine of Siena, and later (possibly in 1378) in Pisa.

Pisa, thus, is a fundamental junction for our research, because it is the meeting point between the two mystical traditions, the Catherinian and the Birgittine one. Alfonso already knew the *signore* of the city, Pietro Gambacorta, because in 1372, they had travelled together, along with Birgitta, to Jerusalem. Pietro is likely to have hosted Alfonso in his house many times, when the latter was traveling to Pisa, and therefore took advantage of his authoritative presence to ask him for advice regarding the situation of his daughter Tora. The latter, a young widow (she was 15), wished to become a nun and had therefore taken refuge with the Poor Clares of San Martino. Her father intervened, however, with armed men on horseback and forced her to return home, where he kept her isolated, preventing future escapes, until she might be given in marriage again. Alfonso, who had been the confessor of Birgitta and had some experience with female spirituality, sensed in Tora a sincere calling and advised her to follow it, after the example of Birgitta, who had also been a widow and was likely to become a saint, due to her works and her commitment to the restoration of the Church. Alfonso also gave her a book with a *istoria* of Birgitta[26] so that she might be inspired by it, if we believe the story recounted by the anonymous hagiographer of Gambacorta.[27] Pietro could not do anything but support the decision of his daughter, who assumed the religious name of Chiara. After spending some years among the Dominicans of Santa Croce in Fossabanda in Pisa, Chiara founded in the same city the first Italian Dominican observant monastery in 1385.

The blending of different kinds of spiritualities—the Franciscan, the Birgittine, and the Dominican—present in the story of Chiara Gambacorta makes clear the close relationship between reformers of different origins and backgrounds. These religious men and women spun networks of solidarity and elective affinities, preparing their much-desired reform. It was natural for Chiara to run away from home and take refuge with the Franciscans of San Martino, who were very close to her, given their penitential spirituality. Yet it was equally natural later to choose the Dominican Order as the foundation of her monastery, since, after all, the Dominicans were the religious family of St. Catherine, whom she admired and knew in person.[28] Still, nothing prevented her from having the church of the convent she founded (S. Domenico in Pisa) decorated with stories taken from the visions of St. Birgitta, under whose aegis Alfonso freed her from her father's "slavery."[29] Also Maria Mancini, Chiara Gamabcorta's visionary sister, is the protagonist of a *vita,* dense of mystical experiences.[30] The *vita* is clearly inspired by the visions of Birgitta, and it is enriched with the insertion of a letter by Alfonso addressed to Maria, apparently sent in response to her doubts regarding the vision of a terrible black horse.[31] This underlines that Alfonso was already a point of reference both for the Birgittine and for the Dominican mystical thought.

It is worth recalling that in Pisa Catherine received the stigmata. Alfonso therefore established a personal relationship not only with Catherine, but also with her circle.[32] Perhaps he was even in Siena with Catherine, but it is certain that Alfonso was close to her when she lived in Rome, since her disciple Stefano Maconi wrote to another of her followers, Neri di Landoccio Pagliaresi, who was in Rome with Catherine: "I beg you that you recommend me to our Mother, and to the others, especially to the bishop Alfonso."[33]

In the same period, Alfonso was engaged in the transcription and dissemination of the *Revelations* of Birgitta, probably through the Naples scriptorium, where he could count on the favor of Queen Johanna I. In 1377 (before 29 May), the first draft of the *Revelations*—containing the books from I to VII with the prologue of Master Mathias of Linköping, *Stupor et mirabilia*—was ready to be delivered to the members of the examining commission set for Birgitta's canonization. In 1378, after the passage of Alfonso and other Roman penitents to the Urbanist party, Alfonso wrote a treatise in the form of a letter to the French cardinals—in the past attributed, perhaps not by chance, to Raymond of Capua—in which he harshly criticized the double papal election carried out by the college of cardinals.[34] In the meantime, with the death of Gregory XI and the election of Urban VI (1378), the commission for the canonization of Birgitta widened and was therefore in need of new copies of the *Revelations* to be delivered to the various members of the curial college. Alfonso compiled a second redaction of the work (*c.*1380), enlarging the previous version. The second redaction contained a preface, the *Epistola solitarii ad reges*, the *Liber celestis imperatoris ad reges*, the *Sermo angelicus*—used for the liturgical office of Matutins by Birgittine sisters—the *Quattuor orationes*, the *Regula Salvatoris* and a *vita* of St. Birgitta.[35] This redaction was the one that circulated more frequently among Catherinian circles of devotees, as we will see. The frequent contacts between Alfonso and the Catherinian circle, and not just with Catherine, as has often been implied, explains the profound understanding of the life and works of Birgitta that the Dominicans revealed. If we should determine a chronology for this type of reciprocal influence, the precedence must undoubtedly be attributed to Birgitta, who began to be appreciated in the Catherinian circle slightly before the Birgittine convents started to copy and read the Catherinian manuscripts.

Birgitta in Catherinian Circles

Tommaso Caffarini was the Dominican friar who was in charge of the promotion of Catherine's cult and directed the Venetian scriptorium where a great number of Catherinian manuscripts were produced. In his deposition at the "Processo Castellano," he provides a detailed account about what precisely the Dominicans knew of Birgitta's doctrine.[36] What Caffarini says is that Birgitta preceded Catherine in Rome and left many *scripturas*.[37] He then lists the seven books of the *Revelations* as they appeared in the definitive redaction of Alfonso, including the *Liber celestis imperatoris ad reges* (dubbed Book VIII), the *Regula*, and the *Sermo angelicus*.[38] In other words, Tommaso offers more than the general information, which would have been available in the Dominican libraries. In fact, he demonstrates that he has read the works of Birgitta, by citing them in several passages and comparing her doctrine to the Catherine's. As a proof of truth, he refers to Books I and IV of the *Revelations* and to the *Sermo angelicus*. Moreover, commenting on the words of Catherine "*Mihi absit gloriari nisi in cruce Christi*" ("But let it be far from me to glory except in the cross of Christ"), Caffarini refers to the same simile that Birgitta used to describe the contrasting sentiment that Mary felt toward her son Jesus, that is, a mixture of joy and pain, as if a rose with thorns grew in her chest.[39] Likewise, in his deposition, Caffarini discusses the cross of Christ at length: how it was made, which kind of wood it was made of, where the nails were, how Jesus was lifted onto it, and the clothes he was wearing. For all these particulars, he relies on Bernard of Clairvaux as well as on Birgitta, who provided him with the details he needed to narrate the story of the crucifixion.[40] Perhaps even more interesting is the parallel set up by Caffarini, in his second deposition, between the political positions of the two saints, both of whom fought for reform of the Church.[41]

As we can see, by the beginning of the fifteenth century, the knowledge of Birgitta's works was not superficial. She was particularly known among the Observant preachers, who easily managed the entire Birgittine corpus, which they had already acquired and which they had provided with indexes and *tabulae ad usum praedicatorum*. This was the result of the tremendous work of collecting and editing completed by Caffarini in Venice, beginning in 1395.

Although it is true that volumes of Birgittine content were already circulating at the end of the fourteenth century, even outside the religious contexts, this was a circulation restricted to specific and elite circles of readers. A good example is the two letters that Ser Lapo Mazzei, a pious, rich, and highly educated Florentine notary, sent to Francesco Datini in November 1395.[42] Ser Lapo tells his friend Francesco that at night, he was reading the *Life and Miracles* of Birgitta. In addition, he was looking forward to reading Birgitta's *Revelations*, which he heard about by a bishop. Mazzei succeeded in procuring the *Regula Salvatoris* and a *Life of Birgitta*, although we do not know which version.[43] He also tells us that, at the end of 1395, it was still difficult to obtain an entire copy of the *Revelations*, demonstrating that these texts were reserved for a privileged audience of the high ecclesiastical spheres.

Ser Lapo's testimony is all the more valuable, as he was in close contact with Antonio di Niccolò degli Alberti, donor of the first house of the Birgittine Order in Italy, the Paradiso outside of Florence. At this time, it was undoubtedly difficult to find or make a copy of the entire book of *Revelations*, which still, apparently, had a limited circulation. Educated laymen had easier access to the hagiographic literature than to the *Revelations*, and it was not difficult for Ser Lapo to obtain a copy of the *Regula*, given his relations with Alberti and with the Paradiso.

A fourteenth-century manuscript, possibly produced before her canonization, provides a sign of an early, but selected, diffusion of texts related to Birgitta. The codex contains, in a significant pairing, the Latin *Vita* (BHL n. 1334b), the *Oraciones*, and the *Regula* (first redaction, in first person), resulting in a volume not dissimilar from the one in the hands of Ser Lapo.[44] A few years later, the vernacular *Lives of Catherine and Birgitta* were copied together in a most significant manuscript: the manuscript Siena, Biblioteca comunale degli Intronati [BCI], T.II.6, that dates back to the early fifteenth century and has richly ornate initials.[45] It includes two of Caffarini's writings: the *Legenda minor*, in the *vetus* redaction (fols. 1a–124b), and the *Sermo de sancta Catherina* (fols. 124b–130b), both translated by Stefano Maconi. In addition, the manuscript contains two hagiographies of Birgitta in Italian: the *Life* (fols. 132a–60b) and *Miracles* (fols. 161a–73a). It is possible that the manuscript could have been copied after 1411, since Maconi's translation was completed only after his return to Milan, at the end of the Schism that had divided his order.[46] In contrast, we know little about the Italian translations of the *vitae* of Birgitta, since there is not yet a complete census of the manuscript witnesses, and so far, the scholarly research has only focused on the translations of the *Revelations*, to which I will soon return.[47]

The translation of the Birgittine texts in the Sienese manuscript was certainly written after the canonization, which is mentioned in the first lines of the incipit.[48] It was probably modeled on one of the longer versions of the first *Vita* (BHL 1334) and the liturgical *Life* written by Birger Gregersson between 1374 and 1383 (BHL 1335).[49] The success of this translation is also measurable by the number of manuscripts that contain the Italian text. These manuscripts were concentrated in the Florentine area, where the Paradiso monastery clearly played a key role in the spread of Birgittine hagiography. For instance, the manuscript Florence, Biblioteca Medicea Laurenziana, San Marco 917 (1490–1520), from a female Dominican nunnery, preserves the *Life* in question at fols. 53r–85v. The Florentine volume, Archivio di Stato di Firenze, Corporazioni religiose soppresse, 179.49 (15th c.), transmits the same *Life* and the *Miracles*, at fols. 1–36r and 36v–52v, and so do the codices Firenze, Biblioteca Nazionale Centrale [BNC], Magl. XXXVIII.15 (15th–16th cent.), fols. 2r–69r, Magl. XXXVIII.93 (sixteenth century), fols. 2r–58v and Magl. XXXVIII.128 (30 November 1458). The three latter manuscripts were copied in the Paradiso monastery by three Birgittine nuns, Sr. Raffaella, Sr. Margherita Niccolini and Sr. Caterina. This confirms, I would argue, the specific interest of the female branch of the order in copying and preserving books, especially those of mystical or hagiographic argument.[50]

While the translator remains anonymous, it is interesting to note the methodological premise he gives in the beginning. He offers precise indications on how to correct any wrong qualifications concerning Birgitta, who by that point—we are after the canonization of 1391, as we have seen—had to be called a saint, and not blessed, in all the places where this title occurs. However, the earliest witness of the Italian translation of the *Life* (BHL n. 1334b), is the MS written in 1399 on behalf of Cristoforo di Gano Guidini, Siena, BCI, I.V.26 (fols. 277r–96v). The manuscript traces back to the Catherinian milieu, which may be considered the origin of the diffusion of the text, if not of the translation.[51]

Cristoforo di Gano Guidini

Let us for a moment return to Ser Lapo's letter, dated November 1395. On Christmas of the same year, Raymond of Capua handed over to Caffarini, who already lived in Venice at that time, his *Life of Catherine* (*Legenda maior*, BHL n. 1702), so that Tommaso could begin to make copies of it. According to the testimony of Ser Lapo, in Tuscany at the end of the fourteenth century, it was easy to find copies of the *Life and Miracles of Birgitta*, but not so easy to find manuscripts of her *Revelations*. On the contrary, the *Dialogue* of Catherine was already widespread, both in Italian and in Latin, at least since the 1380s—but was not as frequently requested by the laymen such as Ser Lapo, it seems—while Catherine's *Life* was difficult to find.

Four years later (that is, in 1399) the situation had changed radically. Several copies of the Catherine's *vita* were made, and the notary

Cristoforo di Gano Guidini declared the Italian translation of the entire corpus of *Revelations* complete, a project he had undertaken of his own volition.[52] If we examine how Birgitta's writings were read and therefore how her fame spread throughout the spiritual groups connected to the Dominicans, we find, on the one hand, Alfonso of Jaén, representative of the religious factions supporting Pope Urban VI and author of an important editorial work on the *Revelations*. On the other hand, we find Cristoforo di Gano Guidini, scribe and devoted follower of Catherine.

Cristoforo (also Cristofano), was of a modest family, but was educated by his maternal grandfather, so that he learned the *Donato*, that is the principles of grammar and rhetoric, as well as Latin.[53] Having completed his studies in Siena, he settled there. However, Cristoforo expanded his patrimonial interests also to the countryside, where he usually practiced his profession as a notary. After he met Catherine, he was tempted to enter a religious order, but his mother dissuaded him, reminding him of the sacrifices she made as a young widow. Therefore, after asking Catherine's opinion on three possible wives, he married one of them (Mattea di Fede di Turino, not the one Catherine suggested) and had seven children. The plague, which struck the city in 1390, decimated his family, taking away his wife and six children. Cristoforo, left alone with his eight-year-old daughter Nadda, read the event as a divine sign, indeed a punishment for having chosen the marriage instead of dedicating himself to God, as Catherine would have liked. He then sent his surviving daughter to a monastery and took the habit in 1391 as *oblatus* (a sort of lay friar) in the Spedale of S. Maria della Scala in Siena.

At this time, Cristoforo had already completed his Latin translation of Catherine's *Libro*, the *Dialogue*, which she had dictated in Italian vernacular to him and two other scribes of hers. The writing of the Latin version was a long and difficult process, which, as the evidence suggests, dates to the years around 1385, and certainly before 1389.[54] Much later, after Cristoforo's religious conversion in 1391, we can locate the decision to make (or, to have made) an Italian vernacular translation of the *Revelations*, whose oldest manuscript witness is the pair of codices Siena, BCI, I.V.25/26, dated 1399, which also contains a long prologue by the translator.[55]

Cristoforo thus led a process of double translation: first, that of the *Dialogue* of Catherine from vernacular to Latin, which he completed himself; second, the translation of the *Revelations* of Birgitta from Latin to Italian, which he most likely commissioned and not translated himself. The challenge, however, was not out of his reach, given his culture and knowledge of Latin, as is obvious from his translation of the *Dialogue* of Catherine, not to mention his ability in hagiographic writing, a sample of which is found in a volume in Rieti, Biblioteca comunale, I.2.45 (1406), which contains *Legends of saints* in *ottava rima*.[56] Additionally, the testimony of Feo Belcari, who, while he was writing the *vita* of the blessed Giovanni Colombini, mentions a text of the same subject, with a moralizing content, written by the notary Cristoforo Guidini.[57]

The Sienese volumes (I.V.25/26) are certainly the earliest witnesses of the complete Italian translation of the *Revelations*. Domenico Pezzini, who has studied translations of Birgitta's writings, both in English and in Italian, first drew up a list of manuscripts, outlining their possible reciprocal relationships.[58] He observed that, in addition to being some of the earliest manuscripts, the Sienese volumes (I.V.25/26) are also rare witnesses of the entire translation of the *Revelations* in general. I believe that the Oxford manuscript, Bodleian Library, Canon. it. 127 (15th c.), witness of the entire Guidini's version (it omits only the final lines of the text), can be added to the list of complete versions. Considering that several manuscripts of the ancient collection of Matteo Canonici (now in Oxford) came from the ecclesiastical libraries of Venice, we cannot exclude the possibility that this manuscript was also produced there. Perhaps it was produced in the scriptorium of Tommaso Caffarini of Siena in SS. San Giovanni e Paolo, as certainly happened in the case of another volume including the *Legenda maior*.[59]

Apart from the first version of Cristoforo Guidini, Pezzini identifies two other translations. One is the fourth book alone, in a manuscript owned by the Medici family (second redaction).[60] Another one, also partial, dates back to the second half of the fifteenth century (third redaction).[61] Both could be dependent on the version that, for convenience, we will call the Guidini's version, which, at the current stage of research, would appear to have been the undisputed model, at least in Tuscany.

Regarding the translation of the *Revelations*, we can observe the state of the transmission of the manuscript, which is fragmented, partly for the chance occurrences that affect every manuscript transmission, and partly because the length of the text did not often allow it to be contained within a single, moderately-sized volume. Therefore, the process of copying the text required a division of the material into several volumes, which naturally facilitated the dispersion of individual codices. This practice was so common that the manuscript witnesses identified so far contain only some books, like the Florentine manuscripts with the third redaction described by Pezzini. To this, we can add the following manuscripts: Firenze, BNC, Pal. 77 (11 March 1495), from Paradiso, containing Books III–IV; Firenze, Biblioteca Riccardiana, MS 1336 (15th c. in.), with Books V–VIII and MS 1397 (15th c.), with Books I–II. For other manuscripts, on the contrary, the fragmentary nature of the text is a conscious choice: they are miscellanies of spiritual subjects, as often happens, with excerpts of the most requested or most useful mystical texts.[62]

The justification for Cristoforo's translation of the *Revelations*—a process which, if not personally completed, was at least sponsored by him—is the need to provide a solid foundation for those who would have requested these texts, especially rich laymen and nuns. Guidini's translations are complete and well-ordered texts which would have been used to produce more copies on request, either of the text in its entirety or select excerpts. These translations could also easily be (re)translated in the various European vernacular languages, and that was precisely what happened in the case of the *Dialogue* of Catherine.

At least three Latin translations of the *Dialogue* are known, in addition to one which is now considered lost. The first was made by Raymond of Capua and is unfinished. The second translation, by Guidini, was the first to be completed. The third, finally, was made by Stefano Maconi around 1419 and was very successful in both manuscript and print forms.[63] This is the focal point of the entire history of the transmission of Catherine's works: as long as they were not translated into Latin, they had no circulation outside Italy, as Guidini notes in his *Memorial*.[64] Guidini decided to translate the *Dialogue* for himself and for the benefit of those who, being educated, preferred to read Latin writings rather than vernacular texts. After his translation, he sent it to Stefano Maconi in order to have it revised. Moreover, Latin was used to promote the reading of Catherinian works outside the order. In fact, one of the most active channels of the diffusion of mystical works throughout Europe was the network of Carthusian monasteries, which were strongly marked by Catherinian thought, when Maconi was Abbot General. In England, for example, translations were made from Latin texts, and many of these, especially mystical works, were transmitted through the Carthusians. In this regard, the association between the two religious houses on the opposite banks of the Thames, the Charterhouse of Sheen, and the female part of the Birgittine Abbey of Syon, is well explored.[65]

In Syon, the first integral English translation of the *Dialogue* of Catherine, known as *The Orchard of Syon* (1420–30), was conceived. Begun by an anonymous author, it was continued by a certain Dan Jamys, perhaps a Carthusian in Sheen, and was commissioned by Syon, where the nuns seem to have had a more culturally active role than their male counterparts, especially with regard to mystical works, which were generally transmitted by miscellaneous manuscripts, collections of disparate and often heterogeneous texts.[66] These collections were composed in the medieval Carthusian libraries and included the principal spiritual writings of the time (early fifteenth century), among which works by authors such as Walter Hilton, Richard Rolle, and Julian of Norwich. Similar volumes were in the old library of Syon, which also owned at least two copies of the *Dialogue* in English translation.[67] The English translation of Catherine's *Dialogue* does not derive from a Carthusian text. It may have its origin in the translation of Maconi (1419), but as Phyllis Hodgson has demonstrated by comparing extended portions of the Middle English text, the translation probably derives from the Guidini version.[68] We know that the latter's version was reviewed by Maconi and traveled through his network of contacts. The first Catherinian writings to have some audience in restricted English cultural circles were some extracts from the *Dialogue*, transmitted by eight manuscripts,[69] probably translated around 1400. However, none of these extracts is an actual translation of the *Dialogue*. Seven of these are Middle English versions of the *Documentum spirituale* written by William Flete in 1377, under Catherine's dictation and known as *Cleanness of Sowle*.[70] Some years later, *The Orchard of Syon* was edited, the first complete translation of the *Dialogue*, dated to around 1420–30 and transmitted by three manuscripts, one printed volume, and two excerpts.[71]

These pieces of evidence can allow us to draw some preliminary conclusions.[72] First of all, it is clear that, as long as only Flete's *Documentum* was available, this was used as an *accessus* to the Catherinian writings, which were therefore only partially known. It was thus with the arrival of the Carthusians in Sheen, in 1414, and with the start of their cultural exchanges with the Birgittines in Syon (founded in 1415), that the Latin text of Guidini became available for reading and translating. Finally, the complete text of the *Dialogue* and the *Legenda* become, in turn, sources for excerpts, which are then included in the great miscellanies of spiritual writings, which enjoyed success throughout Europe, thanks mainly to the Carthusians.

Conclusion

From our first, though not exhaustive, survey of the extant manuscripts, it appears that there is much evidence testifying that the *Revelations* of Birgitta were read very early (by the end of the fourteenth century) in the Dominican monasteries and in the broader circle of Catherinian devotees. Similarly, it is clear that the works of Catherine were customary reading in the houses of the Birgittine Order, but with significantly later attestations (15th c.). The first reason for the delayed circulation is the late formation of Catherine's hagiography (it happened only after 1395 and the publication of the *Legenda maior*). Second, the vernacular language of Catherine's *oeuvre* limited the international exchanges and had to be translated into Latin in order to get the expected success. Finally, it was not before they had achieved space and means to copy them, as we have seen in the case of the Florence Paradiso and Syon abbey in England, that the Birgittine sisters were able to read other works than those strictly required by the Rule. Not until then could Catherine's works circulate among the Birgittines, and, as we have seen, Catherine's texts came to circulate only within the female branch of the order. Moreover, it can be observed that both the milieus—the Catherinian in a broader sense and the Birgittine in a narrower sense—were the promoters of the spirituality and writings of the other. In cases like these—and perhaps it is possible to extrapolate the results of this inquiry to the discussion of all mystical writings—the mobility of the texts is an extremely important factor in order to evaluate their impact in the cultural and religious evolution of different circles.

Notes

1 See James David Mixson and Bert Roest (eds.), *A Companion to Observant Reform in the Late Middle Ages and Beyond* (Leiden: Brill, 2015).
2 Hans Aili, "The manuscripts of Revelaciones S. Birgittae," in *Santa Brigida, Napoli, L'Italia*, eds. Olle Ferm, Alessandra Perriccioli Saggese, and Marcello Rotili (Naples: Arte tipografica editrice, 2009), 153–60.
3 Silvia Nocentini, "Lo 'scriptorium' di Tommaso Caffarini a Venezia," *Hagiographica* 12 (2005): 79–144; F. Thomas Luongo, *The Saintly Politics of Catherine of Siena* (Ithaca, NY: Cornell University Press, 2006).
4 Luisa Aurigemma, "La tradizione manoscritta del Dialogo della Divina Provvidenza di santa Caterina da Siena," *Critica letteraria* 16 (1988): 237–58. A more detailed list of all manuscripts will appear in the PhD dissertation thesis of Dr. Noemi Pigini (Università degli Studi di Siena, XXXIV ciclo, tutores: Claudio Lagomarsini and Johannes Bartuschat).
5 Birgitta of Sweden, *The Revelations of St. Birgitta of Sweden*, trans. Denis Searby, Introductions and Notes by Bridget Morris, 4 vols (Oxford: Oxford University Press, 2006–15), 1: 6–38.
6 Religious women would, however, soon play a decisive role in manuscript transmission and devotional choices; see, for example, the case of Chiara Gambacorta discussed below.
7 Werner Williams-Krapp, "*Wir lesent daz vil in sölichen sachen swerlich betrogen werdent.* Zur monastischen Rezeption von mystischer Literatur im 14. und 15. Jahrhundert," in *Nonnen, Kanonissen und Mystikerinnen. Religiöse Frauengemeinschaften in Süddeutschland. Beiträge zur interdisziplinären Tagung vom 21. bis 23. September 2005 in Frauenchimiensee*, eds. Eva Schlotheuber, Helmut Flachenecker, Ingrid Gardill (Göttingen: Vandenhoeck & Ruprecht, 2008); "Die Bedeutung der reformierten Klöster des Predigerordens für das literarische Leben in Nürnberg in 15. Jahrhunderts,"in *Studien und Texte zur literarischen und materiellen Kultur der Frauenklöster im späten Mittelalter. Ergebnisse eines Arbeitsgesprächs in der Herzog August Bibliothek Wolfenbüttel, 24.-26. Febr. 1999*, eds. Falk Eisermann, Eva Schlotheuber, Volker Honemann, (Leiden: Brill, 2004).
8 The first and most authoritative Latin *vita* was composed between 1385 and 1395 by her confessor, later Master General of the Dominican Order, Raymond of Capua, and was known as *Legenda maior* (see LM). The following *vitae* are mostly abbreviated texts (*legendae minores* or *minimae*). Among these are worth mentioning the *Legenda minor* of Tommaso Caffarini (1411–15, critical edition available in *Sanctae Catharinae Senensis legenda minor*, ed. Ezio Franceschini [Siena: 1942]) and the one written in 1425 by Jerome of Prague (unpublished). In Catherine's case, Italian texts represent the earliest hagiographic tradition about her, since we know at least three works written before the *Legenda maior*, all reported by *Biblioteca Agiografica Italiana* (BAI). See *Repertorio di testi e manoscritti, secoli XIII–XV*, eds. Jacques Dalarun and Lino Leonardi, 2 vols (Florence: SISMEL, Edizioni del Galluzzo, 2003): the two different recounts of the death of Catherine by Barduccio Canigiani (between 1380 and 1384, BAI nn. 11 and 12), one of which was used by Raymond for his work, and the report of some Catherine's miracles by an anonymous Florentine scribe (between 1374 and 1385, BAI, n. 13).
9 C. Annette Grisé, "Catherine of Siena in Middle English Manuscripts: Transmission, Translations, and Transformation," in *The Theory and Practice of Translation in the Middle Ages*, eds. Rosalyn Voaden et al. (Turnhout: Brepols, 2003).

10 As to the imitable sanctity, see Fernanda Sorelli, *La santità imitabile. "Leggenda di Maria da Venezia" di Tommaso da Siena* (Venice: Deputazione di storia patria per le Venezie, 1984), and Marco Faini and Alessia Meneghin (eds.), *Domestic Devotions in the Early Modern World* (Leiden: Brill, 2018).

11 Not to mention parallel traditions, such as that relating to the so-called *Documentum spirituale*, collected by William Flete around 1377, which had a direct tradition (3 MSS) and an indirect one in the *Libellus de Supplemento* of Caffarini (4 MSS), but which, in turn, is in its content very similar to the letter T64, the one that Catherine sent to Flete himself, so it had circulation, in a colloquial version, even within the tradition of the whole Epistolary. For William Flete, see Silvia Nocentini, "Guillemus Flete," in *C.A L.M.A. (Compendium Auctorum Latinorum Medii Aevi)*, vol. V (Florence: SISMEL, Edizioni del Galluzzo, 2015), 27–8. Editions of the *Documentum* are in: Robert Fawtier, "Catheriniana," *Melanges d'archéologie et d'histoire* 34 (1914): 86–93; and in *Supplementum*: Thomas Antonii de Senis "Caffarini," *Libellus de Supplemento*, 296–300. Edition of letter T64 in Catherine of Siena, *Le Lettere di S. Caterina da Siena ridotte a miglior lezione, e in ordine Nuovo disposte*, ed. Niccolò Tommaseo (Florence: G. Barbera, 1860), vol. 2, 14–22. For the English diffusion of the text see Jennifer N. Brown, "The Many Misattributions of Catherine of Siena: Beyond the Orchard in England," *The Journal of Medieval Religious Culture* 1 (2015): 67–84.

12 Silvia Nocentini, "Il problema testuale del Libro di divina dottrina di Caterina da Siena: questioni aperte," *Revue d'histoire des textes* 11 (2016): 255–94.

13 Catherine of Siena, *Dialogo della divina provvidenza*, ed. Innocenzo Taurisano (Rome: Libreria editrice E. Ferrari, 1928), XXII, n. 1.

14 Simona Brambilla, *"Padre mio dolce." Lettere di religiosi a Francesco Datini. Antologia* (Rome: Ministero per i Beni e le Attività Culturali, 2010), 19. Margherita was the wife of the famous Italian merchant Francesco Datini, who entertained a rich epistolary with various religious figures, among which Chiara Gambacorta, to whom we will return later.

15 Described in Rosanna Miriello, *I manoscritti del Monastero del Paradiso di Firenze* (Florence: SISMEL, Edizioni del Galluzzo, 2007), 151–55.

16 Paradiso was one of the first Birgittine houses in Italy, founded by the Florentine Antonio di Niccolò Alberti in 1390. See Tore Nyberg, *Birgittinische Klostergründungen des Mittelalters* (Leiden: CWK Gleerup, 1965), 84–9; Tore Nyberg, "Paradiso," *Birgittiana*, 1 (1993): 9–14; Miriello, *I manoscritti*.

17 This vernacular version is preceded by the translator's prologue, which is highly important both as to its early date and as to his desire to justify his work as a translator; likewise a similar prologue on prophecy is placed before the vernacular version of the *Revelations* edited by Cristoforo Guidini in 1399 (see below). The *Sermo* in the same Italian version is also in the MS: Firenze, BNC, Conv. Soppr. B.II.1719 (1498).

18 Catherine of Siena, *Le Lettere*, vol. 1, 65–69.

19 Firenze, BNC, Palatino 59 (25 April 1450), with the entire epistolary (170 letters), copied by the Birgittine friar Tommaso di Marco (Miriello, *I manoscritti*, 143–4) and the manuscript Firenze, Riccardiano 1267, copied on 22 December 1485 by sister Raffaella with the *Dialogue*, followed by Catherine's Miracles (Miriello, *I manoscritti*, 147–48).

20 See Williams-Krapp, *"Wir lesent daz vil in sölichen sachen swerlich betrogen werdent,"* 263–78 and Williams-Krapp, *Die Deutschen und Niederländischen Legendare des Mittelalters. Studien zu Ihrer Überlieferungs-, Text- und Wirkungsgeschichte* (Tübingen: Niemeyer, 1986).

21 See his testimony at the so-called Processo Castellano (1411–16), that took place in Venice, where some religious men (and Caffarini between them) were praising Catherine's virtues, although she was not yet canonized, PC, 94 and 142–43. See also the initial quotation in the Introduction to the present volume.

22 On the crucial role of Alfonso, see further Chapter 9 by Camille Rouxpetel in the present volume.

23 The so-called poor friars or *Fraticelli* were groups of penitents, living in hermitages. They were inspired by the Franciscan way of life, but intended it in a more strict sense and, generally, set themselves outside the Minoritic order. Except for Italy, almost everywhere, they incurred in the accusation of heresy and many of them were faced with the Inquisition and burned as heretics.

24 The document has been published by Mario Sensi, "La regola di Niccolò IV dalla Costituzione 'Periculoso' alla bolla 'Pastoralis officii' (1298)," in *La "Supra montem" di Niccolò IV (1289): genesi e diffusione di una regola. Atti del V convegno di studi francescani (Ascoli Piceno, 26–27 ottobre 1987)*, eds. Raffaele Pazzelli and Lino Temperini (Rome: Ed. Analecta TOR, 1988), 180–88, reimpr. in Mario Sensi, *"Mulieres in ecclesia." Storie di monache e bizzoche* (Spoleto: Fondazione Centro Italiano di studi sull'Alto Medioevo CISAM, 2010), vol. 1, 418–26.

25 The project would fail due to the extreme conditions imposed to the various communities, see Mario Sensi, "Alfonso Pecha e l'eremitismo Italiano di fine secolo XIV," *Rivista di Storia della Chiesa in Italia* 47 (1993): 51–80.

26 Many Latin hagiographical recounts was made on Birgitta, as we can see by the BHL: *Bibliotheca hagiographica latina antiquae et mediae aetatis*, eds. Société des Bollandistes, 2 vols (Bruxelles: Société des Bollandistes, 1898–1901), with its *Supplementum* (Bruxelles: Société des Bollandistes, 1986), nn. 1334–59. Here, I briefly outline the earliest that had their origin or some circulation in Italy, while I return later to Italian translations of these *Vitae* (see also BAI, vol. II, p. 124). The first hagiography of Birgitta was written down by her two confessors, Master Peter of Skänninge and Prior Peter of Alvastra and is known in three redactions. The two longer versions are: the so-called Process Vita (BHL n. 1334), included in the Acts of the canonization process, and the Panisperna-Vita (BHL n. 1334b), named after the earliest manuscript witness, the *Liber de miraculis beate Brigide de Suecia*, was made in Rome around 1378, in the monastery of San Lorenzo in Panisperna, where Birgitta's body was preserved before her translation to Vadstena. The third version is the shortest one, and therefore, some scholars tend to think it is the earliest and original *vita* written by the two confessors. A fourth major version of Birgitta's *vita* is the liturgical one, written by Birger Gregersson after 1374 (BHL n. 1335). Edition of BHL n. 1339 by John Kruse, "Vita metrica S. Birgittae," in *Meddelanden från det litteraturhistoriska seminariet i Lund*, I, *Lunds Universitets års-skrift* 28 (1891–92): 10–28; edition of BHL n. 1334b in AP, 614–40; edition of BHL n. 1334 in AP, 73–105. Edition of BHL n. 1335 by Isak Collijn, *Birgerus Gregorii Legenda S. Birgitte* (Uppsala: Almqvist & Wiksells, 1946) and Carl-Gustaf Undhagen, *Birger Gregerssons Birgitta-officium. Birgerus Gregorii, Officium Sancte Birgitte* (Uppsala: Almqvist & Wiksells, 1960). See also: Cordelia Heß, *Heilige machen im spätmittelalterlichen Ostseeraum. Die Kanonisationprozesse von Birgitta von Schweden, Nikolaus von Linköping und Dorothea von Montau* (Berlin: Akademie Verlag, 2008), 99–204; Silvia Nocentini, "Un eremita, due confessori, tre redazioni: i primordi dell'agiografia brigidina in Italia," *Hagiographica* 26 (2019), 289–330.

27 Sylvie Duval, *"La beata Chiara conduttrice." Le Vite di Chiara Gamba-corta e Maria Mancini e i testi dell'Osservanza domenicana pisana* (Rome: Edizioni di Storia e Letteratura, 2016), 142. The *Life of Tora* (later Chiara) was written by an anonymous around 1450 and is handed down by five manuscripts, dated to the period between 1580 and 1620, on this see Duval, *"La beata Chiara conduttrice,"* 33–74.

28 Possibly with the intermediation of Alfonso, see Giles Gérard Meersseman, "Spirituali romani, amici di Caterina da Siena," in *Ordo fraternitatis. Confraternite e pietà dei laici nel Medioevo*, 3 vols (Rome: Herder, 1977), 1: 535–73.

29 The paintings testify that Chiara and her sisters had at their disposal some books with the works and life of Birgitta, although these manuscripts are today to be considered lost or dispersed in other archival collections. See Ann M. Roberts, "Chiara Gambacorta as Patroness of the Arts," in *Creative Women in Medieval and Early Modern Italy: A Religious and Artistic Renaissance*, eds. E. Ann Matter and John Coakley (Philadelphia: University of Pennsylvania Press, 1994); *Dominican Women and Renaissance Art: The Convent of San Domenico of Pisa* (London and New York: Routledge, 2016). For example, the Pisan nunnery exchanged books for copying with the Dominican one in Venice (Corpus Christi), where was copied the MS Venezia, Biblioteca Nazionale Marciana, lat. III. 25 (*c.*1400), containing the first book of the *Revelations*.

30 Maria di Bartolomeo Mancini (d. 1429) was a companion of Chiara Gambacorta, among the first members of S. Domenico in Pisa. She outlived three husbands and many children to become a Dominican sister, first in S. Croce in Fossabanda, then in S. Domenico. Maria experienced many visions, all recorded in her *Vita*. See Duval, *"La beata Chiara conduttrice,"* 75–92 and 175–93, and Roberts, *Dominican Women*, 24–25, 182–83, 202–04.

31 Duval, *"La beata Chiara conduttrice,"* 186–87.

32 Cristoforo di Gano Guidini wrote in his Memorial book, regarding Catherine's followers: "Also was among her sons ... Missere the bishop Alfonso," Carlo Milanesi, "Ricordi di Cristofano di Gano Guidini," *Archivio storico Italiano* 4 (1843): 25–48, at 34. Catherine remembers the circumstances of the delivery of the papal indulgence with these words: "This one was the spiritual father of that countess, who died in Rome, and he is the one who, for the love of virtue, renounced to the bishopric dignity. From the saint Father he came to me, telling me to pray in particular for the Pope." See letter 127 to Tommaso of Siena and Bartolomeo Dominici, in *Epistolario di santa Caterina da Siena*, ed. Eugenio Dupré Theseider (Rome: Istituto storico Italiano per il Medioevo, 1940), 394–97, at 396.

33 Edited in Francesco Grottanelli, *Legenda minore di S. Caterina da Siena e lettere dei suoi discepoli: scritture inedite* (Bologna: Gaetano Romagnoli, 1868), 283 and 363, note 56. On this prominent Carthusian and devoted disciple and scribe of Catherine, see Giovanni Leoncini, "Un certosino del tardo Medioevo: don Stefano Maconi," in *Die Ausbreitung kartäusischen Lebens und Geistes im Mittelalter,* Analecta Cartusiana 63 (Salzburg: 1990), vol. 1, 54–107. On his activity as a Catherinian promoter, see Nocentini, "Lo 'scriptorium'," 87–9, and LM, pp. 8–25.

34 We know two other treatises by Alfonso on the same argument: *Informaciones* (1380) and *Conscripcio bona* (1388), edited by Franz Bliemetzrieder in "Un'altra edizione rifatta del trattato di Alfonso Pecha, vescovo resignato di Iaën, sullo scisma (1387–1388), con notizie sulla vita di Pietro Bohier, Benedettino, vescovo di Orvieto," *Rivista storica benedettina* 4 (1909): 74–100; the *Conscripcio* has been edited by Robert E. Lerner, on the basis

of a different manuscript "Alfonso Pecha's Treatise on the Origins of the Great Schism: What an Insider 'Saw And Heard'," *Traditio* 72 (2017): 411–51.

35 On the various redactions of Alfonso and their dating, see the introduction of the editor (Carl-Gustaf Undhagen), in Rev. I.

36 The "Processo Castellano" was a bishopric survey (1411–16) on the cult of Catherine in the city of Venice.

37 PC, 94, 96–97.

38 PC, 142–43.

39 PC, 166; cf. SA: 16.14–20.

40 PC, 179 and 193. See Rev. IV: 70.1–30, and also Rev. I: 10.108–121; Rev. VII: 15.11–37. In the *Libellus de supplemento*, he includes even the self-inflicted stigmata of Birgitta in his list of similar phenomena, when he has to demonstrate the truth of the invisible signs of crucifixion on Catherine's body (Caffarini, *Libellus de Supplemento*, 124–25).

41 Caffarini, *Libellus*, 434. See also Rev. IV: 33.1–46 and LM, II.10, pp. 319–33.

42 Datini was a rich merchant from Prato, near Florence. He, as an additional demonstration of the continuous and fervid spiritual exchange between lay and religious environments, was recipient and sender of letters from and to a large group of religious persons, including Chiara Gambacorta, see Brambilla, *"Padre mio dolce."* Lapo Mazzei, *Lettere di un notaro a un mercante del secolo XIV. Con altre lettere e documenti*, ed. Cesare Guasti (Florence: Le Monnier, 1880), vol. I, 118–23, letter n. 92 and letter n. 91; now available in a new edition by Gloria Camesasca, "Lettere di ser Lapo Mazzei a Francesco Datini (1390–1399)," (PhD diss., Università Cattolica del Sacro Cuore, Milan, 2012).

43 At that time there were almost three main versions of Birgitta's *Vita*, i.e. BHL 1334, 1334b and 1335, for which see above note 26.

44 Siena, BCI, G.XI.20, 14th c. ex. We do not know if this manuscript—or the one in Ser Lapo's possession—was produced in Tuscany, but it is very likely that both manuscripts were of Tuscan provenance.

45 The volume, wherever was written down, was already in Siena in 1464, since a note in the anterior counterguard registers the snowfall on 26 December, when many roofs collapsed.

46 Stefano had been Abbot General of the Carthusian Order (Urbanist party) from 1398 to 1411, when he renounced his post to promote the order's re-union. He then left the Charterhouse in Seitz (now in Slovenia) and came back to Milan, or better to say, to the new Charterhouse in Pavia, whose foundation was been facilitated by him, in harmony with the Duke.

47 See Domenico Pezzini, *The Translation of Religious Texts in the Middle Ages: Tracts and Rules, Hymns and Saints' Lives* (Bern: P. Lang, 2008).

48 Siena, BCI, T.II.6, fol. 132r.

49 The Latin *Life* was published by Isak Collijn in AP, 614–40 and in *Corpus codicum Suecicorum Medii Aevi* 7 (Hafniae, 1936), 3–41. The Latin version is transmitted by MS: Roma, Archivum generale OFM, MS "Panisperna" (1378), fols. 1r–20v, Siena, BCI, G.XI.20 (14th c. ex.), fols. 2r–26v, Helsinki, UB, MS Nordenskiöld (15th c. in.), fols. 91r–110r, all of which used by Collijn for his edition. In addition, we know also MSS: Augsburg, UB, Cod. II.1.2°.201, fols. 364v–83r (1487) and Göttingen, UB, Theol. 202, fols. 317r–30r (1469). To my knowledge, there has never been done a complete census of manuscripts transmitting the *retractata* version of Birgitta's *Life*, in almost all cases copied with some miracles. A first attempt is made by Silvia Nocentini in "Un eremita, due confessori."

50 See below for similar considerations emerged from the numerous studies focused on the relations between the Charterhouse of Sheen and the Birgittine Abbey of Syon in England.

51 On the other hand, it is surprising that the thematic hagiography compiled by Bertoldo of Rome (BHL n. 1349) had not been traced in Italian catalogues, neither in Latin nor in Italian. Bertoldo was an important exponent of the Birgittine movement in Italy, since he was general confessor of Paradiso in 1429 (Miriello, *I manoscritti*, 23) and he wrote the *Life* around 1434, in order to send it to Vadstena.

52 This is the earliest Italian translation of the *Revelations*, and the following versions will be all related to it. See Domenico Pezzini, "Il primo volgarizzamento italiano delle *Rivelazioni* e degli altri scritti di S. Brigida: il codice I.V.25/26 della Biblioteca degli Intronati di Siena (1399)," in Ferm, Perriccioli Saggese, and Rotili, *Santa Brigida, Napoli, L'Italia*, 67–72.

53 Information on Cristoforo's biography is found in Giovanni Cherubini, "Dal libro di ricordi di un notaio senese del Trecento," in *Signori, contadini, borghesi: ricerche sulla società Italiana del basso medioevo* (Florence: La Nuova Italia, 1974), 393–425 and in Simona Foà, "Guidini, Cristoforo," in *Dizionario Biografico degli Italiani*, vol. 61 (Rome: Istituto storico Treccani, 2004). www.treccani.it/enciclopedia/cristoforo-guidini_(Dizionario-Biografico)/ (Accessed 08.10.2018).

54 Silvia Nocentini, "'Fare per lettera': le traduzioni Latine del *Libro di divina dottrina* di Caterina da Siena," *Studi medievali* 56, no. 2 (2015): 639–80; "Il problema testuale."

55 Prologue edited in Pezzini, "Il primo volgarizzamento." For a discussion of the illuminations in this MS, see Chapter 6 by Maria H. Oen in the present work.

56 L. Buono et al. (eds.), "I manoscritti datati delle province di Frosinone, Rieti e Viterbo," in *Manoscritti datati d'Italia* 17 (Florence: SISMEL, Edizioni del Galluzzo, 2007), 137–8.

57 Cherubini, "Dal libro dei ricordi," 393.

58 Pezzini, *The Translation of Religious Texts*, 381.

59 Oxford, Canon. Misc. lat. 205 (15th c. in.) and LM, 54–5. This manuscript is moreover a precious testimony of the Latin partial version of Catherine's *Dialogue* written by Raymond of Capua. The Canonici collection was undoubtedly exquisite for the quality of its pieces, such as an Italian volume with the *Dialogue* (Canon. it. 283, 15th c.) and a Latin exemplar of the entire *Revelations* (Canon. Misc. 475, 15th c.).

60 Firenze, Biblioteca Medicea Laurenziana, Pl. 27.10 (15th c. in.).

61 Firenze, BNC, II.II.393 (15th c.): Book I, part of II (1–3), III and IV and some orations; Firenze, BNC, II.130 (1494): Books I–II and two letters, coming from Paradiso; Firenze, BNC, II.III.270 (26.4.1495): Books VII–VIII, miracles and two lauds, still from Paradiso. All manuscripts are described in Miriello, *I manoscritti*.

62 For example the manuscripts: Siena, BCI, I.VIII.26 (14th ex.–15th in.), volume owned by the Sienese Olivetans, early witness of the Guidini version, which contains only a passage from Book II, 28 (fols. 62v–63v); Siena, BCI, F.II.18 (second half of 15th c.), which have, at fols. 80v–84v, a single revelation, under the title "Numerus vulnerum Christi secundum praesentem revelationem sunt quinquemilia CCCCLX"; Pescia, Biblioteca Capitolare, XXII.VI.11.11 (15th c.), fols. 150r–60r, with a single prophecy of Birgitta (incipit: "Destati o fier leone al mio gran grido"). Pezzini ("Il primo volgarizzamento") adds the manuscript Firenze, BNC, II.II.391 (15th c.), a collection of diverse passages from *Revelations*, all of them concerning prophecy.

63 Nocentini, "Fare per lettera."

64 Milanesi, *Ricordi*, 37–8.

65 See Ann M. Hutchinson, "What the Nuns Read: Literary Evidence from the English Bridgettine House, Syon Abbey," *Mediaeval Studies* 57 (1995): 207–22.

66 See Vincent Gillespie, "Dial M for Mystic: Mystical Texts in the Library of Syon Abbey and the Spirituality of the Syon Brethren," in *Looking in Holy Books: Essays on Late Medieval Religious Writing in England* (Turnhout: Brepols, 2011); Hutchinson, "What the Nuns Read."

67 In the library of Syon were preserved two manuscripts with the Latin translation of the *Dialogue*, maybe lost: O 70 and M 71. The latter includes, in addition, some excerpts from the *Life of Catherine*. Vincent Gillespie and Anthony Ian Doyle (eds.), *Syon Abbey. With Libraries of the Carthusians* (London and Toronto: British Library and University of Toronto Press, 2001), 243, 330, 647.

68 Phyllis Hodgson, "The Orcherd of Syon and the English Mystical Tradition," in *Proceedings of the British Academy* 50 (1964): 229–49.

69 The list of manuscripts can be found in Dirk Schultze, "Translating St Catherine of Siena in Fifteenth-Century England," in *Catherine of Siena: The Creation of a Cult*, eds. Jeffrey F. Hamburger and Gabriela Signori (Turnhout: Brepols, 2013), 187; and in Brown, "The Many Misattributions," 80–1.

70 The eighth manuscript is a different version of the *Cleanness*, which, according to Jennifer Brown, is a free re-elaboration of the *Dialogue*. See Brown, "The Many Misattributions."

71 The manuscripts with the complete translation are: London, British Library, MS Harley 3432 (15th c.), Cambridge, St John's College, MS C.25 (15th c.) and New York, Pierpont Morgan Library, MS M.162 (1470). For these and the list of extracts, see Schultze, "Translating St Catherine."

72 The evidence is treated more fully in the recent work by Jennifer N. Brown, *Fruit of the Orchard: Reading Catherine of Siena in Late Medieval and Early Modern England* (Toronto: University of Toronto Press, 2019).

6 Ambivalent Images of Authorship

Maria H. Oen

When the works of Birgitta of Sweden and Caterina of Siena started to circulate in the late fourteenth century, the reception of the instructive voice of a woman could be highly unfavorable. The opposition was rooted in a biblical injunction (1 Cor. 14:34–35, 1 Tim. 2:12) codified in *Decretum Gratiani* and much discussed by theologians already in the thirteenth and fourteenth centuries.[1] These debates coincided with a wave of laypeople, many of them women, who expressed themselves publicly on subjects traditionally the privilege of the clergy.[2] When Birgitta's *Revelations* and Catherine's *Letters* and *Libro*, or the *Dialogue*—works which comprised explicit spiritual and political instructions—were made public through widely disseminated manuscripts, they seemed to be transgressing the normative boundaries regulating women's voices.[3]

In both cases, the early transmission of the texts can be traced back to specific scriptoria connected to key figures in the promotion of their respective cults.[4] Regarding Birgitta, her collaborator Alfonso of Jaén, who, according to the primary sources, had been instructed by God through His Swedish conduit to edit and publish her revelations, performed his task with great speed.[5] In 1377, that is, within four years after the visionary's death, a compilation of revelations comprising seven books and an apologetic prologue was submitted to the papal commission charged with evaluating Birgitta's claim to sanctity. After another year or two, the corpus was spread in an augmented version,[6] which was dispersed in deluxe codices produced in a Neapolitan workshop, presumably under the direct supervision of Alfonso.[7] In Catherine's case, her disciple, the Dominican friar Tommaso Caffarini, took charge of the systematic dissemination of her writings.[8] In 1394, 14 years after the death of the author, Caffarini transferred to Venice, where he set up a workshop in the convent of Corpus Domini connected to the Dominican church SS. Giovanni e Paolo.[9] Its purpose was to promote the cult of Catherine through the broad transmission of her writings and images of the saint *in spe*. Both Alfonso and Caffarini were, in other words, particularly motivated to present Birgitta and Catherine in a manner that would ensure the positive reception of their works.[10]

In the manuscripts containing Birgitta's and Catherine's writings, Alfonso and Caffarini made strategic use of visual rhetoric, playing on the value medieval society placed on elements such as page layout and colors for the reading of a text in the sense of committing it to memory.[11] The codices produced in the Neapolitan and Venetian scriptoria employed specific iconographical programs designed to structure how the texts were read and to affect construal of their meanings.[12] This chapter focuses on how these illuminations, and, in particular, the author portraits of the two women, were utilized to shape the readers' understanding of their authorial roles within a cultural climate that was, in accordance with "apostolic authority," skeptical to the female public (/published) voice. The essay opens by drawing attention to some tensions in the textual and visual approaches to authorship and writing in late medieval culture in general, and especially in the material pertaining to Birgitta and Catherine, before analyzing some of their earliest author portraits produced in the milieus around the two women.

To Write or Not to Write

As is well known, authoring or composing in medieval culture was not synonymous with being able to physically write, a task that was often left to a scribe.[13] The commitment of a literary work to a written text on a physical support would usually happen late in the process of authoring, and it was customarily the result of a collaborative effort that involved dictation.[14] For this reason, it is interesting to note that in medieval author portraits, a visual genre inherited from Antiquity, one of the most typical formulas for depicting the author of a work was with a pen in his hand.[15] In the literary works of women, however, the motif of the author holding a pen appears seldom. Lesley Smith's research reveals that aside from a few exceptions, prior to *c*.1400 (after which time some portraits of secular female writers such as Christine de Pizan appear in vernacular manuscripts), there are hardly any author-cum-scribe portraits of women, despite the fact that there were numerous female authors, both within and outside of monasteries, just as there were many women working as scribes in convents and in professional workshops.[16] As I have argued elsewhere, this paucity of images of women writing should perhaps be considered to be related to the anxiety regarding female public voices of this period.[17] Against this background, it is of particular interest in the current context that the only case in which Smith identified a female religious author shown in the act of writing, besides Hildegard of Bingen, is Birgitta in the iconography developed in the Neapolitan scriptorium.[18]

In addition to these incongruences between male and female author portraits, it is curious to notice that, despite the peripherality of the act of writing for the process of composition, when it comes to literature associated with female authors in the later Middle Ages, their ability to physically write, or resistance to this activity, becomes a trope.[19] Concerning this phenomenon, the source material pertaining to Birgitta and Catherine offers interesting examples of how the question of whether or not a woman could physically record her own compositions become a central issue in representations of them, textual and visual. The sources relating to the two saintly authors are replete with tensions and ambivalence concerning their writing and their authorial roles. This is also the case in the iconography of the illuminations that I will analyze here.

The most conspicuous difference between the author portraits of Birgitta and Catherine concerns the representation of writerly agency; whereas the former is given a pen, itself a remarkable attribute for a woman, there is a noteworthy absence of the pen in the case of the latter. This difference in visual strategies is perplexing as the promoters of Catherine were very much aware of the Birgittine campaign from a generation earlier, which would have been a presumptive model, given the extremely wide dissemination of Birgitta's works and the successful outcome of her canonization process in 1391. Caffarini had further reason to look to the program for the circulation of Birgitta's *Revelations*, owing to the similarities between the two women, who are among the very few laywomen of this period to leave a substantial corpus of religious and political instructive literature, a point he himself comments on in his deposition for Catherine's canonization process (1411–16) where he frequently compares the two.[20] In this context, it should also be remembered that a disciple of Catherine, Cristoforo di Gano Guidini, played a key role in the transmission of Birgitta's *Revelations* in the vernacular on the Italian peninsula. Cristoforo was responsible for the production of what Domenico Pezzini has argued to be the first complete Italian translation of the *Revelations*, found in a twin-codex now in Siena's *Biblioteca comunale degli Intronati* (BCI).[21] Whether he commissioned the translation in 1399, as is stated in the two colophons, or personally undertook the task is uncertain. What we know, however, is that Cristoforo translated Catherine's *Dialogue,* originally composed in Italian, into Latin, and that he compiled her letters, which were then brought to Venice by Caffarini in 1398 to serve as sources for his own copies.[22] The Birgittine Siena codex is especially interesting for the present purposes, because it contains an author portrait of the Swedish saint as a scribe that is clearly based on the one developed for the *Revelations* in the Neapolitan scriptorium about 20 years earlier (more on this below).

The absence of a pen in Catherine's images stands out in part because she appears explicitly as a writing agent throughout her corpus, as illustrated in her *Letters,* which typically open with the phrase "I Catherine … am writing to you" (*Io Caterina …scrivo a voi*). This is, of course, an "I" that is an inherent formulaic part of the epistolary genre. However, when approached together with the contents of the letters, for instance, where she discusses the fate of her writings after her death ("take care of the book and any other writing of mine you can find"), it is tempting to see the "I" in the letters as expressing a conscious understanding of her role as the producer of her texts.[23] We should also remember the famous letter addressed to her confessor and hagiographer, Raymond of Capua, in which Catherine asserts her own "aptitude" (*l'attitudine*), to write.[24]

The explicit writing agency of Catherine contrasts sharply with the portrayal of Birgitta in the *Revelations*, where she, despite being the crucial recipient of divine visions, tends to disappear in the text, at least concerning her role as a writer, which, as we will see, was so important for her hagiographers. In the *Revelations*, Birgitta is usually referred to as "a person" who experiences visions, or formulaically as "the bride of Christ." The first person "I" appears rarely, and when it does, it is mainly at the service of describing the visual experience of a vision ("I saw").[25] This could be interpreted as a strategy in the text, by Birgitta and/or her editors, to eliminate the historically contingent person from her celestial visions claimed to originate in God. The hagiography, though, offers a different stance concerning the visionary's role in the production of the text.

The portrayal of the two women in relation to writing in their respective *vitae* takes yet another surprising turn. Birgitta is explicitly presented by her hagiographers as someone who could read *and* write. It is even stated that she usually recorded her revelations in Swedish "in her own hand" (*manu sua propria*) before these were translated into Latin by her confessors; knowing Latin, she then verified that these were translated correctly.[26] In contrast, Catherine's writing skills appear, strangely enough, as a point of disaccord between Raymond of Capua and Caffarini.[27] Raymond was, in fact, the addressee of the abovementioned letter in which Catherine maintained that she had written it herself, but in his *Legenda maior*, he does not acknowledge her ability to write. Caffarini, however, is more than eager to convey that Catherine certainly could write—in his words, by a miracle.[28] But if Caffarini was so concerned with demonstrating Catherine's power to physically shape letters as a part of her saintly persona, why did he not represent her as such in the author portraits in the manuscripts produced under his supervision, particularly given the acceptance of this model provided in the campaign for the promotion of the recently canonized Birgitta? Could it have been a deliberate choice for Caffarini to *not* show Catherine as a scribe, despite her literacy being of such importance to his hagiographical presentation of her?

The Elusive Evangelist

It has long been established that the three oldest preserved codices containing Birgitta's *Revelations*, dated to *c*.1377–81, can be traced back to the same workshop in Naples and that these contain a fixed cycle of illuminations that was reproduced in later codices stemming from all over Europe.[29] This elaborate program includes, in addition to a set of historiated initials, three full-page illuminations serving as a frontispiece for the entire corpus as well as for Books V and VIII. Several of the images stand out as author portraits, most notably the first and the last of the three larger miniatures.

The frontispiece, here from the New York codex (Figure 1.1, see Chapter 1), presents Birgitta as a widow, wearing a dark robe with a white wimple. A rayed halo surrounds her head, visually manifesting her status as *beata*. The visionary is placed in the lower right corner, seated next to a writing desk. An open codex rests in her lap, and she holds a pen in her raised right hand. Birgitta's gaze is turned up toward the center uppermost section of the page, where Christ and the Virgin are seated inside a *mandorla*. The heavenly couple looks back at Birgitta and sends forth rays of light from their hands, which cut diagonally across the folio and culminate at the head of the writer. Birgitta is situated in an earthly realm with a golden background and a wall-hanging behind her, clearly distinguished from the celestial sphere above rendered in blue. Heaven is divided into horizontal registers that form a hierarchy: on top is the *mandorla* encircled by red seraphs and flanked by angels, which together make up the nine groups of the hierarchy of angels. Beneath them are rows of seated apostles, divided into two groups, with figures representing King David, Abraham, and John the Baptist immediately below Christ and the Virgin. In the bottom register are two groups of saintly men and women.

The miniature depicts Birgitta receiving one of her revelations, which she records immediately, in accordance with the account in her *Vita*. In the lower left corner, sharing her terrestrial realm, and yet placed in another time and space as indicated by different backgrounds and the rendering of the foundation, is a priest celebrating Mass while attended by a servant. The scene, which illustrates Birgitta's vision—we can see the host elevated in the hands of the priest miraculously transforming into a human figure—is linked to the visionary by the bust of an angel pointing in both directions while looking at Birgitta. The perspective employed, understood in part through the diminishing sizes of the celestial figures, emphasizes the central role of the writer.

As first noted by Sara Ekwall and more recently discussed by Anette Creutzburg, the motif of the divinely inspired writer Birgitta is shown in accordance with the iconography of the evangelist author portrait.[30] This visual formula was established already in the sixth century, and by the late fourteenth, it was found in gospel books throughout Christendom. According to this portrait type, the biblical author is typically shown at a desk or seated with a book in lap and a pen in hand while gazing up at the divine source of inspiration in the form of the evangelist symbols, the dove of the Holy Spirit, the hand of God, or the bust of

Christ.[31] The model was so well known that the beholder of Birgitta's author portrait could not have failed to recognize it, and consequently to elide the visionary with the biblical prototype.

The choice of the highly revered iconographical model of the writing evangelist complies with and enhances the rhetorical strategies for the presentation of Birgitta's authorial role opted for in the textual sources. In fact, in her *Vita*, Birgitta is explicitly compared to the evangelists.[32] Moreover, throughout the *Revelations*, she is portrayed as the channel of God; thus, it seems that she is not the origin of the writings contained in the books; God is the source and she the chosen conduit. As such, Birgitta plays the part of God's "human pen," just like the authors of the Gospels. This bold characterization of the origin of the *Revelations* implies an even bolder one concerning the status of the text: it is equal to Scripture. In following, this means that the *Revelations* manuscripts, in text and in image, ask that the work be approached not as the writings (or the teachings) of a woman, but as heavenly messages received spiritually in Birgitta's mind by divine agency, as affirmed by the host of saintly and angelic witnesses in the illuminations.

This tactic, it seems, would also be the most efficacious way of legitimizing the public voice of Birgitta. As a divinely chosen prophet speaking on behalf of God in a time of great instability and crisis (caused by the "Avignon Captivity" and the lax morals of priests, she argued), Birgitta conforms to the only exception allowed by theologians such as Henry of Ghent to the injunction against women instructing men.[33] Additionally, the use of the evangelist iconography for Birgitta in the frontispiece makes a subtle and yet quite explicit statement regarding her authorial role. She is not simply a vessel chosen by God; her role in relation to her writings, and indeed the status of text itself, is as *auctor*, just like the "originating texts" (*originales libri*), as Jerome termed the Scriptures, which implies that the *Revelations* belong at the very inception of literary authority (*auctoritas*).[34] In other words, the visionary conforms to the most authoritative category within the medieval discourse on authorship, and consequently she, and more importantly her text, is "worthy of faith and obedience."[35] The argument negates Birgitta's authorship in modern usage, i.e. as the creative individual behind the *Revelations*, but in its historical context, where *auctor/auctoritas* was traditionally characterized by divine origin and/or historical remoteness, it accords her the highest standing possible.

The third full-page illumination in the program, found in the same manuscript (Figure 1.3, see Chapter 1), is on the verso side, facing the opening of *Epistola solitarii ad reges*, Alfonso's treatise on the authenticity of Birgitta's visions that serves as the prologue to his compilation of her visions on secular rule, called *Liber celestis imperatoris ad reges* (Book VIII). This, too, can be seen as an author portrait whose iconography illustrates the title of the work by displaying its celestial sender and the royal recipients. However, it is also a depiction of the publication of the *Revelations*. As in the first miniature, this image is divided horizontally into several registers. In the uppermost tier, Christ and the Virgin are placed in the middle of the blue, star-spangled heavenly sphere, where they are flanked by groups of haloed saints that appear as witnesses. With his right hand, Christ extends a book to Birgitta, placed on the left side in the tier below. On the central vertical axis, directly below the heavenly couple, are two kneeling men, identifiable by their robes as Alfonso and Prior Peter Olofsson, one of Birgitta's two Swedish confessors. They are about to receive a book from Birgitta's right hand, identical to the one she accepts from Christ with her left. Behind the two men, on the opposite side of the register, is a writing desk. In the section below is a row of alternating seated kings and queens, and among these, placed on the central vertical axis, is a king on an elaborate throne. Kneeling at his feet are Birgitta's two collaborators, shown for the second time; they present the king with the book displayed twice above. In the lowest corners of the folio are two groups of figures beholding the presentation scene; those on the left side are dressed in various secular attire implying different stations, and those on the right in clerical and religious garments of various orders and ranks.

The illumination communicates three significant points. First, it again emphasizes the heavenly origin and thus the authority of the *Revelations,* here symbolized by the codex given by Christ to Birgitta. Second, it shows the universal validity of the book, illustrated by the figures of all social classes in the lowest register, and, not least, the acceptance and authorization of the work by the secular ruler receiving it. Third, it demonstrates the relationship between Birgitta and her collaborators, and, significantly, their role in the publication process. The placement of the men between Birgitta and the writing desk underlines their important functions in the recording, translation, and compilation of the work, and the publication illustrated by both the desk, where the written word is produced, and by the presentation scene below, where it is made public. Birgitta is thus literally pushed out of the center and seemingly marginalized in the composition of the miniature. It is the confessors who take pride of place on the central vertical axis between the sender and receiver of the revelations. Indeed, the heavenly couple point down at the two men while they look towards Birgitta in the act of receiving the revelations, thus making manifest that their role in the publication is performed on divine command.

The motif of Birgitta simultaneously receiving and presenting the revelations in the form of a book to her confessors creates the impression of her as a vessel rather than an agent, and suggests that she does not profess to grasp the significance of the message, but immediately confesses, so to speak, the mystery to her spiritual supervisors (a point they also render explicit in the *Vita*). The image thereby seems to counter the powerful assertion of Birgitta's *auctoritas* on the frontispiece to the codex, and instead elevates the roles of her male collaborators. Yet this is only one reading of the image. For at the same time the illumination clearly displays Birgitta as the only figure in the earthly realm in contact with the heavenly one: not her confessors, and certainly not the bishop and friars or any other figure in the illumination who represents the Church, who occupy the place in the folio that is farthest away from Christ. The key to the rhetorical strategies employed in the illuminations program of the *Revelations* thus appears to be the ambivalence of the visual medium; Birgitta is cast as the evangelical *auctor* of a text whose status is equal to Scripture. At the same time, she is a humble vessel, submitting herself to the control and supervision of her confessors, who act as intermediaries in the publishing process, thereby absolving Birgitta from "illegal" public preaching.

Comparing the latter miniature with the frontispiece, it is curious that whereas the first author portrait visualizes an elevation of Birgitta's status to that of biblical *auctor*, this illumination seems to take a quite surprising approach to the notion of authorship considered in its medieval context. Here, Birgitta is removed from the focal point, both in terms of axial composition and perspective. Instead, clearly foregrounded are the two men, who, within the traditional medieval discourse on authorship, serve far less distinguished roles in the production of the text, that of *scriptor* (Prior Peter, who records and translates the revelations) and *compilator* and *commentator* (Alfonso, who compiles the texts into manuscripts and writes commentaries in the form of his prologues).[36] Not only do they occupy the center of the image, but they are presented to the reader, and thus accentuated, by means of the gestures of Christ and the Virgin. This may be a device to subvert the implication that Birgitta is an agent of public instruction. Yet, when we acknowledge that here, the *scriptor*, *compilator*, and *commentator* take an equally (if not even more) important position as the *auctor*, the miniature becomes a most interesting document, bearing testimony to the transformation that the discourse on *auctoritas* was undergoing during this particular period.[37]

The novel image of the writing Birgitta became a fixed motif in later illuminated copies of the *Revelations*.[38] The Sienese codex with the Italian translation of the *Revelations*, commissioned by Catherine's disciple Cristoforo, also contains a portrait of Birgitta with a pen in her hand.[39] On fol. 11v (I.V.25.), approximately two-thirds of the folio is taken up by a framed rectangle containing an image of the visionary seated at a desk at work over a codex (Figure 6.1). With the necessary tools for writing in her hands, she gazes up towards a miniature representation of Christ, in half-length, held up by a host of seraphs. The large figure of the writer has a round halo around her head, visually emphasizing her canonization by the time of the image's production.

Figure 6.1 Author portrait of Birgitta of Sweden writing down her revelations. Siena, Biblioteca comunale degli Intronati, I.V.25, fol. 11v. Date: 1399. Photo: Biblioteca comunale degli Intronati.

Conspicuous in this transformed version of the author-cum-scribe portrait compared with the original in the Neapolitan codex is the removal of all witnesses, combined with the evident focus on the prominent figure of the author, whose importance in the image is increased at the expense of the divine source of inspiration, here reduced considerably in size. In the New York frontispiece, although the perspective is from Birgitta's angle, the celestial sphere takes up the bulk of the folio. Here, the scribe at work is manifestly the principal motif. The display of the pen and knife in Birgitta's hands, together with ink spilled over the desk, further emphasizes human labor and the practical conditions related to the production of the physical text. In other words, although clearly based on the Neapolitan model, the Sienese author portrait seems to attribute even more value to the saint's active involvement in the production of the work. As such, the Sienese Birgitta calls to mind the contemporary evangelist portraits that Laura Kendrick has identified as visual expressions of what was a new approach in scholastic exegesis regarding the role of the human authors of Scripture.[40] As argued famously by Alastair Minnis, in university circles in the thirteenth and fourteenth centuries, there was a great interest in the individual intentions of the human writers of the scriptural texts, believed to be expressed in the literal sense (*sensus literalis*) of the Bible.[41] This perspective on the function of God's "human pens" offered a solution to the problem of concordance between the various biblical books, notably the Gospels, and implied an acknowledgment of the cooperation between the individual writer and divine will. Kendrick has drawn a connection between what she perceives to be not only a renewed interest in the evangelist author portrait in this very period but also the particular emphasis on the manual labor in these illuminations and the contemporary scholastic approach to the intentions of the human authors of the Bible.[42] It is tempting to see the similar highlighting of Birgitta's labors as a scribe in the Siena codex as another example of this particular attitude to the biblical *auctores*. Indeed, the very concept of Birgitta, a contemporary woman, writing Scripture bears testimony to this transformed understanding of the associations between divine and human authorship and thus also of literary *auctoritas*.[43]

As noted above, the Sienese Birgitta manuscript plays an important role in the context of this study as it manifests knowledge among the followers of Catherine of the specific visual and textual strategies used to legitimize the public voice of the Swedish saint. Moreover, the author portrait in Cristoforo's codex has been attributed to various artists who were crucial in the promotion of the cult of Catherine.[44] Nevertheless— and despite the proclamation of Birgitta's sanctity a few years before, which suggests that she could make an excellent model for Catherine's author portrait—when Caffarini initiated his broad publication enterprise around 1400, noted above, he chose a very different visual strategy for the author portrait of Catherine.

The Saintly *doctrix*

Just as with the Birgittine manuscripts from Naples, the illuminations in the codices made in Caffarini's Venetian scriptorium approximately one generation later display a distinct iconography developed for the saintly image of Catherine.[45] According to Lidia Bianchi and Diega Giunta, this visual formula aims to show Catherine not only as a saint but also as a teacher. The attributes and gestures are taken from the medieval iconographical tradition pertaining to the Doctors of the Church.[46] An example of the Caffarinian iconography is found in a historiated initial (Figure 6.2) introducing the second prologue of Raymond of Capua's *Legenda maior*, which in this particular manuscript (Siena, BCI, T.II.4, fol. 5v) serves as an opening to Cristoforo's Latin translation of Catherine's *Dialogue*. The initial offers a frontal image of the author with a polygonal halo that appears ambiguous compared with the "proper" rayed halo of the *beata*, as exemplified by the Neapolitan miniature of Birgitta. Catherine's is more suggestive of the round shape of a saint's halo, though its vague angles keep it from appearing as such.[47] Catherine wears a tunic and veil in white with a black "mantello," the colors of which also reflect the distinct black-and-white Dominican habit.[48] In her hands, she holds the attributes of a book, a white lily, and a crucifix, all of which become part and parcel of the Caffarinian iconography. According to Bianchi and Giunta, these attributes are not only indicative of teaching and preaching, but they also give Catherine a noticeable Dominican appearance. Turning to the next, and arguably more obvious, author portrait of Catherine in the same codex containing her *Dialogue*, I would like to elaborate further on the significance and extent of this Dominican "doctrinal" quality and how it helps to visually substantiate Catherine's authority and sanctity.

Although there are no depictions of Catherine with a pen in her hand in the Venetian manuscripts, the scriptorium did produce a distinct author portrait of Catherine in the act of composing. An example is found in the form of the historiated initial that opens her text on fol. 6v (Figure 6.3) in the same manuscript as the previous initial. The author is here dressed as a *mantellata* in accordance with the description above and equipped with the same ambivalent halo as in the preceding illumination. She stands with her arms folded across her chest in the pose of humility while gazing up towards the half-length figure of Christ that appears in the upper right corner of the letter. Beneath the Savior, two men dressed in secular attire are seated and engaged in the act of writing on scrolls. Both hold a pen in their right hand and an inkhorn in the left.

The iconography of the initial reflects the circumstances of the production of the *Dialogue,* which, according to numerous testimonies, was dictated by Catherine while she was absorbed in ecstasy and under divine inspiration.[49] That she is not holding the pen in this image does not make it any less of an author portrait. As noted above, dictation was perhaps the most common method of authoring, as there would often be a scribe performing the task of writing down the composition. Indeed, there is an established tradition for portraying *auctores* dictating to their scribes in the presence of a symbol of divine inspiration. Two classic examples are St. John, who, in traditional Byzantine iconography,

Figure 6.2 Catherine of Siena (historiated initial opening Raymond of Capua's prologue to *Liber divine doctrine*). Siena, Biblioteca comunale degli Intronati, T.II.4, fol. 5v. Date: first quarter of fifteenth century. Photo: Biblioteca comunale degli Intronati.

pro salute aīaꝛ. quē libꝛ ipa existente a sensibꝰ rapta ita q̄ solitꝛ ꝗ g̃. est usus loꝗ̃di relictus sins stᵽtoribꝰ ī suo uulgari natino ipo dō eidē ugini īspirate atꝗ ruelante dictauit. Et h̄ t̄ c̄ āños dn̄i · 1377 ·

tē maxio desideꝛio anxia ꝑ longi aliꝰ tꝑis spaciuꝛ ī habitaiata ꝰ tute solliate se exꝰens ꝛ gmorata ī cella coḡcois siu ipius ut bōitate dī melꝰ coḡnostert ī se ipa qm̄ post

Figure 6.3 Catherine of Siena dictating to scribes (historiated initial opening *Liber divine doctrine*). Siena, Biblioteca comunale degli Intronati, T.II.4, fol. 6v. Date: first quarter of fifteenth century. Photo: Biblioteca comunale degli Intronati.

dictates *Revelation* to his scribe Prochorus while gazing at a symbol of divine inspiration, and Gregory the Great, who, from Carolingian times and onwards is often shown dictating to his scribe in the presence of the white dove of the Holy Spirit. In the particular case of Catherine, however, I would like to suggest that the model, and the intended *auctor* with which the viewer/reader is invited to align her, is the Dominican saint and doctor Thomas Aquinas.

In addition to casting Catherine as a divinely inspired author dictating to her scribe in the same fashion as the Evangelist and the Church Father, this visual formula evokes a number of her "authorly" miracles described both by Raymond and Caffarini, which correspond to those of Thomas. One of these, clearly alluded to in this initial, was Catherine's ability to dictate to several scribes at the same time. The miracle is described, for instance, in the prologue to Raymond's *Legenda*, part of which in the present manuscript also appears as an introduction to the *Dialogue*, in other words, appearing just before this initial. In the text, the confessor expresses his astonishment that Catherine can dictate simultaneously to two secretaries on different topics in letters addressed to different people.[50] He then goes on to note in amazement that other followers had seen her dictate to three and four scribes at the same time, and, moreover, that "she dictated quickly without even short pauses to think, as if she were reading whatever she was saying from some book placed before her."[51] There are, to my knowledge, no parallels to dictation-miracles of this kind in the *vitae* of other holy women or female mystics associated with the production of texts. However, the legends pertaining to one of the principal saints of the Dominican Order—and one with whom Raymond, Caffarini, as well as Catherine herself, sought to associate her—that is, Thomas Aquinas, is replete with references to such miracles. Examples can be taken from Bernard Gui's *vita* from the mid-1320s, in which he refers to the testimony of several of Thomas's pupils, where it was claimed that Thomas could dictate to many of them at the same time on different topics, and that, on other occasions, his dictation—similar to that of Catherine's in Raymond's words quoted above—was so clear and swift, as if he was reading from a book.[52]

Raymond's prologue and the author portrait that opens the text in the *Dialogue* manuscript—in which she appears in the unmistakable colors of the Dominican habit, performing the same miracles as Thomas—invites the viewer/reader to associate Catherine directly with the saintly doctor, and also to connect the authority of her teaching, laid out in the text introduced by the illumination, to that of the "Saint Doctor," as Thomas is typically referred to by Caffarini.[53]

The presence of the symbol of divine inspiration in Catherine's author portrait and her apparent state of spiritual ecstasy when dictating can also be understood to link her to Thomas. We should not forget that in his canonization process, the "Saint Doctor's" knowledge was attributed to God—as supreme *auctoritas* certainly would be—and was his primary saintly attribute. Consequently, the hagiographical image of him often emphasizes his spiritual ecstasies and celestial communications when he is composing, traits that are not the prerogative of female "illiterate" mystics. For while Catherine is at times portrayed as such a mystic, most notably by Raymond, she is also presented as a *doctrix*. Indeed, in Caffarini's words, Catherine "advanced so much with regard to knowledge of divine matters that she could discuss questions of divine relations acquired or attributed, be it in speech or in writing or in prayer, as if she had studied at a university."[54] He then adds that this was evident from Catherine's discussions not only with her confessor Raymond, who, as Caffarini takes care to stress, was a professor of sacred theology, but also with Tommaso da Venezia, a doctor of canon law, who is said to have learned more from his conversations with her than from his university studies.[55] It seems thus that Catherine is not necessarily represented as the converse to the intellectual institutions from which her sex barred her; on the contrary, she frequently emerges as a doctor according to the very definition of those institutions. But, as a woman and thereby naturally excluded from theological studies at the university, Catherine's authority as a teacher is presented by way of her association with St. Thomas, saint and doctor.

Returning to the author portrait of the dictating Catherine, I would like to argue that this image, too, like that of Birgitta, employs the ambiguity of the visual medium as its primary strategy for establishing Catherine's sanctity and the authority of her teachings while also seeking to avoid potential criticism of the female public voice. On the one hand, in the initial, the *mantellata*, like the Swedish visionary, seems to be a vessel: someone who receives the word of God, by *His* choice, and immediately relates/confesses it to someone else. Furthermore, the presence of the scribes in Catherine's portrait makes it clear that she is not the publisher of her—or, rather, Christ's—teachings; instead, the men in the image are. On the other hand, taking her particular supernatural methods of composition into consideration, as well as Catherine's distinct habit—and remembering Caffarini's desire to promote her as a *Dominican* saint—the ecstatic and miraculous dictation under heavenly inspiration suggests that Catherine is a saintly doctor equal to Thomas. This is an association that perhaps would not have been so strange for the Catherine we encounter in her *Letters*. Here, in the epistle that is generally perceived to mark the beginning of her work on the *Dialogue*, she attributes the inspiration for her "aptitude for writing" to St. Thomas and to St. John. Interestingly, the manner in which Catherine refers to the teaching role of the two saints is not so different from how Thomas, in the *vita* of Bernard Gui, receives assistance from saints Peter and Paul when he encounters an intellectual problem.[56]

Figure 6.4 Catherine of Siena offering her letters to cardinals. Siena, Biblioteca comunale degli Intronati, T.II.2, fol. 25v. Date: First quarter of fifteenth century. Photo: Biblioteca comunale degli Intronati.

The author portrait of Catherine dictating appears in other Caffarinian manuscripts, not only those containing the *Dialogue*, but also the *Letters*.[57] In another well-known copy of her epistles, a twin-codex from the same Venetian workshop—Siena, BCI, T.II.2/3—a different visual formula is utilized, one apparently unique to this manuscript.[58] Here, the letters are organized into two separate volumes. The first contains those sent to ecclesiastical and religious men and women, compiled into groups and placed hierarchically with letters to popes first and those addressed to religious women last. The second volume is organized according to the same hierarchical principle concerning rank and gender, but here are collected all the letters addressed to laypeople. Each group of epistles, in both volumes, is introduced by a colored pen drawing of the author and her addressees, placed inside a large rectangle that occupies about one-third of the folio. The drawing of fol. 25v of T.II.2 (Figure 6.4) serves to illustrate the formula. The miniature opens the section with epistles to cardinals, as rendered visible in the picture.

Catherine is shown frontally in half-length figure in the middle of the upper section. The author, always dressed as a *mantallata*, appears from a cloud, hovering in the air, while holding out in each of her hands three long scrolls. On the ground below are two groups of three men, all dressed as cardinals. They look up toward Catherine while reaching out for her scrolls. Interestingly, symbols of divine inspiration are entirely missing in this visual formula, which allows Catherine to appear as the sole author figure in the image. The same scheme is found throughout the illuminations in the codex, 19 in total, with variation in the number and the appearance of the recipients of Catherine's letters, as these are adjusted to illustrate the addressees described in the text.

The iconography of these miniatures, which should also be understood to belong to the genre of author portraits, evokes a tradition of representing St. Paul—the other authority to which both Raymond and Caffarini seek to compare Catherine.[59] Luba Eleen has studied the iconography of numerous author portraits in manuscripts containing the Pauline epistles, which emerge in the late twelfth and early thirteenth centuries, and she has shown that the apostle is typically represented writing on scrolls or offering these to the addressees. Furthermore, whether he is shown as a scribe, an attesting figure, or as the sender of letters, the visual formula typically includes no symbol of divine inspiration of the sort found in the evangelist portraits—just as in the images of Catherine.[60]

In the Pauline author portraits, the scroll is the principal symbol for the letter, as it is likewise in the Catherinian miniatures. Additionally, scrolls often indicate speech in medieval iconography.[61] This further explains the relationship between the depicted scroll and the signified letter, as this particular textual genre stands for the *speech* of its absent sender. With this in mind, Catherine, like Paul, appears in her author portrait as an absent sender whose speech is present in the form of her letters, thereby also making her present through them. This is visualized in the miniatures by the placement of Catherine's half-length figure in the sky, emerging from a cloud, while she holds out the material tokens of her voice in the form of the letters/scrolls. The association with the foremost letter writer in medieval texts, Paul—who is frequently also placed in a manner indicating presence and absence at the same time in relation to the recipients of his letters—emphasizes Catherine's role as apostle and also as one who *speaks*: her role of preacher. The visual impression of the latter is strengthened by the colors of Catherine's habit that intimately tie her to the Order of Preachers. Yet again, the gist of the visual rhetorical strategies at work in these miniatures is the inherent ambiguous properties of the medium. While the *mantellata* here proves to be a "Pauline" author of epistles, and a preacher whose sermons have universal validity, which is underlined by the great variety in the stations of the depicted addressees throughout the image cycle, her placement in the sky indicates a removal from the public context that Paul has banned her from.[62] Thus, Catherine appears as a preacher and apostle, whose voice is omnipresent to her recipients through her letters, which they visibly reach out for despite her physical absence; and yet, at the same time, she is absolved from any allegation of public preaching and instruction as she is, ostensibly, *not there.*

Conclusion

Although opting, in general, for different iconographical strategies in the illuminations, the Neapolitan and Venetian manuscripts containing the *Revelations*, the *Dialogue*, and the *Letters* utilize the equivocality of the visual medium to their advantage. In both the Birgittine and the Catherinian manuscripts produced a generation later, the iconography has the effect of simultaneously bolstering the authority of the female authors through association with accepted and universally revered models and visual prototypes recognizable to the original audience, while concurrently presenting the women as the instruments of God, acting through His will and not by their own agency. Certain concrete visual approaches are common to the author portraits of both: the inclusion of witnesses, earthly or heavenly, who serve to guarantee the veridicality of what is demonstrated in the images; the universal validity of the texts, made manifest through the presence of numerous recipients who, based on attire, represent a multitude of stations; and, finally, the indirectness of their words with respect to publishing.

In conclusion I would like to return to the question of why Caffarini chose not to render Catherine as a writer, when this particular faculty was of such importance in his hagiographical presentation of her. As is clear from the above discussion, we know that he could not have been ignorant of the visual strategy used to substantiate the authority of Birgitta's *Revelations*. To answer this question, I suggest that we look to the period and context in which Caffarini produced the manuscripts considered here, which was about two decades after Birgitta's canonization. According to Bianchi, these Caffarinian codices were made in direct response to the convocation of the Council of Constance in 1413—the very council where Jean Gerson proclaimed his famous attack on Birgitta's *Revelations* in 1415.[63] We can presume that voices expressing the same kind of criticism had been heard for some time.[64] Central to Gerson's attack was what he deemed to be a violation of the Pauline injunction against women's public teaching, and he was particularly concerned about women writing—something he opposed vehemently.[65] It is tempting to see Caffarini's choice to *not* portray Catherine in accordance with the most typical variant of author portraits as a conscious tactic to not assert her writerly agency too much, and certainly not indicate that she was an author of Scripture. In the case of Birgitta, by this time, her scribal portrait had spread all over Europe in various media and was now a pivotal feature of her saintly image—and arguably becoming problematic for it. From the very day of her canonization in 1391, the heavenly status of the *Revelations* and that of Birgitta as an evangelist, and thus an *auctor*, were under constant debate. At the next major church council, in Basel in 1436, a judgment was passed prohibiting the publication of the work as divinely inspired and equal to Scripture, thus also officially depriving Birgitta of her evangelical standing and her work of its scriptural *auctoritas*.[66]

The campaign for the promotion of Birgitta and her canonization was based on trial and error. There was no obvious model to follow, as the widowed laywoman Birgitta's primary claim to sanctity was encapsulated in a literary corpus containing a call for spiritual and political reform. In Catherine's case, her supporters could look to the campaign of Birgitta and, more importantly, its consequences, and adapt accordingly, as did the promoters of other holy women and visionaries coming after Birgitta.[67] The deliberations over the status of the *Revelations*, and thus implicitly over Birgitta's authorial role, continued for centuries, giving rise to a number of treatises arguing for and against their authority and scriptural validity.[68] Significantly, in the earliest printed editions of the work, from Lübeck (1492) and Nuremberg (1500), parts of a treatise by Cardinal Johannes Turrecremata defending the authenticity of Birgitta's *Revelations* is included together with Boniface IX's canonization bull of 1391 as well as Martin V's confirmation bull of 1419. Although the printed editions contain an elaborate set of illustrations, comprising initials and full-pages images just as in the first manuscripts produced under Alfonso of Jaén, the iconography is here significantly altered. In the Lübeck edition, commissioned by the Birgittine monastery in Vadstena, as well as in the Nuremberg edition whose illustrations are based on the former, the portrayal of Birgitta as an evangelist recording the *Revelations* has been replaced by presentation scenes (Birgitta offering a book to its addressees or to her confessor) and, more strikingly, by what may best be described as dictation scenes. Now, Birgitta is shown with her hands folded in prayer in front of an open book while her pen has been given to one of her confessors.

Notes

1 Emil Friedberg (ed.), *Corpus Juris Canonici* (Leipzig: 1879–81, reprint Graz, 1955), 1: col. 86. The highly influential theologian Jean Gerson, makes it explicitly clear that he sees women's voices in published writings as equal to their prohibited oral instruction in public. See Jean Gerson, "De examinatione doctrinarum," in *Oeuvres completes*, ed. Polémon Glorieux, 9: 467: "sexus muliebris ab apostolica prohibetur auctoritate ne palam doceat; doctrinam intellige, seu verbo seu scripto, nomine suo publicatam, maxime si fuerit ad viros...." ("the female sex is by apostolic authority forbidden to teach in public; that is, teaching, either in words or in writing, which is published in her name, even more so if it is directed at men ...."). All translations are my own unless otherwise noted. The research for this chapter was generously supported by a grant from Stiftelsen Gihls Fond (The Royal Swedish Academy of Letters, History and Antiquities), Sven och Dagmar Saléns Stiftelse, the Research Council of Norway, and the European Research Council (European Union's Seventh Framework Programme for research, technological development and demonstration under Marie Curie grant agreement no

608695). I would like to express my gratitude to Unn Falkeid, F. Thomas Luongo, Stefano Fogelberg Rota, and Kathryn Boyer for their invaluable readings of and assistance with the text.

2 On medieval attitudes towards women's religious instruction, see Alastair Minnis, "Religious Roles: Public and Private" and John Coakley, "Women's Textual Authority and the Collaboration of Clerics," both in *Medieval Holy Women in the Christian Tradition, c.1100–c.1500*, eds. Alastair Minnis and Rosalynn Voaden (Turnhout: Brepols, 2010); Dyan Elliott, "*Dominae* or *Dominatae?* Female Mysticism and the Trauma of Textuality," in *Women, Marriage, and Family in Medieval Christendom: Essays in Memory of Michael M. Sheehan, C.S.B.*, eds. Constance M. Rousseau and Joel T. Rosenthal (Kalamazoo: Medieval Institute Publications, 1998).

3 See also Joan Isobel Friedman, "Politics and the Rhetoric of Reform in the Letters of Saints Bridget of Sweden and Catherine of Siena," in *Livres et lectures de femmes en Europe entre Moyen Âge et Renaissance*, ed. Anne-Marie Legaré (Turnhout: Brepols, 2007).

4 On this subject, see also Silvia Nocentini's Chapter 5 in this volume.

5 On the editor's divine mission, see AP, 98; Rev. II: 31; Extrav., 49. For Alfonso, see further Chapters 1, 5, and 9 in the present volume.

6 For Alfonso's editions, see the editor's introduction by Carl-Gustaf Undhagen in Rev. I, and by Hans Aili in Rev. VIII.

7 On Alfonso and the Neapolitan scriptorium, see Anette Creutzburg, *Die heilige Birgitta von Schweden. Bildliche Darstellungen und theologische Kontroversen im Vorfeld ihrer Kanonisation (1373–1391)* (Kiel: Verlag Ludwig, 2011); F. Thomas Luongo, "Inspiration and Imagination: Visionary Authorship in the Early Manuscripts of the Revelations of Birgitta of Sweden," *Speculum* 93 (2018): 1102–50.

8 Other disciples of Catherine, such as Neri di Landoccio Pagliaresi and Stefano Maconi, also collected and copied her writings from early on; see Suzanne Noffke, "The Writings of Catherine of Siena: The Manuscript Tradition," in *A Companion to Catherine of Siena*, eds. Carolyn Muessig, George Ferzoco, and Beverly Mayne Kienzle (Leiden: Brill, 2012). The majority of the oldest extant codices are from Caffarini's scriptorium.

9 On the scriptorium, see E. Messerini, "Lo *scriptorium* di Fra Tommaso Caffarini," *S. Caterina da Siena* 19 no. 1 (1968): 15–21; Silvia Nocentini, "Lo 'scriptorium' di Tommaso Caffarini a Venezia," *Hagiographica* XII (2005): 79–144.

10 Their advocacy of the two authors should also been seen in connection to their involvement in the Observant Reform movement, as discussed by Silvia Nocentini and Camille Rouxpetel in the present volume.

11 More on this in Mary Carruthers, *The Book of Memory: A Study of Memory in Medieval Culture*, 2nd edn. (Cambridge: Cambridge University Press, 2008), esp. ch. 7.

12 For their discussions of the MSS, see Alfonso's letter to the archbishop in Uppsala, Sweden, on 15 January 1378 (SDHK 11166 in the database of the National Archives in Sweden: https://sok.riksarkivet.se/sdhk); and Caffarini's statements in PC, *passim*. On the early manuscript reception of Catherine's works, see F. Thomas Luongo, "Saintly Authorship in the Italian Renaissance: The Quattrocento Reception of Catherine of Siena's Letters," in *Catherine of Siena: The Creation of a Cult*, eds. Jeffrey F. Hamburger and Gabriela Signori (Turnhout: Brepols, 2013).

13 On this, see also F. Thomas Luongo's Chapter 1 in this volume.

14 See, for instance, Carruthers, *The Book of Memory*. On the gradual changes in literary composition and manuscript culture in the late medieval period, see Daniel Hobbins, *Authorship and Publicity Before Print: Jean Gerson*

and the Transformation of Late Medieval Learning (Philadelphia: University of Pennsylvania Press, 2009).

15 On author portraits, see Laura Kendrick, *Animating the Letter: The Figurative Embodiment of Writing from Late Antiquity to the Renaissance* (Columbus: Ohio State University Press, 1999), Ch. 6; Giovanna Lazzi and Paolo Vitti (eds.), *Immaginare l'autore. Il ritratto del letterato nella cultura umanistica* (Florence: Polistampa, 2000); Eric Palazzo, "Le portrait d'auteur dans les manuscrits du Moyen Âge," in *Portraits d'écrivains. La représentation de l'auteur dans les manuscrits et les imprimés du Moyen Âge et de la première Renaissance* (Paris: Fédération française pour la coopération des bibliothèques, des métiers du livre et de la documentation, 2002).

16 Lesley Smith, "*Scriba, Femina*: Medieval Depictions of Women Writing," in *Women and the Book: Assessing the Visual Evidence*, eds. Lesley Smith and Jane H.M. Taylor (London and Toronto: The British Library and University of Toronto Press, 1996). See also Katrin Graf, *Bildnisse schreibender Frauen im Mittelalter, 9. bis Anfang 13. Jahrhundert* (Basel: Schwabe, 2002).

17 Maria H. Oen, "The Iconography of *Liber celestis revelacionum*," in *A Companion to Birgitta of Sweden and Her Legacy in the Later Middle Ages*, ed. Maria H. Oen (Leiden: Brill, 2019).

18 Two manuscripts from the late twelfth and the early thirteenth centuries, which contain Hildegard's *Scivias* (Wiesbaden, Hessische Landesbibliothek, Cod. 1, only preserved in facsimile) and *Liber divinorum operum* (Lucca, Biblioteca statale, 1942), respectively, show the author in the act of recording a text on a wax tablet while she is receiving a vision. On Hildegard's author portrait, see Katrin Graf, "Les portraits d'auteur de Hildegarde de Bingen," *Scriptorium 55*, no. 2 (2001): 179–96.

19 On this, see, for instance, Elliott, "*Dominae* or *Dominatae?*"; Jane Tylus, "Mystical Literacy: Writing and Religious Women in Late Medieval Italy," in Muessig, Ferzoco, and Kienzle, *A Companion to Catherine of Siena*; Jennifer Summit, "Women and Authorship," in *The Cambridge Companion to Medieval Women's Writing*, eds. Carolyn Dinshaw and David Wallace (Cambridge: Cambridge University Press, 2003), espeically 97.

20 See PC, especially 93–94; 96–97; 142–43.

21 Siena, BCI, I.V.25/26; Domenico Pezzini, "Il primo volgarizzamento italiano delle Rivelazioni e degli altri scritti di S. Brigida: Il codice I.V.25/26 della Biblioteca degli Intronati di Siena (1399)," in *Santa Brigida, Napoli, L'Italia*, eds. Olle Ferm, Alessandra Perriccioli Saggese, and Marcello Rotili (Naples: Arte tipografica, 2009). For a further discussion of Cristoforo and his contribution to the circulation of the Catherinian and Birgittine texts, see Nocentini's Chapter 5 in the present volume.

22 PC, 41, 54, and 73.

23 See Letter T373: "vi prego che el Libro e ogni scrittura la quale trovaste di me, voi ... ve le rechiate per le mani; e fatene quello che vedete che sia più onore di Dio." On Catherine as a writer, see Jane Tylus, *Reclaiming Catherine of Siena: Literacy, Literature, and the Signs of Others* (Chicago, IL: The University of Chicago Press, 2009).

24 Letter T272. The letter is quoted and discussed by Luongo in Chapter 1 in the present volume. For a discussion of the statement and a survey of the various attitudes concerning its authenticity and implications, see Catherine Mooney, "Wondrous Words: Catherine of Siena's Miraculous Reading and Writing According to the Early Sources," in Hamburger and Signori, *Catherine of Siena*.

25 There are, however, explicit reflections in the text concerning what it means to write down divine revelations, on this, see Luongo, "Inspiration and Imagination."

26 AP, 84.

27 The disaccord between Raymond and Caffarini is summed up in Jane Tylus, "Writing versus Voice: Tommaso Caffarini and the Production of a Literate Catherine," in Hamburger and Signori, *Catherine of Siena*; "Mystical Literacy"; *Reclaiming Catherine of Siena*. On writing and authorship, see also Luongo's Chapter 1 in the present volume.

28 He frequently returns to this subject in all of his writings on her. For a presentation of Catherine's writing miracles, see Caffarini's *Libellus de supplemento legende prolixe virginis beate Catherine de Senis*, eds. Giuliana Cavallini and Imelda Foralosso (Rome: Edizioni Cateriniane, 1974), *pars prima*; PC, 62–63. Silvia Nocentini has also shown that Caffarini actually "emends" Raymond's *Legenda* by adding information on her writing ability in the MSS from his scriptorium; see Nocentini, "Lo 'scriptorium'."

29 The oldest MSS are: Warszawa, Biblioteka Narodowa, 3310; Palermo, Biblioteca Centrale della Regione Siciliana, IV.G.2; New York, Pierpont Morgan Library, M. 498. The coherent program was first identified by Carl Nordenfalk, "Saint Bridget of Sweden as Represented in Illuminated Manuscripts," in *De Artibus Opuscula XL. Essays in Honor of Erwin Panofsky*, ed. Millard Meiss (New York: New York University Press, 1961). For thorough treatments of the manuscripts with further bibliographical references regarding the scriptorium and the artists, see Hans Aili and Jan Svanberg, *Imagines Sanctae Birgittae: The Earliest Illuminated Manuscripts and Panel Paintings Related to the Revelations of St. Birgitta of Sweden*, 2 vols (Stockholm: The Royal Swedish Academy of Letters, History and Antiquities, 2003); Creutzburg, *Die heilige Birgitta von Schweden*. The complete cycle of images is also found in a later manuscript ascribed to the same workhop: Torino, Biblioteca Nazionale Universitaria, I.III.23 (early 15th c.), and in two codices of Northern European origin: Berlin, Staatsbibliothek zu Berlin. Preußischer Kulturbesitz, theol.lat.fol. 33 (mid-15th c.) and Stockholm, Kungliga biblioteket, A 70 b (first half of 15th c.). Excerpts of the iconographical program are found in numerous copies from different social, geographical, and linguistic contexts, see Oen, "The Iconography."

30 Sara Ekwall, "Ett ikonografiskt Birgittaproblem: Har förebilden till den skrivande Birgitta i Vadstena varit den skrivande evangelisten?," *Konsthistorisk Tidskrift* 37, no. 1 (1968): 1–20; Anette Creutzburg, "Darstellungen von göttlicher Inspiration in der Neapeler Buchmalerei. Zur Visualisierung von *auctoritas* in der Autorenbildern der hl. Birgitta von Schweden," in *Buchschätze des Mittelalters. Forschungsrückblicke – Forschungsperspektiven*, eds. Klaus Gereon Beuckers, Christoph Jobst, and Stefanie Westphal (Regensburg: Schnell & Steiner, 2011).

31 For the evangelist portraits, including numerous reproductions, see A. M. Friend, "The Portraits of the Evangelists in Greek and Latin Manuscripts. Part 1," *Art Studies* 5 (1927); "The Portraits of the Evangelists in Greek and Latin Manuscripts. Part 2," *Art Studies* 7 (1929); Carl Nordenfalk, "Der Inspirierte Evangelist," *Wiener Jahrbuch für Kunstgeschichte* 36 (1983).

32 AP, 86.

33 See Minnis, "Religious Roles."

34 Carruthers, *The Book of Memory*, 236.

35 Albert Russel Ascoli, *Dante and the Making of a Modern Author* (Cambridge: Cambridge University Press, 2008), 5. For an introduction to the medieval concept of *auctor/auctoritas*, see Ascoli's Introduction and Ch. 2. See also Marie-Dominique Chenu, "Auctor, Actor, Autor," *Bulletin du Cange: Archivium Latinitas Medii Aevi* 3 (1927); Alastair Minnis, *Medieval Theory of Authorship: Scholastic Literary Attitudes in the Later Middle Ages*, 2nd edn. (Philadelphia: University of Pennsylvania Press, 2009).

36 On the roles of the scribe, compiler, and commentator in relation to the *auctor*, see Ascoli, *Dante*, 81.

37 As such, the *Revelations* and the construction of Birgitta's authorial role merits a further study in comparison with other "modern authors" who contribute to the transformation of the concepts of *auctor/auctoritas* in the later Middle Ages such as Birgitta's contemporary Petrarch, and Dante, who, like the Swedish saint, is presented as a visionary in his *Divine Comedy*. For Dante and the transformation of the role of the *auctor*, see Ascoli, *Dante*. For a further discussion of the roles of Birgitta's confessors, especially Alfonso of Jaén, as well as her own role, in the communication of the words of God, see Luongo's Chapter 1 in the present volume.

38 Oen, "The Iconography."

39 Siena, BCI, I.V.25/26.

40 Kendrick, *Animating the Letter*, 192.

41 Minnis, *Medieval Theory of Authorship*.

42 Kendrick, *Animating the Letter*, 192.

43 See Luongo, "Inspiration and Imagination."

44 The illumination has been attributed to Catherine's friend, Andrea Vanni, see Grazia Vailati Schonenburg Waldenburg, "Le Rivelazioni di Santa Brigida MS. I V 25/26 della Biblioteca Comunale di Siena," in *La miniatura italiana in età romanica e gotica*, ed. Grazia Vailati Schonenburg Waldenburg (Florence: Olschki, 1979), 553–74; to Andrea di Bartolo who also worked for Caffarini in Venice, see Giulietta Chelazzi Dini, in *Il gotico a Siena* (Florence: Centro Di, 1982), 317–18; and to the anonymous Sienese artist "Maestro delle Rivelazioni di Santa Brigida di Siena," see Gaudenz Freuler, "La miniatura senese degli anni 1370–1420," in *La miniatura senese 1270–1420*, ed. Cristina De Benedictis (Milan: Skira, 2002), 179–80.

45 The artists behind the Caffarinian illuminations remain anonymous. All that can be maintained is that there are several hands involved in the making of the illuminations; see Lidia Bianchi, "Il carattere dottrinale della santità di Caterina da Siena nella iconografia del primo Quattrocento," in *Atti del Congresso Internazionale di Studi Cateriniani Siena–Roma 24–29 aprile 1980* (Rome: Curia Generalizia O.P., 1981), 570–79. Carl Huter attributes certain illuminations to Cristoforo Cortese and claims that he was the "official illuminator." See "Cristoforo Cortese in the Bodleian Library," *Apollo* January (1980): 10–17, at 13, n. 32. See also Silvia Fumian, "Cristoforo Cortese e i Domenicani a Venezia: di alcuni manoscritti Cateriniani," in *Le arti a confronto con il sacro. Metodi di ricerca e nuove prospettive di indagine interdisciplinare*, eds. Valentina Cantone and Silvia Fumian (Padua: CLEUP, 2009).

46 Lidia Bianchi and Diega Giunta, eds., *Iconografia di S. Caterina da Siena. 1. L'Immagine* (Rome: Città Nuova Editrice, 1988), 76–88; Diega Giunta, "Gli attributi del Dottorato nella iconografia cateriniana," *Rivista dell'istituto nazionale d'archeologia e storia dell'arte* 6–7 (1983/84); Bianchi, "Il carattere dottrinale"; "Caterina da Siena," in *Enciclopedia dell'arte medievale*, ed. Angiola Maria Romanini (Rome: Istituto della Enciclopedia Italiana, 1991–2002), 4: 488–90.

47 On the particular halo in the Caffarinian iconography, see Fabio Bisogni's, "Raggi e aureole ossia la distinzione della santità" and "Il 'Libellus' di Tommaso d'Antonio Caffarini e gli inizi dell'iconografia di Caterina," both in *Con l'occhio e col lume*, eds. Luigi Trenti and Bente Klange Addabbo (Siena: Cantagalli, 1999), 255–56 and respectively 267.

48 Initials with the same iconography can be found in other Caffarinian MSS, such as Siena, BCI, T.I.2, fol. 4v; and Siena, BCI, T.I.1., fol. 1v (here also with a white dove over her head); Venezia, Biblioteca Nazionale Marciana, 2977, fol. 2.

49 LM, I. 1. prol.21, p. 120; PC, 51.
50 LM, I. 1. prol.21, p. 120. See also PC, 51.
51 LM, I. 1. prol.20, p. 120: "... dictabat velociter absque cogitationis etiam modico intervallo ac si legeret in aliquo libro ante se posito quicquid dicebat."
52 Bernard Gui, "Vita S. Thomae Aquinatis" in *Fontes Vitae S. Thomae Aquinatis notis historicis et criticis illustrati,* eds. Dominicus Prümmer and M. H. Laurent (Toulouse: 1911–34), 161–263, at 184–85.
53 PC, *passim.* It can also be noted that while the book is his primary attribute, in the iconography from this period Thomas Aquinas is never portrayed with a pen in his hand. I would like to thank F. Thomas Luongo for drawing my attention to this fact.
54 PC, 118: "In tantum etiam erga notitiam de divinis profecit ut ita de divinis relationibus appropriates vel attributis sive loquendo sive scribendo sive orando ita dissereret ac si in aliquius universitatis studio processisset."
55 PC, 118.
56 Letter T272. For Thomas, see Bernard Giu, "Vita S. Thomae," Ch. 16. On Catherine and Thomas Aquinas, see also Constant J. Mews, "Thomas Aquinas and Catherine of Siena: Emotion, Devotion and Mendicant Spiritualities in the Late Fourteenth Century," *Digital Philology: A Journal of Medieval Cultures* 1, no. 2 (2012): 235–52.
57 Città del Vaticano, BAV, Barb. Lat. 4063, fol. 6r has the dictating author portrait opening the text of the *Dialogue*. Here, there are three scribes taking dictation. There is also another *mantellata* seated at Catherine's feet who holds a codex but not a pen, unlike the three others. There is also a dictating portrait in Modena, Archivio della Cattedrale, MS Confraternità Annunziata, fol. 1r (containing the *Letters*). Also here there is another *mantellata* present, who unlike the three scribes does not write.
58 For a discussion with reproductions of all the miniatures, see Bisogni, "Il 'Libellus'."
59 Paul is frequently evoked in connection to Catherine by Raymond in LM and by Caffarini in PC.
60 See Luba Eleen, *The Illustration of the Pauline Epistles in French and English Bibles of the Twelfth and Thirteenth Centuries* (Oxford: Clarendon Press, 1982), with numerous reproductions from MSS.
61 An illustrating example is found in the Birgittine codex, Warszawa, Biblioteka Narodowa, 3310, fol. 224v.
62 1 Cor. 14:34–35; 1 Tim. 2:12.
63 For a discussion of Jean Gerson's attack on Birgitta with further bibliographical references, see Anna Fredriksson, "The Council of Constance, Jean Gerson, and St. Birgitta's *Revelaciones,*" *Mediaeval Studies* 76 (2014): 217–39. In this connection it should also be noted that Gerson was an extremely influential writer, see Hobbins, *Authorship and Publicity.*
64 This is implied by the presence of the apologetic treatise of Alfonso of Jaén, the *Epistola*, which he included in his edition of the *Revelations* in the second half of the 1370s, and which has been part and parcel of the corpus ever since. See also Fredriksson, "The Council of Constance," 218–19.
65 See n. 1 above. See also Tylus, "Mystical Literacy," 177–78.
66 This did not prevent the Birgittine brethren in Vadstena Abbey to continue to quote the *Revelations* on par with Scripture in their sermons. On this, see Roger Andersson's Chapter 7 in this volume. On the discussions of the origin of the *Revelations* at the Council of Basel, see Anna Fredriksson Adman, *Heymericus de Campo. Dyalogus super Reuelacionibus beate Birgitte. A Critical Edition with an Introduction* (Uppsala: Uppsala University, 2003).

67 A clear example is Dorothy of Montau (d. 1394) and her promoter John of Marienwerder (d. 1417) in the late fourteenth century. On Dorothy, John, and the model of Birgitta, see Dyan Elliott, "Authorizing a Life: The Collaboration of Dorothea of Montau and John Marienwerder," in *Gendered Voices: Medieval Saints and Their Interpreters*, ed. Catherine M. Mooney (Philadelphia: University of Pennsylvania Press, 1999). Another example is Francesca Romana (d. 1441) who, though much influenced by Birgitta, in her *vita* is presented as humbly refusing to write down and publish her revelations, activites which are here explicitly associted with the devil. The example is discussed in Elliott, "*Dominae* or *Dominatae?*" and Tylus, "Mystical Literacy."

68 In addition to Jean Gerson's treatise from the Council of Constance, *De probatione spirituum* (1415) and his *De examinatione doctrinarum* (1423), Birgitta had been criticized in Henry of Langenstein's *Concilium pacis* (1383), and later in an anonymous tract known from the English cardinal Adam Easton's refutation of it in his tract defending the authenticity of the saint in 1390 (*Defensorium Sancte Birgitte*). Other treatises defending the heavenly status of the *Revelations* are Birger Gregersson's *Epistola contra calumpniantes sanctissima reuelaciones beate Birgitte* (between 1384–91); Heymericus de Campo's *Dyalogus super Reuelacionibus beate Birgitte* and Cardinal Johannes de Turrecremata's *Defensorium super Reuelationes celestes Sancte Birgitte*, both stemming from the Council of Basel. In 1484, Sixtus IV revoked the 1436 judgment of the Council of Basel. Yet the status of the text and Birgitta's role was still uncertain, as the inclusion of apologetic tracts in the early printed editions of the *Revelations* bear testimony to. Bridget Morris notes that "Rumblings of discontent continued intermittently against Birgitta's canonization and it was not until the post-medieval period, with Benedict XIV's pontificate (1740–58), that a bull 'De servorum Dei beatificactione et beatorum canonizatione' was issued which silenced the critics of the canonization of the three great women saints of the later medieval period, Hildegard of Bingen, Caterina of Siena and Birgitta of Sweden," in *St Birgitta of Sweden* (Woodbridge: Boydell Press, 1999), 158. See also Claire L. Sahlin, *Birgitta of Sweden and the Voice of Prophecy* (Woodbridge: Boydell Press, 2001), 159–68.

7   Saints Catherine and Birgitta as Received by Preachers

Roger Andersson

Many historians have asked themselves whether there was any direct contact between Catherine of Siena and Birgitta of Sweden. After all, they were more or less contemporaries, and despite the distance between Siena and Rome, where Birgitta lived after having left her native country, the two women could very well have met. But no such evidence is at hand. The closest we can get is probably a small piece of information contained in one of Birgitta's *vitae*, a rather obscure version called *Vita Anglica*, appearing in English sources.[1] It states that upon her return from her pilgrimage to the Holy Land, Birgitta planned to travel to Vadstena to die instead of going back to Rome and that, on this journey, she wanted to stop in Siena and pay a visit to St. Catherine.[2] However, Christ appeared and told her to go back to Rome instead, and obviously, if the *Vita Anglica* is a trustworthy source, Birgitta followed this advice. To some extent, the older Swedish saint served as a role model for the younger Catherine or, to be more precise, for the men promoting her cult. A prominent example of this is provided by one of the key figures in the campaign for Catherine's sanctity, Tommaso d'Antonio da Siena, known as Caffarini. In his supplement to Raymond of Capua's *Legenda maior*, when discussing Catherine's stigmatization, Caffarini mentions Birgitta, together with several other saints, as an exemplary model of self-flagellation, itself an action worthy of imitation.[3] In the transmission of a work known as *Remedies Against Temptations* (*De remediis contra temptationes*), originally composed by Catherine's friend William Flete, interpolations from the *Revelations* of Birgitta are used to provide a good example in the art of resisting temptations.[4] Later, we can see that at least some followers of Birgitta were interested in the writings of Catherine. For instance, the sisters at Paradiso, the Birgittine monastery in Florence, copied Catherine's *Dialogue* and letters alongside the *Revelations* of Birgitta,[5] and the same *Dialogue* was translated into Middle English for the nuns at Syon abbey, the Birgittine house in England.[6] More interesting for us, and definitely less well known, is the fact that Catherine is, at least occasionally, put forward as a model female saint for the sisters in Vadstena abbey, the motherhouse of Birgitta's monastic order. In the sermons, or *collationes*, he preached before the sisters, Nicolaus Ragvaldi, who was confessor general in the beginning of the sixteenth century, sometimes quotes from the *Legenda maior*. He relates short episodes from Catherine's *vita* to prove the point that she was a saint worthy of imitation.[7] This is of particular interest, since there are no traces of Catherine of Siena in medieval Swedish sources up to this point.

The many similarities and dissimilarities between Catherine and Birgitta are dealt with elsewhere in this book, so there is no need to remind the reader about the common claim of divine inspiration, the way in which they received their message, or how it was dictated to secretaries or confessors. In both cases, their texts were considered by their followers to be true expressions of the word of God, something which gave both women the highest authority, on a linguistic as well as religious level. In the case of Catherine, it was discussed by her followers to what extent one was allowed to make alterations to the text, and in Birgitta's case, it is described in the *Vita* how she herself controlled that the (Latin) text she had dictated to her confessors was indeed in accordance with the revelation she had experienced.[8] For both saints, we have information about how the texts were meant to be disseminated in order to reach their intended recipients and have the full effect on whoever was reading them.

The topic of the present chapter is the preaching that took place after the remarkable lives and deaths of these two future saints. When the relics of Birgitta were brought back to Sweden, having been transferred from Rome to Vadstena in the period 1373–74, one of the first priest brothers at Vadstena abbey, Johannes Giurderi, more commonly known as Johannes Præst, is said to have preached assiduously every day during the whole period of Lent. It is reported that:

> In the beginning, when the relics of our holy mother Saint Birgitta were translated from Rome to Vadstena, this worthy servant of God preached excellently and with the highest and utmost devotion every day of Lent to the people coming in crowds from all parts of the land.[9]

Obviously, this was an event of considerable importance and Katarina Ulfsdotter, Birgitta's daughter, reports that bringing home her mother's bones also brought peace not only to Vadstena, but also to the previously tormented kingdom of Sweden.[10]

A similar kind of Lenten preaching took place in Italy for Catherine. Caffarini himself reports that he, in 1396, preached about Catherine every day throughout Lent:

> I say that I preached not only the three days of Easter, but also for the whole preceding Lenten season in the aforementioned church of San Zanipolo, about this virgin's similarity to the seraphic crucifix that seraphically appeared to Francis one day, and especially how this seraphic woman was an imitator of the seraphic crucifix of Christ.[11]

Thus, in the cases of both Birgitta and Catherine, there was an intense preaching activity during Lent with the obvious purpose of promoting their cults prior to their respective canonizations. Caffarini's Lenten cycle, itself representing only part of the vast oeuvre of Catherinian sermons, which he would continue to preach for many years to come, provides an excellent point of departure for a comparison between preaching on Catherine, and preaching on Birgitta. The sermons by the Swedish preacher Johannes Præst have unfortunately not been preserved, but there are good reasons to propose that he, like Caffarini, was preaching in favor of future canonization. Shortly after Birgitta's relics had been transferred to Sweden, Johannes appears as a member of the group commissioned by Bishop Nicolaus Hermanni to examine the authenticity of the miracles that had been ascribed to the saint *in spe*.[12] Regarding Caffarini's aims, however, there is absolutely no doubt. He was, as Carolyn Muessig points out, "the most active figure in the promotion of [Catherine's] cult."[13] As far as the popular veneration of Catherine and Birgitta is concerned, there was probably not much need for promotion or propaganda: They were both practically regarded as saints even before their canonization.[14] Nevertheless, the formal cults still required papal approval.

Were there any differences in the reception of the saintly lives of these two women by the preachers? To some extent, Birgitta and Catherine seem to represent two different types of saintly personalities, and the general character of their respective literary legacies does not wholly correspond. In the following, I explore the portrayal of Catherine and Birgitta in sermons, and the extent to which their own literary works played a role in that portrayal.

The Divine Catherine

The earliest preserved sermon on Catherine seems to be one composed by the abovementioned William Flete in 1382. According to Muessig, this sermon is also particularly important as it sets the general tone for subsequent Catherinian preaching: "The sermon contains several precedents for many themes that we will see repeated in pastoral literature on Catherine for the next 200 years."[15]

Among the more prominent themes Muessig identifies in Flete's sermon are Catherine as the spouse of Christ, her bodily mortifications, the comparison with St. Paul, Catherine's defense of the papacy and promotion of a crusade against the infidels, and her role as a mediator assisting Christ in the salvation of humankind. In my own reading of this sermon, I am particularly struck by its loose structure.[16] In the sermon, which was preached (or at least composed) two years after her death, William Flete addresses both Catherine herself, as "our beloved mother," and the (sinful) citizens of Siena who did not live according to her teachings. It is difficult to analyze the composition according to the standard terminology and concepts of the medieval *ars praedicandi*: it does not start from a scriptural *thema*, nor is the structure derived from a clear division or by means of distinctions. Some passages from Scripture are important and subjected to exegesis and application, such as Apoc. 12:1–2 in the latter part of the discourse: "And a great sign appeared in heaven. A woman clothed with the sun and the moon under her feet and on her head a crown of twelve stars." The woman in the Book of Revelation is interpreted by Flete as Catherine, and this is only one example of the apocalyptic dimension of her portrayal that emerges from his sermon.

Another striking aspect is the sermon's contents. With the exception of a discussion of the situation in Rome and Avignon in the middle of the sermon, the entire discourse concerns Catherine and nothing else. Sometimes, Flete refers to her confessor, Raymond of Capua, whose *Legenda maior* was not yet written, but other parts seem to be taken from Flete's own experiences. We must remember that he had been a close friend of Catherine himself and had acted as her confessor. There is no chronological recapitulation of the events of her life; instead, different aspects of Catherine's sanctity are brought forward. The subject of her bodily mortifications is so flagrant that it deserves a special note. Bodily mortification is also a common theme in the *Legenda maior* and other writings on Catherine's sanctity.[17] Flete narrates an episode in which she actually died one day, her soul flying up to heaven, where it remained for a while and whence it could see "from a far the hidden things of God and wonders which may not be spoken of."[18] And, Flete continues, this life is to be considered death more than life for which reason "each additional day of her [Catherine's] life was an additional death." Having seen what she saw, Catherine died spiritually each time she witnessed an offense against God. In Flete's sermon, her corporeal sufferings are treated in this context:

> How much bodily suffering, how many bodily deaths, how many truly unbearable afflictions, how many infirmities she endured from the beginning to the end! Who could count how many in her head, in her chest, her stomach, her intestines, her bones, all over indeed, throughout her whole body?[19]

Further on in the sermon, Flete informs us that miracles were worked through divine power. Indeed, Catherine's whole life is presented as a miracle since it was a martyrdom, a constant suffering. Thus, there was a purpose to her bodily pains, in that they could "impose justice":

> The greatest saints and chosen ones of God took natural refreshment in health and in sickness, but we see that in this regard she lived beyond nature. If ever some water or liquid nourishment

entered her body she cleansed her stomach and imposed justice, that is, vengeance, on herself, with what suffering God alone knows. If she experienced no other suffering than that involved in cleansing her stomach it would have been too much for her. When she was unable to cleanse her stomach she had suffering upon suffering since she was unable to impose justice on herself.[20]

Being a martyr who could impose justice, Catherine made herself partake in the work that Christ had already begun, namely that of saving mankind. The topic of her union with, and even transformation into, Christ is well known to Catherinian scholars (particularly in connection with her stigmatization), and is also expressed in Flete's sermon when he claims that Christ actually ate Catherine ("At this time it was Christ who ate her"), thereby echoing a phrase in St. Augustine's *Confessions*.[21] When Flete addresses the "ungrateful men of Siena," he urges them to remember "how you were saved by her merits."[22] The idea that Catherine's sufferings were for the sake of the sins and salvation of mankind reappears again and again in the sermon. Flete speaks of Catherine as someone who came down from heaven to earth for the sake of man's salvation and states that God "for the salvation of the human race... raised her up and breathed into her face the breath of life."[23] He declares:

> Let us always remember that she endured intolerable sufferings for our sins; let us remember how daily a new eagerness and fervor was kindled in her to give her life for us, a hundred times were it possible, and how many graces we have received from her mind. Let us remember that from her rising to her setting there rose up in her more and more abundant sufferings and torments for the Church of God and the sins of the people.[24]

In other words, Catherine's whole life, as well as the way she tragically languished away, were other means of transmitting the messages contained in her own preaching and teaching. But how does that come through in the text at hand?

Catherine was one of the most productive writers of her age, yet there are no direct quotations from her texts in Flete's sermon. This does not, however, mean that Catherine does not "speak" in the text. Since the preacher had known her personally, he frequently refers to the words she had spoken directly to him. This lends a degree of authenticity to Flete's sermon, which appears as an eyewitness account. When he talks about how Catherine had died and then returned to life, Flete states that "she told me so herself."[25] Sometimes, Catherine is also quoted directly: "She in a rapture once said: 'Lord, punish the sins of the whole world in this poor body, even though it is not sufficient to carry the penalty for its own sins.'"[26] Similar expressions appear in Catherine's *Dialogue*, but no direct source of the quote has been found, thereby making it plausible that Flete is speaking honestly when he says that Catherine actually said this to him.

> Often she used [to] say: "Lord, I want you to allow me to sleep." So willingly did she sleep that she had to be physically shaken to awake: no wonder, for in her rapture the Lord sent his hand and touched her mouth and filled it with *a spirit of wisdom and understanding* (Is. 11:2), saying: "You are my servant, in you shall I glory; I have given you as a light to the nations, that you may be my salvation to the ends of the earth (Is. 49:3, 6)." She replied: "You are my glory, you are my protector, Lord, for *you sent from on high* at my passing *and received me and took me out of many waters* (Ps. 17:17)."[27]

Interestingly, in this last quote Catherine's own words are merged into the words of Scripture in a way that makes it difficult to tell the one from the other (were it not for the editor's use of italics). Thus, in Flete's homiletical discourse, a first person pronoun can refer to God, Christ, or to Catherine (potentially simultaneously). Thus, there is a linguistic counterpart to Catherine's transformation into Christ, her assisting Christ in the redemptory work for the sins of Man, and even her performing it herself through her sufferings. We close the section on Catherine with another quote which proves the same point. The identification with Christ is never as evident as when she, as Flete reports, speaks the words of the Gospel as if they were emanating from her own invention:

> At the hour of her passing she could say: "It is time for me to return to him who sent me; my sons, do not be sad, *let not your hearts be troubled* (Jn 14:27) or in fear; I shall ask the Father to guard you. The scripture says: *Unless I go away the paraclete will not come to you* (Jn 16:7). When I have been taken up my spouse will send him to you. *If you love me keep my commands*, keep my teachings, and *I will ask the Father and he shall give you another paraclete, the spirit of truth, to remain with you forever. I will not leave you orphans; I will come to you* (Jn 14:15–18)." She could say those words of the gospel: *A little while now and the world shall not see me, but you,* my sons, *shall see me,* that is, through faith, *for I live and you shall live* (Jn 14:19).[28]

The Human Birgitta

We now turn to the early preaching on St. Birgitta. As mentioned above, the Lenten sermons preached by Johannes Præst in connection with the return of Birgitta's bodily remains to Vadstena have not been preserved.

What we have from Johannes is a copy of his *sermones de tempore*, possibly compiled not long after his death in 1391. Even if we had had a collection of *sermones de sanctis*, this would probably not have included a sermon for Birgitta, since she was canonized the same year as Johannes died. Johannes's assiduous preaching in Vadstena in 1374 would probably have found its way into some other type of sermon manuscript, such as a collection of either *reportaciones* or *sermones quadragesimales*.

Concerning the portrait of Birgitta emerging from sermon evidence from Vadstena, we can profit from a brief yet thorough survey by Monica Hedlund.[29] The different motifs she identifies are quite common in sermons for female saints in general, and so it is interesting to note how, already in the earliest sermons, the Birgittine preachers were eager to make their saint conform to the established hagiographical patterns, and to the traditional qualities of female sainthood. One such recurring image is that of Birgitta as a widow, widowhood of course being highly praised by medieval hagiographers, following the words of St. Paul: "*Viduas honora quae vere viduae sunt*" ("Honor widows, that are widows indeed," 1 Tim. 5:3), a quotation which was occasionally used as theme for the sermons.[30] According to Hedlund, this motif was crucial already in the sermon preached by Pope Boniface IX on the occasion of the Canonization festivities in October 1391, which most certainly influenced the preaching on Birgitta in the years to come. A number of homilies compare Birgitta to Judith in the Old Testament who functions as *typos* of the pious widow. Here other qualities, common to Judith and Birgitta, are also emphasized: Birgitta's wisdom (*sapientia*), strength (*fortitudo*), diligence (*diligentia*), persistence (*sedulitas*), and her fear of God (*timor Dei*). Likewise, as Hedlund observes, Birgitta is sometimes, albeit not very frequently, portrayed as a prophet, one who preaches the joy of the elect and the severe judgment of the unrighteous and who claims divine inspiration for her teachings. Birgitta's quality of a prophet is particularly interesting since the question of whether her *Revelations* were inspired by God (or, as the adversaries thought, by the devil) was much debated at the great church councils in the fifteenth century.[31]

There are several general similarities between St. Birgitta and St. Elizabeth of Hungary (1207–31), and preaching on Birgitta may very well to some extent have been modeled upon the preaching on Elizabeth.[32] Both holy women are often called "the bride of Christ."[33] This is a hagiographic commonplace, but additionally, we see also that they were both widows, a motif that occurs frequently in sermons on Elizabeth, often prefigured by Judith.[34] It should also be mentioned that extracts from the legend were read at table in the sisters' convent Vadstena on Elizabeth's feast day (19 November).[35] Even though Johannes Præst's collection of Sunday sermons does not contain any preaching for the feast day of Birgitta, she is nevertheless omnipresent in these sermons, in one respect in particular: they are imbued with quotations from the

Revelations. There is nothing surprising about that since this was more or less required in the legislative documents regulating the religious life at Vadstena. The basic document on the preaching duty of the Birgittine priests is Chapter 15 of the *Regula Salvatoris*:

> The thirteen priests should only apply themselves to the divine office, to study and to prayer without involving themselves in other activities or tasks. They should explain the gospel of the day in their native language every Sunday with everyone in attendance. They should also preach publicly on every solemnity preceded by a vigil of fasting on bread and water as well as on other feasts that have vigils.[36]

In an amplification of this chapter, contained in Chapter 23 of the *Revelaciones extravagantes*, it is stated among other things the following:

> They [the thirteen priest brothers] should discuss the Bible along with these words of mine and of my beloved Mother and my saints; the lives of the Fathers; the miracles of the saints, the profession of faith; as well as countermeasures against temptations and vices, all of this according to the capacity of the listeners.[37]

The expression "these words of mine and of my beloved Mother and my saints" clearly refer to the *Revelations*, since in them it is normally Christ and Mary who speak, and sometimes also other saints.[38] The *Revelations* are quoted already in the earliest preserved Vadstena sermons, if not always extensively then at least regularly. In the beginning of the fifteenth century, the authenticity of Birgitta's revelations was debated among theologians. These intense discussions eventually resulted in a formal judgment pronounced at the Council of Basel in 1436, with the implication that the priests were no longer allowed to call the revelations "heavenly," nor to "pronounce or disseminate in public such things."[39]

Before we return to the practice of quoting from the *Revelations*, we shall take a closer look at what appears to be the earliest sermon for one of Birgitta's feast days, not counting the Canonization sermon by Pope Boniface from 1391. The homily in question is found in Uppsala University Library (UUB), MS C 259.[40] A note at the end of this manuscript in combination with the shelf mark system used to indicate its position in the monastic library allows us to safely state that the book was written (or finished) in Vadstena in the year 1400. Paleographic evidence further suggests that it was written by Thorirus Andreae, who was one of the 13 priest brothers between 1392 and 1418.

UUB, C 259 contains a collection of sermons of different kinds (*sermones varii*), both Sunday sermons and sermons for saints' feasts. The sermon for St. Birgitta (fols. 59r–61r) remains unedited and has received little attention. If the normal pattern for the model collection is to give ordered series of either *sermones de tempore* (the dates vary from year to year) or *sermones de sanctis* (celebrated on fixed dates), here we see a mixture of these two organizing principles. Given the order of Sunday sermons and sermons for saints' days, and how these sometimes coincide, it has been possible to support the idea that the sermons entered in the manuscript appear in the same order that they were actually preached, or intended for preaching, and they thus represent the preaching calendar for Thorirus Andreae for the years 1392–1400. According to this reconstruction, the Birgitta sermon was preached or intended for preaching on 7 October 1397.[41] In it, Thorirus follows a model which is also represented in several other sermons on Birgitta, and which is also quite common in sermons for other female saints. However, apart from the standard repertoire of virtues (see below), there is a characteristic voice speaking precisely about Birgitta and no one else. Thorirus sets out from the theme *Ora pro nobis quoniam mulier sancta es* ("Now therefore pray for us, for thou art a holy woman," Judith 8:29). This is an excellent choice of theme since it allows the preacher to touch upon both human shortcomings here on earth, and on the eternal bliss in the afterlife.[42] As far as the structure is concerned, the text is mainly organized according to the requirements of the normal thematic sermon, and there is not much complexity in terms of subdivisions, different sets of forewords (*prothema, introductio*), or such matter. In the main development of the theme, the preacher focuses on the word *sancta*, leading us to believe that his main message is to promote the idea that Birgitta is in fact a holy person. We need someone to pray for us, and since Birgitta is holy, she is well fitted for this. However, Thorirus is eager to point out that she was not only holy but also had other qualities.[43] In addition, the rest of the sermon is derived from this fourfold distinction, stating that she was wise (*sapiens*), strong (*fortis*), diligent (*diligens, sedula*), and God-fearing (*timorata*).

When speaking of Birgitta's *wisdom* the preacher likens her to a wise architect who builds her house on a solid ground and foundation. This metaphor is applied to the virtue of humility, but in this context, it is natural to also think about Birgitta as a well-respected matron of a large household. Thorirus further quotes from the *Vita* and in particular from those passages where Birgitta's generosity and mercifulness are brought to the fore.[44] It is told how Birgitta constantly gave alms to the poor, how she in Rome repaired hospitals and visited sick people. The wisdom of Birgitta consists in struggling along the right path,[45] and this wisdom did not come from herself alone, it was also necessary to have wise teachers, and here, Thorirus makes a reference to one of her *Revelations* on this topic.[46] The solid foundation of the wise architect is Birgitta's virtuous life, and this enables us to get an idea about the nature of her wisdom. The main ingredients in this wisdom are the merciful deeds she performed, and that she turned her eyes away from the temporal delights and instead directed them to the desire for the eternal things.[47] The visual sign of her wisdom is the splendor in her face, which was shining like the sun, and here Thorirus uses the same passage from the Biblical Revelation 12 that we just saw in William Flete's sermon for St. Catherine: "And a great sign appeared in heaven, a woman clothed with the sun" (Apoc. 12:1).[48]

The section on Birgitta's *strength* dwells mainly on her patience and her widowhood. Being strong is equivalent to being patient and suffering afflictions without complaining. However, considerably less emphasis is put on Birgitta's bodily mortifications here compared to what we saw in Flete's sermon. Birgitta is portrayed as extremely aware of her own sinfulness and self-accusations are frequent. But she does not, at least not in this sermon, suffer much herself.[49] When Catherine is presented as starving herself as a means of assisting Christ in saving souls, Birgitta rather appears as a helping friend in this world. She is not like ordinary women who are too weak: "many women are weak and cannot sustain sickness or other misfortunes; they are effeminate, cry often, and are inclined to slandering."[50] In contrast, Birgitta was patient in suffering any discomfort. The preacher relates an episode from the *Vita* concerning one of her enemies who did not believe a word of what she was telling.[51] He did not dare to speak against her himself but instead incited another person to shout insulting words at her while pretending to be drunk. This he did,[52] and those standing near wanted to punish him, but Birgitta immediately forgave him, saying that she had sought her own praise all her life, and why should she not now hear what is only right?[53] Indeed, although it is a good example of self-effacement, the point made by the preacher is of course that it takes much inner strength to persevere in the good under harsh circumstances and in opposition to the enemies of God.

Birgitta was also a *widow*, and in this, she should be honored, following the words of St. Paul about the true widow and with Judith as the Old Testament *typos* (see above). A *true* widow in this context is not only one who has lost her husband but also a widow who has renounced the love for worldly things, and this is given support from none other than Birgitta's confessor Master Mathias of Linköping.[54] Widowhood, however, is also a dangerous state. There is no one there to console them, and widows are constantly running the risk that both neighbors and strangers will want to draw them back to worldly delights. According to our preacher, this has to do with the fact that widows are especially prone to diabolical instigations. And all the more do they risk such things if they have not their heads covered.[55] One may indeed wonder why this is so important for him; would it not have been more fruitful for everyone if he had raised a topic more revealing of Birgitta's character and of more immediate relevance for the moral of the listeners than this? But, as we will soon see, Thorirus will come back to the topic of women's clothing further on in the sermon.

In the section on Birgitta's *diligence* Thorirus dwells on her attentiveness in serving God, and in particular on her generosity in helping
people in need. Many men, Thorirus claims, love women who are at-
tentive and diligent in their services.[56] And this is precisely why Christ
loved Birgitta, because she was so eager to serve him. Again the preacher
quotes from the legend where it is said that Birgitta did not spare any
effort in helping poor and sick people. It is especially pointed out how
she administered food to twelve poor whose feet she would wash each
Friday. And whenever Birgitta heard about leprous or sick people, she
visited them and treated their wounds with her own hands without fear.
She even urged her daughters to follow her example in this, but she was
criticized for having the children perform this work at their young age
because of the high risk of infection. To this, Birgitta simply answered
that the girls by this means should learn and understand that serving the
poor and sick was a way to serve God.[57] As we see, even in this section
there is much emphasis on how Birgitta devoted great care to the temporal anxieties. This is probably not a general description of her character,
but it seems to be the picture the preacher wants to transmit. It may not
be a coincidence that Thorirus is especially urgent to compare Birgitta to
Martha, the servant who was so diligent in serving her Master.[58]

In the concluding paragraphs, Birgitta's *fear of God* is discussed. Sur-
prisingly, much of this section is devoted to questions about the importance of avoiding pride in clothing. One aspect of fearing God is not to
care about corporeal beauty, and Birgitta certainly did not do that.[59]
Thorirus deplores those worldly people who by sheer pride unduly dec-
orate themselves.[60] Christ had prescribed to Birgitta that there should
not be a single thread in her clothes that was a sign of pride. These
women, on the other hand, do not want to wear clothes in which any
single thread is *not* the sign of pride.[61] The theme is developed at length,
among other with the help of rather substantial quotations from Vincent
Ferrer, the influential Dominican from Valencia (and a contemporary of
Thorirus) who was, however, hardly known in Sweden at all. The main
idea that Thorirus seems eager to drive home from this is that taking
pride in fancy clothing is almost the worst thing one can do. Such or-
nament is the sign of spiritual death in a similar way as when a cloth is
laid over the bier where a dead body is lying: A woman unduly ornate
is nothing but the bier of a dead soul.[62] As if this was not enough, the
preacher exclaims that a woman should despair more if her daughter
dresses with pride than if she falls down dead right in front of her.[63]

As we have seen from the comparison between Flete's 1382 sermon
for Catherine and Thorirus's 1397 sermon for Birgitta, there are some
recurring differences. The focus for Flete was Catherine's corporeal sufferings and the way in which these helped saving man from sin. Together
with her near identification with and transformation into Christ (exemplified by her stigmata),[64] Flete almost presents Catherine as a godly

figure. Birgitta, on the other hand, is presented more in her capacity of a loving woman in this world. True, she is a marvelous example of self-effacement and patience, but Birgitta remains rooted in this temporal life. She is a strong widow; she is a Martha, not a Mary, occupied with serving God as well as she can, helping the poor and avoiding dressing with pride. It is perhaps significant that Catherine is often called "mother" in Flete's sermon, a word which in the Birgittine context normally is reserved for the Mother of God. In this and other respects, it might be justified to speak about the divine Catherine and the human Birgitta. Accordingly, the power to perform miracles after the death is brought more to the fore in the case of Birgitta. It goes without saying that this is part of the sanctity of both women, but there is significantly less emphasis on the miracles in the documents relating to the canonization process of Catherine (the *Processo Castellano*) than in those pertaining to Birgitta (*Acta et processus*). In his study of the former, George Ferzoco writes: "Most atypically for a canonized saint, miraculous cures are comparatively minor in number and in emphasis."[65] The image of Birgitta, which our preacher wants to transmit to his audience, is not completely consistent with other aspects of her person and life. She is often portrayed as a true prophet engaged in ecclesiastical and political affairs on the highest level, but such aspects are not at all brought to the fore in this homiletical context. This only proves that her sanctity and her quality as role model are multifaceted and diverse.

Revelations as Scripture

As mentioned above, Birgitta's *Revelations* were quoted extensively in the Vadstena sermons. This practice begins already in the earliest homilies, and certainly not only in those intended for her feast days. I have elsewhere argued that the function of such quotations from Birgitta's writings were threefold: *auctoritas*, *exemplum*, and *structura*.[66] The function of *auctoritas* often involves precise imperative statements aimed at the instruction of the audience, and *exempla* are normally used to touch the feelings of the listeners: bad examples to induce fear and conscience of one's own sin, good examples to produce feelings of relief, hope, and trust. The function of *structura* is prevalent in those cases where the *Revelations* are used to structure if not an entire sermon at least a substantial part thereof, such as one of its main sections (*principalia*).

The *authority* of the *Revelations* in this context is evident already from the passage in *Revelaciones extravagantes* quoted above. Here, Christ himself speaks about "these words of mine" and requires the priests to use them in their sermons. And not only do the Vadstena priests quote from them together with the standard repertoire of patristic and medieval ecclesiastical authorities, such as Augustine, Gregory the Great,

Bernard of Clairvaux, Thomas Aquinas, and so on—a close scrutiny of how the *Revelations* are used as theological arguments reveals that they are actually used on a par with Scripture itself. This remarkable claim is of course what caused so much concern for the theologians at the Council of Basel and earlier. The 1436 judgment declares that it is prohibited to equate the authority of the *Revelations* with that of the Gospels. We know that the priests quoted from the *Revelations* in the early years in the history of the abbey, but did they continue after the Council of Basel? The answer to this is conclusively affirmative: there is no decrease in the frequency of quoting from the *Revelations* in this function from the 1430s and onward. In this particular respect, the priests, if not actually disobeying the judgment, at least seem to have disregarded one of the most crucial parts thereof.[67] After all, we should remember that in his early defense of Birgitta (from the 1340s), known as *Stupor et mirabilia*, a text usually published as a prologue to the *Revelations*, Master Mathias of Linköping had argued Christ's revelation to Birgitta was "even more amazing than the one by which he showed himself in the flesh."[68] This is confirmed by the iconographic tradition in which the representation of the writing Birgitta was taken from the well-established iconography of the evangelist as a scribe.[69] Thus, also in paintings Birgitta's *Revelations* are put on a par with the Gospels.

I will give a couple examples of how Birgitta's *Revelations* are quoted with a similar function in the sermons.[70] The first is taken from a sermon for the Eighth Sunday after Trinity (UUB C 270, fols. 110v–113v) by the already-mentioned Johannes Præst, who was preaching in connection with the translation of Birgitta's relics. In this sermon, Johannes quotes St. Augustine who claims that love is the only virtue by which the sons of the heavenly kingdom can be distinguished from the sons of perdition.[71] The pains of the latter are explored with some care after which the preacher sets out to prove that anyone who does not act according to the love of God does not deserve to enter the kingdom of heaven:

> According to what Christ says in the second heavenly book, chapter 5: "Only a person who has charity can obtain my kingdom"[Rev. II: 5.21]. I Corinthians 13 [.1–3)]: "If I speak with the tongues of men and of angels" etc. up to "and if I should distribute all my goods to feed the poor, and if I should deliver my body to be burned, and have not charity, it profits me nothing."[72]

Here, the words of Christ transmitted in Book II of Birgitta's *Revelations* are quoted together with the words of St. Paul.

One of the most prominent of all Vadstena preachers was Johannes Borquardi. Even though he was professed in 1428, the main part of his time as one of the 13 priest brothers and preachers (he also served as confessor general for a short period, 1443–44), occurred after the 1436 judgment. Therefore, one would expect a lower frequency of quotations from the *Revelations* in comparison with his precedents. This, however, is not the case: as we can see from his sermons, Johannes Borquardi also continues to quote from the *Revelations* in the same way as his predecessors did. In a sermon intended for the feast St. Peter *ad vincula* (1 August) which was an important day for pilgrimage in Vadstena, Johannes Borquardi speaks about different forms of chains or bonds (*vincula*), such as the bond of obedience. By this bond, the preacher explains, humans were chained in baptism to keep and to observe the Ten Commandments.[73] As we see in the following quotation, taken from the passage on the seventh Commandment, Johannes uses quotations from the *Revelations* as *auctoritates* in the same context and with the same function as the quotation from the Church Father Augustine of Hippo.

> We see this in the robbers, both here in this kingdom and in other places. In the future, they will be punished with eternal damnation if they do not emend, as Augustine says: "Sin is not forgiven unless emended and removed." And in the *Revelations* Christ says: "What do men of the world think, those who have an evil faith, who retain what is unjustly acquired? Surely not that they will enter Heaven. Definitely, they will not do this anymore than Lucifer!"[Rev. VI: 85.4].[74]

As we see, Johannes Borquardi's aim of "proving" that stealing will be severely punished receives ample support from the writings of Birgitta. This is a very short quotation from the sermon, but it could easily be multiplied. Innumerable examples from Johannes's fellow priest brothers or those who served after him all the way up to the beginning of the sixteenth century could be cited to prove that the practice of putting the *Revelations* on par with Scripture continued.[75]

In the bull *Spectat ad Romani* from 1472, Pope Sixtus IV prohibited not only the depiction of St. Catherine with stigmata but even the mere mentioning of it in sermons.[76] This is reminiscent of the prohibition to quote from Birgitta's *Revelations* in the 1436 judgment just discussed but does not contradict what appears to be one of the most important differences between how the two female saints were received by preachers. To my knowledge, the writings of Catherine were never quoted in this way in sermons, or, for that matter, quoted at all. We know that the preachers who had known her personally, such as for example William Flete, do not hesitate to use her own words in her sermons. And of course, the remarkable events of her life also provided rich material for preachers, and thus the *Legenda maior* was certainly quoted once it had been completed.

At first glance, this seems a bit peculiar, given how much Birgitta's and Catherine's respective written legacies have in common. The *Dialogue* is organized as a dialogue between the eternal Father and a human soul, and the status of the work as a true expression of the Word of God seems not to have been contested even in Catherine's lifetime. The *Revelations* of Birgitta are not in total structured as a dialogue, but a great number of the chapters use this literary device, and most certainly, God the Father, his Son, and the Virgin speak frequently in the texts. In Catherine's *Dialogue*, the spiritual life of humankind is treated and discussed by means of analogy, allegory, and metaphor, and likewise the pictorial language and extensive use of metaphors have justly been described as one of the most salient characteristics of Birgitta's style. To give but one example: The image of nursing, and Christ feeding with blood, according to Jane Tylus "the most Catherinian of metaphors,"[77] is also frequently used in Birgitta's writings; then again, however, it can almost be regarded as a commonplace. Furthermore, both texts contain strong evidence for the need of ecclesiastical reform and advice aiming at the cultivation of virtue, prayers, and obedience. Disregarding such general things that both works have in common, I would like to propose a few reasons as to why the texts are treated so differently by preachers.

One reason which immediately strikes me is the fact that the practice of quoting from the *Revelations* was stipulated in the rule of Birgitta's own new monastic order. Catherine, who became a *mantellata* herself and established a house for women, never founded a new order as such.

A second reason for the different treatment of their literary works in sermons is related to language. Catherine wrote in her own vernacular, the Tuscan dialect. And, while it is true that Birgitta's *Revelations* were probably first written in Swedish (as her hagiographers explain, and several witnesses in the canonization process bear testimony), they were almost immediately translated into Latin, and it is in this form that they are rendered in the sermons. Given that these Latin sermons, as they appear in the surviving manuscripts, were probably used as a point of departure for vernacular preaching, we must assume that they were translated more or less *ad hoc* into Swedish at the preaching occasion, possibly with the help of notes in the margins or similar. However, their authority certainly must have something to do with the fact that they were preserved in a written, reasonably fixed, Latin form. The *volgare* of Catherine on the other hand did not entail such an authority. It was too connected to the orality of her religious experience, something which has been discussed with much care by Tylus. As a matter of fact, this was an important issue already in the sixteenth and seventeenth centuries not only in the circles of the Academia della Crusca but even before: "The Academia della Crusca...was hardly the first to ignore Catherine as a textual authority."[78]

A third reason has to do with the metaphorical style itself. In sermons to a non-learned audience, one would expect a vivid use of metaphors, allegories, and similes. This is precisely what we find in the *Revelations*.

Birgitta's imagery has been described as very concrete and innovative. It is further extremely systematic, in that the imagery is almost always used as a point of departure for an application on the morals, the religious life, catechetical topics, teachings on society, Church, and such things. There are many famous examples of metaphors taken from the daily life on the countryside, such as tools, houses on a farm, animals, etc. According to Bridget Morris:

> Birgitta's mind is encyclopaedic and synthetic, her imagination fierce and fertile, and she shows sharp powers of observation and a keen intelligence and understanding. Striking images in unusual juxtapositions frequently form the nucleus of the visionary experience, in a succession of points that are sharp enough to fix themselves in her mind in discrete parcels.[79]

Most certainly, Catherine also uses imagery and overarching symbols (such as the famous bridge) extensively in the *Dialogue*. But their persuasive power may be diminished by the associative style in which she presents them. Therefore, her visionary experience may be less suited for the edificatory purpose of a popular preacher. Already in 1906 Algar Thorold writes:

> St. Catherine has no style as such; she introduces a metaphor and forgets it; the sea, a vine, and a plough will often appear in the same sentence, sometimes in the same phrase.[80]

And even though Tylus rightly speaks about Catherine's "vibrant and particularly visual metaphors," she also refers to another scholar who claims that Catherine "simply wallows in examples without explaining them" and that she uses metaphors that "do not appeal to the listener's rational sensibility."[81]

Conclusion

In the preceding paragraphs, I have compared the ways in which Catherine of Siena and Birgitta of Sweden were received by preachers and presented in these preachers' sermons. As far as the general image of the two saints is concerned, I notice that Catherine appeared as an almost godly figure, practically identifying herself with Christ and with the remarkable claims of having the capacity to save mankind, partly by means of her corporeal sufferings and bodily mortifications. Birgitta, on the other hand, is presented as a strong, virtuous, and self-effacing widow. It is true that she constantly turned her prophetic mind toward the eternal things, but in the sermons, substantially more emphasis is put on her love and good deeds. This is the reason why I, in a slightly provocative wording, spoke of the *divine* Catherine and the *human* Birgitta. I also noticed a difference in how their respective literary legacies were used. Whereas the *Revelations* of Birgitta are quoted in the Swedish sermons already from the start and throughout the Middle Ages, we see no such comparable practice in the case of Catherine. Furthermore, when quoting from Birgitta's texts, the Vadstena priests ascribe them such a high theological authority that they practically put them on a par with Scripture itself.

One could say that both saints convey the evangelical message, but they do it in different ways. Likewise, the preachers use two different strategies of demonstrating how this is done: in Catherinian preaching, mostly the life and fate of the *person* is at stake. In Birgittine preaching, the authority contained in the *texts* plays the most prominent role. Only a limited number of sources have been used for this preliminary study. Hopefully, future research will be able to judge if the results have a more general applicability.

Notes

1 Stephan Borgehammar, "*Vitae Birgittae*. En översikt och tre editioner," in *Humanitas. Festskrift till Arne Jönsson*, eds. Astrid M. H. Nilsson, Aske Damtoft Poulsen, and Johanna Svensson (Gothenburg: Makadam, 2017), 185–86.

2 Borgehammar, "*Vitae Birgittae*," 186: "Et cogitauit pergere Sweciam ad terram suam et ibi perpetuo manere in monasterio suo quod fundauerat, usque ad mortem. Concupiuit eciam ex longo desiderio transire per ciuitatem Senensem, vt visitaret et salutaret beatissimam uirginem Katerinam de Senis, cuius fama mire sanctitatis per orbem diuulgabatur."

3 See Chapter 8 by Gábor Klaniczay in the present work.

4 See Roger Ellis, "'Flores ad fabricandam … coronam.' An Investigation into the Uses of the Revelations of St Bridget of Sweden in Fifteenth Century England," *Medium Ævum* 51 (1982): 163–86, at 175. However, since these interpolations occur only in one manuscript, they were most likely not in Flete's original: "But this particular attempt to remodel Flete's work evidently remained a sport, without offspring" (Benedict Hackett O.S.A, Eric Colledge, and Noel Chadwick, "William Flete's 'De Remediis contra Temptaciones' in its Latin and English Recensions," *Mediaeval Studies* 26 (1964): 210–30, at 219.

5 See Rosanna Miriello, *I manoscritti del monastero del Paradiso di Firenze* (Florence: SISMEL, Edizioni del Galluzzo, 2007). On the crossing traditions in the textual history of Birgitta's and Catherine's writings, see also Chapter 5 by Silvia Nocentini in the present volume.

6 The translated text is known as *The Orchard of Syon*. On the impact of Catherine at Syon Abbey, see, for example, Jane Chance, "St Catherine of Siena in Late Medieval Britain: Feminizing Literary Reception through Gender and Class," *Annali d'Italianistica* 13 (1995): 163–203.

7 See Maria Berggren (ed.), *Homiletica Vadstenensia ad religiosos et sacerdotes* (Turnhout: Brepols, 2009), 83 and 123.

8 AP, 84; Birgitta of Sweden, *The Revelations of St. Birgitta of Sweden*, trans. Denis Searby, Introductions and notes by Bridget Morris, 4 vols (Oxford: Oxford University Press, 2006–15), 1: 12.

9 Uppsala, UUB, C 270, fols. 156r–v. Quoted from *Mittelalterliche Handschriften der Universitätsbibliothek Uppsala. Katalog über die C-Sammlung*, eds. Margarete Andersson-Schmitt, Håkan Hallberg, and Monica Hedlund, 8 vols (Uppsala: Uppsala university 1988–95), 3: 233: "Et in primordio quando reliquie sacrosancte matris nostre sancte byrghitte de roma watzstena sunt translate iste dignus dei famulus quolibet die per totam xl^{mam} egregie predicauit plebi ex omnibus finibus terre cateruatim venienti cum summa et maxima deuocione."

10 André Vauchez, *Sainthood in the Later Middle Ages*, trans. Jean Birrell (New York: Cambridge University Press, 1997 [1981]), 465, quoting from AP, 313–4.

11 Quoted from Carolyn Muessig, "Catherine of Siena in Late Medieval Sermons," in *A Companion to Catherine of Siena*, eds. Carolyn Muessig, George Ferzoco, and Beverly Mayne Kienzle (Leiden: Brill, 2012), 210 (where also the Latin of the source text is given).

12 Anders Fröjmark, *Mirakler och helgonkult. Linköpings biskopsdöme under senmedeltiden* (Uppsala: Uppsala universitet, 1992), 32 and 106. He died on 11 June 1391.

13 Muessig, "Catherine of Siena," 209.

14 See also Vauchez, *Sainthood*, 97.

15 Muessig, "Catherine of Siena," 204.

16 I have used the translation by Benedict Hackett in *William Flete, O.S.A. and Catherine of Siena. Masters of Fourteenth Century Spirituality* (Villanova, PA.: Augustinian Press, 1992), 185–220. For the Latin source text see Robert Fawtier, "Catheriniana," *Mélanges d'archéologie et d'histoire* 34, no. 1 (1914): 40–75.

17 See also for example Vauchez, *Sainthood*, 409.

18 Hackett, *William Flete*, 188.

19 Hackett, *William Flete*, 188.

20 Hackett, *William Flete*, 194.

21 Hackett, *William Flete*, 200; Augustine of Hippo, *Confessiones* VII.10: "Cresce et manducabis me. Nec tu me in te mutabis sicut cibum carnis tuae, sed tu mutaberis in me."

22 Hackett, *William Flete*, 205.

23 Ibid., 207.

24 Ibid., 211–12.

25 Ibid., 188.

26 Ibid., 192.

27 Ibid., 196.

28 Ibid., 203.

29 Monica Hedlund, "Vadstenapredikanter om Birgitta," in *Heliga Birgitta – budskapet och förebilden. Föredrag vid jubileumssymposiet i Vadstena 3–7 oktober 1991*, eds. Alf Härdelin and Mereth Lindgren (Stockholm: KVHAA, 1993), 311–27.

30 The theme or *thema* is the short biblical quotation that serves as a point of departure for the discourse. Normally, the division of the theme generates the different principal sections of the sermon.

31 See the exhaustive discussion in Claire L. Sahlin, *Birgitta of Sweden and the Voice of Prophecy* (Woodbridge: Boydell Press, 2001).

32 Hedlund, "Vadstenapredikanter om Birgitta," 318.

33 Ottó Gescer, *The Feast and the Pulpit: Preachers, Sermons and the Cult of St. Elizabeth of Hungary, 1235–ca. 1500* (Spoleto: Fondazione Centro Italiano di studi sull'Alto Medioevo, 2012), 6.

34 Gescer, *The Feast*, 157–59.

35 Jonas Carlquist, *Vadstenasystrarnas textvärld. Studier i systrarnas skrift-brukskompetens, lärdom och textförståelse* (Uppsala: SFSS, 2007), 295–97.

36 Birgitta of Sweden, *The Revelations*, 4: 136.

37 Birgitta of Sweden, *The Revelations*, 4: 245.

38 Roger Andersson and Stephan Borgehammar, "The Preaching of the Birgittine Friars at Vadstena Abbey (c. 1380–1515)," *Revue Mabillon*, Nouvelle série 8, vol. 69 (1997): 206–36, at 232–33.

39 Anna Fredriksson Adman, *Heymericus de Campo: Dyalogus super Reuelacionibus beate Birgitte. A Critical Edition with an Introduction* (Uppsala: Uppsala University, 2003), 29.

40 *Mittelalterliche Handschriften*, 3: 186–93.

41 Roger Andersson, "Sermon Manuscripts of Different Kinds," *Medieval Sermon Studies* 55 (2011): 39–41.

42 UUB, C 259, fol. 59r: "Et possunt verba ista sumi ad commendacionem sancte Byrgitte et sunt verba degencium in hoc mundo et implorancium suffragium sancte Byrgitte regnantis in celo. In quibus verbis duo describuntur. Primum miserabilis defeccio, que est in statu vie. Secundum venerabilis perfeccio, que est in statu patrie. Primum ibi *Ora pro nobis*, secundum ibi *quoniam mulier sancta es* ...." Quotations from this sermon are taken from an unpublished transcription by Maria Berggren for the project *Vadstenabrödernas predikan*; it has been checked against the manuscript by myself.

43 UUB, C 259, fol. 59r: "Notandum ergo est, quod sancta Byrgitta fuit non simpliciter sancta ...."

44 Quoting from the *Vita* is normal in all *de sanctis* preaching and eminently so in the preaching on St. Elizabeth of Hungary, one of the hagiographic models for the medieval preaching on Birgitta. The events in her life proves her be worthy of praise for certain virtues. Gescer, *The Feast*, 196–97.

45 UUB, C 259, fol. 59v: "Veram vtique sapienciam elegit, quia attendebat, quod dicit Augustinus: *Spiritualis sapiencia est via recta ducens ad finem rectum* ...."

46 UUB, C 259, fol. 59v: "Nec mirum, quod ista sancta mulier sapiens erat. Nam sapientissimum habuit doctorem. Vnde ii libro celesti xxii: *Maria loquitur* ...."

47 UUB, C 259, fol. 59v: "Scilicet per sua virtuosa opera intelligi potest, quam sapiens erat et potentissimus faciem illius commutabit scilicet ab amore temporalium ad desiderium eternorum."

48 UUB, C 259, fol. 59v: "Hoc signatum fuit, quando Rome facies eius visa est aliquibus resplendere ad modum solis, vt dicatur: *Mulier amicta sole.* Apocalypsis xii." The resplendent beauty as a visual sign of sainthood is a hagiographic commonplace and is also attributed to Catherine. Vauchez, *Sainthood*, 435.

49 Throughout her *Revelations* Birgitta often speaks in favor of moderation. Avoiding gluttony does not mean starving; no spiritual exercises should be performed that could be harmful to the fragile nature of the human body. On the different roles of physical tokens of sanctity in the cases of Catherine and Birgitta, see Chapter 8 by Gábor Klaniczay in this volume.

50 UUB, C 259, fol. 59v: "Multe sunt mulieres fragiles ad sustinendum infirmitates vel aduersitates, molles ad flendum, prone ad maledicendum."

51 UUB, C 259, fol. 59v: "Vanum enim est verbis tuis dare fidem." See also AP, 493.

52 UUB, C 259, fol. 59v: "O domina, nimis sompnias, nimis vigilas. Expedit tibi plus bibere et plus dormire."

53 UUB, C 259, fols. 59v–60r: "Cumque ita loqueretur, circumstantes vole-bant vindicare in eum, sed ipsa per nomen Iesu Christi prohibuit eis dicens: 'Permittite eum loqui, quia Deus misit eum. Ego enim, que in tota vita mea quesiui laudem meam et blasphemaui Deum meum, quare non audiam iusti-ciam meam? Omnes, qui plus laudabant me, adulabantur michi.'"

54 UUB, C 259, fol. 60r: "Vere vidue sunt, dicit magister Mathias in concor-danciis: Que sicut a vita, ita a mundi amore destitute." Apparently Mathias is here in his *Alphabetum distinctionum* quoting Peter the Lombard (*In epistolam I ad Thimothaeum*, Ch. 5). There is not much evidence of Mas-ter Mathias being quoted in the Vadstena sermons, but recent research has drawn attention to the fact that his *Homo conditus* was actually used by the brothers for sermon composition; see Roger Andersson, "Messenger Manu-scripts and Mechanisms of Change," in *Continuity and Change: Papers from the Birgitta Conference at Dartington 2015*, eds. Elin Andersson, Claes Ge-jrot, E. A. Jones, and Mia Åkestam (Stockholm: KVHAA, 2017), 31–34.

55 UUB, C 259, fol. 60r: "Consuetudo enim dyaboli est, quod multas aduersitates excitat viduis et precipue illis, que nubere nolunt, nunc per propinquos, nunc per extraneos, vt eas ad amorem mundi retrahat vel saltem impacientes efficiat."

56 UUB, C 259, fol. 60r: "Multi viri diligunt mulieres, que sedule et diligentes sunt in suis obsequiis."

57 UUB, C 259, fol. 60r: "Et quando aliqui redarguebant dominam Brigidam eo, quod ducebat filias suas ad illos infirmos in tam tenera etate, vt non inficerentur fetoribus et infirmitatibus ipsorum, respondit sancta Byrgitta, quod vtique hoc faceret, vt ibidem addiscerent seruire Deo in infirmis et in pauperibus eius."

58 UUB, C 259, fol. 60v: "Et quia sedula fuit in seruicio Christi prefigurata fuit per Martham, de qua dicitur Luce x [Luc. 10:40]: *Martha satagebat circa frequens ministerium.*"

59 Ibid.: "Certe hec sancta Birgitta fauorem hominum non curauit nec pulchri-tudinem corporis reputauit sed Deum timens omnem diligenciam apposuit, ne ipsum offenderet."

60 Ibid.: "O, quam longe est timor Dei ab istis mundialibus, qui se tam superbe contra Dei voluntatem ornant diuersis vestimentis!"

61 Ibid.: "Christus enim precepit sponse sue sancta Birgitte [see Extrav. 75.19], ne quidem vnum filum haberet in vestibus suis, in quo notaretur superbia. Sed iste domine econuerso nolunt portare vnum filum in vestibus suis, in quo non appareat superbia."

62 Ibid.: "Talis ornatus signum est mortis spiritualis. Quando pannus ponitur super feretrum, signum est cadaueris mortui et quod ibi iaceat mortuus. Sic in corpore ornato signum est, quod anima est ibi mortua, et sic mulier or-nata non est nisi feretrum anime mortue."

63 Ibid.: "Vnde pocius deberet mulier plangere super filiam suam superbe orna-tam, quam si viderit eam ante se iacentem mortuam in corpore."

64 The coincidental fact that she—like Christ—lived for thirty-three years rather strengthens this identification with the Savior.

65 George Ferzoco, "The *Processo Castellano* and the Canonization of Cather-ine of Siena," in Muessig, Ferzoco, and Kienzle, *A Companion to Catherine of Siena*, 200.

66 Roger Andersson, "Birgitta and Her Revelations in the Sermons of the Vad-stena Brothers," in *A Companion to Birgitta of Sweden and Her Legacy in the Later Middle Ages*, ed. Maria H. Oen (Leiden: Brill, 2019).

67 Besides the official response to the judgement there seems to have developed an unofficial attitude towards it: "They never in their hearts nor in their own writings recognized the judgement" (Fredriksson Adman, *Heymericus*, 48).

For examples from the sermon material of the three functions of *auctoritas*, *exemplum*, and *structura*, see Andersson, "Birgitta and her Revelations."

68 Prol. M., 21: "Sane stupendior est hec apparicio illa, que se per carnem monstrauit." The text was included by the principal editor of the *Revelations*, Alfonso of Jaén, as a prologue to the corpus.

69 See further Chapter 6 by Maria H. Oen in this volume.

70 These examples are also discussed in Andersson, "Birgitta and her Revelations."

71 Augustine of Hippo, *De Trinitate*, cap. 18 (PL 42, col. 1082).

72 UUB, C 270, fol. 113r: "Vnde dicit Christus ii libro celesti v: 'Nullus, nisi qui caritatem ad me habuerit, regnum meum optinere poterit.' 1 Cor xiii: 'Si linguis hominum loquar et angelorum' etc vsque 'Si distribuero in cibos pauperum omnes facultates meas, et si tradidero corpus meum ita vt ardeam, caritatem autem non habeam, nichil michi prodest.'"

73 UUB, C 331, fol. 170r: "Hiis vinculis siue isto vinculo obediencie ligari debet quilibet christianus ad tenendum et obseruandum precepta Dei et hoc fit in baptismo, quando homo abrenunciat dyabolo et omnibus pompis eius et ligatur vinculo obediencie ad obediendum Deo et eius preceptis."

74 UUB, C 331, fol. 172r: "Sicut videmus in raptoribus hic in regno et alibi. In futuro punientur eterna dampnacione nisi restituerint, quia dicit Augustinus: 'Peccatum non dimittitur nisi restituatur ablatum'. Et in Reuelacionibus dicit Christus: 'Quid credunt homines in mundo male fidei possessores, qui retinent iniuste obtenta. Numquid credunt quod intrabunt celum? Certe non magis quam Lucifer!'"

75 See further Andersson, "Birgitta and her Revelations."

76 Otfried Krafft, "Many Strategies and One Goal: The Difficult Road to the Canonization of Catherine of Siena," in *Catherine of Siena. The Creation of a Cult*, eds. Jeffrey F. Hamburger and Gabriela Signori (Turnhout: Brepols, 2013), 40.

77 Jane Tylus, *Reclaiming Catherine of Siena: Literacy, Literature, and the Signs of Others* (Chicago, IL: The University of Chicago Press, 2009), 3.

78 Tylus, *Reclaiming Catherine of Siena*, 9.

79 Birgitta of Sweden, *The Revelations*, 1: 27–28. See also Birger Bergh, *Heliga Birgitta. Åttabarnsmor och profet* (Lund: Historiska Media, 2002), 121–30.

80 Algar Thorold, *The Dialogue of the Seraphic Virgin Catherine of Siena* (London: 1907), 13.

81 Tylus, *Reclaiming Catherine of Siena*, 186–87, quoting Vittorio Coletti, *Parole dal pulpito. Chiesa e movimenti religiosi tra latino e volgare nell'Italia del Medioevo e del Rinascimento* (Casala Monferrato: Marietti, 1983).

8 The Mystical Pregnancy of Birgitta and the Invisible Stigmata of Catherine

Bodily Signs of Supernatural Communication in the Lives of Two Mystics

Gábor Klaniczay

Body and soul are intricately interrelated in visionary experience, and communication with the supernatural frequently left visible marks on the body, which also served as proofs of contact with divine forces. The broader context of bodily signs includes trance, rapture, and ecstasy, each of which has its own physiological consequences and mythological background.[1] With such a condition, the body of the mystic might become a channel through which divine revelations can reach the believers. The negative variants of all this, bodily vexations and tribulations received from diabolic apparitions and the spectacular bodily manifestations of diabolical possession, are perceived and described according to a similar logic.

In an even broader sense, the body can become a vehicle for mystical experience: various traits of asceticism such as fasting, self-flagellation, and bodily mortification can prepare for and contextualize the encounter with the agents of the supernatural. Research in recent decades has dealt much with these phenomena, and found a privileged field of inquiry in the lives and writings of late medieval religious women; many insightful studies followed a psychologically and anthropologically founded concept of female "somatic religiosity."[2]

Caroline Bynum put Catherine of Siena in the center of her inspiring analysis of this phenomenon, as a prime example of using the body as a vehicle of mystical experience.[3] As regards her excessive fasting, Bynum debates the "holy anorexia" thesis proposed by Rudolph Bell,[4] and suggests a rich panorama of symbols that might explain the abstinence from food in the lives of female mystics:[5] food as control of the body (a potential location of sin), food as control of circumstance (relations to family and religious roles), food and flesh as pleasure and pain, and woman's body as food. Besides this central feature, Bynum provides an analysis of how blood and the heart became dominant symbols for Catherine. Another crucial dimension was her attention to the body of Christ, shown in her devotion to his circumcision, her eucharistic piety, her compassionate admiration of Christ's Passion, expressed in her physical contact with his side-wound (whence she could drink his life-giving blood), in her desire to share suffering with him,[6] both by self-flagellation with chains and by asking to receive the crown of thorns—and, above all, by her stigmatization.

In comparison, if one regards the life and the work of Birgitta of Sweden, the other most important visionary in Rome in those decades and the immediate predecessor of Catherine of Siena, she is almost entirely missing from the overview of Caroline Bynum and the studies on the subsequent large wave of research on somatic religiosity. Such bodily phenomena were, indeed, comparably less in the center of Birgitta's religiosity than they were with Catherine, but they are not entirely absent there either. Her mystical pregnancy, bodily penance, and ascetic practices after being widowed merit attention in this respect.

Nevertheless, because of this disproportion, here I will reverse the historical order. I will discuss first the stigmatization of Catherine and the related bodily signs of her ongoing close contact with Christ and his Passion, and then turn to the mystical pregnancy of Birgitta, an imitation of the body of the Virgin Mary instead of that of Christ.

The Road to the Stigmata of Catherine of Siena

Stigmatization, as we know, is the appearance of Christ's passion wounds on the body of a living devout believer. When Christ transforms his or her body into His own divine body and shares His suffering with this person, He allows him or her to share His redemptive role as well.[7] The Church recognized this greatest possible miracle only twice in the Middle Ages: for Francis of Assisi and Catherine of Siena. Both claims were received and supported with enthusiasm by their own orders, but generated skeptical critiques and sometimes strong counter-reactions from the other order and from the broader public of believers. These discourses provide valuable source material for understanding the significance that the contemporary public attributed to these bodily signs of supernatural communication, and at the same time they can also illustrate their controversial nature.

Disputes over the stigmata of Catherine were preceded by the controversy over the stigmata of St. Francis and the rivalries provoked by this miracle, which have been analyzed by André Vauchez,[8] Chiara Frugoni,[9] and many others.[10] Besides formulating skeptical views on the cult of the stigmatized *Alter Christus* of the Franciscans, the Dominicans, Cistercians, and Augustinians also strove to find a stigmatic of their own. Roughly forty years after the death of St. Francis, in 1267, the fame of two stigmatized Beguines started to spread: in the diocese of Liège Elizabeth Spalbeek, patronized by the Cistercian abbot Philippe de Clairvaux,[11] and in Cologne Christina of Stommeln, discovered by

Peter of Dacia, a Dominican friar originally from Gotland.[12] Lukardis of Oberweimar, a Cistercian nun since the age of 12, supervised by two Dominican confessors, was stigmatized according to her legend in 1281 and lived with those marks for almost three decades.[13] The Augustinian nun, Clare of Montefalco, bore the signs of the suffering Christ not on the outside of her body but inside her heart, planted there by Christ himself during one of her visions.[14]

The strongest endeavor to find a female stigmatic counterpart of St. Francis manifested itself among the Dominicans. After having patronized Beguines and Cistercian nuns, in the fourteenth century there was a remarkable attempt to attribute a stigmatic reputation to the only Dominican nun who was at that time close to being officially recognized as a saint: the Hungarian princess Margaret, daughter of King Béla IV. There was an unfinished canonization process around her person between 1273 and 1276 (only concluded in 1943).[15]

The oldest testimony of this reputation, born in Italy, is the panel painting by the Master of the Dominican Effigies (*c*.1350) in Santa Maria Novella, Florence, where Margaret, with a visible stigma on her right hand, figures prominently in the group of Dominican saints surrounding the Virgin. A fresco in San Domenico, Perugia, dated to 1368, shows her in a scene reminiscent of the iconography of the stigmatization of St. Francis, where she receives the stigmata from a flying seraph-Christ while her crown rests on the ground beside her feet. A description of her stigmatization also surfaced in a passage inserted into her legend probably in Italy, in the 1370s.[16] All this is not well known, so it merits emphasizing. The stigmatized fame of Margaret of Hungary paved the way for the Dominican Order's ultimately successful breakthrough in this field: the stigmatization of Catherine of Siena.[17]

Controversies on the Invisible Stigmata of Catherine

According to the report in *Legenda maior* (II, 6) of Raymond of Capua, this event occurred on Palm Sunday—1 April 1375—in Pisa, where Catherine was on an important political mission with a group of her closest disciples.[18] She went to hear Mass by her confessor in a chapel dedicated to St. Bartholomew and St. Christina, she took communion, and thereafter she fell into ecstasy.

> Suddenly, before our eyes, [Catherine's body] which had been prostrate on the ground, rose up to a kneeling position; she stretched out her arms and hands to their full length; her face grew radiant. For a long time she knelt like that, bolt upright, her eyes closed. Then, while we still looked on, all of a sudden she pitched forward on the ground as if she had received a mortal wound. A few minutes later she returned to her senses. In a little while, she sent for me, and

spoke to me privately apart from the others. "Father," she said, "I must tell you that, by his mercy, I now bear the stigmata of the Lord Jesus in my body."..."I saw our Lord fastened to the cross, coming down upon me in a blaze of light. With that, as my spirit leaped to meet its Creator, this poor body was pulled upright. Then I saw, springing from the marks of his most sacred wounds, five blood-red rays coming down upon me, directed towards my hands and feet and heart. Realizing the meaning of this mystery, I promptly cried out: "Ah, Lord God, my God, I implore you not to let the marks show outwardly on my body." While these words were still upon my lips, before the rays had reached me, their blood-red color changed from blood red to radiant brightness, and it was in the form of clearest light that they fell upon the five points of my body—hands, feet and heart....[19]

This eye-witness account was only written down more than a decade later, sometime between 1385 and 1395, and no contemporary sources report this extraordinary event, which is quite surprising since according to Raymond's description it happened during a spectacular ecstasy, in front of a large group of her devout followers, that is in public, and not alone in a hermitage as was the case with St. Francis.

Jörg Jungmayr remarked recently that Catherine makes no reference to this event in Pisa in her numerous letters or in her *Dialogue* (although there are two places, in Letters T92 (May 1374) and T142 (from early 1375), which could be interpreted as hints for a desired stigmatization).[20] Concerning the earliest iconographic proof, the fresco by Andrea Vanni for the Cappella delle Volte in Siena, made in 1380/81, immediately after Catherine's death, there has been a debate whether the mark visible in the painting was originally there on her hand, being kissed by a follower, or only added subsequently. The restoration of 1950 voted for its originality.[21] The earliest sermon on Catherine, by one of her closest friends and admirers, the Augustinian hermit William Flete of Lecceto in 1382, two years after her death, makes the first public statement:

She endured many crosses in this world, and was often crucified, in many and varied ways, in spirit, in soul and in body, perhaps without our knowing it. Hence it was not without great significance that she received on her body the wounds of our Lord Jesus Christ in Pisa, as I heard.[22]

Flete calls her "a true disciple of the Apostle Paul," and cites her speaking of the pains in her body with the words: "I do not live, Christ lives in me" (*non vivo ego, vivit in me Christus*).

We know more about the general climate of opinion in the years when Raymond of Capua formulated the description of this stigmatization in the *Legenda maior* and brought it to the public. Catherine's former confessor was then the Master General of the Dominican Order and one of the chief proponents of the unfolding Observant movement which was supposed to restore the order's original purity.[23] The self-affirmation of the Dominicans was also directed against their chief rivals, the Franciscans, who, in precisely in the same years, reached an extreme position stressing the God-likeness of their stigmatized founder. Between 1385 and 1390 Bartolomeo da Pisa wrote his mighty treatise, the *Liber de conformitate beati Francisci ad vitam domini Iesu*, which was disseminated in 1395, at the very same time as *Legenda maior*.[24]

The renewal of the Order of Preachers was closely bound to the rise of the cult of their new candidate for sainthood, who was presented as a counterpart to St. Francis, of equal value. After the city of Siena petitioned for the initiation of a proper papal canonization process, also supported by the Master General of the Dominicans, Raymond of Capua, in 1396 an intensive campaign began for Catherine's canonization. The two principal actors in this enterprise were two Sienese compatriots and disciples of Catherine, Stefano Maconi, her *"discepolo prediletto,"* who after her death became a leading reformer of the Carthusian Order,[25] and Tommaso d'Antonio da Siena, known in modern research as Caffarini, prior of the convent of Dominican Tertiaries Corpus Domini in Venice.[26] Caffarini made Catherine's stigmata a sign of election, the central feature of the campaign for her canonization. In 1396 he made Catherine's similarity to Christ and her stigmatization the principal theme of his Lenten sermons. An important number of these sermons dealt with the parallels between Catherine and Francis. This campaign can well be considered as a Dominican reaction to the book by Bartolomeo da Pisa.[27]

A witness's testimony almost twenty years later confirms this impression: Bartolomeo Dominici (d. 1415), one of Catherine's confessors, describes her stigmatization with the following words: "The people present could see how she reached out with her hands and legs, just the same way as Blessed Francis had received the stigmata."[28] The experience Catherine had when she received her stigmata was indeed not independent of the visual representations of the stigmatization of Francis: the blood-red rays, Giotto's invention as pointed out by Chiara Frugoni, defined imperatively, how subsequent stigmatizations were lived.[29]

Caffarini also attributed great significance to images. The first representations of Catherine's stigmata were probably due to his initiative, such as the polyptych by Andrea di Bartolo, where Catherine is depicted with four Dominican *mantellate*, with the scene of her stigmatization on the predella,[30] and the initials in the copies of the *Legenda maior* by Raymond of Capua, prepared in Caffarini's scriptorium.[31] At the same time, he kept on gathering supportive materials for Catherine's canonization. He compiled a *Libellus de supplemento* to the legends of Catherine between 1411 and 1416; the most important part, chapter VII, is a long *Tractatus de stigmatibus*, which probably repeated much of the material of the 1396 Lenten sermons.[32]

Caffarini also intended to discuss stigmata based on precedents, he juxtaposed the way the most prominent stigmatics he knew of had received the stigmata. As shown in the illustrations of his manuscript prepared by the Bolognese circle of Cristoforo Cortese,[33] besides St. Francis and St. Catherine he included two more Dominicans, the thirteenth-century friar Walter of Strasbourg, whose invisible but painful stigmata were described by Gerard of Frachet in his *Vitae fratrum*,[34] and another thirteenth century figure, the Dominican-supervised Beguine, Helen of Hungary.[35] Caffarini learnt about Helen, when he inquired among his confreres about the much-represented stigmata of Margaret of Hungary. Gregory, the Hungarian provincial, informed him that the fame of Margaret's stigmata was inaccurate. Nevertheless, he sent him the legend of Margaret's *magistra*, Helen, who was "indeed" stigmatized—I strongly suspect that the charming legend of Helen was reworked for this occasion. In any case, the original story of her alleged stigmatization, according to which lilies sprang from her stigmatic wounds, was welcomed by Caffarini in his stigmata typology.

Caffarini also supported his campaign for Catherine with an ample collection *de omnibus speciebus stigmatum* (going beyond the five wounds of Christ, adding also other bodily injuries) from the hagiographies of other saints and from St. Catherine's legend. His list included scars from demonic vexations, self-flagellation or special *signa* received in visions, such as wounds from the Crown of Thorns or the Nails of the Crucifixion, or the miraculous exchange of hearts with Christ. The long series of precedents started with St. Dominic and St. Peter Martyr, and included Clare of Montefalco, Gertrude the Great, and the Dominican tertiary Margaret of Città di Castello. For the discussion in our volume, it is especially interesting that Birgitta of Sweden is also included in this list of Catherine's precedents, as "having poured upon her naked flesh drops of burning wax which left traces."[36] In the eyes of Caffarini, the wounds caused by such an ascetic exercise were also a form of stigmata. This broad interpretation ranged all bodily injuries stemming from Passion-centered devotional practices to the same category as the wounds received from the crucified Seraph by Francis. The readers could not escape the conclusion that in this field the Christ-related *signa* acquired by Catherine were as impressive as those of Francis (if not more so).[37]

Despite all his efforts, even organizing an irregular canonization hearing in 1411, the "Processo Castellano," Caffarini could not achieve an initiation of proceedings for Catherine.[38] Giovanni Dominici spoke in vain in her interest at the Council of Constance,[39] where important authorities, among them the Paris Chancellor Jean Gerson, were strongly against this kind of female, mystical, ecstatic spirituality so closely related to such bodily signs.[40]

After several more decades, Catherine was finally canonized in 1461, by the Sienese Pope Pius II.[41] This met, however, with an immediate malignity from the side of the Franciscans. The Franciscan bishop Roberto Caracciolo da Lecce was charged with celebrating the festive Mass after the canonization. After having read out the entire text of Catherine's stigmatization from the legend of Raymond of Capua, Caracciolo continued with the following words:

> ...on the basis of this vision of hers, in many places St. Catherine had been depicted as receiving the stigmata from Christ. This was probably done with the intention of making the invisible things known by the visible, and by this painting indicate the real, uncontrollable pain—all this could probably be tolerated, despite the error which followed from this: to make believe that she had in fact received visible stigmata. I have seen and read several such writings praising this saint, but I was unable to find anything else in them than the pain she suffered from during her ecstatic rapture, without any further signs. And even if we want to call this pain by the name of stigmata, it does not contain nor imply the same miraculous conditions as the stigmata of St. Francis.... This does not diminish in any way the sanctity of Catherine.[42]

When, a decade later, Pope, Sixtus IV came from the Franciscan Order, this conflict worsened considerably. In the bull *Spectat ad Romani* of September 1472 he prohibited representations of St. Catherine *cum stigmatibus Christi ad instar beati Francisci* ("with the stigmata of Christ, similarly to Blessed Francis"), even the mentioning of it in sermons, and he repeated this prohibition in 1475 and 1478.[43]

The counter-reaction to this prohibition from the Dominican Order did not fail to resurface after the death of Sixtus IV (1484). During the papacy of Alexander VI (1492–1502), a new series of stigmatized images of Margaret of Hungary appeared. She did not figure in the pontifical prohibition and could strengthen the claim for the representation of St. Catherine's stigmata. As a print from around 1500 shows, Margaret continued to be depicted as a surrogate stigmatic, reminding everyone of the invisible stigmata of St. Catherine.[44] But this was not enough; in the 1490s, to prove the truthfulness of St. Catherine's stigmata, also a host of new Dominican stigmatics appeared on the scene: a group of charismatic women of unusual vigor. As Ann Matter; Gabriella Zarri; and, more recently, Tamar Herzig have revealed in a series of fascinating studies, the Savonarolan movement assigned a significant leading role to these "*sante vive*," in the footsteps of St. Catherine of Siena.[45]

The most noteworthy of these "new Catherines" was the Dominican tertiary Lucia Brocadelli, also known as Lucia of Narni (d. 1544). In the city of Viterbo, on 25 February 1496, during a meditation on the Passion on Good Friday, bleeding stigmata appeared on her hands, feet, and side. She claimed she was publicly exposing her bleeding stigmata on the recommendation of St. Catherine as a testimony to the veracity of her invisible stigmata.

The celebrity of Lucia's stigmata, which brought her to the protection of the mighty Duke Ercole II d'Este, were seen personally by Pope Alexander VI, and were examined several times by inquisitors and physicians, will not detain us here, besides the fact that it intended to underline one of the singular aspects of Catherine's stigmata, i.e. their invisible nature.

Visibility and Invisibility of the Stigmata

The dilemma of visibility and invisibility of marvelous bodily phenomena, and the task of interpreting the *signa* in relation to divine, supernatural agents is a central feature in the lives of mystics and visionaries, a crucial aspect of understanding the relation between body, soul, and the spiritual dimensions.[46] It is no wonder that this aspect was also present in the history of stigmatizations from the outset. In the founding miracle, that of Francis, after Thomas of Celano's first famous description of the stigmatizing apparition of the Seraph at Mount La Verna in 1224, a second torrent of legends appeared. The *Legend of the Three Companions* (1240) and the *Second Life of St Francis* (2Cel) (1247) enriched the supernatural bond of Francis by the earlier communication with the *croce dipinta* at San Damiano, and thus developed substantially the concept of stigmatization: "the wounds of the sacred Passion were impressed deep in his heart, though not yet on his flesh [2Cel]."[47] The *Tractatus de miraculis* (3Cel) (1254), continues in this vein: "just as, internally, his mind had put on the crucified Lord, so, externally, his whole body put on the cross of Christ ...."[48]

The internal, miraculous bodily secrets manifest themselves in perceptible traces and, sooner or later, they also show externally. For Francis, it happened in his lifetime but he kept them secret and they were revealed to the public only on his dead body. Other, already mentioned stigmatics, such as Elizabeth Spalbeek, Christine of Stommeln, and Lukardis of Oberweimar showed their wounds to devout onlookers as ultimate proof. At the same time, in Gerard Frachet's description of the Dominican prior, Walter of Strasbourg, the concept of aching, painful, but invisible stigmata appears as a different, spiritualized way of participating in the bodily suffering of Christ:

> He entered to pray in Colmar in the house of the Friars minor and meditated on the bitter suffering of the Lord, and felt in his body on five places such a strong pain that he could not withhold himself and he cried out in a loud voice, and since then he keeps feeling bitter pain on these five places.[49]

Clare of Montefalco also suffered painful invisible wounds, placed into her heart by Christ during a vision in the form of the *arma Christi*—a hidden but quite corporeal phenomenon she talked about in her life which was eagerly discovered in her extracted heart by the nuns after her death.[50]

There were multiple reasons for the invisibility of Catherine's stigmata in Raymond of Capua's description and Tommaso Caffarini's explanation.[51] Modesty, the will to avoid vainglory was certainly one, although not stressed explicitly by these hagiographers. There was also a strong desire among the Dominicans to juxtapose the stigmata of St. Francis to something slightly different but arguably of the same value. As for the experience of the invisible but painful bodily perception of Christ's wounds, besides the example of Walter of Strasbourg they could rely upon an entire Dominican tradition. The late thirteenth-century *Nine Ways of Prayer* attributed to St. Dominic popularized a more disciplined, ascetic, and interiorized assimilation of Christ's suffering.[52] The stigmata of Lukardis of Oberweimar, the Cistercian nun patronized by Dominican confessors, also appeared first in a painful but invisible form, to become visible only in a renewed encounter with Christ.[53]

To put it briefly: the claim of invisible stigmata was a paradox, because it lacked precisely the most striking feature of this miracle, the immediate, tangible visibility of the bloody impact of the crucified Christ upon the stigmatic's body. At the same time, it was anchored in an increase in late medieval passion devotion and made itself convincing through a broad spectrum of ascetic, penitential, and visionary practices. This cultural context is what explains the durable popularity of the invisible stigmata among the mystics of the early modern times: such as Maria Maddalena dei Pazzi and Marie de l'Incarnation (Madame Acarie);[54] the same kind of invisibility characterized the transverberation of Theresa of Avila.[55] And, as in the case of Clare of Montefalco, invisibility still required some kind of proof; as with Clare's heart, the injuries of transverberation were also discovered in the heart of Theresa of Avila after her death. The corporeal relics of Catherine of Siena also came to support the veracity of her stigmata; from the sixteenth century, the stigmata, unseen in her lifetime, could be indeed perceived on her mummified hand- and feet-relics.[56]

The long-drawn-out debate on the invisible stigmata of Catherine, which stimulated polemical and partisan tracts in the sixteenth century,[57] came to a standstill with the treatise of Gregorio Lombardelli commissioned by Clement VIII.[58] The treatise reflects the changed attitudes, after the council of Trent, concerning the representation of the supernatural phenomena.[59] The truthfulness of Catherine's stigmata was justified by Lombardelli: "if indeed the wounds were not seen by everyone, it does not follow on account of this that she did not have the wounds; because Balaam did not see the angel, and yet the angel was there and the ass saw the angel."[60] He also returns to the argument of Roberto Caracciolo: "Just as in books, one reads things, that teach the invisible through the visible; just so the visible wounds of St. Catherine, in images, teach [about] the invisible [wounds] which she carried whilst alive; and therefore it is no error to paint her with stigmata."[61]The treatise continues with complex theological argumentation: can one doubt the real presence of Christ in the host only because it is not visible? Lombardelli concludes with visual proof, the fact that he personally saw the stigmata on Catherine's relics in Rome at the Jubilee of 1600.

The Mystical Pregnancy of Birgitta

Let me turn now, after this detailed discussion of Catherine's invisible stigmata, to another invisible supernatural bodily manifestation: the mystical pregnancy Birgitta of Sweden. While Catherine's stigmata became a core symbol of the *imitatio Christi*, in Birgitta's life, one can observe the manifestation of a similarly significant model, the *imitatio Mariae*. Like the imitation of Christ, and especially the body of Christ, this model also emerged in the twelfth-century renewal of medieval Christianity.[62] Devotion to Christ and the Virgin Mary, as the monumental work of Rachel Fulton[63] demonstrates, had a parallel and intertwined unfolding in Latin Christianity, which intensified from the twelfth century.[64] Identification with the Virgin Mary provided a privileged road to express their devotion to Christ for female mystics, especially lay women, who turned to the religious life being widowed or even while still living in marriage. Rosalynn Voaden has recently provided an overview of three crucial aspects: the devotion to the Christ child, whom they could approach with motherly love; the desire to embrace Christ as an attractive adult man, as a "Bride of Christ" (also a central, and paradoxical, epithet of the Virgin), and compassion as a mourning mother for Christ's suffering at the crucifixion.[65] From the twelfth and thirteenth centuries a broad set of examples is illustrative, from Beguines such as Marie of Oignies, Ida of Louvain, Hadewych,[66] the companion of St. Francis, Clare of Assisi,[67] to late medieval lay female mystics such as Angela of Foligno[68] and Margery Kempe.[69] These three approaches provided opportunities for a close personal encounter with Christ, a possibility for a mystical union.

An ingenious addition to this complex was the idea of mystical pregnancy claiming ecstatic-visionary participation in the bodily experience of the Virgin, thus sharing with her both the glorious task of bringing the Savior to this world and achieving a mystical union by holding the unborn Christ in their bodies. Illuminated from this internal presence, they felt superbly authorized to speak in his name.

This idea of mystical pregnancy could have emerged parallel to the thirteenth-century news of the stigmatization of Francis, the claim for a total bodily identification of an *alter Christus* with the Savior.

A similarly close assimilation of a female mystic to the Virgin Mary, not only in her virginity, but even in her supernatural pregnancy contained the same—almost sacrilegious—ambition of deification, as the appearance of the wounds of Passion on the body of a believer.

The changing content of Marian devotion contributed to the formation of this claim. The motherhood of Mary became more and more central,[70] supported by her multiplying joint representations with the infant Christ, also related to the impact of the Byzantine *Hodegetria* type of icon in the West after the sack of Constantinople in 1204.[71] It is emblematic that the female counterpart of Francis, Elizabeth of Hungary (d. 1231), was described by her maids, after the birth of her child, with the following words: "Following the example of the blessed Virgin, Elizabeth carried her child in her own arms and offered it on the altar along with a candle and a lamb."[72] Female mystics started to strive for having access to the child Christ by the Virgin, appearing to them together in visions. Already Marie of Oignies (d. 1213) felt as if she were cuddling the baby Jesus between her breasts and observed him crying in the cradle and feeding from the breasts of Mary.[73] Others asked for the privilege of holding him in their hands, nursing him with motherly care.[74] With this triumph of the cult of the Virgin, motherhood appeared more compatible with female sanctity than before, and Birgitta became an important emblem of this evolution.[75]

The first, unclear, hints to the phenomenon of mystical pregnancy came from a heretical background: Margaret, the lover of the heresiarch Fra Dolcino, who burned with him in 1300, was claimed by followers to have been pregnant with the Holy Spirit, as was, some two decades later, Na Prous Boneta, a Beguine in Provence.[76] The Franciscan tertiary, Agnes Blannbekin (d. 1315), who became notorious for having the foreskin of Christ appear miraculously in her mouth, could also feel a swelling in her womb at Christmastime.[77] Christina Ebner, a Dominican nun in Engelthal (d. 1356), dreamt that "she was pregnant with our Lord... and after a while she dreamt how she would bear him without pain."[78] Another Dominican nun in Mödingen, Margaretha Ebner (d. 1351), perhaps a cousin of Christina, had the visionary experience of being admonished by a statue of the infant Christ to suckle him, and, subsequently, "as an apogee of corporeal *imitatio Mariae*, the Sister's own body reproduced the birth of Christ," with three sisters holding her while she had spasms of pain.[79]

These data show, with the precedents for the stigmatization of St. Francis,[80] and with the ampler series leading to the stigmatization of Catherine of Siena, that the general spiritual context was already prepared when Birgitta[81] received the famous vision one Christmas Eve, in the Cistercian monastery Alvastra (Rev. VI: 88.1). She experienced "such a great and wonderful feeling of exultation ...in [her] heart that she could scarcely contain herself for joy...a wonderful sensible movement in her heart like that of a living child turning and turning around."[82]

Her confessors, Master Mathias of Linköping and Prior Peter of Alvastra, present at this event, could observe and sense these movements, and the latter gave a detailed testimony of it at Birgitta's canonization process.[83]

This vision has been analyzed by Claire L. Sahlin in the context of fourteenth-century spirituality, and in the light of subsequent theological explanations for the birth of Christ in the heart.[84] She reached back to patristic precedents, quoting Origen on the word of God conceived in human hearts just like Christ was born in Mary. Eloquent formulations of Ambrose, Augustin, and the twelfth-century Cistercian Guerric of Igny are added to the description of the formation of this "affective spirituality" where believers are solicited to give birth to Christ "in the womb of their hearts."[85] While hinting at the, almost contemporary precedents of mystical pregnancy whom Birgitta probably did not know, Sahlin points to two models that probably did influence her thinking because they were known by her confessors Master Mathias and Prior Peter: the life of Mary of Oignies by Jacques de Vitry, and the twelfth-century treatise *Speculum virginum*, exhorting virgins to give birth to Christ spiritually.[86]

As regards the spiritual meaning of mystical pregnancy for Birgitta, Sahlin points out that the vision on mystical pregnancy "represented her difficult decision to place her spiritual vocation above the attachments to her biological children and suggested that she was filled with divine wisdom." Her "identification with the Virgin Mary became her model for giving flesh to divinity. ...Birgitta felt authorized through her maternal role... to serve as outspoken prophet and vehicle of divine revelation."[87]

The ingenuity of using the association with the Virgin in a much more powerful script for imitation than any other mystic before her is emphasized by Miri Rubin in her recent monograph on the cult of the Virgin Mary: "Bridgettine Mary was an agent of redemption, a public actor in Christian history. She was also a private sufferer with her son. Like Mary, whose heart was pierced by the pain of the Crucifixion, Birgitta felt through her heart, where her spiritual child was born."[88]

These issues have been treated again in the monograph of Päivi Salmesvuori who observed that the mystical pregnancy had a special significance at the beginning of Birgitta's religious career as a widow. The Christmas miracle, when Birgitta felt that Christ was born in her heart, compensated for the lack of virginity, a serious obstacle on the road of religious perfection. By regarding her body "as similar to Mary's body," by feeling Jesus inside herself, she could feel like she was both a mother and a virgin, like Mary.[89]

Conclusion

The visionary life of Catherine of Siena, her experience of personal encounters with Christ, who put the Crown of Thorns on her head, who thrust a nail of his crucifixion through her hand, causing immense pain, who exchanged hearts with her, who allowed her to drink his blood from his side-wound, and, finally, who impressed in her body the invisible but painful stigmata, can be counted as a prime example of "corporeal visions," according to the well-known classification of Augustine (*De Genesi in Litteram*, XII).[90]

Birgitta's revelations, in comparison, except for her early experience of mystical pregnancy, rather belonged to the second and the third type of visions: "spiritual" and "intellectual." She did include some hints Mary gave to her own body in the *Revelations* (the suffering in her heart when Christ was crucified [Rev. VII: 15], the absence of pain at the Nativity [Rev. VII: 21]), but the body of Birgitta is rather absent through all of her eight books. Was this due to the influence of her confessor Alfonso of Jaén, who, in constructing her behavior within the discourse of *discretio spirituum*, "obliterated her body," as Rosalynn Voaden has claimed?[91]

Bodily symbols are indeed less present in Birgitta's career as a prophet than in the passion-centered spirituality of Catherine of Siena. In this respect, Salmesvuori points to a relevant episode in the life of Birgitta. At the beginning of her religious career, in the second year after she came to the monastery of Alvastra, Birgitta became very ill because, like many female ascetics since the time of St. Jerome, she refused to bathe for a long time, and only reluctantly accepted the advice of the doctors and Master Mathias to abandon this excess. As her confessor Prior Peter later narrated, a revelation also helped her to find a model of "suitable asceticism,"[92] a moderation in this field. This principle is subsequently recurring in the *Revelations*: "The body should not be killed but cleansed through abstinence so that the words of God can be spread abroad by means of it" (Rev. III: 34.4). In Rev. VI: 122 Christ encourages a woman to moderate her gestures in public.[93]

Nevertheless: Birgitta's mystical pregnancy, the "marvelous and great exultation of her heart" had a huge influence upon the integration of motherly corporeality into the symbols of somatic female religiosity. Like the stigmata of St. Francis, it also inspired emulation. The first paragon was Dorothy of Montau (d. 1394), a Prussian mystic, almost stigmatic,[94] who was present in Danzig when Birgitta's remains were carried through that city, from Rome to Vadstena, Sweden. She also felt that her uterus swelled, and that God turned within her like an unborn child. Her confessor, Johannes Marienwerder reported of her vision at this occasion, hearing from God:

> If St Birgitta had not reported that a living fetus had appeared and moved back and forth in her heart and uterus, you, moreover, could not have manifested this very similar thing concerning yourself. But, nevertheless, you actually exhibited more of this than she. I magnified your heart and uterus more than hers.[95]

This emulation of the mystical pregnancy of Birgitta became in her order, the Birgittine sisters of Vadstena, a liturgically framed Christmas
ritual by the end of the fifteenth century. A book of liturgical readings
copied in 1502 (Stockholm, Kungliga Biblioteket, A 3) describes in the
rubric "Concerning our Lord Jesus Christ's childhood and growth. How
he spiritually shall be born and raised in the human heart and soul,"
how the passage of Birgitta's *Revelations* (Rev. VI: 88) should be read
to the sisters, instructing them to become spiritual mothers of Christ
themselves.[96]

Mystical pregnancy continued to be cultivated, in the early modern
times, not only by Birgittine sisters, but appeared also in the somatic
spiritual manifestations of other orders, such as the Clarisse of Spain
(Magdalena de la Cruz, d. 1544)[97] the Carmelites in France,[98] or the
Devonshire prophetess Joanna Southcott (d. 1814).[99]

Notes

1 Gábor Klaniczay, "The Process of Trance: Heavenly and Diabolic Apparitions in Johannes Nider's *Formicarius*,"in *Procession, Performance, Liturgy, and Ritual*, ed. Nancy van Deusen (Ottava: Institute of Medieval
  Music, 2007).
2 Caroline Walker Bynum, *Holy Feast and Holy Fast: The Religious Significance of Food to Medieval Women* (Berkeley: The University of California
  Press, 1987); Nancy Caciola, *Discerning Spirits: Divine and Demonic Possession in the Middle Ages* (Ithaca, NY: Cornell University Press, 2003);
  Dyan Elliott, "The Physiology of Rapture and Female Spirituality," in *Medieval Theology and the Natural Body*, eds. Peter Biller and Alastair Minnis
  (York: York Medieval Press, 1997); *Proving Woman: Female Spirituality
  and Inquisitional Culture in the Later Middle Ages* (Princeton, NJ: Princeton University Press, 2004); "Flesh and Spirit: The Female Body," in *Medieval Holy Women in the Christian Tradition, c. 1100–c. 1500*, eds. Alastair
  Minnis and Rosalynn Voaden (Turnhout: Brepols, 2010); Rosalynn Voaden,
  "Mysticism and the Body," in *The Oxford Handbook of Medieval Christianity*, ed. John H. Arnold (Oxford: Oxford University Press, 2014).
3 The General Index of her book provides an analytic list of some 60 entries;
  see Bynum, *Holy Feast and Holy Fast*, 423.
4 Rudolph Bell, *Holy Anorexia* (Chicago, IL: The University of Chicago Press,
  1985); Bynum, *Holy Feast and Holy Fast*, 189–208.
5 A constant phenomenon until our days. See Jacques Maître, *Anorexies religieuses, anorexie mentale. Essai de psychanalyse sociohistorique. De Marie
  de l'Incarnation à Simone Weil* (Paris: Le Cerf, 2000).
6 See Esther Cohen, *The Modulated Scream: Pain in Late Medieval Culture*
  (Chicago, IL: The University of Chicago Press, 2010).
7 Pierre Adnès, "Stigmates," in *Dictionnaire de spiritualité ascétique et mystique. Doctrine et histoire*, vol. 14, (Paris: 1988); Joachim Bouflet, *Les stigmatisés* (Paris: Cerf, 1996); Gábor Klaniczay (ed.), *Discorsi sulle stimmate
  dal Medioevo all'età contemporanea – Discours sur les stigmates du Moyen
  Âge à l'époque contemporaine*, in *Archivio italiano per la storia della pietà*
  26 (2013): 7–385.

8 André Vauchez, "Les stigmates de Saint François et leurs détracteurs dans les derniers siècles du moyen âge," *Mélanges de l'École française de Rome* 80 (1968): 595–625; *Francis of Assisi: The Life and Afterlife of a Medieval Saint* (New Haven, CT: Yale University Press, 2012).

9 Chiara Frugoni, *Francesco e l'invenzione delle stimmate. Una storia per parole e immagini fino a Bonaventura e Giotto* (Turin: Einaudi, 1993).

10 Arnold Davidson, "Miracles of Bodily Transformation, or, How St. Francis Received the Stigmata," in *Picturing Science, Producing Art*, eds. Caroline A. Jones, Peter Gallison, and Amy Slaton (London: Routledge, 1998); Richard Trexler, "The Stigmatized Body of Francis of Assisi: Conceived, Processed, Disappeared," in *Frömmigkeit im Mittelalter. Politisch-soziale Kontexte, visuelle Praxis, körperliche Ausdrucksformen*, eds. Klaus Schreiner and Marc Müntz (Munich: Wilhelm Fink, 2002); Jacques Dalarun, "The Great Secret of Francis," in *The Stigmata of Francis of Assisi: New Studies New Perspectives*, eds. Jacques Dalarun, Michael Cusato, and Carla Salvati (St. Bonaventure, NY: The Franciscan Institute, 2002); Solanus M. Benfatti C.F.M, *The Five Wounds of Saint Francis* (Charlotte, NC: TAN Books, 2011).

11 Walter Simons and J. E. Ziegler, "Phenomenal Religion in the Thirteenth Century and Its Image: Elisabeth Spalbeek and the Passion cult," in *Women in the Church*, eds. W. J. Sheils and Diana Wood (Oxford: Basil Blackwell, 1990); Walter Simons, "Reading a Saint's Body: Rapture and Bodily Movement in the *Vitae* of Thirteenth-Century Beguines," in *Framing Medieval Bodies*, eds. Sarah Kay & Miri Rubin (Manchester: Manchester University Press, 1994).

12 John Coakley, "Friars as Confidants of Holy Women in Medieval Dominican Hagiography," in *Images of Sainthood in Medieval Europe*, eds. Renate Blumenfeld-Kosinski and Timea Szell (Ithaca, NY: Cornell University Press, 1991); Aviad M. Kleinberg, *Prophets in Their Own Country: Living Saints and the Making of Sainthood in the Later Middle Ages* (Chicago, IL: The University of Chicago Press, 1992).

13 Kleinberg, *Prophets in Their Own Country*, 101–11; Piroska Nagy, "Sensations et émotions d'une femme de passion: Lukarde d'Oberweimar († 1309)," in *Le sujet de l'émotion au Moyen Age*, eds. Damien Boquet and Piroska Nagy (Paris: Beauchesne, 2009).

14 Cordelia Warr, "Re-reading the Relationship between Devotional Images, Visions, and the Body: Clare of Montefalco and Margaret of Città di Castello," *Viator* 38 (2007): 217–49.

15 Gábor Klaniczay, *Holy Rulers and Blessed Princesses: Dynastic Cults in Medieval Central Europe* (Cambridge: Cambridge University Press, 2002), 195–279; Viktória Hedvig Deák, *La légende de sainte Marguerite de Hongrie et l'hagiographie dominicaine* (Paris: Cerf, 2013); Ildikó Csepregi, Gábor Klaniczay, and Bence Péterfi (eds.), *Legenda Vetus, Acta Processus Canonizationis et Miracula Sanctae Margaritae de Hungaria – The Oldest Legend, Acts of the Canonization Process and Miracles of Saint Margaret of Hungary* (Budapest: CEU Press, 2017).

16 This legend was discovered and published by Caffarini. Thomas Antonii de Senis "Caffarini," *Libellus de supplemento, Legende prolixe virginis beate Catherine de Senis*, eds. Giuliana Cavallini and Imelda Foralosso (Roma: Edizioni Cateriniane, 1974), 175.

17 Gábor Klaniczay, "Le stigmate di santa Margherita d'Ungheria: immagini e testi," *Iconographica. Rivista di iconografia medievale e moderna* 1 (2002): 16–31; "On the Stigmatization of Saint Margaret of Hungary," in *Medieval*

Christianity in Practice, ed. Miri Rubin (Princeton, NJ: Princeton University Press, 2009).

18 On Catherine's political missions see F. Thomas Luongo, *The Saintly Politics of Catherine of Siena* (Ithaca, NY: Cornell University Press, 2006).

19 LM, II. 6.35–37, p. 259. Translated in Raymond of Capua, *The Life of Catherine of Siena.* trans. Conleth Kearns (Wilmington, DE: Glazier, 1980), 186–7.

20 Jörg Jungmayr, "Ekstase und politische Mission. Die Stigmata der Caterina von Siena (1347–80)," in *Zwischen Himmel und Erde. Körperliche Zeichen der Heiligkeit,* eds. Waltraud Pulz et al. (Stuttgart: Steiner 2012), 61–77.

21 Diega Giunta, "L'affresco di Andrea Vanni," in Lidia Bianchi and Diega Giunta, *Iconografia di S. Caterina da Siena. 1. L'immagine* (Roma: Città Nuova, 1988); "The Iconography of Catherine of Siena's Stigmata," in *A Companion to Catherine of Siena,* eds. Carolyn Muessig, George Ferzoco, and Beverly Mayne Kienzle (Leiden: Brill, 2012), 263.

22 Robert Fawtier (ed.), "Catheriniana," *Mélanges d'archéologie et d'histoire* 34 (Rome: École française de Rome, 1914), 49–50; Benedict Hackett, *William Flete, O.S.A., and Catherine of Siena* (Villanova, PA.: Augustinian Press, 1992), 194; Carolyn Muessig, "Catherine of Siena in Late Medieval Sermons," in Muessig, Ferzoco, and Kienzle, *A Companion to Catherine of Siena,* 204. On this sermon, see also Chapter 7 by Roger Andersson in the present volume.

23 André Vauchez, *Catherine de Sienne. Vie et passions* (Paris: Cerf, 2015), 129–34.

24 Bartholomaeo de Pisa, *De Conformitate vitae beati Francisci ad vitam Domini Iesu, Analecta Franciscana,* IV–V (1906–12).

25 David Movrin, "The Beloved Disciple: Stephen Maconi and St. Catherine of Siena," *Annual of Medieval Studies at Central European University* 10 (2004): 43–53.

26 Otfried Krafft, "Many Strategies and One Goal: The Difficult Road to the Canonization of Catherine of Siena," in *Catherine of Siena: The Creation of a Cult,* eds. Jeffrey F. Hamburger and Gabriela Signori (Turnhout: Brepols, 2013), 26–30. On Maconi's and Caffarini's instrumental roles in the diffusion of Catherine's writings—an important strategy in their promotion of her sanctity—see also Chapter 5 by Silvia Nocentini in the present volume.

27 Alessandra Bartolomei Romagnoli, "La disputa sulle stimmate," in *Virgo digna coelo: Caterina e la sua eredità,* eds. Alessandra Bartolomei Romagnoli, Luciano Cinelli, and Pierantonio Piatti (Vatican City: Libreria editrice vaticana, 2013), 417.

28 "… visa est a circumstantibus manus et pedes extendere, sicut depingi consuevit B. Franciscus cum sacra stigmata scribitur recepisse," PC, 342; George Ferzoco, "The *Processo Castellano* and the Canonization of Catherine of Siena," in Muessig, Ferzoco, and Kienzle, *A Companion to Catherine of Siena,* 185–203.

29 Frugoni, *Francesco e l'invenzione delle stimmate,* 210–22.

30 Giunta, "The Iconography of Catherine of Siena's Stigmata," 285–87.

31 Silvia Nocentini,"Lo 'scriptorium' di Tommaso Caffarini a Venezia," *Hagiographica* 12 (2005): 79–144. On the role of illuminations in Caffarini's manuscripts, see Chapter 6 by Maria H. Oen in the present book.

32 "Caffarini," *Libellus de supplemento,* 121–266; Fernanda Sorelli, "La production hagiographique du dominicain Tommaso Caffarini," in *Faire croire. Modalités de la diffusion et de la réception des messages religieux du XIIe au XVe siècle,* ed. André Vauchez (Rome: École française de Rome, 1981).

33 Fabio Bisogni, "Il Libellus di Tommaso d'Antonio Caffarini e gli inizi dell'iconografia di Caterina," in *Con l'occhio e col lume,* eds. Luigi Trenti e

Bente Klange Addabbo (Siena: Cantagalli, 1999); Emily Ann Moerer, "The Visual Hagiography of a Stigmatic Saint: Drawings of Catherine of Siena in the 'Libellus de Supplemento'," *Gesta* 44 (2005): 89–102; Jane Tylus, *Reclaiming Catherine of Siena: Literacy, Literature, and the Signs of Others* (Chicago, IL: The University of Chicago Press, 2009).

34 Gerardi de Fracheto O.P., *Vitae fratrum Ordinis Praedicatorum*, ed. Benedikt Maria Reichert, Monumenta Ordinis Fratrum Praedicatorum Historica 1 (Lovanii, 1896), 223.

35 Robert Fawtier (ed.), "La vie de la bienheureuse Hélène de Hongrie," *Mélanges d'archéologie et d'histoire* 33 (1913): 3–23; AASS, Nov. IV (Bruxelles: 1925), 267–76; Deák, *La légende de sainte Marguerite de Hongrie*, 162–68.

36 "... ipsa stillante ardentis cerei stillas flammigeras super nudam carnem, exinde quedam note et signa relinquebantur," "Caffarini," *Libellus de supplemento*, 124.

37 Carolyn Muessig, "The Stigmata Debate in Theology and Art in the Late Middle Ages," in *The Authority of the Word: Reflecting on Image and Text in Northern Europe, 1400–1700*, eds. Celeste Brusati, Karl Enenkel, and Walter Melion (Leiden: Brill, 2012).

38 Ferzoco, "The *Processo Castellano*."

39 Krafft, "Many Strategies and One Goal," 30.

40 Klaniczay, "The Process of Trance," 230–41.

41 Krafft, "Many Strategies and One Goal," 31–41.

42 Giunta, "The Iconography of Catherine of Siena's Stigmata," 262.

43 Giunta, "The Iconography of Catherine of Siena's Stigmata," 267–69.

44 Diega Giunta, "La questione delle stimmate alle origini della iconografia cateriniana e la fortuna del tema nel corso dei secoli," in Trenti and Addabbo, *Con l'occhio e col lume*, 345, 442, Fig. 225.

45 E. Ann Matter, "Prophetic Patronage as Repression: Lucia Brocadelli da Narni and Ercole d'Este," in *Christendom and its Discontents: Exclusion, Persecution, and Rebellion, 1000–1500*, eds. Scott L. Waugh and Peter D. Diehl, (Cambridge: Cambridge University Press, 1995); E. Ann Matter and Gabriella Zarri (eds.), *Una mistica contestata. La vita di Lucia da Narni (1476–1544) tra agiografia e autobiografia* (Rome: Edizioni di Storia e Letteratura, 2011); Gabriella Zarri, *Le sante vive. Profezie di corte e devozione femminile tra '400 e '500* (Turin: Rosenberg & Sellier, 1990); Tamar Herzig, *Savonarola's Women: Visions and Reform in Renaissance Italy* (Chicago, IL: The University of Chicago Press, 2008); *Christ Transformed into a Virgin Woman. Lucia Brocadelli, Heinrich Institoris, and the Defense of the Faith* (Rome: Edizioni di Storia e Letteratura, 2013).

46 Giselle de Nie, Karl F. Morrison, and Marco Mostert (eds.), *Seeing the Invisible in Late Antiquity and the Early Middle Ages* (Turnhout: Brepols, 2005).

47 Thomas of Celano, "The Remembrance of the Desire of the Soul," in *Francis of Assisi: Early Documents*. Vol. II. *The Founder*, eds. Regis J. Armstrong, J A. Wayne Hellmann, and William J. Short (New York: New City Press, 1999), 249.

48 Thomas of Celano, "The Treatise on the Miracles of Saint Francis," in Armstrong, Hellmann, and Short, *Francis of Assisi*, 401.

49 Gerardi de Fracheto O.P., *Vitae fratrum*, 223.

50 See n. 14 above.

51 David Ganz, "The Dilemma of a Saint's Portrait: Catherine's Stigmata between Invisible Body Trace and Visible Pictorial Sign," in Hamburger and Signori, *Catherine of Siena*, 239–62.

52 Paul Philibert, "Roman Catholic Prayer: The *Novem modi orandi sancti Dominici*," in *Contemplative Literature: A Comparative Sourcebook on*

Meditation and Contemplative Prayer, ed. Louis Komjathi (New York: SUNY Press, 2015).

53 See n. 14.

54 Christian Mouchel, *Les femmes de douleur. Maladie et sainteté dans l'Italie de la Contre-Réforme* (Paris: PUF, 2007); Antoinette Gimaret, "Corps manqués et stigmates invisible dans le biographies spirituelles du XVIIe siècle," in Klaniczay, *Discorsi sulle stigmate*, 239–58.

55 Jodi Billinkoff, *The Avila of Saint Teresa. Religious Reform in a Sixteenth-Century City* (Ithaca, NY: Cornell University Press, 1989).

56 Michael Hohlstein, "'Sacra lipsana': The Relics of Catherine of Siena in the Context of Propagation, Piety, and Community," in Hamburger and Signori, *Catherine of Siena.*

57 Alessandra Bartolomei Romagnoli, "Un trattatello cinquecentesco in difesa delle stimmate di Caterina da Siena," in Klaniczay, *Discorsi sulle stimmate.*

58 Gregorio Lombardelli, *Sommario della disputa. A difesa della Sacre Stigmate di Santa Caterina da Siena* (Siena: 1601).

59 Cordelia Warr, "Visualizing Stigmata: Stigmatic Saints and Crises of Representation in Late Medieval and Early Modern Italy," in *Studies in Church History* 47 (2011): 228–47; Bartolomei Romagnoli, "La disputa sulle stimmate," 432–35.

60 Lombardelli, *Sommario,* 31.

61 Lombardelli, *Sommario,* 32. (I cite the translation by Cordelia Warr).

62 Giles Constable, "The Imitation of the Body of Christ," in *Three Studies in Medieval Life and Social Thought: The Interpretation of Mary and Martha, The Ideal of the Imitation of Christ, The Orders of Society* (Cambridge: Cambridge University Press, 1995), 143–247.

63 Rachel Fulton, *From Judgement to Passion: Devotion to Christ and the Virgin Mary, 800–1200* (New York: Columbia University Press, 2002).

64 Miri Rubin, *The Mother of God: A History of the Virgin Mary* (New Haven, CT: Yale University Press, 2009).

65 Voaden, "Mysticism and the Body," 401–08.

66 Walter Simons, *Cities of Ladies: Beguine Communities in the Medieval Low Countries* (Philadelphia: University of Pennsylvania Press, 2001).

67 Catherine M. Mooney, "*Imitatio Christi* or *Imitatio Mariae?* Clare of Assisi and Her Interpreters," in *Gendered Voices: Medieval Saints and Their Interpreters*, ed. Catherine M. Mooney (Philadelphia: University of Pennsylvania Press, 1999).

68 Cristina Mazzoni, "Angela of Foligno," in Minnis and Voaden, *Medieval Holy Women*, 581–600.

69 Clarissa W. Atkinson, *Mystic and Pilgrim: The Book and the World of Margery Kempe* (Ithaca, NY: Cornell University Press, 1983).

70 Rubin, *The Mother of God,* 257–67.

71 Hans Belting, *Likeness and Presence. A History of the Image before the Era of Art* (Chicago, IL: The University of Chicago Press, 1994), 73–77, 200–07.

72 Kenneth Baxter Wolf, *The Life and Afterlife of St. Elizabeth of Hungary* (Oxford: Oxford University Press, 2011), 198.

73 Jacques de Vitry, *The Life of Marie of Oignies*, trans. Margot H. King (Toronto: Peregrina, 1993), 112.

74 Rosemary Hale, "*Imitatio Mariae*: Motherhood Motifs in Devotional Memoirs," *Mystics Quarterly* 16 (1990): 193–203.

75 Jeannette Nieuwland, "Motherhood and Sanctity in the Life of Saint Birgitta of Sweden: An Insoluble Conflict?" in *Sanctity and Motherhood: Essays on Holy Mothers in the Middle Ages*, ed. Anneke B. Mulder-Bakker

(New York: Garland, 1995). Birgitta's *imitatio Mariae* is also discussed in detail by Unn Falkeid in Chapter 3 in the present volume.

76 Barbara Newman, *From Virile Woman to WomanChrist* (Philadelphia: University of Pennsylvania Press, 1995), 195–98, 208–09, 215–18.

77 Dyan Elliott, *Fallen Bodies: Pollution, Sexuality and Demonology in the Middle Ages* (Philadelphia: University of Pennsylvania Press, 1999), 124–25.

78 Hale, "*Imitatio Mariae*,"193–95.

79 Hale, "*Imitatio Mariae*,"196–97; Barbara Koch, "Margaret Ebner," in Minnis and Voaden, *Medieval Holy Women*, 403.

80 Carolyn Muessig, "Signs of Salvation: The Evolution of Stigmatic Spirituality before Francis of Assisi," *Church History* 82 (2013): 40–68.

81 Bridget Morris, *St Birgitta of Sweden* (Woodbridge: Boydell Press, 1999); Pavlína Rychterová, *Die Offenbarungen der heiligen Birgitta von Schweden. Eine Untersuchung zur alttschechischen Übersetzung des Thomas von Štítné* (Cologne: Böhlau, 2004).

82 Rev. VI: 88.1: "Nocte natalis Domini tam mirabilis et magna aduenit sponse Christi exultacio cordis, ut vix se pre leticia tenere posset, et in eodem momento sensit in corde motum sensibilem admirabilem, quasi si in corde esset puer viuus et voluens se et reuoluens."

83 *Deposicio copiosissima domini prioris de Aluastro*, in AP, 484; Tore Nyberg, "The Canonization Process of St. Birgitta of Sweden," in *Procès de canonisation au MoyenÂge. Aspects juridiqueset religieux – Medieval Canonization Processes. Legal and Religious Aspects*, ed. Gábor Klaniczay (Rome: École française de Rome, 2004); Cordelia Heß, *Heiligemachen im spätmittelalterlichen Ostseeraum. Die Kanonisationsprozesse von Birgitta von Schweden, Nikolaus von Linköping und Dorothea von Montau* (Berlin: Akademie Verlag, 2008), 99–172.

84 Claire L. Sahlin, "A Marvelous and Great Exultation of the Heart: Mystical Pregnancy and Marian Devotion in Bridget of Sweden's Revelations," in *Studies in Saint Birgitta and the Brigittine Order*, ed. James Hogg, vol. 1 (New York: Edwin Mellen, 1993), 108–09; *Birgitta of Sweden and the Voice of Prophecy* (Woodbridge: Boydell Press, 2001), 78–109.

85 Sahlin, *Birgitta of Sweden*, 85–86.

86 Sahlin, *Birgitta of Sweden*, 88–90; *Speculum virginum*, ed. Jutta Seyfarth (Turnhout: Brepols, 1990).

87 Sahlin, *Birgitta of Sweden*, 84.

88 Rubin, *The Mother of God*, 347. On Birgitta's use of the model of Mary, see also Chapter 3 by Unn Falkeid in the present volume.

89 Päivi Salmesvuori, *Power and Sainthood: The Case of Birgitta of Sweden* (New York: Palgrave Macmillan, 2014), 80–91.

90 Augustine, *The Literal Meaning of Genesis*, trans. John H. Taylor, vol. 2. Books 7–12 (New York: Newman, 1982), 185.

91 Rosalynn Voaden, *God's Words, Women's Voices: The Discernment of Spirits in the Writing of Late-Medieval Women Visionaries* (York: York Medieval Press, 1999), 92–93.

92 Voaden, *God's Words, Women's Voices*, 76–80.

93 Voaden, *God's Words, Women's Voices*, 197.

94 Heß, *Heilige machen*, 245–331.

95 Max Töppen (ed.) "Aus dem Septililium venerabilis domine Dorothee," in *Scriptores rerum Prussicarum: die Geschichtsquellen der preussischen Vorzeit*, eds. Theodor Hirsch, Max Töppen, and Ernst Strehlke (Leipzig: Verlag von S. Hirzel, 1863), vol. 2, 365; I cite the translation of Sahlin, *Birgitta of Sweden*, 105.

96 Sahlin, *Birgitta of Sweden*, 106–07.
97 Maurice Garçon, *Magdeleine de la Croix abbesse diabolique* (Grenoble: Jérôme Millon, 2010 [1939]), 181–84.
98 Valerio Marchetti, "Il re bambino. Cronologia e geografia di un culto monarchico," in *Infanzie. Funzioni di un gruppo liminale del mondo classico all'Età moderna*, ed. Ottavia Niccoli (Florence: Ponte alle Grazie, 1993).
99 Susan Juster, "Mystical Pregnancy and Holy Bleeding. Visionary Experience in Early Modern Britain and America," *William and Mary Quarterly*, 3rd series 57 (2000): 249–88.

9 The Crossing Paths of Birgitta of Sweden, Catherine of Siena, and Alfonso of Jaén

Camille Rouxpetel

One man connects Birgitta of Sweden and Catherine of Siena more than any: Alfonso Pecha de Vadaterra, former bishop of Jaén.[1] As confessor of both Birgitta and Pedro of Luna, the cardinal of Aragon and future Benedict XIII (1394–1423), the Spaniard also links Birgitta with the Iberian Peninsula. Alfonso had been created Bishop of Jaén in Andalusia in 1359, but already by 1368, he had given up the ecclesiastical career to become a Hieronymite hermit, just like his brother Pedro. The genesis of this order is linked to the spiritual Franciscans of Umbria and Tuscany, who announced the coming of the Holy Spirit in Spain.[2] If the early links between Italian hermits and spirituals, on the one hand, and the Spanish pre-Hieronymites, on the other hand, are difficult to establish, these connections become much more obvious after the foundation of the order, through the action and the path of Alfonso of Jaén.

Alfonso joined the Order of Hieronymites and became one of the main architects of the rapprochement between Spanish and Italian hermits. He met Birgitta of Sweden soon after his conversion, having just arrived in Italy.[3] His entry into the circle of Birgitta, of whom he became the last confessor, gave him access to the Avignon Curia and, by extension, to Pope Gregory XI. Upon Birgitta's death (23 July 1373), instead of escorting the funeral procession to Vadstena, Alfonso returned to Italy, where Gregory XI (1370–78) had given him missions in Pisa, in the Patrimony of St. Peter, and in Sicily, in order to lay the groundwork for a large union of the many varieties of hermit communities on the peninsula. A letter sent by Alfonso of Jaén to the hermits of Santa Maria del Santo Sepolcro (Florence), undated but received by its addressees on 15 March 1374, makes it possible to specify the nature of this mission: he asked them to receive and instruct some hermits and informed them that the pope had authorized him to found an eremitic-cenobitic congregation of Italian Hieronymites, on the model of the Spanish Hieronymites, both in central Italy and in the Kingdom of the Two Sicilies.[4] It was during this time that he met Catherine of Siena; his role in the canonization process of his former penitent, Birgitta, then introduced him into Roman reform circles. There he met the cardinal of Aragon, Pedro of Luna, whose confessor he became. Pedro of Luna, papal legate for the kingdoms of the

Iberian Peninsula, later pope under the name of Benedict XIII, never stopped supporting the Hieronymites.

This chapter functions as a "step sideways"—a study of both the role of Birgitta of Sweden and Catherine of Siena from an outside perspective and, in a broader context, that of the reformists of the late fourteenth century. This shift demands a change in point of view; by moving the analysis of these figures to areas of contact between them.[5] My aim is not to compare their ecclesiological thoughts, but rather to study a group of Observants and Spirituals through the interactions between Alfonso, Birgitta, and Catherine, and the larger network to which they belonged. These interactions take place during a period marked by the Great Western Schism (1378–1417) and the Reform of Observance.[6] Appearing at the end of the fourteenth century, this reform consisted of an attempt to find an answer to the Church's troubles, symbolized by the Schism, as well as a desire for renewal. This desire was paradoxically founded on a return to a previous order, and a return to a stricter obedience to the primitive rule in the case of monastic orders. The Reform of Observance concerned both levels: the Church's head (*in capite*), as well as its grassroots level (*in membris*)—such as monasteries, as we will see through the example of the abbey of Subiaco (Lazio). This "hierarchical reform" was intended to operate first on the Church's head but also to have an impact on all the members (*reformatio in capite et in membris*). In that regard, Birgitta of Sweden's and Catherine of Siena's reform efforts also focused on both levels. While they spoke directly to the pope, their efforts also focused on the religious orders with which they were connected: the Birgittine Order, founded by Birgitta herself, and, in Catherine's case, the Dominicans.

The Role Assigned to Birgitta of Sweden in the Urbanist Strategy of Alfonso of Jaén

In 1374, on his return to Rome from a mission in Castile to preach a crusade in order to redeem captives, Alfonso of Jaén encountered Katarina Ulfsdotter, Birgitta's daughter and first abbess of the Birgittine monastery in Vadstena.[7] Katarina had traveled there to prepare the process of beatification of her mother. Pedro of Luna, the cardinal of Aragon, was chosen to conduct investigations. This choice was anything but fortuitous: Pedro of Luna's house in Rome was the meeting place for the partisans of the Observance, and one of his two confessors was, as noted above, Alfonso of Jaén. Furthermore, Raymond of Capua, the leader of the Observant Dominicans, was one of Pedro's familiars. The future Master General of the Dominican Order, Raymond was then the prior of the monastery of Santa Maria sopra Minerva—and the confessor of Catherine of Siena. All were close relatives of Bartolomeo Prignano, who was considered to be one of the main promoters of the reform of the Church.

Dated by Robert Lerner to 1385/86, Alfonso's treatise on the schism and the circumstances of the election of Bartolomeo Prignano as Pope Urban VI (1378–89), entitled *Conscriptio bona sub triplici via de electione sanctissimi in Christo patris ac domini, domini Urbani pape sixti*, gives some indications of the relations between Alfonso, Pedro of Luna, the Benedictine bishop and reformist Pierre Bohier,[8] and Birgitta of Sweden.[9] The three *viae*, or paths, referred to in the title are the *via spiritus* ("spiritual path"), the *informatio facte* ("factual information"), and the *via iuris* ("juridical path"). In the section devoted to the spiritual path, the *via spiritus*, Alfonso begins by quoting Birgitta:

> On the first point, i.e. about the teaching by the spiritual way, it seems to me established and I say this: before the jubilee year of the pontificate of Clement VI, while Birgitta, a native of the kingdom of Sweden, was in this kingdom and prayed alone, our Lord Jesus Christ appeared to her and, speaking with her, made two revelations to her: the first, which she was to immediately send to Pope Clement, and the other to the kings of France and of England.[10]

Here, Birgitta serves the reforming project of Alfonso in two ways: by legitimizing the prophecy and by her reforming action toward the pope (*reformatio in capite*). A little later, when writing about Urban V, Alfonso makes a link between himself and Birgitta: "St. Birgitta herself presented this revelation to Pope Urban, written by my hand at Montefiascone, before he returned the day before the Assumption of the Blessed Virgin Mary."[11] Then, exploring the second path (*informatio facte*), in a section devoted to the facts of the miracle and Prignano's election, Alfonso presents himself as a witness, as the confessor of Pedro of Luna, the cardinal of Aragon: "And I was, though unworthy of it, the confessor of one of these cardinals, who often confided his secrets to me and asked me for advice on difficult subjects outside the confession."[12] During the few days preceding the conclave, Alfonso once again refers to Birgitta upon encountering her daughter who came to Rome for the canonization of her mother:

> And then, three or four days before the beginning of the conclave, I went to find Katarina, the daughter of St. Birgitta of Sweden, and told her to go immediately to the Archbishop of Bari, humbly to pay her homage and to entrust to him the canonization of her mother, Blessed Birgitta, a canonization that was then debated and instructed at the curia in the presence of Pope Gregory, but to say nothing to the archbishop about the election.[13]

Alfonso's advice to Katarina shows how much the issues of her mother's canonization process were political—"to entrust to him the canonization

of her mother ... but to say nothing to the archbishop about the election."
In Alfonso's description, the role assigned to Birgitta, dead five years before Prignano's election, is beyond doubt: her revelations demonstrated
that Urban VI was the true pope [*verus papa*]. After recalling a central
theme in Birgitta's revelations, namely the importance of the pope's return from Avignon to Rome, Alfonso concluded:

> Therefore, by virtue of all that precedes, I firmly believe that Urban,
> and not Clement, is the true pope [*verum papam*] according to the
> will of God and the power of the keys. All this confirmed to me
> that my belief was true: after the birth of schism, many and great
> servants and friends of God, both hermits and other holy men and
> women of great virtue and leading a life known to be exemplary,
> from Germany, from Italy, from Sweden, from Spain, which I inter-
> viewed separately ...assured me.[14]

Alfonso finally explores the third path, the *via iuris* ("the legal path"):
"Thirdly, I said that I kept my information on the truth of this matter
from the legal track."[15] If they all are bound by a common will to reform
the Church, Alfonso assigned to each a specific method of legitimizing
the reform: Birgitta through her prophetic revelations, Alfonso with his
testimony on the various events surrounding the election of Prignano to
the pontificate, and Bishop Pierre Bohier by his expertise as a lawyer.
The first path (*via spiritus*) is then linked to Birgitta, the second one
(*informatio facte*) to Alfonso as eyewitness, and the third and last one
(*via iuris*) to Pierre Bohier:

> Then a man of virtue and holy intention, that is to say, Brother Pierre,
> monk of Saint Benedict, a native of Gaul, of the city of Narbonne,
> formerly bishop of Orvieto, doctor of canon law, told me, fully in-
> formed of this reality related to the pontificate through his former
> secretary, that while still bishop, tormented by his conscience, he
> left the antipope and the curia to reside in Paris at the monastery of
> Celestines and advise Charles, King of France.[16]

Reform Monasticism—An Ideal Shared by Alfonso and Birgitta: The Abbey of Subiaco, Center and Observatory of the Reform Project

Having reproduced the letter written by Pierre Bohier to Pope Urban VI
to return under his obedience, Alfonso composed a short biography
of the Benedictine bishop aimed at supporting his friend: "It is indeed
impossible for me to explain how much the aforementioned bishop is
virtuous, conscientious, and moral."[17] In his praise of Bohier, Alfonso

highlighted three elements: his stay in Subiaco, his expertise in canon law, and his intellectual honesty.

Why was his stay in Subiaco important? First, this was the place of the meeting of Alfonso of Jaén and Pierre Bohier. Their friendship was based on a common action in favor of the Observance. It is probably to Subiaco that their bonds of friendship were tied—perhaps through Brother Maurus, a monk at Sacro Speco, one of the two monasteries of the Abbey of Subiaco, and of Castilian origin (Brother Maurus will be mentioned again later). Overlooking the valley of the Aniene, the Abbey of Subiaco is one of the three great Benedictine abbeys of Lazio, along with Montecassino and Farfa. The church of San Lorenzo in Subiaco testifies to an early Christianization of the region; probably going back to the second half of the fourth century, it predates the presence of Benedict of Nursia, founder of the abbey. Benedict's presence and actions in Subiaco are reported by Gregory the Great in the second book of the *Dialogues*, composed between 593 and 594. Fleeing Rome and the world in search of a "desert" to which to withdraw, Benedict settled in a cave in the territory of Subiaco to live as a hermit. Called by the brothers of a neighboring community to lead them, he left and, according to Gregory the Great, founded twelve monasteries; the Abbey of Subiaco was the descendent of at least one of these. This single abbey in fact comprised two communities, that of St. Scholastica and that of Sacro Speco, which had a more eremitical vocation and was assembled at the supplementary place of the cave of Benedict.

The community of the Sacro Speco acquired renewed importance in the fourteenth century, in the wake of the Benedictine monastic reforms. The Franciscan spiritual Angelo Clareno was probably the first reformer of the monastery. Clareno found refuge there between 1318 and 1334, during the tenure of the Abbot Bartholomeus II. Clareno left for Subiaco after the death of his protector, Cardinal Giacomo Colonna, whose family played a leading role in the monastery. From 1362, under the impulse of the Abbot Bartholomew III of Siena (1362–69), Subiaco became the epicenter of a reform movement of Benedictine monasticism, promoting a more interiorized version of the rule and redefining the role of the abbot and of the two monastic communities. From there, the monastery became a meeting place for men favorable to church reform; their efforts contributed greatly to the election of Prignano to the pontificate in 1378. Among these men were Alfonso of Jaén and Pierre Bohier. Furthermore, it was precisely to Subiaco that Bohier withdrew to write his second commentary on the Rule of Benedict from an observant perspective.

What precisely did Alfonso say about Bohier and Subiaco in his treatise?

> I indeed saw this man, while he exercised his episcopal responsibilities in a spirit of peace, come to the holy Benedictine monastery of

the Speco, to the abbey of Subiaco, which is 32 miles from Rome and where is observed honorably the Rule of St. Benedict. After having in my presence called the prior and the monks of this monastery, he announced to them that he wanted to build in this valley a monastery dedicated to St. Jerome, placed under the rule of St. Benedict and endowed with twelve monks. He told them that he wanted to give up his episcopal functions, to retire to the monastery, to become a monk in order to live here as a true monk, poorly and by obeying the Rule. And immediately, he built the aforementioned monastery of St. Jerome. I personally went to this new little monastery. But because of the schism in the Church of God, he had to give up fulfilling his desire.[18]

Birgitta—who strongly supported a stricter observance of the Augustinian rule within the order she founded—Bohier, and Alfonso joined in renouncing worldly life in favor of a monastic life influenced both by a strong ascetic ideal and an observant ideal, reinforced by the duplication of *observatur regula* and *in observantia regule*: *laudabiliter observatur regula* ("is observed honorably the Rule of St. Benedict")... *ac eciam renunciare et dimittere suum episcopatum et in ipso monasterio se includere et monachare ut verus monachus in observancia regule et in paupertate ibidem vivere* ("to give up his episcopal functions, to retire to the monastery, to become a monk in order to live here as a true monk, poorly and by obeying the Rule"). But Brigitta, Bohier, and Alfonso also shared the desire to exert a real political influence: Birgitta, like Catherine, never eased her campaign for the restoration of the Holy See to Rome. As for Bohier and Alfonso, both were deeply involved in the resolution of the Schism, with Birgitta's canonization process being a part of their action. Bohier and Alfonso both seem to have taken three intersecting paths: a willingness to give up their episcopal careers in favor of the monastic life; the figure of St. Jerome; and Subiaco.

Thus, in the first lines of his treaty, Alfonso justified his own status as a witness in the investigation carried out by the kings of Castile and Aragon on the election of Urban VI:[19] "I was also heavily questioned because I resigned from my episcopate, renounced a high office, thus abandoning my patrimony for God's sake, as well as all earthly riches and vain worldly honors."[20] In saying this, he turned around the argument of his opponents—*vel forte interrogatus sum* ("I was heavily questioned") in order to make an argument for his reliability—his *contemptus mundi* ("contempt for the world")—and therefore his commitment to the observance; this maneuver legitimized his testimony. Regarding St. Jerome, it is not his role as the cardinal-doctor of the Church that is invoked here. Rather, notwithstanding the brevity of his sojourn in the Chalcis desert, it is instead his role as a hermit, a penitent of the desert that is evoked. Jerome had already acquired this identity after both the traditional and mendicant monastic orders had cast him as a "reform saint." The new spiritual demands of the reformers of the fourteenth century, who promoted a return to the monastic origins and a more internalized version of the Rule, are particularly consonant with the eremitic and penitential dimension of both Benedict, linked to Subiaco, and Jerome. Indeed, in the fourteenth century, several spiritual and reforming attempts were directly connected with Jerome: the order of the clerics of St. Jerome, the Jesuates, founded in 1367 by Giovanni Colombini of Siena; several communities in Tuscany and the Marches; and the Order of Hieronymites, approved by Gregory XI in 1373 with the bull *Salvatoris humani generis*. One of the founders of this order was Pedro Fernandez Pecha, the widowed royal treasurer, first superior general of the Spanish Hieronymites, and brother of Alfonso of Jaén.

In 1383, Alfonso founded an abbey dedicated to St. Jerome in Quarto near Genoa.[21] Evoking Peter, the *infante* of Aragon (1305–81), a key figure in Aragonese prophetism and Franciscanism and partisan, along with Birgitta and Catherine, of the pope's return to Rome,[22] Alfonso specified:

> This brother Peter [of Aragon] told me all this seriously, although I was unworthy, before the schism, at the time when Pope Gregory was in Avignon, the year 1372. He gave me all this written by the hand of Brother Raymond [of Capua], his confessor, and I keep these writings in our monastery of St. Jerome at Genoa.[23]

According to the inscription placed on Alfonso's tomb in Quarto, the first community was formed by Spanish brothers, who remained loyal to Urban VI and were disappointed at Aragon's entrance into the Clementine obedience:

> Here is the venerable Father dom. Alfonso de Vadaterra, of the Hispanic nation, who shared his own patrimony for God and gave up his bishopric of Jaén to become poor, follow the poor Christ, and lead an eremitic life. Then, arriving at Genoa, he founded this church, intended for alms to the poor and dedicated to St. Jerome, which he obtained from the king through the venerable Olivetan monks. Finally, he joined the Lord on 19 August 1388.[24]

The foundation of a monastery dedicated to St. Jerome in Italy but populated with Spaniard monks testifies to the success of one of the axes of the reforming policy of Alfonso: the rapprochement between Italian and Spanish hermits in an eremitic-cenobitic community. This foundation and this rule constitute one of the foundations of the reform desired by both Alfonso and those around him, including Birgitta and Catherine. Let us recall that the eremitic-cenobitic model is the foundation of the

Augustinian rule, also given to the Birgittine Order. When he was with Birgitta in Montefiascone in the summer of 1370, Alfonso was probably already living either in solitude or in a house of hermits (perhaps in the Spanish community at Montefalcone according to Eric Colledge).[25] He was also working toward the rapprochement between Italian and Spanish hermits, as evidenced by a passage from Alfonso's testimony at Birgitta's canonization process, which evokes brother Maurus of Spain:

> Lady Laetitia reported these facts on 9 November 1370, at the castle of Genenciani, in the presence of three witnesses: dom. Alfonso, brother Maurus of Spain, monk at the Benedictine monastery of Speco, and Thomasa, handmaid or servant of the same lady Laetitia.[26]

Two years later, in 1372, Maurus made monastic profession at the Sacro Speco community. Given the year of the novitiate, Maurus entered the abbey as early as 1371. In view of the links maintained by Alfonso of Jaén with the Benedictine abbey, and especially with the monastery of Speco, we can surmise that he was the origin of Maurus's choice to make his monastic profession there. Maurus, a native of Toledo (he is called "of Toledo" in several acts preserved in the library of Santa Scolastica in Subiaco), might have come to Italy with Alfonso, or he may have joined the hermits of the region of Toledo, among whom was Alfonso's brother, Pedro.

It was therefore in Subiaco that, in 1374, Alfonso met this other reformer, Benedictine Bishop Pierre Bohier. This was probably not the first time the two men met, though the place and date of their first meeting are unknown. The meeting of 1374 is nevertheless important for our purposes. In this year, depending on the exact moment when Pierre Bohier made his request, three or five Spanish brothers were already present at the Speco. Two of them, Donatus de Toledo and Jeronimus de Aragonia, appear in the archives of the monastery in the year in which Alfonso was present. Considering the origin of Brother Donatus, prior of the Speco in 1374, one could even hypothesize an earlier connection with the former bishop of Jaén. Just before his departure for Italy, Alfonso frequented the pre-Hieronymite eremitic community that his brother had joined in 1366. Like Maurus, sometimes called "of Hispania," sometimes "of Toledo," Donatus of Toledo could have come with Alfonso from the Iberian Peninsula to settle in Italy. Although we cannot confirm this, we can note that in 1374 two Spaniards appeared at the Speco. Alfonso of Jaén and Pierre Bohier were also present, the latter nurturing the project to install a monastery dedicated to St. Jerome near the Speco.[27]

Within the curial circles in which Alfonso moved, we also find the English Benedictine Adam Easton. A staunch supporter of Urban VI,

Easton was one of five witnesses summoned by Alfonso in the process of the canonization of Birgitta of Sweden. On 21 December 1381, Urban made him cardinal. The context of one of Easton's works, the *Defence* of Birgitta, is of special interest. Indeed, this episode is particularly relevant to precisely the network to which Birgitta's partisans belonged in the specific context of her process of canonization.

Easton's *Defence* is a response to an attack on Birgitta issued in Perugia by an unknown opponent.[28] That the attack came from Perugia is not coincidental: the city was home to the *fraticelli*, Franciscan Spirituals who were in favor of a reform of both their order and of the Church (*in capite et in membris*). Alfonso had been in contact with the *fraticelli* when he first left Jaén; indeed, as early as 1368 Alfonso's presence is attested in Perugia—a region marked by the influence of the Franciscan Tertiary Tomasuccio da Foligno (1319–77)—and this happened at the moment when the Inquisition struck the *fraticelli*.[29] The links established with the main city of Umbria do not stop there. The Santa Maria Novella monastery in Perugia (now San Benedetto Novello) was indeed one of the two main Italian Hieronymite foundations; in 1408, the monastery received the authorization, which had been sought for some time, to take the title and vocation of St. Jerome. Alfonso's connections with the hermit centers were used against him and the reform for which he had campaigned. These attacks most likely originated from the same source as those made against Birgitta, to which Easton had replied. Fittingly, Easton sent his work, the *Defence* of Birgitta, to Alfonso of Jaén and the nuns of Vadstena.

The Diversity of the Ecclesiological Thoughts within the Reform Network of Alfonso: Catherine of Siena, Pierre Bohier, and the Anonymous Author of the *Liber dialogorum hierarchie subcelestis*

Between Bohier and the Sienese environment, the *Liber dialogorum hierarchie subcelestis*, an anonymous Dominican treatise dated from 1388, forges another connection. It depicts a fictitious dialogue between a master, called "orthodox," and his disciple, Paucastius, a catechumen who had rejected his baptism because of the many questions raised by the Schism. In the *Liber*, the anonymous author compares the two schisms, that of the Eastern and Western Churches, and he seeks solutions from the Greek-Orthodox Church to the challenges facing the Roman Church, which suffered from its pontifical monarchy. The author also discussed the two foundations of the papal monarchy: the Petrine primacy and the Donation of Constantine, and denounced the latter as apocryphal in chapter XXI, which closed the second book of the treatise.

How should we understand the nature and purpose of the *Liber*? As the work of a Dominican whose order is nevertheless a staunch defender of papal primacy? As a reformist treatise questioning the government of the church and promoting a conciliar way? As an historical and philhellenic text? There is no need to choose between these different facets. The question is how to articulate them. It thus becomes necessary to broaden the framework of research in order to examine the *Liber*'s resonances with the events and debates of the time, and to consider the diffusion of the text.

Three contextual links are of particular interest: that between the anonymous Dominican text and Pierre Bohier; that between the anonymous author of the *Liber* and Subiaco; and that between the anonymous text, Siena, and the Dominicans of Siena, including Catherine.

In the *Liber*, the anonymous author said that he met Pierre Bohier several times, both at the court of the French king, Charles V, and in Rome. The author of the *Liber* also cited two other names: the secular canon and professor of theology Guillaume of Salvarville, to whom he credited the explanation of the word "synagogue"; and the Dominican altarist, i.e. the priest responsible of the high altar of the basilica of the Vatican, Brother Gonzalvus, who allowed him to consult the ancient registers of the Church of Rome. In a 2008 article, Hélène Millet demonstrated the connections between the anonymous author of the *Liber* and these three men based on their writings and ideas on reform, and based on the friendship they developed at the Benedictine Abbey of Subiaco.[30]

Let us return for a moment to the figure of Brother Gonzalvus. This Aragonese preacher, prior of Santa Sabina, the Dominican convent on the Aventine Hill in Rome, was the confessor of Pedro of Luna, as was also Alfonso of Jaén. On the basis of his studies in canon law in Montpellier (1361–70) and his participation in the April 1378 papal election, Pedro of Luna finally rallied the cardinals; citing the climate of terror surrounding the election of Bartolomeo Prignano, and relying on the decretal *De his quae vi metusve causa fiunt* (I, 40), Pedro suggested having Prignano's elevation nullified and proceeding to the election of a new pontiff. Having left Rome for Anagni at the end of June, in August, Pedro sent one of his confessors, the Aragonese brother Gonzalvus OP, to persuade Urban VI to renounce the pontificate. Far from obeying the Aragonese cardinal, the Dominican made a stop at Subiaco and went immediately to the Speco with his compatriots, in order to remain apprised of the turnaround of Pedro of Luna. He reported this interview in his deposition during the Castilian inquiry of Medina del Campo, conducted in 1379 on the events of 1378 by the Dominican Cardinal Nicolas Misquinus:

> Leaving Anagni, I arrived at the Monastery of Speco, at the Abbey of Subiaco, where are some monks totally withdrawn from the world, for what I know, come from the regions of Spain, devotees and known to the cardinal of Luna. They were kept informed of many subjects by Cardinal of Luna himself. While I was exposing to

them the malignancy of the situation that had led to the schism, one of them said to the assembly: "See brothers: the nave of the church has been dislocated in the open sea and everyone is in this world to deal with the salvation of the soul, which is why, because we were separated from every other community, everyone must speak according to what God has inspired him, in order to preserve with more safety and usefulness the wood of this broken nave." At these words, after having heard all the arguments, it appeared to all of us in this place that to follow the path or the pact of the cardinals and their words was to go straight to hell, following the devil, while to follow the vicar of Christ, whom they [the cardinals] had elected for his holiness, his spirituality in all things, and the skill which he displayed in his acts, was to follow the way of truth to the Lord Christ and our Savior. And so everything was accomplished and decided.[31]

Brother Gonzalvus explicitly linked the Aragonese cardinal with the brothers "from the regions of Spain" residing at the Speco—links based on loyalty, on belonging to the same nation, and on exchanging information "of many subjects" (*in multis*), presumably the sending of letters or emissaries.[32] Who were these emissaries? Brother Gonzalvus, confessor of Pedro of Luna? One of Speco's Spanish brothers?

Strong ties unquestionably bind the cardinal to the Spanish monastic community of Subiaco. At the announcement of Pedro of Luna's position in favor of the cardinals assembled at Anagni, one of the Spanish monks spoke immediately: he led, according to Gonzalvus, all the brothers present, including him—*de omnibus nobis*—to support Urban VI in not following the Aragonese cardinal. The Dominican therefore presented his visit as a kind of meeting between reformers who had just been betrayed by one of their own. He would not have convinced the Aragonese monks to follow the path which he himself had already followed, but would have come to consult men to whom he was bound by spiritual and national ties, transcending their reciprocal monastic affiliations. Revealing a striking contrast between the incipit—*devoti et noti cardinali de Luna* ("devotees and known to the cardinal of Luna")—and the explicit—*sequi viam vel amicitiam cardinalium et dicta eorum esset ire ad infernum post diabolum* ("to follow the path or the pact of the cardinals and their words was to go straight to hell, following the devil")—this short testimony is the story of a real drama, proportionate to the shock provoked by the reversal of the cardinal, one of the most reliable supporters of the reformers up to this point.

The anonymous author of the *Liber* completed his work, in a revised version extant in a manuscript now in Madrid, by saying:

Thus ends the "Dialogue of the Subcelestial Hierarchy" between an Orthodox and a Catechumen, named Paucastius, divided into four books and composed in Siena, from the Holy Scripture, the holy canons and sentences of the Fathers, the year of the Lord 1388, by a certain brother of the order of Preachers, bishop. May his name be erased from the book of the living on earth to be inscribed in the book of life in eternity.[33]

In the explicit, the author gives three clues to his identity: he was a Dominican, a bishop, and he had composed his treatise in Siena, in 1388, i.e. eight years after the death of Catherine of Siena. Although, unlike Catherine, the anonymous author fought against the pontifical monarchy, both of them supported Urban VI. The anonymous author might be one of the French followers of Urban VI who had to leave for Italy when it became impossible both to stay in France and to support Urban. But the integration of the anonymous author into the milieu of the Dominicans of Siena and his links with the thought of Catherine are for the moment only speculation. It is nonetheless possible to connect them by means of common acquaintances and their membership in a common framework. To this end, two intermediaries appear again as particularly interesting: Alfonso of Jaén and Pierre Bohier.

Ecclesiology of the fourteenth century, whether it is dominant ecclesiology or alternative, unconventional ecclesiology, such as that of Catherine or the anonymous Dominican author, focuses mainly on the question of the modes of government.[34] The doctrine of the *plenitudo potestatis* of the pope and the cardinals is based on a definition of the Roman Church as universal church, heir to the privileges of St. Peter and of the apostolic college. The Roman Church is thus defined as a body whose pope is the head and the cardinals are the members.

Making the reform of the mystical body dependent on that of the head, the reformist reflection, the social and political implications of which are far from negligible, focused on the questions of the schism and of the government, from the monastery to the Church in general. The effect of the Great Schism made the debate on the question of the modes of government, the papal monarchy, and the role of the college of cardinals more acute, while at the same time exploring the legal and spiritual basis for the legitimacy of the 1378 election.

Catherine of Siena and the anonymous Dominican bishop, author of the *Liber* composed in Siena in 1388, agreed on the question of the place and status of the cardinals.[35] Established in the context of the Gregorian reform of the eleventh century, the College of Cardinals was intended to assist the Roman pontiff in governing the Church and ensuring the legality of the papal election. The cardinals' power increased considerably in the first decades of the fourteenth century, in reaction to the autocratic tendencies of Boniface VIII (1294–1303). The pinnacle of the cardinals' power came during the electoral capitulation of 1352, when they realized their claim to participate fully in the *plenitudo potestatis*. In 1378, the double pontifical election that gave birth to the Great Schism modified not only the concept of the power of the council, but also the power of the cardinals. The authority of the pope, vicar of St. Peter and then, from Innocent III (1198–1216), vicar of Christ, appeared now in competition with the authority emanating from the apostolic succession of cardinals. Cardinals were no longer simply created by the pontiff; their legitimacy, and hence their authority, emanated directly from the apostolic community as a whole. This interpretation threatened to set the authority of the council above that of the pontiff. The conciliarist movement thus shifted the center of gravity of the debate from the *Ecclesia romana* to the *Ecclesia universalis* and to the institution, which formalized it the best: the general council.

Both Catherine and the anonymous Dominican Bishop condemned the excesses of the cardinals' power. In her letters, Catherine repeatedly criticized the corruption of the papal curia. According to the anonymous author of the *Liber*, the curia was not an honor but a horror. He thus entitled Chapter VII of Book IV *Quando et sub quo potestas plenaria, camera et curia ceperunt in Romana ecclesia, a quibus tribus videmus omnia mala* ("When and under whose power appeared the plenary power, the *camera* and the *curia*, from which we see all the evils coming"). In chapter VIII of the same book, the Orthodox, answering a question of the Catechumen, enumerates the turpitudes of the curia:

> It is quite the contrary, my son, the opposite, as we said above, and they oppose each other. Thus, our elders affirmed that the Roman curia dishonored the Church and the prelates that compose it, because they founded the churches and the rules of life. The curia indeed seeks the splendor and the pomp; the Church tends towards humility. The curia amasses wealth for its own superfluous needs; the Church disperses them and gives them to the poor. The curia attracts her, as St. Bernard said, and, considering this, toward her converge from all over the world the ambitious, the misers, the simoniacs, the sacrilegious, the concubines, the incestuous, and the monstrous beings of this kind, while the Church avoids and shuns any such relationship.[36]

In opposing the Church and the curia, these criticisms are reflected in the reforms of Urban VI, which sought to put the cardinals' behavior and their lifestyle in harmony with evangelical ideals by reducing of the importance of their *familia*, fighting against the plurality of their benefits, controlling links with the sovereigns, struggling against the diversion of church property to the benefit of members of their families, and so on.

In the writings of Catherine, the very concept of *Ecclesia romana* disappears. She rejected what she saw as a false idea used to increase the prerogatives of the Sacred College and to diminish the power of the pope. Then again, in the *Liber* the concept of *Ecclesia romana* or *sedes romana* is repeated, but without favoring the power of the cardinals:

> However the Roman See, i.e. the Roman Church, can change place, provided that all the Roman nation change its place. But the nation living faithfully in the same place, the Apostolic See and the Roman See, will retain in this place the first rank.[37]

The *Ecclesia romana* is first a local church, the church of Rome. This very same definition is found in the writings of Bohier, who made a distinction between *Ecclesia romana* and *Ecclesia catholica*: "Church: i.e. catholic, not only Roman."[38] Further, when commenting on the investiture of Clement by Pierre, Bohier wrote:

> Church: i.e. all the faithful who were then in the city of Rome. In fact, the gathering of Catholic human beings forms the Catholic Church.... On the contrary, in them lies the Catholic Church itself.... As for the other Apostles, they have their own apostolic churches, i.e. congregations, which form a single Church, true and Catholic, spread throughout the world.[39]

There follows the proposition of Bohier and the anonymous author to put an end to the Schism: the meeting of a provincial council and not of an ecumenical council, the question not belonging to the Church as a whole but only to the Church of Rome. The meeting of an ecumenical council must be reserved for the union with the Greek Church. Rather, for Catherine, the *Ecclesia romana*, as an institution of Salvation, can only be the *Ecclesia universalis*.

Thus a central issue divided Catherine of Siena and the anonymous Dominican bishop and author of the 1388 treatise the *Liber*, namely the papal monarchy. For Catherine, the pope is "Christ on earth." The formulation then spreads among his followers.[40] The pope thus holds the supreme authority as *vicarius Christi* and *vicarius Dei*. As *vicarius Christi* and successor of St. Peter, he holds the power of the keys.

The view of the papacy is very different in the *Liber*. The anonymous author created a parallel between the schism of the Eastern and Western churches and sought solutions in the East to reform the Roman Church, made "sick" by pontifical monarchy. To that end, he addressed the two foundations of the papal monarchy: the Petrine primacy and the Donation of Constantine.

According to the anonymous text, Peter is the *coapostolus* of the other apostles: "Because the See of Peter or Apostolic See is nothing but the house of God, or the church in which Peter or his companions, his co-apostles [*coapostolis*], preach the faith of Christ."[41] In the middle of

Book I, having dealt with the parity of the apostolic sees, the anonymous author treated the parity of the apostles:

> Concerning the equality of the apostles: how far is the tradition of the keys of the churches, how is Peter [Petrus] called the prince or the greatest of the apostles, and how is the stone [pietra] called the foundation of the churches?
>
> CATECHUMEN: I beg you, tutor, say if the equality of which you say exists between the apostolic churches existed also between the apostles when the Lord handed them the keys [of the Church].
>
> ORTHODOX: I think that it was, my very dear, since all the apostles received parity at the same time and from the same Lord, after his Resurrection, the honor and the power of the keys, according to John the Evangelist .... As Jesus said: "As the Father has sent Me, so also I am sending you. Receive the Holy Spirit. If you forgive anyone his sins etc. [Jn. 20:21–22]."[42]

The anonymous Dominican bishop then based his demonstration on a commentary of Matt. 16:18. In chapter XXI, which closed the second book, the author tackled the second foundation of the papal monarchy, denouncing the Donation of Constantine as apocryphal.[43]

How can we understand such a criticism, leveled by a man whose order was one of the principal defenders of the papal monarchy? In 1367, Pierre Bohier, the pope's vicar in Rome, was commissioned by Gregory XI to accompany the envoys of the Byzantine emperor John V Palaeologus, who had come to prepare a possible ecumenical council to establish a union between the two churches. Bohier's enthusiasm for the Greek patristics and the legacy of the ecumenical councils undoubtedly dates from this period, as evidenced in his second commentary on the Rule of St. Benedict, written at the Abbey of Subiaco, in 1373. It is probable, given some remarks evoking direct contact with his Eastern Oriental co-religionists, that the anonymous author of the *Liber* was either present himself alongside the Byzantine emperor's ambassadors, or that he was informed of this embassy by Bohier, one of his close relations.[44] Two years later, in 1369, this first embassy led to the personal conversion of the emperor, who came to the West to receive baptism from the hands of the pontiff. This disagreement between the Dominican anonymous author and Catherine of Siena on the highly essential topic of the pontifical monarchy indicates the existence of different currents, certainly several years apart, among the Dominicans of Siena who supported Urban VI. One of the factors explaining these divergences could be the consideration of the Greek Church in the definition of the *Ecclesia universalis*. Indeed, seen from the observant perspective, the Greek Church presented a model of collegiality, from monasteries devoid of rule in the Latin sense, to the pentarchy, an institution corresponding to the formalization of the five major sees—Rome, Constantinople, Alexandria, Antioch, and Jerusalem—who assumed the collective responsibility of the direction of the Church. The meeting of the Greek ambassadors seems to me to be decisive here in better understanding the ecclesiological thinking of both Bohier and the author of the *Liber*, as well as their originality within the reforming network to which they belonged, alongside Alfonso, Catherine or Birgitta.[45]

Conclusion

To conclude, two ideas seem to underlie the crossing paths of Birgitta of Sweden, Catherine of Siena, and Alfonso of Jaén: their thoughts, in their historical context, and the networks they belonged to, reflecting the interconnected history of religious orders at the turn of the fourteenth and fifteenth centuries.

Importantly, the men and women whose paths we have just followed are as much theoreticians of governance as they are actors of the government of the Church. They drew from their personal experiences the seeds of their ideas and beliefs. Several elements bear witness to this point: the extensive correspondence maintained by Catherine of Siena; the official functions assumed by several actors; the influence of Bohier's experience as Bishop of Orvieto on the abuses of the pontifical government; and the influence of the 1367 meeting with the Greek ambassadors.

A connected history of religious orders: three "ancient" orders—the Benedictine, the Dominican, the Franciscan—are connected with two "recent" orders—the Hieronymites and the Birgittines. More than orders, it is the individuals who connect. They become mediators as they transgress the boundaries defined by their orders. Moreover, even though Birgitta died before the beginning of the schism and Catherine barely two years after, their insertion in the network of which Alfonso was the center acquires its meaning in the context of the Great Schism. In speaking on behalf of the two saints, Alfonso pursued their common reform objectives, but in a different context: the Great Schism. Birgitta's and Catherine's interests first intersected with those of Alfonso in the context of a reformist quest highlighting an eremitic—or both eremitic and cenobitic—way of life. They then continued to converge after the death of the two saints in the reforming attempts to resolve the schism and whatever the party chosen by the various reformers, that of Urban VI or that of Clement VII. It is undoubtedly in their common reforming ideals that existed before the Schism that we must look for the roots of this convergence beyond death and the fractures of the Schism.

The links between Pedro of Luna, Alfonso of Jaén, and Pierre Bohier were numerous and seem to have resisted the fissures caused by the Schism. On 1 August 1386, Pierre Bohier left Paris for Genoa, where he found Urban VI, from whom he obtained pardon. He then wrote to

Pedro of Luna announcing his withdrawal from the Clementine obedience and his return to Urban VI. It is to Alfonso that he addressed and entrusted his letter, with the burden of forwarding it to the addressee. He died soon after, on 3 March 1388.

How did these men and women, with their conflicting and diverse identities, come to have such common aspirations—and how did they manage to follow paths opposed to their national or monastic allegiances? How can we grasp these historical moments and environments in all their complexity? Two of the safest means of achieving this are to follow singular, unusual paths; and to consider outcomes that could have but did not come to pass by examining the precise historical moments when such outcomes were still in the realm of possibility. Following these paths, which are strongly out of tune with the historical narrative imposed by the victors, allows us to avoid a teleological view of history by not privileging those who imposed their views from the start, as the beginning of a larger movement, the prefiguration of models. It thus becomes possible to define the contours of a network, understood here as a set of relations between social actors operating at different scales, aiming not at the individual properties of the actors studied but the relations between them. In the decades immediately preceding the Great Schism, Birgitta of Sweden and Catherine of Siena were key actors in the reformist debates that agitated the Western Church. Far from thinking, living, and acting in isolation, they evolved within larger networks; the solutions they advocated constituted, along with many others, an alternative or unconventional ecclesiology. Alfonso of Jaén emerges as a central, if not the main, intermediary of this broad network.

Notes

1 I am very grateful to Prof. Jesse Rodin and Dr. Diana Bullen Presciutti for proofreading this paper.
2 The Franciscan spirituals of Umbria and Tuscany, associated with Tommasuccio of Siena (d. 1377), are referred to as *fraticelli* by Mario Sensi, and as tertiary Franciscan by others. See Mario Sensi, "Il beato Tommasuccio: biografi, biografe e culto," in *Il b. Tommasuccio da Foligno, terziario francescano ed i movimenti religiosi popolari Umbri nel Trecento. Ciclo di conferenze alla Biblioteca Jacobilli (Foligno, 13–18 novembre 1978)*, ed. Raffaele Pazzelli (Rome: 1979); Sophie Coussemacker, "L'ordre de saint Jérôme en Espagne, 1373–1516" (PhD Diss., Paris X-Nanterre: 1994), 4. It is likely that many of Tommasuccio's disciples, or at least disciples of his master, Peter Rigali or Gualdo, left for the Iberian Peninsula between 1343, the date of the arrival of Tommasuccio within the community gathered around the hermitage of Peter in the Serra Santa di Gualdo Tadino, and 1367, the date of the death of Peter Gualdo. They would then have joined the hermits of Guisando, one of the eremitic nuclei at the origin of the Order of Hieronymites. The date of 1367 coincides with the eremitic vocation of Pedro Fernandez Pecha, Alfonso's brother, who joined, with Fernando Yañez, another founder of the order, the hermits of the region of Toledo in

the second half of 1366. Alfonso, Pedro's younger brother, then gave up his position in July 1368. If it is not established that Alfonso spent some time in his brother's hermit community in Villaescusa and then in Lupiana, it is likely to have at least influenced his decision to leave his episcopacy in Jaén. Shortly after, during the summer, Alfonso traveled to Rome and entered the service of Birgitta of Sweden. On Alfonso and Birgitta, see Arne Jönsson, *Alfonso of Jaén: His Life and Works with Critical Editions of the Epistola Solitarii, the Informaciones and the Epistola Serui Christi* (Lund: Lund University Press, 1989).

3 On the particular friendship of Alfonso of Jaén and Birgitta of Sweden, see Giulia Puma, "Brigitte de Suède et Alfonso de Jaén: une 'amitié spirituelle' à la fin du xIVᵉ siècle," *Arzanà* 10 (2013): 329–64.

4 Mario Sensi, "Alfonso Pecha e l'eremitismo italiano di fine secolo XIV," *Rivista di Storia della Chiesa in Italia* XLVII (1993): 51–80, at 73–74.

5 On this issue, see Julia Bolton Holloway, "Saint Birgitta of Sweden, Saint Catherine of Siena: Saints, Secretaries, Scribes, Supporters," *Birgittiana* 1 (1996): 29–45. On the reception of the Birgittine and Catherinian text within the Observant Reform movement, see also Chapter 5 by Silvia Nocentini in the present volume.

6 Hélène Millet, "Un réseau international d'ermites et de réformateurs en quête d'une nouvelle spiritualité dans la seconde moitié du xIVᵉ siècle," in *La circulation des élites européennes*, eds. Henri Bresc, Fabrice d'Almeida, and Jean-Michel Sallmann (Paris: SeliArslan, 2002), 100–22. For an update on the Great Western Schism see Joëlle Rollo-Koster and Thomas H. Izbicki (eds.), *A Companion to the Great Western Schism (1378–1417)* (Leiden: Brill 2009).

7 Alfonso was in Tuscany, engaged in establishing eremitic-cenobitic communities (see above), when Gregory XI ordered him to return to Avignon to entrust him with this mission in Castile to redeem Christian prisoners from Muslims.

8 Pierre Bohier was the abbot of St-Chinian (near Béziers in the diocese of Saint Pons de Tomières) when he was elected bishop of Orvieto 16 November 1364. In 1378, at the early beginning of the Great Schism, Bohier took the party of Clement VII; as a result Urban VI excommunicated him and removed him from his bishopric. Writing a commentary on the *Liber Pontificalis*, he changed his mind and took up the cause for Urban VI. He left France on 1 August 1386 to enter the urbanist obedience. He then chose Alfonso of Jaén as an intermediary to make contrition with the Roman pope (see Konrad Eubel, *Hierarchia catholica…*, vol. 1: 508 and Enzo Petrucci, "Bohier Pietro," *Dizionario Biografico degli Italiani* 11 (1969): 193–203).

9 Edition available in Franz Bliemetzrieder, "Un'altra edizione rifatta del trattato di Alfonso Pecha, vescovo resignato di Iaën, sullo scisma (1387–1388), con notizie sulla vita di Pietro Bohier, Benedettino, vescovo di Orvieto," *Rivista storica benedettina* 4 (1909): 74–100; Robert E. Lerner, "Alfonso Pecha on Discriminating Truth about the Great Schism," in *Autorität und Wahrheit. Kirchliche Vorstellungen, Normen und Verfahren*, ed. Gian Luca Potestà (Munich: De Gruyter, 2012), 127–46.

10 Bliemetzrieder, "Un'altra edizione," 83–84: "De primo autem, id est, de informatione per viam spiritus, constat mihi et dico, quod ante annum Iubilei tempore papa Clementis sexti beata Birgitta de regno Suecie essendo in regno Suecie sola in oracione, dominus noster Jesus Christus apparuit ei et loquendo cum ea et dedit sibi duas revelaciones, unam, quam deberet statim mittere domino Clementi pape, et aliam Regibus Francie et Anglie." All translations from this work are my own.

11 Ibid., 85: "Quam revelationem ipsa domina beata Brigida presentavit dicto Urbano pape scriptam de manu mea in Monteflasconis, antequam ipse recederet, in vigilia Assumpcionis beate Marie virginis."

12 Ibid., 90: "Et tunc ego eram licet indignus confessor unius ipsorum cardinalium, qui me de suis secretis et arduis consiliis extra confessionem sepius requirebat."

13 Ibid., 92: "Et tunc ego per 3 vel 4 dies ante introitum conclavis ivi ad dominam Katherinam filiam beate Brigide de regno Suecie et dixi ei, quod statim iret ad dictum dominum archiepiscopum Barensem et faceret ei humiliam reverenciam et recommendaret ei efficaciter negocium canonizacionis matris sue beate Brigide, quod tunc pendebat et tractabatur in curia coram papa Gregorio, sed nichil diceret archiepiscopo de materia electionis."

14 Ibid., 88: "Propterea credo firmiter ex predictis Urbanum esse verum papam secundum voluntatem Dei, et non Clementem, quantum ad claves Ecclesie, et hanc meam credulitatem veram esse confirmarunt mihi, postquam scisma est ortum, multi et magni servi et amici Dei, tam heremite quam alii sancti viri et sancte mulieres magne virtutis et singularissime vite note de Alemannia, de Ytalia, de Suecia et de Yspania, quos ego rogavi singillatim ... me certificarent."

15 Ibid., 97: "Dixi tercio quod eram informatus per viam iuris de veritate in ista materia."

16 Ibid., 98: "Preterea postea eciam quidam virtuosus et sancta intencionis vir, scilicet dominus frater Petrus monachus sancti Benedicti, natione Gallicus civitatis Narbonensis, quondam episcopus Urbevetanus, decretorum doctor egregius, me in hac veritate de papatu per suum quondam secretarium plenissime informavit, qui episcopus dimisit antipapam et curiam suam propter stimulum consciencie, quem habebat, et postea per suasionem Karoli regis Francie Parisiis residebat in monasterio Celestinorum."

17 Ibid., 99: "Quante enim virtutis et bone consicencie ac perfeccionis hic predictus episcopus est, non sufficio enarrare."

18 Ibid., 99:

> Vidi enim, dum ipse suum episcopatum pacifice possidebat, anno Domini millesimo ccc° LXX quarto, quod ipse pervenit ad sanctum monasterium Specus sancti Benedicti in Abbatia Sublacensi prope Romam ad 32 miliaria, ubi beati Benedicti laudabiliter observatur regula. Et vocatis in mei presencia priore ipsius monasterii et monachis, proposuit se velle in illa valle edificare quodam monasterium sub vocabulo beati Ieronimi et sub Benedicti Regula et dotare illud pro XII monachis, ac eciam renunciare et dimittere suum episcopatum et in ipso monasterio se includere et monachare ut verus monachus in observancia regule et in paupertate ibidem vivere, statimque fecit fabricari in illa valle dictum cenobium sancti Ieronimi. In quo quidam monasteriolo novo ego fui personaliter. Sed quia istud scisma in ecclesia Dei supervenit, ideo desiderium suum adimplere nequivit.

19 Bartolomeo Prignano was elected pope under the name of Urban VI in April 1378. The violent disagreements that opposed him to the cardinals led them to elect in the summer a competing pope, Robert of Geneva, who took the name of Clement VII. This double election marked the beginning of the Great Schism, which lasted until the election of Martin V in 1417.

20 Bliemetzrieder, "Un'altra edizione," 83: "... vel forte interrogatus sum, quia meum episcopatum dimisi et renunciavi dignitati, relinquens eciam patrimonium meum propter amorem Christi, omnesque divicias terrenas et mundanos vanos honores."

21 Coussemacker, "L'ordre de saint Jérôme en Espagne," 181–3; Lancellotto, "De monasterio Quartano," in *Id.*, *Historiae Olivetanae* II, 15 (Venice: 1623), 171–2; A. Donatelli, "Le origini del Monastero di S. Gerolamo di Quarto," *L'Ulivo* (1972) : 47–50; Eric Colledge, "*Epistola solitarii ad reges*: Alphonse of Pecha as Organizer of Birgittine and Urbanist Propaganda," *Mediaeval Studies* 18 (1956): 19–49, at 26–27.

22 Regarding Peter of Aragon, see José M. Pou y Marti, *Visionarios, beguinos y fraticelos catalanes (siglos* XII–XV) (Madrid: Colegio "Cardenal Cisneros," 1992), 370–2.

23 "Que omnia narravit mihi indigno seriose dictus frater Petrus ante tempus scismatis tempore pape Gregorii Avinione anno Domini millesimo CCC° LXXII et dedit mihi omnia in scriptis de manu fratris Raymundi confessoris sui et habeo omnia ista in monasterio nostro sancti Ieronimi in Ianuam," (Bliemetzrieder, "Un'altra edizione," 85).

24 "Hic jacet Reverendus Pater Dominus Alphonsus de Vadaterre, Natione Hispanus, qui disperse Patrimonio proprio propter Deum, relictoque Episcopatu Geennense, ut pauper Christum pauperem sequeretur Eremeticam vitam duxit. Tandem Ianuam veniens Eleemosynis fidelium sub vocabulo Beati Hieronymi hanc fundavit Ecclesiam, quam regi obtinuit per Venerabiles Monachos Ordinis Montis Oliveti. Demumque migravit ad Dominum Anno MCCCLXXXVIII, die 19 Augusti," Lancelletto, "De monasterio Quartano," 172.

25 Colledge, "*Epistola solitarii ad reges*," 27.

26 AP, 402: "Hec narravit dicta domina Leticia nona die novembris in Castro Genenciani anno Domini millesimo cccmo lxxmo, presentibus isto teste domino Alfonso, et frate Mauro de Yspania, monacho monasterii Specus beati Benedicti, et Thomasa ancilla seu pedisequa eiusdem domine Leticie."

27 Camille Rouxpetel, "Subiaco à l'épreuve du Grand schisme d'Occident: la mainmise espagnole sur le Sacro Speco (1378–1401)," in *Gli spazi della vita comunitaria*, ed. Letizia Panni Ermini (Spoleto: Centro Italiano di studi sull'alto medioevo, 2016): 419–39.

28 Margaret Harvey, *The English in Rome, 1362–1420: Portrait of an Expatriate Community* (Cambridge: Cambridge University Press, 1999), 204–05.

29 Mario Sensi, "Alfonso Pecha."

30 Hélène Millet, "Le *Liber dialogorum hierarchie sub cœlestis* (1388)," in *Vaticana et medievalia. Études en l'honneur de Louis Duval-Arnould*, eds. Jean-Marie Martin, Bernadette Martin-Hisard and Agostino Paravicini Bagliani (Florence: SISMEL, Edizioni del Galluzzo, 2008).

31 *Archivium Fratrum Praedicatorum*, t. 25–7 (1955–57), III, 247, § 26:

> Veniendo de Anagnia veni ad monasterium de Specu, abbacia Sublacensi, ubi sunt quidam monachi ad plenum, ut opinor, non amatores mundi, de partibus Yspanie, devoti et noti cardinali de Luna. Qui eciam in multis informati erant ab ipso cardinali de Luna. Quibus cum dispositionem malam scismatis narrarem, fuit qui [one of the Spanish monks] in consilio illo dixit: 'Videte fratres: Navis ecclesie in medio pelagi dissoluta est, et quilibet est in mundo isto pro procurando salutem anime. Et ideo hic—quod eramus ab omni alio consorcio segregati sub quadam arbore—dicat unusquisque secundum quod Deus sibi spiraverit, quod lignum de ista nave rupta securius et utilius tenendum.' Ad quod verbum, consideratis omnibus argumentis, visum fuit ibi de omnibus nobis, quod sequi viam vel amiciciam cardinalium et dicta eorum esset ire ad infernum post diabolum, et sequi vicarium Christi, quem illi tamquam sanctiorem et omnino spiritualem et expertum in agendis eligerant, esset ire per viam veritatis ad Christum dominum et salvatorem nostrum. Et ita fuit ibit erminatum et difinitum,

Gilles-Gérard Meersseman "Études sur l'ordre des frères prêcheurs au début du Grand Schisme."

32 Rouxpetel, "Subiaco à l'épreuve du Grand schisme d'Occident."

33 Madrid, Biblioteca Nacional, MS 54, fol. 25r: "Explicit Dyalogus ierarchie subcelestis inter catholicum orthodoxum et cathecuminum Paucastium in quatuor libros divisus et recollectus in Senis ex sacre Scripture, canonumque sacrorum et patrum sentenciis, anno Domini millesimo octuagesimo octavo per quondam fratrem de ordine predicatorum et episcopum, cuius nomen utinam de libro vivencium [deleatur] temporaliter ut scribatur eternaliter libro vite."

34 Enzo Petrucci, "L'ecclesiologia alternativa alla vigilia e all'inizio del grande scisma: S. Caterina da Siena e Pietro Bohier vescovo di Orvieto," in *Atti del Simposio Internazionale Cateriniano–Bernardiniano, Siena 17–20 aprile 1980*, eds. Domenico Maffei and Paolo Nardi (Siena: Accademia Senese degli Intronati, 1982).

35 For a broader context, see Unn Falkeid, *The Avignon Papacy Contested: An Intellectual History from Dante to Catherine of Siena* (Cambridge, MA: Harvard University Press, 2017).

36 Città del Vaticano, Biblioteca Apostolica Vaticana, Reg. Lat.715, fols. 37v–38r: "Ymo sunt vere, mi fili, in contrarie, ut supra fuit dictum, et sibi invicem adversantur. Unde nostri seniores asserunt quod Romana curia dehonestavit ecclesiam et quod similiter curie prelatos eo quod ecclesias fundaverunt et vitas. Curia namque querit fastum et pompam ; Ecclesia stare secum ad humilitatem. Curia divicias congregat pro suis superfluitatibus ; Ecclesia illas dispergit et dat pauperibus. Curia trahit ad se, iuxta dictum beati Bernardi, et ad illam de toto orbis, illud considerandus, confluunt ambiciosi, avari, symoniaci, sacrilegi, concubinarii, incestuosi et istius modi monstra hominum; Ecclesia vero vitat et fugit contubernia talium."

37 BAV, Reg. Lat.715, fol. 18r: "Romana tamen sedes, id est Romana ecclesia, transmutari valet, si totus Romanus populus mutaretur. Sed ibidem remanente fideli populo illic sedes apostolica et sedes Romana dignitate etiam prima remanebit."

38 "Ecclesia: scilicet catholica, non tantum Romana," Pierre Bohier in *Liber pontificalis nella recensione di Pietro Guglielmo OSB e del cardinale Pandolfo, glossato da Pietro Bohier OSB, vescovo di Orvieto*, ed. Ulderico Přerovský, 3 vols, "*Studia Gratiana*," XXI, XXII e XXIII (Rome, 1978), III, Glosse, 8.

39 "Ecclesia: Id est omnes fideles qui tunc erant in Urbe. Nam collection catholicorum hominum Ecclesia catholica est … immo et in eis est ipsa catholica Ecclesia … Alii eciam apostoli suas habent apostolicas ecclesias, id est congregationes, quae tamen unam faciunt veram et catholicam Ecclesiam per totum mundum dispersam," Pierre Bohier (ibid., 12), quoted in Petrucci, "L'ecclesiologia alternativa," 248).

40 Petrucci, "L'ecclesiologia alternativa," 218–19.

41 BAV, Reg. Lat.715, fol. 17v: "Quia sedes Petri vel apostolica nil aliud est quam Dei domus, vel ecclesia in qua Christi fides predicata a Petro vel a suis sociis coapostolis."

42 BAV, Reg. Lat.715, fol. 10r: "De parilitate apostolorum: quoad traditionem clavium ecclesiarum esse, et qualiter Petrus princeps vel maior dicitur apostolorum, et quomodo petra dicitur vel fundamentum ecclesiarum? Catechumenus: Modo oro, preceptor, dic si equalitas quam dicis esse in apostolicis ecclesiis fuit eciam inter apostolos in clavium traditarum a Domino dispensacione. Orthodoxus: Fuit ut reperio, carissime, quoniam omnes apostoli una hora et ab uno Domino post eius resurrectionem pari consorcio honorem et

potestatem clavium, secundum Johannis evangelium, acceperunt .... Sicut inquit Jhesus: 'misit me pater et ego mitto vos. Accipite spiritum sanctum quorum remiseritis peccata et caetera ....'"

43 BAV, Reg. Lat.715, fol. 26v. See Daniele Menozzi, "La critica alla autenticità della Donazione di Costantino in un manoscritto della fine del XIV secolo," *Cristianesimo nella Storia* I (1980): 123–54.

44 *Liber* II, 15; BAV, Reg. Lat.715, fol. 23v: "Catechumenus: Tuis preceptor stupeo fatibus et iam amare Grecos incipio. Sed rogo te si sunt Greci in humanis virtutibus et viribus virtuosi? Orthodoxus: Sunt et pulcriores carissime ceteris hominibus in aspectu in affatibus placidiores et pacifici inter gentes."

45 Camille Rouxpetel, "Philhellénisme et réforme pendant le Grand schisme: Guillaume Saignet et les Grecs," in *Humanisme et politique en France à la fin du Moyen Âge. Hommage à Nicole Pons*, eds. Carla Bozzolo, Claude Gauvard, and Hélène Millet (Paris: Éditions de la Sorbonne, 2018): 123–39.

Epilogue

André Vauchez

It is odd that historians, who often cite the names of these two great figures of fourteenth-century spirituality together, have never before—at least to my knowledge—undertaken an investigation about their relationship. Such a topic makes this volume particularly interesting. Certainly, Birgitta and Catherine were not, strictly speaking, contemporaries, separated from each other by a generation. If, as it is believed, the Sienese mystic was born in 1347, then the Swedish prophetess would already have been 44 years old, and it is almost certain that they never met during their lifetimes. Catherine's public career, marked by her first interventions in the life of the Church, began only in 1374, whereas Birgitta had already died on 23 July 1373. But this entrance into public life by the Sienese *Mantellata* is not devoid of any connection to the death of the "Sibyl of the North." A letter sent by Catherine on 26 March 1374 to two Dominicans of her entourage—Bartolomeo Dominici and Tommaso d'Antonio Caffarini—mentions Birgitta in the following way:

> I announce to you that the pope has sent us one of his vicars. *He is the spiritual father of this countess who died in Rome, who refused, out of love of virtue, the title of bishop.* He came to find me, while telling me that the Holy Father is asking me to pray for him and for the Holy Church; and, as a sign of his mission, he brought me a plenary indulgence. So, therefore, rejoice and be glad because the Holy Father has begun to turn his attention towards the honor of God and the Holy Church [italics added].[1]

The person who had sought out Catherine on behalf of Pope Gregory XI (1371–78) was not just anyone. It was Alfonso Pecha, the former bishop of Jaén in Andalusia. He was born in Guadalajara around 1330, resigned his office in 1368, and settled in Italy, where, until his death in 1389, he played an important role in the expansion of religious orders of an eremitical orientation. His brother Pedro Pecha, on the other hand, was the founder of the Order of Saint Jerome (Hieronymites), approved by Gregory XI in 1373.[2] The importance of this figure, long relegated to the shadows, is now widely recognized. During the 1370s and 1380s,

Alfonso of Jaén was, in effect, a point of reference for all who were aspiring to reform the Church; he worked alongside his friend Pierre Bohier, a French monk, later the bishop of Orvieto, who, like Alfonso, had considered resigning his post to withdraw into a convent dedicated to Saint Jerome, which he'd had built close to the Sacro Speco of Subiaco.[3] In 1374, upon his return from Avignon, the Spanish prelate went to find the Sienese *Mantellata* to bestow on her the pope's blessing and an indulgence; and it seems quite certain that the purpose of this encounter was to find a successor to Birgitta, for whom he had been both spiritual director and redactor, organizing her revelations into books and then disseminating them throughout Christendom. Moreover, we know through other sources that Alfonso of Jaén played an important role in arranging for Tora, daughter of Pietro Gambacorta, lord of Pisa, to enter into religious life. She had been widowed at the age of 15 and refused to remarry, in spite of the insistence of her father. Informed of the situation by Alfonso in 1374, Catherine wrote two letters to the young woman urging her to persevere in her widowhood and to commit herself to the religious life.[4] Taking the name Chiara (Clare), she first entered the Poor Clares, but then established the convent of San Domenico in Pisa in 1386. This marked the beginning of the Observant movement among Dominican women, founded upon the teachings and model of Catherine of Siena.[5] Alfonso had inspired in Chiara a lively devotion for Birgitta, and the Pisan monastery became a center of the cult of the saint after her canonization, in 1391, as attested to by the biography of its third prioress, Maria Mancini. This text contains a letter that Chiara sent to Alfonso about certain dreams as well as his answer sent in response.[6]

There are other indications of contact between Alfonso of Jaén and Catherine beyond the letter cited at the beginning of this text. Indeed, one of her secretaries—the Sienese notary Cristofano (also Cristoforo) di Gano Guidini—lists in his *Ricordi* the members of the saint's *famiglia* and notably includes "Missere lo vescovo Alfonso" (the Lord Bishop Alfonso). We also know that this close friend of Catherine financed the Italian translation of the *Revelations* of Birgitta during the 1390s, as evinced by two manuscripts extant in Siena's Biblioteca comunale degli Intronati.[7] As to this last matter, it is important to emphasize the fact that, with respect to the reception of the writings of Birgitta and Catherine, often the same people and the same groups procured them in order to draw inspiration from them.

Alfonso had further opportunities to collaborate with Catherine when, at the end of 1378, she settled in Rome to support the cause of Urban VI. As is known, the election of this pope was soon contested by the cardinals, who ended up choosing from among themselves a different pontiff, who took the name of Clement VII. Catherine was horrified by this schism and did all that she could to impede its spreading. Toward that end, she again approached Alfonso of Jaén, who was then spiritual adviser to Cardinal Pedro de Luna, a man considered to be a virtuous prelate and supporter of efforts to reform the Church. When the cardinal then abandoned the camp of Urban VI, Alfonso, Catherine of Siena, and her confessor and future biographer, the Dominican Raymond of Capua, wrote an anonymous text called the "Urbanist Manifesto" of 1379, which strongly condemned the behavior of the schismatic cardinals and vigorously took the side of the Roman pontiff.[8] Alfonso continued to criticize the adversaries of Urban VI by writing various treatises or pamphlets, including the *Informationes domini Alphonsi eremitae... super creatione Urbani VI* ("Considerations of Lord Alfonso the Hermit about the Election of Urban VI"), in which he fulminates against Robert of Geneva—the antipope Clement VII—whom he portrays as the "executioner of Cesena" and a slaughterer of Christians.[9] Within this same context, it is asserted that Catherine of Siena and Katarina Ulfsdotter—Birgitta's daughter—were to have been sent to Queen Johanna I in Naples to prevail on her to support the camp of Urban VI. But Raymond of Capua dissuaded his spiritual daughter from continuing this project. This sovereign, to whom Catherine had addressed several emotional letters in the attempt to get her to return to the right path, was very attached to the memory of Birgitta, whom she had met several times during her sojourns to Naples;[10] and the queen had written to Popes Gregory XI and Urban VI to request the opening of Birgitta's process of canonization, where the visionary's promoter would be Alfonso of Jaén.

All these events confirm that, far from being coincidental or occasional, the meeting of Catherine and Alfonso in 1374 signaled the beginning of a lasting collaboration between them. And in many respects, it can be argued that the Sienese *Mantellata* did, in fact, take the baton from the Swedish prophetess at the request of Alfonso and Pope Gregory XI, and that, in large measure, she relied on the same networks to promote the return of the papacy to Rome and reform within the Church—both of which she, no less than Birgitta, considered to be urgent. They were convinced that for the pope to fulfill his duties for the good of Christianity, he needed to reside in the city of which he was its bishop—not merely as its sovereign but as its pastor, in a spirit of humility and charity. Despite differences in form, there is a strong thematic continuity in the writings of the two women. As Pierre Bohier tells us in his *Treatise on the Schism*, Birgitta, in a revelation addressed to Gregory XI in 1371 or 1372, said

> ... that the will of God was that he return with the Curia immediately to Rome and that he come reside in Rome in his Apostolic See, not in pomp but in humility and paternal charity; and that he then reform the universal Church; and that he root out sins that were rampant in the Roman Curia.[11]

She then threatened Gregory with the fury of Christ if he did not act on her message in the shortest time possible. Niccolò Orsini, one of the friends and protectors of the Swedish saint, carried this text to Avignon, after which the pope, duly impressed, charged Gérard du Puyand Alfonso of Jaén with a "special mission" to Birgitta to confer with her and ask for a sign confirming the authenticity of her divine mission.[12] After the Swedish saint's death, in July 1373, Catherine wrote to the pope on these same subjects in more or less the same terms, but she added a third aim for Gregory XI upon his return to Rome and reformation of the Curia: the organization of a crusade, which would open the door to the reunification of Christians warring with each other. They could join in a common struggle for the recovery of the Holy Land and conversion of the Muslims. At the end of her life, Birgitta became hostile to these crusading projects, which she considered to be a waste of time and energy. For her, the absolute priority was the return of the papacy to Rome. But aside from this small difference, the messages of the two women were identical, and they used the same verbal frankness with the papacy. Birgitta knew personally Cardinal Pierre Roger de Beaufort, whose nephew, also a cardinal, had once provided her lodging in his Roman palace. In 1370, he had introduced her to Pope Urban V. After the cardinal was elected as Pope Gregory XI, he became the privileged recipient of Catherine's letters, 15 of which have survived. However, the first correspondents of the ecclesiastical hierarchy with whom the Sienese saint had communicated were Bérengar de Lézat and Gérard du Puy, papal *nuncii* in Italy, both of whom sought her advice on how to remedy the evils afflicting the Church.[13]

These were people with whom Birgitta had dealt at the end of her life; and thus at this level as well there exists a real continuity regarding groups who supported both women. Compared with Birgitta, Catherine obviously had the advantage of being able to rely upon a religious order—namely, the Dominicans. Additionally, when she traveled to Rome in 1378 to defend the cause of Urban VI, she received a warm welcome from several important aristocratic families influential at the Curia, including the Papazzuri and the Orsini, who had previously supported the activities of Birgitta. Niccolò Orsini, count of Nola and governor of Perugia, in particular had welcomed Birgitta in Montefiascone in 1368 when she met Urban V for the first time. And afterwards he had delivered her last revelations—which were increasingly threatening—to Avignon, where the pope had returned in 1370. It is the same with respect to the Italian clergy. Thus, Giacomo of Itri, bishop of Otranto and close associate of Gregory XI, to whom Catherine wrote a long letter in 1375, had supported Alfonso of Jaén in his efforts to federate the hermits of central Italy into a single eremitical order. This was a project that Andrea da Lucca and the hermits of Monteluco near Spoleto were also associated with—whose help Catherine had enlisted, in 1379, when she was endeavoring to persuade these "spiritual friends" to take part in a "council of holy ones" that she was trying to gather in Rome to support Urban VI.[14]

Let us also add—to round out this picture—that both women aspired to found a religious order or a community. We are well informed about the efforts expended by Birgitta to obtain Urban V's approval of the Constitutions of the Order of the Holy Savior, which she had established in Vadstena; the results were ultimately disappointing for her, in as much as the most original aspects of her rule were not included by the Holy See, at least not at first. We know less about Catherine's numerous personal appeals to Gregory XI to obtain permission to found a female monastery at Belcaro, near Siena, which was actually under construction when she died but did not survive her. However, the spirit that inspired this foundation was rekindled after her death in the Observant monastery of San Domenico, formed in Pisa in 1386 by Chiara Gambacorta, who, as noted above, had similarly been influenced by Alfonso of Jaén.

Now that we have set out the parallels between these two pious women who had dedicated themselves to the service of the Church and its head and who expressed their support of similar issues in like manner, it is well that we ask ourselves if they were, for all of that, mirror images of each other and interchangeable figures. Obviously, this is not the case and the differences that existed between them are not less striking than are the resemblances. Birgitta was an aristocrat, a princess, even, if we believe the acts of her canonization process, where she is described as a "*principissa Nericie.*" She had been married a long time before being widowed in the mid-1340s, and was the mother of eight children. Catherine, by contrast, was the daughter of a cloth-dying artisan who was ruined by the economic crisis that hit Siena in 1360. But she relied especially on aristocratic families, and she gave evidence of being very critical of the communal regime of the "popular" sort in Siena that held sway at that time in the city. She was similarly contemptuous, though, toward the hard-scrabble workers in the textile industry—the "Ciompi"—who rebelled in Florence in 1378 and nearly succeeded in assassinating her. At an early age, she had made a vow of chastity and she never let herself be deterred by the efforts of her mother, who wanted her to marry at all costs.

But these differences of a social-economic order are not as determinative as one might imagine. Birgitta, formed by the reading of certain works of Ambrose, made known that she was very attached to virginity and to continence; and she denounced with real vehemence—as did Catherine in her *Dialogue*—the moral failures of the clergy, in particular in the domain of sexuality. Though born into very different milieus, they were both laywomen, thus "unlettered" in the medieval sense of the term, to the extent that they did not know Latin and had to make a valiant effort to learn it: Birgitta, with Mathias of Linköping and her Swedish confessors who followed her to Rome; Catherine, with the Dominicans of her entourage—especially her cousin Tommaso della Fonte—thanks to whom she gained a certain familiarity with and comprehension of the Bible, sacred texts, as well as moral theology. In general, even the educated women of this period were not able to write, and they were thus subject to the "power" of a male: first, that of their fathers, then of their husbands.[15] Birgitta, who belonged to the upper nobility, was probably introduced to writing in her youth; Catherine had to learn it herself, and she described this extraordinary experience in a letter addressed to Raymond of Capua:

> In my ignorance, I was deprived of all consolation. God remedied that by giving me the ability to write, in order that, in coming back down from the heights where I was, I could in some small way comfort my heart, lest it break. Not yet willing to pull myself away from this shadowy life, he etched this ability into my heart, as a mother does with a child, by showing me how to do it.[16]

In actual practice, however, both women preferred to dictate their revelations or visions to their entourage, composed mostly of clerics (for Birgitta) and lay notaries (for Catherine). For as F. Thomas Luongo and Maria H. Oen have demonstrated, although women were not forbidden to write, the recognition of their status as messengers of God depended on the collaboration of one or several churchmen who alone could "authorize" their works and approve them for dissemination.[17]

The most significant differences between the two women are, in fact, of a different kind. One variance concerns the nature of their relationship with Rome. Both considered the city to be profoundly central to Christianity. They urged the pope leave Avignon because of its close proximity to France and the paralyzing political pressures that lay there. He should return to reside in the only place where his authority could be fully exercised on behalf of the reform of the Church. Birgitta went to Rome in 1349 in anticipation of the Jubilee of 1350, fervently hoping to travel through this holy city where, she believed, "the streets are paved with gold reddened with the blood of saints," and from which the Christian faith had been spread throughout the West all the way to distant Sweden.[18] She was, above all else, a figure from the margins, a pilgrim from distant Sweden ("*ab Aquilone,*" as Pope Boniface IX said in his canonization sermon in 1391) who arrived in Rome hoping to obtain indulgences, and alert to the Christian myth of Rome.[19] Once there, though, despite experiencing the joy of witnessing Pope Urban V and Emperor Charles IV enter the city together in 1368, the overriding feeling she carried with her was one of disappointment. In her *Revelations,* Rome looks like a city in utter decadence: its churches are in ruins; the faithful have abandoned it; and a den of unscrupulous thieves, licentious monks, and laymen and women disregard papal excommunications. She responded to what she saw with repeated invectives against the fallen city and its inhabitants, some of whom replied in kind, mocking her and even physically threatening her during her peregrinations from one basilica to another, calling her a witch! Having made herself unpopular among the Roman people, she worked few miracles there, except in the aristocratic families—the Colonna and especially the Orsini—whom she often visited.

In contrast, when Catherine left Siena for Rome during the fall of 1378, it was not owing to any interest in the city itself but to rush to support the papacy, and not for her own salvation, but for that of the Church. Housed in modest lodgings in a neighborhood located near the Dominican convent of Santa Maria sopra Minerva, where numerous Tuscans lived, she was sensitive to the difficulties that faced the sick and poor as well as the victims of various mishaps. On their behalf, she performed many miracles, later described in her *vita* and in the "Processo Castellano," which took place in Venice between 1411 and 1416. The dispiriting spectacle that surrounded her is absent from the letters that she wrote right up until her death, in April 1380. Catherine never lost sight of the sacred character of Rome, which was essential as the springboard for reforming the Church, for which she prayed every morning at St. Peter's.[20]

In some works about religious life at the end of the Middle Ages, Birgitta of Sweden and Catherine of Siena are considered together under the term "mystics," a word often not clearly defined. I would argue that it many ways the term is misapplied and that the two women's specific spiritual experiences are not interchangeable. If by mystic one means

> the desire of man to have immediate contact with God, already in this life, through personal experience, sentiments and reflections of man along the road to this contact and finally the fulfillment of this desire ... perceived as a fleeting annulment of the difference between the subject of desire—the human soul, and the object for which it longs—God,[21]

then it seems to me that this definition corresponds much more to the experience of Catherine than to that of Birgitta. Certainly, Christ speaks to the latter several times while characterizing her as "my spouse" (*sponsa mea*); but this title aims to legitimize her claim to be the spokesperson of God among men and women rather than to give expression to an experience of mystical union. Moreover, He addresses her most often by calling her "my daughter" (*filia mea*). The Swedish saint is, first of all, a visionary in the tradition of Hildegard of Bingen, and she refers to herself as a "channel" between God and humanity, to whom she has been called to transmit the "spiritual and heavenly secrets," which God has allowed her to see and hear. For her, the revelation initiated by Christ and sustained through his friends—the prophets and apostles—is continued through her. Thus, she does not hesitate to refer to Alfonso of Jaén, who rendered her *Revelations* into Latin and disseminated them, as *"evangelista meus."*[22] Kari Børresen noted aptly "Christ locates Birgitta's proclamation of God's justice and mercy as part of the unfolding revelatory process."[23] In her *Revelations,* one does not find any references to mystical states (raptures, ecstasies) or to phenomena such as the kiss, the exchange of hearts, or the marks of the stigmata that would attest to a temporal realization of a perfect union with Christ.[24] Love is surely very much present here; but it is a love due every creature by reason of His incarnation, passion, and sufferings that He endured for our salvation. Unlike Catherine, Birgitta does not describe her interior experience; she is content to be mankind's spokesperson of the infinite love of Christ, who for her is more a master than a lover; her key word is mediation. Contrary to Catherine's world, Birgitta's remains static. Her vision does not prompt the general movement proper to the mystic who, according to Michel de Certeau, "submits the signs to a variety of displacements."[25]

Putting an even finer point on it, there is another important difference between Birgitta and Catherine. Whereas Catherine communicates directly with Christ, developing in her *Dialogue* a veritable theological vision of "Christ-the-Bridge" between divinity and humanity, Birgitta, in her *Revelations,* communicates more often with the Virgin Mary, who explains to her the mysteries of salvation. The voice of Mary becomes for her the voice of heaven.[26] As Børresen has observed, "Instead of metaphorically feminizing the Godhead, Birgitta attempts to divinize femaleness by describing Mary as Christo-typic, whilst Catherine tries to actualize her parity with godlike men by 'becoming male' in Christ and transforming her feminine weakness into perfect maleness."[27] It is significant in this regard that, in her letters, the Sienese *Mantellata* almost always exhorts her correspondents—be they men or women—to be "virile" and to conduct themselves "virilely," that is, like men, or in a manly manner. The Virgin Mary is not absent from her writings, but she appears there more in the role of a mother-in-law who tenderly looks upon the mystical marriage of her Son with Catherine. In contrast, Birgitta grants a dominant role to the Mother of God and presents her as an active partner in salvation history by emphasizing her participation in the sufferings of Christ, with whom she shares the same heart: "Just as Adam and Eve sold the world for a single apple, you might say that my Son and bought the world back with a single heart" (Rev. I: 35.7). For Birgitta, Mary, *mater dolorosa* and queen of the Church, plays a co-redemptrix role for humanity, to the point of appearing, as it were, like a fourth person attached to the Trinity. Birgitta considered herself to be, for her own time, the continuator of this specific female mission, imitating the role played by Mary in the incarnation of Christ by bringing into the world— both at the carnal and spiritual levels—children of God. Through this claim, Birgitta affirms the primacy of the feminine, thereby challenging the archetypical male model of Christianity. In this regard, she can be considered, in spite of appearances, more original than Catherine.

In addition to "mystic," another term frequently used with respect to both saints is that of "prophetess."[28] Here, too, it is important to look at things more closely. Undoubtedly, Birgitta places herself in the lineage of biblical prophecy. She herself defined her prophetic vocation in her *Revelations*, where she says that God would have charged her "to spiritually see, hear, and understand so that you may reveal to others that which you hear in the Spirit" (Rev. III: 5.8), and that she considered herself an apostle and a prophet of God, a new instrument through which he is speaking to Christians (see, e.g. Extrav., 47). Birgitta forcefully challenged the powers of this world—clergy as well as laity—and did not hesitate to announce to Urban V—when he was considering returning from Rome to Avignon in 1370—that if he made this bad decision, he would not have long to live. When he then died two months after his return to France, this news helped bolster the reputation of the Swedish saint, to whom was attributed, from that point forward, the ability to predict imminent dramatic events; indeed, in her *Revelations,* the eschatological perspective is always present. And Roger Ellis is correct in talking about a "spirituality of crisis and judgment," noting in reference to her: "we may say that she inhabits not only the present in which her fellows are confined but also a future not yet available to them."[29] If she brandishes threats, it is not to terrorize her contemporaries but to urge them to repentance and to a greater holiness of life. Her moral instruction is illustrated with numerous concrete examples, presented in a style marked by a frantic agitation and undergirded by an awareness of the omnipresence of evil and the acute need to escape it.

Catherine of Siena, for her part, never presented herself as a prophetess, although some of her contemporaries considered her as such. Her prophecy had nothing to do with the "Pursuit of the Millennium" (in a letter to a cleric of Naples, she condemns the apocalyptic speculations that were ever prevalent in his day)[30] nor with the announcement of events to come, despite Raymond of Capua's attributing to her the prediction, a few months in advance, of the 1378 break of the Schism. But, more broadly, one may typify as "prophetic" every systemic attempt to interpret historical events in the light of a higher plan and to establish a connection between present events and God's plan in a manner that persuades believers to involve themselves in this endeavor. She felt called in a particular way to this mission on 1 April 1376, after a vision that she interpreted as a kind of prophetic investiture.[31] According to Catherine, Christ asked her at that time to lead the pope, the clergy, and the Christian people in a movement of reform, where the outcome could only be positive, in spite of present difficulties, as God had assured her of the final triumph of the Church. Keeping in mind the prohibition of women from speaking publicly in church (based on 1 Tim. 11:13), Catherine could not throw herself into any kind of preaching campaign; in fact, she seems to have preached only one time, in 1379 in Rome, in front of the cardinals and at the request of Pope Urban VI. Nonetheless, through the letter-writing that she undertook with all kinds of people—from popes and kings to simple lay people—she attempted to foreground the spiritual meaning of contemporary events and to incite them to return to the root causes of religious and moral crises the Church was experiencing, which she considered to be the result of the abandonment of gospel values, prompted by pride and the pursuit of power and pleasure. Catherine practiced a kind of epistolary prophesying to the extent that, in her letters, she sought to elevate human beings by inviting them to return to the central place of the divine law in individual and collective existence. This often leads her to neglect the institutional or structural causes of failures and abuses, which Birgitta is more sensitive to. But Catherine emphasizes less the anger of God than his mercy; and she accords a greater importance to the role played by true servants of God—that small number of spiritual men and women whom she calls "pillars" of the Church and tried in vain to assemble in Rome in 1379. It is certainly possible to contest the authenticity of her inspiration, and, in fact, some of her adversaries did just that. But for her, the authority of her words were guaranteed by her own spiritual experience, especially by the special privileges—the ring, the exchange of hearts, the stigmata—that Christ had granted to her. Her first and chief biographer, the Dominican Raymond of Capua, was happy to present her as a weak unlettered woman on whom God had chosen to rely in order to confound the wise and the powerful who disdained His grace and who had distanced themselves from Him. But Catherine, like Birgitta, corresponded well to the biblical model of the strong and wise woman (*mulier fortis*), such as is depicted in Proverbs (Prov. 31:25–31), and one who did not hesitate to engage in political activities, as Luongo has demonstrated so well.[32]

I therefore think that one can say that Birgitta and Catherine were authentic prophetesses, each in her own way. But it is remarkable that this charisma was scarcely recognized by the Church of their day. In his sermon delivered on the occasion of Birgitta's canonization in 1391, the Roman pontiff Boniface IX compared her to Judith, Esther, and Miriam: three female figures of the Old Testament who had distinguished themselves through their obedience to God and their courage in the service of the people of Israel. The bull of canonization simply states that some of the things that she had announced had actually transpired since her time.[33] But, in the context of the Great Schism then raging, the pope was especially acquainted with her, owing to her insistence that the successor of Peter had to reside in Rome and nowhere else. All others seem to have shared the sentiment of the Swedes who, in the petitions they sent to the Holy See during the 1380s and 1390s, emphasized that the majority of prophecies that the saint had made during her lifetime about her own country had recently come to pass. Similarly, in 1461, Pius II, in the sermon that he delivered at the time of the canonization of Catherine of Siena, praised the charity that had led her to intervene in the affairs of the Church; he credited her with the distinction of having brought the papacy back from Avignon to Rome and of having promoted the cause of the crusade, dear to the heart of this pope, who sought until his death to organize one against the Turks.[34]

It is true that between the two canonizations, two councils had convened: Constance, in 1415—where influential theologians like Jean Gerson had cast doubt on the holiness of Birgitta and the prophetic inspiration of Catherine; and Basel, where in 1434 Louis Allemand demanded the condemnation of some of Birgitta's disciples, who were elevating the *Revelations* to the same level as the Gospels—thus prompting a lively reaction in her defense from Heymericus de Campo and the Dominican Juan de Torquemada (Johannes Turrecremata).[35] The extent to which prophetic revelations that were proliferating throughout the Christian world during the last third of the fourteenth century raised a great deal of perplexity and mistrust among much of the clergy. For this reason, one can understand how the papacy in this period might not have wanted to pronounce definitively on the question of the authenticity of the *Revelations* of Birgitta of Sweden—who, nevertheless, was canonized a second time in 1415 by John XXIII and a third time by Martin V in 1419—nor on the veracity of the stigmata of Saint Catherine of Siena. But papal recognition of their holiness favored the diffusion of their works throughout Christendom—a diffusion that was considerable in the fifteenth and sixteenth centuries. Thus, for the first time in Christian history, two women—Birgitta and Catherine—were regarded as authentic sacred authors and their writings as sources of valuable inspiration for all the faithful.

Notes

1 Author's translation. For the letter, see Catherine of Siena, Letter 127 in *Epistolario di Santa Caterina da Siena*, ed. Eugenio Duprè-Theseider (Rome: Istituto storico Italiano per il Medioevo, 1940), 1: 88: "E cio fue el padre spirituale di quella contessa che mori a Roma, ed è colui che rinuntio al vescovado per l'amore della virtù."

2 On Alfonso of Jaén, see Eric Colledge, "Epistola solitarii ad reges: Alphonse of Pecha as Organizer of Birgittine and Urbanist Propaganda," *Mediaeval Studies* 18 (1956): 19–49; Arne Jönsson, *Alfonso of Jaén: His Life and Works with Critical Editions of the Epistola solitarii, the Informaciones and the Epistola Serui Christi* (Lund: Lund University Press, 1989); Mario Sensi, "Alfonso Pecha e l'eremitismo di fine secolo XIV," *Rivista di storia della Chiesa in Italia* 47 (1995): 51–80.

3 See Camille Rouxpetel, "Subiaco à l'épreuve du Grand schisme d'Occident: la mainmise espagnole sur le Sacro Speco (1378–1401)," in *Gli spazi della vita comunitaria*, ed. Letizia Panni Ermini (Spoleto: Centro Italiano di studi sull'alto medioevo, 2016), and Chapter 9 by Camille Rouxpetel in this volume.

4 Catherine of Siena, Letters T194 and T262.

5 See Sylvie Duval, *"La beata Chiara conduttrice." Le Vite di Chiara Gamba-corta e Maria Mancini e i testi dell'Osservanza domenicana Pisana* (Rome: Edizioni di storia e letteratura, 2016).

6 Duval, *"La beata Chiara conduttrice,"* 26–28, 187.

7 Carlo Milanesi, "Ricordi di Cristofano di Gano Guidini," *Archivio storico italiano* 4 (1843): 34–35. See Chapter 5 by Silvia Nocentini and Chapter 6 by Maria H. Oen in this volume.

8 See Gilles Gérard Meersseman, "Spirituali romani, amici di Caterina da Siena," in *Ordo fraternitatis. Confraternite e pietà dei laici nel Medioevo*, eds. Gilles Gérard Meersseman and Gian Piero Pacini (Rome: 1977), vol. 1, 563–64.

9 Critical edition available in Jönsson, *Alfonso of Jaén*, 185–203.

10 Catherine of Siena, Letters T133; T138; T143; T312; T317; T348 and T362.

11 *Conscripcio bona sub triplici via de electione sanctissimi in Christo patris ac domini domini Urbani VI*, ed. F. P. Bliemetzrieder, "Un'altra edizione del Trattato di Alfonso Pecha, vescovo resignato di Iaên sullo scisma (1387–1388), con notizie sulla vita di Pietro Bohier Benedettino, vescovo di Orvieto," *Rivista storica benedettina* 4 (1909): 74–100, at 86.

12 See Alfonso of Jaén, *Informaciones domini Alphonsi heremite olim episcopi Gihennensis super Creatione Urbani*, in Jönsson, *Alfonso of Jaén*, 189.

13 Catherine of Siena, Letter T109.

14 See Mario Sensi, *"Mulieres in ecclesia." Storie di monache e bizzoche*, 2 vols (Spoleto: Fondazione CISAM, 2010), vol. 1, 385–436, at 40; André Vauchez, *Catherine de Sienne. Vie et passions* (Paris: Cerf, 2015), 97–98.

15 On this, see Jane Tylus, *Reclaiming Catherine of Siena: Literacy, Literature, and the Signs of Others* (Chicago, IL: The University of Chicago Press, 2009).

16 Catherine of Siena, Letter T272. Author's translation.

17 See Chapter 1 by F. Thomas Luongo and Chapter 6 by Maria H. Oen in this volume.

18 AP, 94.

19 Boniface IX, The canonization bull of St. Birgitta of Sweden, *Ab origine mundi*, in AASS, Oct. IV, cols. 468–72.

20 On this subject, see Arnold Esch, "Tre sante e il loro ambiente sociale a Roma: S. Francesca Romana, S. Brigida di Svezia e S. Caterina da Siena," in *Atti del Simposio Internazionale Cateriniano-Bernardiniano, Siena 17–20 aprile 1980*, eds. Domenico Maffei and Paolo Nardi (Siena: Accademia degli Intronati, 1982), 89–120; Ludovico Gatto, "La Roma di Caterina," in *La Roma di Caterina da Siena*, ed. Maria Grazia Bianco (Rome: Edizioni Studium, 2001), 13–48.

21 Peter Dinzelbacher, "Saint Bridget and Mysticism of Her Time," in *Santa Brigida - profeta dei tempi nuovi. Atti dell'incontro internazionale di studio, Roma 3–7 ottobre 1991/Saint Bridget Prophetess of New Ages. Proceedings of the International Study Meeting, Rome, October 3–7 1991* (Rome: Casa generalizia Suore Santa Brigida, 1993), 338–72, at 340.

22 Extrav., 47.1–4 and 49.

23 Kari Elisabeth Børresen, "Bridget of Sweden as Model of Theological Inculturation," in *Santa Brigida - profeta dei tempi nuovi*, 197.

24 The fact that Birgitta had, on several occasions, experienced the pains of childbirth when thinking of Christ is, above all, a testimony to her desire to imitate, in everything, the Virgin Mary. On this subject, see Chapter 8 by Gábor Klaniczay in this volume.

25 Michel de Certeau, *La fable mystique* (Paris: Gallimard, 1982).

26 See Chapter 3 by Unn Falkeid in this book.

27 Børresen, "Bridget of Sweden as Model of Theological Inculturation," 189.

28 As the Florentine chronicler Marchione di Coppo Stefani writes with regard to Catherine of Siena in *Cronaca fiorentina* (1378) (in *Rerum italicarum Scriptores*, ed. N. Rodolico, vol. XXXI, 2nd edn. [Città di Castello, 1903]), 306: "Those of *la Parte* [=the Guelphs] held her for a prophetess and the others for a bad woman."

29 See Roger Ellis, "The Swedish Woman, the Widow, the Pilgrim, and the Prophetess: Images of St. Bridget in the Canonization Sermon of Pope Boniface IX," in *Santa Brigida - profeta dei tempi nuovi*, 97.

30 Catherine of Siena, Letter T343.

31 Catherine of Siena, Letter T219.

32 F. Thomas Luongo, *The Saintly Politics of Catherine of Siena* (Ithaca, NY: Cornell University Press, 2006).

33 Ellis, "The Swedish Woman," 95–98 and 116–20.

34 See Vauchez, *Catherine de Sienne*, 115–16.

35 Anna Fredriksson Adman, Anna. *Heymericus de Campo: Dyalogus super Reuelacionibus beate Birgitte. A Critical Edition with an Introduction* (Uppsala: Uppsala University, 2003); Juan de Torquemada, *Declarationes revelationum sanctae Birgittae* (1435–36) ed. in *Sacrorum Conciliorum Nova Amplissima Collectio* (1692–1769), vol. 30, cols. 699–814.

Bibliography

Cited Manuscripts

Augsburg, Universitätsbibliothek, Cod. II.1.2°.201
Berlin, Staatsbibliothek zu Berlin. Preußischer Kulturbesitz, theol.lat.fol. 33
Cambridge, St John's College, MS C.25
Città del Vaticano, Biblioteca Apostolica Vaticana, Barb. Lat. 4063
Città del Vaticano, Biblioteca Apostolica Vaticana, Reg. Lat. 715
Firenze, Archivio di Stato di Firenze, Corporazioni religiose soppresse, 179.49
Firenze, Biblioteca Medicea Laurenziana, Pl. 27.10
Firenze, Biblioteca Medicea Laurenziana, San Marco 917
Firenze, Biblioteca Nazionale Centrale, II.130
Firenze, Biblioteca Nazionale Centrale, II.II.391
Firenze, Biblioteca Nazionale Centrale, II.II.393
Firenze, Biblioteca Nazionale Centrale, II.III.270
Firenze, Biblioteca Nazionale Centrale, Conv. Soppr. B.II.1719
Firenze, Biblioteca Nazionale Centrale, Magl. XXXVIII.15
Firenze, Biblioteca Nazionale Centrale, Magl. XXXVIII.93
Firenze, Biblioteca Nazionale Centrale, Magl. XXXVIII.128
Firenze, Biblioteca Nazionale Centrale, Palatino 59
Firenze, Biblioteca Nazionale Centrale, Palatino 77
Firenze, Biblioteca Riccardiana, MS 1336
Firenze, Biblioteca Riccardiana, MS 1345
Göttingen, Universitätsbibliothek, Theol. 202
Helsinki, Universitetsbiblioteket, MS Nordenskiöld
London, British Library, MS Harley 3432
Lucca, Biblioteca statale, 1942
Madrid, Biblioteca Nacional, MS 54
Modena, Archivio della Cattedrale, MS Confraternita Annunziata
New York, Pierpont Morgan Library, M. 162
New York, Pierpont Morgan Library, M. 498
Oxford, Bodleian Library, Canon. it. 127
Oxford, Bodleian Library, Canon. it. 283
Oxford, Bodleian Library, Canon. Misc. lat. 205
Oxford, Bodleian Library, Canon. Misc. 475
Palermo, Biblioteca Centrale della Regione Siciliana, IV.G.2
Pescia, Biblioteca Capitolare, XXII.VI.11.11
Rieti, Biblioteca comunale, I.2.45
Roma, Archivum generale OFM, MS Panisperna

Siena, Biblioteca comunale degli Intronati, F.II.18
Siena, Biblioteca comunale degli Intronati, G.XI.20
Siena, Biblioteca comunale degli Intronati, I.V.25/26
Siena, Biblioteca comunale degli Intronati, I.VIII.26
Siena, Biblioteca comunale degli Intronati, T.I.1
Siena, Biblioteca comunale degli Intronati, T.II.2/3
Siena, Biblioteca comunale degli Intronati, T.II.4
Siena, Biblioteca comunale degli Intronati, T.II.6
Stockholm, Kungliga Biblioteket, A 3
Stockholm, Kungliga biblioteket, A 70 b
Torino, Biblioteca Nazionale Universitaria, I.III.23
Uppsala, Uppsala Universitetetsbibliotek, C 259
Uppsala, Uppsala Universitetetsbibliotek, C 270
Uppsala, Uppsala Universitetetsbibliotek, C 331
Venezia, Biblioteca Nazionale Marciana, 2977
Venezia, Biblioteca Nazionale Marciana, lat. III. 25
Warszawa, Biblioteka Narodowa, 3310
Wiesbaden, Hessische Landesbibliothek, Cod. 1

Primary Sources

Acta et processus canonizacionis b. Birgitte. Edited by Isak Collijn. SFSS. Ser. 2. Latinska skrifter 1. Uppsala: Almqvist and Wiksell, 1924–31.

Acta sanctorum. Edited by Johannes Bollandus, Godefridus Henschenius, et al. 68 vols. Antwerp and Brussels, 1643–1940.

Augustine of Hippo. *De Trinitate.* In *Patrologia latina cursus completus: Series latina.* Edited by Jacques-Paul Migne, vol. 42. Paris, 1841–64.

———. *The Literal Meaning of Genesis.* Translated by John H. Taylor, vol. 2. Books 7–12. New York: Newman, 1982.

Bartholomaeo de Pisa. *De Conformitate vitae beati Francisci ad vitam Domini Iesu. Analecta Franciscana,* IV–V (1906–12).

Berggren, Maria, ed. *Homiletica Vadstenensia ad religiosos et sacerdotes.* Turnhout: Brepols, 2009.

Biblioteca Agiografica Italiana [BAI]. *Repertorio di testi e manoscritti, secoli XIII-XV.* Edited by Jacques Dalarun and Lino Leonardi. 2 vols. Florence: SISMEL, Edizioni del Galluzzo, 2003.

Bibliotheca hagiographica latina antiquae et mediae aetatis [BHL]. Edited by Société des Bollandistes. 2 vols. Brussels: Société des Bollandistes, 1898–1901.

Birgitta of Sweden. *Reuelaciones Extrauagantes.* Edited by Lennart Hollmann. SFSS. Ser. 2. Latinska skrifter. Uppsala: Almqvist and Wiksell, 1956.

———. *Revelaciones Book VII.* Edited by Birger Bergh. KVHAA. Uppsala: Almqvist and Wiksell, 1967.

———. *Revelaciones Book V.* Edited by Birger Bergh. KVHAA. Uppsala: Almqvist and Wiksell, 1971.

———. *Opera minora II: Sermo angelicus.* Edited by Sten Eklund. KVHAA. Uppsala: Almqvist and Wiksell, 1972.

———. *Opera minora I: Regvla Salvatoris.* Edited by Sten Eklund. KVHAA. Stockholm: Almqvist and Wiksell, 1975.

———. *Revelaciones Book I.* Edited by Carl-Gustaf Undhagen. KVHAA. Stockholm: Almqvist and Wiksell, 1977.

———. *Life and Selected Revelations.* Edited by Marguerite Tjader Harris. Translated by Albert Ryle Kezel. New York: Paulist Press, 1990.

———. *Opera minora III: Quattuor oraciones.* Edited by Sten Eklund. KVHAA. Stockholm: Almqvist and Wiksell, 1991.

———. *Revelaciones Book VI.* Edited by Birger Bergh. KVHAA. Stockholm: Almqvist and Wiksell, 1991.

———. *Revelaciones Book IV.* Edited by Hans Aili. KVHAA. Stockholm: Almqvist and Wiksell, 1992.

———. *Revelaciones Book III.* Edited by Ann-Mari Jönsson. KVHAA. Stockholm: Almqvist and Wiksell, 1998.

———. *Revelaciones Book II.* Edited by Carl-Gustaf Undhagen and Birger Bergh. KVHAA. Stockholm: Almqvist and Wiksell, 2001.

———. *Revelaciones Book VIII.* Edited by Hans Aili. KVHAA. Stockholm: Almqvist and Wiksell, 2002.

———. *The Revelations of St. Birgitta of Sweden.* Translated by Denis Searby, with Introductions and Notes by Bridget Morris. 4 vols. Oxford: Oxford University Press, 2006–15.

Bliemetzrieder, Franz. "Un'altra edizione rifatta del trattato di Alfonso Pecha, vescovo resignato di Iaën, sullo scisma (1387–1388), con notizie sulla vita di Pietro Bohier, Benedettino, vescovo di Orvieto." *Rivista storica benedettina* 4 (1909): 74–100.

Brambilla, Simona. *"Padre mio dolce." Lettere di religiosi a Francesco Datini. Antologia.* Rome: Ministero per i Beni e le Attività Culturali, 2010.

Cachey, Theodore, ed. and trans. *Petrarch's Guide to the Holy Land: Itinerary to the Sepulcher of Our Lord Jesus Christ.* Notre Dame, IN: University of Notre Dame Press, 2002.

Camesasca, Gloria. "Lettere di ser Lapo Mazzei a Francesco Datini (1390–1399)." PhD dissertation, Università Cattolica del Sacro Cuore, Milan, 2012.

Catherine of Siena. *Le lettere di S. Caterina da Siena, ridotte a miglior lezione, e in ordine nuovo disposte con premio note di Niccolò Tommaseo.* Edited by Niccolò Tommaseo. 4 vols. Florence, 1860.

———. *Dialogo della divina provvidenza.* Edited by Innocenzo Taurisano. Rome: Libreria editrice E. Ferrari, 1928.

———. *Epistolario di santa Caterina da Siena.* Edited by Eugenio Dupré Theseider. Rome: Istituto storico Italiano per il Medioevo, 1940.

———. *Le Orazioni di S. Caterina da Siena.* Edited by Giuliana Cavallini. Siena: Cantagalli, 1993.

———. *Il Dialogo della divina Provvidenza: ovvero Libro della divina dottrina.* Edited by Giuliana Cavallini. Rome: Edizioni Cateriniane, 1968. 2nd edn. Siena: Cantagalli, 1995.

———. *Santa Caterina da Siena: Opera Omnia. Testi e concordanze.* Edited by Fausto Sbaffoni. Pistoia, 2002. CD-ROM Edition.

———. *The Letters of Catherine of Siena.* Edited and translated by Suzanne Noffke. 4 vols. Tempe: Arizona Center for Medieval and Renaissance Studies, 2000–08.

Corpus codicum Suecicorum Medii Aevi 7. Hafniae, 1936.

Csepregi, Ildikó, Gábor Klaniczay, and Bence Péterfi, eds. *Legenda Vetus, Acta Processus Canonizationis et Miracula Sanctae Margaritae de Hungaria – The Oldest Legend, Acts of the Canonization Process and Miracles of Saint Margaret of Hungary.* Budapest: CEU Press, 2017.

Dante. *Purgatorio.* Translated by Allen Mandelbaum. New York: Bantam, 1984.

Eubel, Konrad. *Hierarchia catholica medii aevi...6* vols. Monasterii: Sumptibus et Typis Librariae Regensbergianae, 1913–67.

Fawtier, Robert, ed. "La vie de la bienheureuse Hélène de Hongrie." *Mélanges d'archéologie et d'histoire* 33 (1913): 3–23.

——— ed. "Catheriniana." *Mélanges d'archéologie et d'histoire* 34. Rome: École française de Rome (1914): 3–96.

Fredriksson Adman, Anna. *Heymericus de Campo: Dyalogus super Reuelacionibus beate Birgitte. A Critical Edition with an Introduction.* Acta Universitatis Uppsaliensis, Studia Latina Uppsaliensia. Uppsala: Uppsala University, 2003.

Friedberg, Emil, ed. *Corpus Juris Canonici.* 2 vols. Leipzig: 1879–81, repr. Graz, 1955.

Gerardi de Fracheto O.P. *Vitae fratrum Ordinis Praedicatorum.* Edited by Benedikt Maria Reichert. Monumenta Ordinis Fratrum Praedicatorum Historica 1. Lovanii, 1896.

Gerson, Jean. "De examinatione doctrinarum." In *Œuvres complètes.* Edited by Palémon Glorieux, vol. 9, 458–75. Paris: Desclée & Cie, 1960–73.

Grottanelli, Francesco. *Leggenda minore di S. Caterina da Siena e lettere dei suoi discepoli: scritture inedite.* Bologna: Gaetano Romagnoli, 1868.

Gui, Bernard. "Vita S. Thomae Aquinatis." In *Fontes Vitae S. Thomae Aquinatis notis historicis et criticis illustrate.* Edited by Dominicus Prümmer and M. H. Laurent. Toulouse, 1911–34.

Hackett, Benedict, O.S.A, Eric Colledge, and Noel Chadwick. "William Flete's 'De Remediis contra Temptaciones' in its Latin and English Recensions. The Growth of a Text." *Mediaeval Studies* 26 (1964): 210–230.

———. *William Flete, O.S.A. and Catherine of Siena. Masters of Fourteenth Century Spirituality.* Edited by John E. Rotelle, O.S.A, with a Foreword by Francis X. Martin, O.S.A. Villanova, PA: Augustinian Press, 1992.

Hodgson, Phyllis, and Gabriel M. Liegy, eds. *The Orcherd of Syon.* Early English Text Society 258. London, 1966.

Jacques de Vitry. *The Life of Marie of Oignies.* Translated by Margot H. King. Toronto: Peregrina, 1993.

Jerome. *Select Letters.* Translated by F.A. Wright. Cambridge, MA: Harvard University Press, 1933.

Juan de Torquemada. *Declarationes revelationum sanctae Birgittae.* Edited in *Sacrorum Conciliorum Nova Amplissima Collectio,* vol. 30, cols. 699–814. 1692–1769.

Jönsson, Arne. *Alfonso of Jaén: His Life and Works with Critical Editions of the Epistola Solitarii, the Informaciones and the Epistola Serui Christi.* Studia Graeca et Latina Lundensia. Lund: Lund University Press, 1989.

Kruse, John. "Vita metrica S. Birgittae." In *Meddelanden från det litteraturhistoriska seminariet i Lund,* I, *Lunds Universitets årsskrift* 28 (1891–92): 10–28.

La Chanson de Roland. Edited by Joseph Bédier. Paris: H. Piazza, 1921.

Laurent, Marie-Hyacinthe, ed. *Il Processo Castellano. Con appendice di documenti sul culto e la canonizzazione di S. Caterina*. Fontes Vitae S. Catharinae Senensis Historici 9. Milan, 1942.

Lerner, Robert E. "Alfonso Pecha's Treatise on the Origins of the Great Schism: What an Insider 'Saw And Heard'." *Traditio* 72 (2017): 411–51.

Liber pontificalis nella recensione di Pietro Guglielmo OSB e del cardinale Pandolfo, glossato da Pietro Bohier OSB, vescovo di Orvieto. Edited by Ulderico Přerovský. 3 vols. "Studia Gratiana," XXI, XXII e XXIII. Rome, 1978.

Lombardelli, Gregorio. *Sommario della disputa. A difesa della Sacre Stigmate di Santa Caterina da Siena*. Siena, 1601.

Matter, E. Ann and Gabriella Zarri, eds. *Una mistica contestata. La vita di Lucia da Narni (1476–1544) tra agiografia e autobiografia*. Rome: Edizioni di Storia e Letteratura, 2011.

Mazzei, Lapo. *Lettere di un notaro a un mercante del secolo XIV. Con altre lettere e documenti*. Edited by Cesare Guasti. 2 vols. Florence: Le Monnier, 1880.

Meersseman, Gilles-Gérard. "Études sur l'ordre des frères prêcheurs au début du Grand Schisme." *Archivium Fratrum Praedicatorum*. T. 25–27 (1955–57).

Milanesi, Carlo. "Ricordi di Cristofano di Gano Guidini." *Archivio storico Italiano* 4 (1843): 25–48.

Paulsson, Göte, ed. *Chronica Visbycensis, 815–1444*. In *Annales Suecici Medii Aevi*. Lund: Gleerup, 1974.

Petrarca, Francesco. *Letters of Old Age: Rerum Senilium Libri I–XVIII*. Edited and translated by Aldo S. Bernardo, Saul Levin, and Reta A. Bernardo, vol. II. Baltimore, MD: Johns Hopkins University Press, 1992.

Raymond of Capua. *The Life of Saint Catherine of Siena by Raymond of Capua*. Translated by Conleth Kearns. Wilmington, DE: Michael Glazier, 1980.

———*Die Legenda Maior (Vita Catharinae Senensis) des Raimund von Capua*. Edited by Jörg Jungmayr. 2 vols. Berlin: Weidler Buchverlag, 2004.

———. *Legenda maior sive Legenda admirabilis virginis Catherine de Senis*. Edited by Silvia Nocentini. Florence: SISMEL, Edizioni del Galluzzo, 2013.

Rerum italicarum Scriptores. vol. XXXI, 2nd edn. Città di Castello, 1903.

Scriptores rerum svecicarum medii aevi. Edited by Claudius Annerstedt, vol. 3. Uppsala: E. Berling, 1871 and 1876.

Speculum virginum. Edited by Jutta Seyfarth. Turnhout: Brepols, 1990.

Supplementum. Edited by Société des Bollandistes. Brussels: Société des Bollandistes, 1986.

The Prayers of Saint Bridget: The Fifteen Oos. Thesaurus Precum Latinarum: Treasury of Latin Prayers. Compiled by Michael Martin Online in Latin and English. www.preces-latinae.org/thesaurus/Filius/StBrigid.html [Accessed 05.10.2018].

Thomas Antonii de Senis. "Caffarini." *Sanctae Catharinae Senensis legenda minor*. Edited by Ezio Franceschini. Siena, 1942.

———. *Libellus de supplemento, Legende prolixe virginis beate Catherine de Senis*. Edited by Giuliana Cavallini and Imelda Foralosso. Roma: Edizioni Cateriniane, 1974.

Thomas of Celano. "The Remembrance of the Desire of the Soul." In *Francis of Assisi: Early Documents*. Vol. II. *The Founder*. Edited by Regis J. Armstrong,

J A. Wayne Hellmann, and William J. Short, 233–395. New York: New City Press, 1999.

———. "The Treatise on the Miracles of Saint Francis." In *Francis of Assisi: Early Documents*. Vol. II. *The Founder*. Edited by Regis J. Armstrong, J A. Wayne Hellmann, and William J. Short, 397–470. New York: New City Press, 1999.

Töppen, Max, ed. "Aus dem Septililium venerabilis domine Dorothee." In *Scriptores rerum Prussicarum: die Geschichtsquellen der preussischen Vorzeit*. Edited by Theodor Hirsch, Max Töppen, and Ernst Strehlke, vol. 2. Leipzig: Verlag von S. Hirzel, 1863.

Wolf, Kenneth Baxter. *The Life and Afterlife of St. Elizabeth of Hungary*. Oxford: Oxford University Press, 2011.

Secondary Materials

Adnès, Pierre. "Stigmates." In *Dictionnaire de spiritualité ascétique et mystique. Doctrine et histoire*, vol. 14, 1211–43. Paris: 1988.

Aili, Hans. "St. Birgitta and the Text of the *Revelationes*. A Survey of Some Influences Traceable to Translators and Editors." In *The Editing of Theological and Philosophical Texts from the Middle Ages*. Edited by Monika Asztalos, 75–91. Stockholm: Almqvist and Wiksell, 1986.

———."The Manuscripts of Revelaciones S. Birgittae." In *Santa Brigida, Napoli, L'Italia*. Edited by Olle Ferm, Alessandra Perriccioli Saggese, and Marcello Rotili, 153–60. Naples: Arte tipografica editrice, 2009.

Aili, Hans and Jan Svanberg. *Imagines Sanctae Birgittae: The Earliest Illuminated Manuscripts and Panel Paintings Related to the Revelations of St. Birgitta of Sweden*, 2 vols. Stockholm: Royal Academy of Letters, History and Antiquities, 2003.

Andersson, Aron. *Guds moder och den heliga Birgitta: En antologi*. Vadstena: Vadstena Affärstryck, 1978.

Andersson, Roger. "Sermon Manuscripts of Different Kinds." *Medieval Sermon Studies* 55 (2011): 39–41.

———."Messenger Manuscripts and Mechanisms of Change." In *Continuity and Change: Papers from the Birgitta Conference at Dartington 2015*. Edited by Elin Andersson, Claes Gejrot, E. A. Jones, and Mia Åkestam, 24–39. Stockholm: KVHAA, 2017.

———. "Birgitta and Her Revelations in the Sermons of the Vadstena Brothers." In *A Companion to Birgitta of Sweden and Her Legacy in the Later Middle Ages*. Edited by Maria H. Oen, 159–85. Leiden: Brill, 2019.

Andersson, Roger and Stephan Borgehammar. "The Preaching of the Birgittine Friars at Vadstena Abbey (c. 1380–1515)." *Revue Mabillon*, Nouvelle série 8, 69 (1997): 206–36.

Ascoli, Albert Russel. *Dante and the Making of a Modern Author*. Cambridge: Cambridge University Press, 2008.

Atiya, Aziz Suryal. *The Crusade in the Later Middle Ages*. London: Methuen, 1938.

Atkinson, Clarissa W. *Mystic and Pilgrim: The Book and the World of Margery Kempe*. Ithaca, NY: Cornell University Press, 1983.

Aurigemma, Luisa. "La tradizione manoscritta del Dialogo della Divina Provvidenza di santa Caterina da Siena." *Critica letteraria* 16 (1988): 237–58.

Bartolomei Romagnoli, Alessandra. "Un trattatello cinquecentesco in difesa delle stimmate di Caterina da Siena." In *Discorsi sulle stimmate dal Medioevo all'età contemporanea – Discours sur les stigmates du Moyen Âge à l'époque contemporaine*. Edited by Gábor Klaniczay. Rome: Edizioni di Storia e Letteratura = *Archivio italiano per la storia della pietà* 26 (2013): 177–226.

———. "La disputa sulle stimmate." In *Virgo digna coelo: Caterina e la sua eredità. Raccolta di Studi in occasione del 550° anniversario della canonizzazione di santa Caterina da Siena (1461–2011)*. Edited by Alessandra Bartolomei Romagnoli, Luciano Cinelli, and Pierantonio Piatti, 405–44. Vatican City: Libreria editrice vaticana, 2013.

Beattie, Blake. "Catherine of Siena and the Papacy." In *A Companion to Catherine of Siena*. Edited by Carolyn Muessig, George Ferzoco, and Beverly Mayne Keinzle, 73–98. Leiden: Brill, 2012.

Bell, Rudolph. *Holy Anorexia*. Chicago, IL: The University of Chicago Press, 1985.

Belting, Hans. *Likeness and Presence: A History of the Image before the Era of Art*. Chicago, IL: The University of Chicago Press, 1994 [1990].

Benfatti, Solanus M. C.F.M. *The Five Wounds of Saint Francis*. Charlotte, NC: TAN Books, 2011.

Bergh, Birger. *Heliga Birgitta. Åttabarnsmor och profet*. Lund: Historiska Media, 2002.

Bianchi, Lidia. "Il carattere dottrinale della santitá di Caterina da Siena nella iconografia del primo Quattrocento." In *Atti del Congresso Internazionale di Studi Cateriniani Siena–Roma 24–29 aprile 1980*, 563–95. Rome: Curia Generalizia O.P., 1981.

———. "Caterina da Siena." In *Enciclopedia dell'arte medievale*. Edited by Angiola Maria Romanini, vol. 4, 86–92. 12 vols. Rome: Istituto della Enciclopedia Italiana, 1991–2002.

Bianchi, Lidia and Diega Giunta. *Iconografia di S. Caterina da Siena. 1. L'immagine*. Roma: Città Nuova, 1988.

Billinkoff, Jodi. *The Avila of Saint Teresa. Religious Reform in a Sixteenth-Century City*. Ithaca, NY: Cornell University Press, 1989.

Bisogni, Fabio. "Il 'Libellus' di Tommaso d'Antonio Caffarini e gli inizi dell'iconografia di Caterina." In *Con l'occhio e col lume*. Edited by Luigi Trenti e Bente Klange Addabbo, 253–68. Siena: Cantagalli, 1999.

———. "Raggi e aureole ossia la distinzione della santità." In *Con l'occhio e col lume*. Edited by Luigi Trenti and Bente Klange Addabbo, 349–51. Siena: Cantagalli, 1999.

Blumenfeld-Kosinski, Renate. *Poets, Saints, and Visionaries of the Great Schism, 1378–1417*. University Park: Pennsylvania State University Press, 2006.

———. "Philippe de Mézières's *Life of Saint Pierre de Thomas* at the Crossroads of Late Medieval Hagiography and Crusading Ideology." *Viator* 40 (2009): 223–48.

———. "Roles for Women in Colonial Fantasies in Fourteenth-Century France: Pierre Dubois and Philippe de Mézières." In *The French of Outremer: Communities and Communications in the Crusading Mediterranean*. Edited by Laura Morreale and Nicholas Paul, 247–81. New York: Fordham University Press, 2018.

Borgehammar, Stephan. "*Vitae Birgittae.* En översikt och tre editioner." In *Humanitas. Festskrift till Arne Jönsson.* Edited by Astrid M. H. Nilsson, Aske Damtoft Poulsen, and Johanna Svensson, 177–200. Gothenburg: Makadam, 2017.

Bouflet, Joachim. *Les stigmatisés.* Paris: Cerf, 1996.

Bräm, Andreas. *Neapolitanische Bilderbibeln des Trecento. Anjou-Buchmalerei von Robert dem Weisen bis zu Johanna I.* 2 vols. Wiesbaden: Reichert, 2007.

Brown, Jennifer N. "The Many Misattributions of Catherine of Siena: Beyond the Orchard in England." *The Journal of Medieval Religious Culture* 1 (2015): 67–84.

——. *Fruit of the Orchard: Reading Catherine of Siena in Late Medieval and Early Modern England.* Toronto: University of Toronto Press, 2019.

Brown, Peter. *Augustine of Hippo: A Biography.* 2nd edn. Berkeley: University of California Press, 2000.

Brundage, James A. *Law, Sex, and Christian Society in Medieval Europe.* Chicago, IL: The University of Chicago Press, 1987.

Brundin, Abigail. *Vittoria Colonna and the Spiritual Poetics of the Italian Reformation.* Aldershot: Ashgate, 2008.

Buono, L. et al., eds. *I manoscritti datati delle province di Frosinone, Rieti e Viterbo.* Manoscritti datati d'Italia 17. Florence: SISMEL, Edizioni del Galluzzo, 2007.

Bynum, Caroline Walker. *Holy Feast and Holy Fast: The Religious Significance of Food to Medieval Women.* Berkeley: The University of California Press, 1987.

Bysted, Ane, Carsten Selch Jensen, Kurt Villads Jensen, and John H. Lind, eds. *Jerusalem in the North: Denmark and the Baltic Crusades, 1100–1522.* Turnhout: Brepols, 2012.

Børresen, Kari Elisabeth. "Bridget of Sweden as Model of Theological Inculturation." In *Santa Brigida – profeta dei tempi nuovi. Atti dell'incontro internazionale di studio, Roma 3–7 ottobre 1991/Saint Bridget Prophetess of New Ages. Proceedings of the International Study Meeting, Rome, October 3–7 1991,* 188–200. Rome: Casa generalizia Suore Santa Brigida, 1993.

Cachey, Theodore. "'Peregrinus (quasi) ubique': Petrarca e la storia del viaggio." *Intersezioni: Rivista di storia delle idee* 17, no. 3 (1997): 369–84.

Caciola, Nancy. *Discerning Spirits: Divine and Demonic Possession in the Middle Ages.* Ithaca, NY: Cornell University Press, 2003.

Capecelatro, Alfonso. *Storia di Santa Caterina e del papato del suo tempo.* Florence: Barbera, Bianchi, 1858.

Cardini, Franco. "L'idea di crociata in Santa Catarina da Siena." In *Atti del Simposio Internazionale Cateriniano–Bernardiniano, Siena 17–20 aprile 1980.* Edited by Domenico Maffei and Paolo Nardi, 57–87. Siena: Accademia Senese degli Intronati, 1982.

Carlquist, Jonas. *Vadstenasystrarnas textvärld. Studier i systrarnas skriftbrukskompetens, lärdom och textförståelse.* Uppsala: SFSS, 2007.

Carruthers, Mary. *The Book of Memory: A Study of Memory in Medieval Culture.* 2nd edn. Cambridge: Cambridge University Press, 2008.

Casteen, Elizabeth. *From She-Wolf to Martyr: The Reign and Disputed Reputation of Johanna I of Naples.* Ithaca, NY: Cornell University Press, 2016.

Chance, Jane. "St Catherine of Siena in Late Medieval Britain: Feminizing Literary Reception through Gender and Class." *Annali d'Italianistica* 13 (1995): 163–203.

Chareyron, Nicole. *Pilgrims to Jerusalem in the Middle Ages*. Translated by Donald W. Wilson. New York: Columbia University Press, 2005 [2000].

Chelazzi Dini, Giulietta. *Il gotico a Siena*. Florence: Centro Di, 1982.

Chenu, Marie-Dominique. "Auctor, Actor, Autor." *Bulletin du Cange: Archivium Latinitas Medii Aevi* 3 (1927): 81–6.

Cherubini, Giovanni. "Dal libro di ricordi di un notaio senese del Trecento." In *Signori, contadini, borghesi: ricerche sulla società Italiana del basso medioevo*, 393–425. Florence: La Nuova Italia, 1974.

Chollet, Loïc. "Croisade ou évangélisation? La polémique contre les chevaliers teutoniques à l'aune des témoignages des voyageurs français de la fin du moyen âge." *Ordines militares* 20 (2015): 175–203.

Christiansen, Eric. *The Northern Crusades: The Baltic and the Catholic Frontier 1100–1525*. Minneapolis: University of Minnesota Press, 1980.

Coakley, John. "Friars as Confidants of Holy Women in Medieval Dominican Hagiography." In *Images of Sainthood in Medieval Europe*. Edited by Renate Blumenfeld-Kosinski and Timea Szell, 222–45. Ithaca, NY: Cornell University Press, 1991.

———. "Women's Textual Authority and the Collaboration of Clerics." *Medieval Holy Women in the Christian Tradition, c.1100–c.1500*. Edited by Alastair Minnis and Rosalynn Voaden, 83–104. Turnhout: Brepols, 2010.

Cohen, Esther. *The Modulated Scream: Pain in Late Medieval Culture*. Chicago, IL: The University of Chicago Press, 2010.

Coletti, Vittorio. *Parole dal pulpito. Chiesa e movimenti religiosi tra latino e volgare nell'Italia del Medioevo e del Rinascimento*. Casala Monferrato: Marietti, 1983.

Colledge, Eric. "*Epistola solitarii ad reges*: Alphonse of Pecha as Organizer of Birgittine and Urbanist Propaganda." *Mediaeval Studies* 18 (1956): 19–49.

Constable, Giles. "The Imitation of the Body of Christ." In *Three Studies in Medieval Life and Social Thought: The Interpretation of Mary and Martha, The Ideal of the Imitation of Christ, The Orders of Society*. 143–247. Cambridge: Cambridge University Press, 1995.

Coussemacker, Sophie. "L'ordre de saint Jérôme en Espagne, 1373–1516." PhD dissertation, Paris X-Nanterre, 1994.

Cox, Virginia. *Lyric Poetry by Women of the Italian Renaissance*. Baltimore, MD: The Johns Hopkins University Press, 2013.

Creutzburg, Anette. "Darstellungen von göttlicher Inspiration in der Neapeler Buchmalerei. Zur Visualisierung von *auctoritas* in der Autorenbildern der hl. Birgitta von Schweden." In *Buchschätze des Mittelalters. Forschungsrückblicke – Forschungsperspektiven*. Edited by Klaus Gereon Beuckers, Christoph Jobst, and Stefanie Westphal, 265–79. Regensburg: Schnell & Steiner, 2011.

———. *Die heilige Birgitta von Schweden. Bildliche Darstellungen und theologische Kontroversen im Vorfeld ihrer Kanonisation (1373–1391)*. Kiel: Verlag Ludwig, 2011.

Dalarun, Jacques. "The Great Secret of Francis." In *The Stigmata of Francis of Assisi: New Studies New Perspectives*. Edited by Jacques Dalarun, Michael

Cusato, and Carla Salvati, 9–26. St. Bonaventure, NY: The Franciscan Institute, 2002.

Davidson, Arnold. "Miracles of Bodily Transformation, or, How St. Francis Received the Stigmata." In *Picturing Science, Producing Art*. Edited by Caroline A. Jones, Peter Gallison, and Amy Slaton, 101–24. London: Routledge, 1998.

Deák, Viktória Hedvig. *La légende de sainte Marguerite de Hongrie et l'hagiographie dominicaine*. Paris: Cerf, 2013.

De Certeau, Michel. *La fable mystique*. Paris: Gallimard, 1982.

De Nie, Giselle, Karl F. Morrison, and Marco Mostert, eds. *Seeing the Invisible in Late Antiquity and the Early Middle Ages*. Turnhout: Brepols, 2005.

Denis-Boulet, Noële. *La carrière politique de Sainte Cathérine de Sienne: Étude historique*. Paris: Desclée et Brouwer, 1939.

Del Pozzo, Joan Patterson. "Speaking in Imagery, Speaking in Ecstasy: A Discussion of Saint Catherine of Siena's Language and Style." PhD dissertation, The Johns Hopkins University, 1991.

Dinshaw, Carolyn and David Wallace. "Introduction." In *The Cambridge Companion to Medieval Women's Writing*. Edited by Carolyn Dinshaw and David Wallace, 1–10. Cambridge: Cambridge University Press, 2003.

Dinzelbacher, Peter. "Saint Bridget and Mysticism of Her Time." In *Santa Brigida – profeta dei tempi nuovi. Atti dell'incontro internazionale di studio, Roma 3–7 ottobre 1991/Saint Bridget Prophetess of New Ages. Proceedings of the International Study Meeting, Rome, October 3–7 1991*, 338–72. Rome: Casa generalizia Suore Santa Brigida, 1993.

Donatelli, A. "Le origini del Monastero di S. Gerolamo di Quarto." *L'Ulivo* (1972).

Dupré Theseider, Eugenio. "Caterina da Siena." In *Dizionario biografico degli Italiani* 22, 361–79. Rome: Istituto della Enciclopedia Italiana, 1979.

Duval, Sylvie. *"La beata Chiara conduttrice." Le Vite di Chiara Gambacorta e Maria Mancini e i testi dell'Osservanza domenicana pisana*. Rome: Edizioni di Storia e Letteratura, 2016.

Echart, Kevin Scott. "Birgitta of Sweden and Medieval Prophecy." PhD dissertation, Yale University, 1993.

Edbury, Peter W. "The Crusading Policy of King Peter I of Cyprus, 1359–1369." In *The Eastern Mediterranean Lands in the Period of the Crusades*. Edited by P. M. Holt, 90–105. Warminster: Aris and Phillips, 1977.

Ekdahl, Sven. "Crusade and Colonisation in the Baltic: A Historiographical Analysis." In *The North-Eastern Frontiers of Medieval Europe*. Edited by Alan V. Murray, 1–42. Farnham: Ashgate, 2014.

Ekwall, Sara. "Ett ikonografiskt Birgittaproblem: Har förebilden till den skrivande Birgitta i Vadstena varit den skrivande evangelisten?" *Konsthistorisk Tidskrift* 37, no. 1 (1968): 1–20.

Eleen, Luba. *The Illustration of the Pauline Epistles in French and English Bibles of the Twelfth and Thirteenth Centuries*. Oxford: Clarendon Press, 1982.

Elliott, Dyan. "The Physiology of Rapture and Female Spirituality." In *Medieval Theology and the Natural Body*. Edited by Peter Biller and Alastair Minnis, 143–73. York: York Medieval Press, 1997.

———. *"Dominae or Dominatae?* Female Mysticism and the Trauma of Textuality." In *Women, Marriage, and Family in Medieval Christendom: Essays in*

Memory of Michael M. Sheehan, C.S.B. Edited by Constance M. Rousseau and Joel T. Rosenthal, 47–77. Kalamazoo: Medieval Institute Publications, 1998.

———. "Authorizing a Life: The Collaboration of Dorothea of Montau and John Marienwerder." In *Gendered Voices: Medieval Saints and Their Interpreters.* Edited by Catherine M. Mooney, 168–91. Philadelphia: University of Pennsylvania Press, 1999.

———. *Fallen Bodies: Pollution, Sexuality and Demonology in the Middle Ages.* Philadelphia: University of Pennsylvania Press, 1999.

———. *Proving Woman: Female Spirituality and Inquisitional Culture in the Later Middle Ages.* Princeton, NJ: Princeton University Press, 2004.

———. "Flesh and Spirit: The Female Body." In *Medieval Holy Women in the Christian Tradition, c.1100–c.1500.* Edited by Alastair Minnis and Rosalynn Voaden, 13–46. Turnhout: Brepols, 2010.

Ellis, Roger. "'Flores ad fabricandam … coronam.' An Investigation into the Uses of the Revelations of St Bridget of Sweden in Fifteenth Century England." *Medium Ævum* 51 (1982): 163–86.

———. "The Divine Message and its Human Agents: St. Birgitta and her Editors." *Studies in St. Birgitta and the Brigittine Order* 35 (1993): 209–33.

———. "The Swedish Woman, the Widow, the Pilgrim, and the Prophetess: Images of St. Bridget in the Canonization Sermon of Pope Boniface IX." In *Santa Brigida – profeta dei tempi nuovi. Atti dell'incontro internazionale di studio, Roma 3–7 ottobre 1991/Saint Bridget Prophetess of New Ages. Proceedings of the International Study Meeting, Rome, October 3–7 1991,* 93–120. Rome: Casa generalizia Suore Santa Brigida, 1993.

Esch, Arnold. "Tre sante e il loro ambiente sociale a Roma: S. Francesca Romana, S. Brigida di Svezia e S. Caterina da Siena." In *Atti del Simposio Internazionale Cateriniano-Bernardiniano, Siena 17–20 aprile 1980.* Edited by Domenico Maffei and Paolo Nardi, 89–120. Siena: Accademia degli Intronati, 1982.

Faini, Marco and Alessia Meneghin, eds. *Domestic Devotions in the Early Modern World.* Leiden: Brill, 2018.

Falkeid, Unn. *The Avignon Papacy Contested: An Intellectual History from Dante to Catherine of Siena.* Cambridge, MA: Harvard University Press, 2017.

Fennell, John L. I. "The Campaign of King Magnus Eriksson against Novgorod in 1348: An Examination of the Sources." *Jahrbücher für Geschichte Osteuropas.* Neue Folge, Bd. 14, H. 1 (1966): 1–9.

Ferm, Olle. "Heliga Birgittas program för uppror mot Magnus Eriksson: En studie i politisk argumentationskonst." In *Heliga Birgitta – budskapet och förebilden. Föredrag vid jubileumssymposiet i Vadstena 3–7 oktober 1991.* Edited by Alf Härdelin and Mereth Lindgren, 125–43. Stockholm: KVHAA, 1993.

Ferzoco, George. "The *Processo Castellano* and the Canonization of Catherine of Siena." In *A Companion to Catherine of Siena.* Edited by Carolyn Muessig, George Ferzoco, and Beverly Mayne Kienzle, 185–203. Leiden: Brill, 2012.

Finegan, Jack. *The Archaeology of the New Testament: The Life of Jesus and the Beginning of the Early Church.* Princeton, NJ: Princeton University Press, 1992.

Foà, Simona. "Guidini, Cristoforo." In *Dizionario Biografico degli Italiani*, vol. 61. Rome: Istituto storico Treccani, 2004. www.treccani.it/enciclopedia/cristoforo-guidini_(Dizionario-Biografico)/ [Accessed 08.10.2018].

Fonnesberg-Schmidt, Iben. *The Popes and the Baltic Crusades 1147–1254*. Leiden: Brill, 2007.

Foucault, Michel. "What is an Author." In *The Foucault Reader*. Edited by Paul Rabinow, 101–20. New York: Pantheon Books, 1984.

Fredriksson, Anna. "The Council of Constance, Jean Gerson, and St. Birgitta's *Revelaciones*." *Mediaeval Studies* 76 (2014): 217–39.

Freuler, Gaudenz. "La miniatura senese degli anni 1370–1420." In *La miniatura senese 1270–1420*. Edited by Cristina De Benedictis, 177–207. Milan: Skira, 2002.

Friedman, Joan Isobel. "Politics and the Rhetoric of Reform in the Letters of Saints Bridget of Sweden and Catherine of Siena." In *Livres et lectures de femmes en Europe entre Moyen Âge et Renaissance*. Edited by Anne-Marie Legaré, 279–94. Turnhout: Brepols, 2007.

Friend, A. M. "The Portraits of the Evangelists in Greek and Latin Manuscripts. Part 1." *Art Studies* 5 (1927): 115–47.

———. "The Portraits of the Evangelists in Greek and Latin Manuscripts. Part 2." *Art Studies* 7 (1929): 3–29.

Frosini, Giovanna. "Lingua e testo nel manoscritto viennese delle lettere di Caterina." In *Dire l'ineffabile. Caterina da Siena e il linguaggio della mistica. Atti del Convegno (Siena, 13–14 novembre 2003)*. Edited by Lino Leonardi and Pietro Trifone, 91–126. Florence: SISMEL, Edizioni del Galluzzo, 2006.

Frugoni, Chiara. *Francesco e l'invenzione delle stimmate. Una storia per parole e immagini fino a Bonaventura e Giotto*. Turin: Einaudi, 1993.

Fröjmark, Anders. *Mirakler och helgonkult. Linköpings biskopsdöme under senmedeltiden*. Uppsala: Uppsala universitet, 1992.

Fulton, Rachel. *From Judgement to Passion: Devotion to Christ and the Virgin Mary, 800–1200*. New York: Columbia University Press, 2002.

Fumian, Silvia. "Cristoforo Cortese e i Domenicani a Venezia: di alcuni manoscritti Cateriniani." In *Le arti a confronto con il sacro. Metodi di ricerca e nuove prospettive di indagine interdisciplinare*. Edited by Valentina Cantone and Silvia Fumian, 101–09. Padua: CLEUP, 2009.

Ganz, David. "The Dilemma of a Saint's Portrait: Catherine's Stigmata between Invisible Body Trace and Visible Pictorial Sign." In *Catherine of Siena: The Creation of a Cult*. Edited by Jeffrey F. Hamburger and Gabriela Signori, 239–62. Turnhout: Brepols, 2013.

Garçon, Maurice. *Magdeleine de la Croix abbesse diabolique*. Grenoble: Jérôme Millon, 2010 [1939].

Gardener, Edmund G. *Saint Catherine of Siena: A Study in the Religion, Literature and History of the Fourteenth Century in Italy*. London: J. M. Dent, 1907.

Gatto, Ludovico. "La Roma di Caterina." In *La Roma di Caterina da Siena*. Edited by Maria Grazia Bianco, 13–48. Rome: Edizioni Studium, 2001.

Gescer, Ottó. *The Feast and the Pulpit: Preachers, Sermons and the Cult of St. Elizabeth of Hungary, 1235–ca. 1500*. Spoleto: Fondazione Centro Italiano di studi sull'Alto Medioevo, 2012.

Gilkær, Hans Torben. *The Political Ideas of St. Birgitta and her Spanish Confessor, Alfonso Pecha. Liber Celestis Imperatoris ad Reges: A Mirror of Princes.* Translated by Michael Caine. Odense: Odense University Press, 1993.

Gillespie, Vincent. "Dial M for Mystic: Mystical Texts in the Library of Syon Abbey and the Spirituality of the Syon Brethren." In *Looking in Holy Books: Essays on Late Medieval Religious Writing in England*, 175–207. Turnhout: Brepols, 2011.

Gillespie, Vincent and Anthony Ian Doyle, eds. *Syon Abbey. With Libraries of the Carthusians.* London and Toronto: British Library and University of Toronto Press, 2001.

Gimaret, Antoinette. "Corps manqués et stigmates invisible dans le biographies spirituelles du XVIIe siècle." In *Discorsi sulle stimmate dal Medioevo all'età contemporanea – Discours sur les stigmates du Moyen Âge à l'époque contemporaine.* Edited by Gábor Klaniczay. Rome: Edizioni di Storia e Letteratura = *Archivio italiano per la storia della pietà* 26 (2013): 239–58.

Giunta, Diega. "Gli attributi del Dottorato nella iconografia cateriniana." *Rivista dell'istituto nazionale d'archeologia e storia dell'arte* 6–7 (1983/84): 355–85.

———. "La questione delle stimmate alle origini della iconografia cateriniana e la fortuna del tema nel corso dei secoli." In *Con l'occhio e col lume.* Edited by Luigi Trenti e Bente Klange Addabbo, 319–48. Siena: Cantagalli, 1999.

———. "The Iconography of Catherine of Siena's Stigmata." In *A Companion to Catherine of Siena.* Edited by Carolyn Muessig, George Ferzoco, and Beverly Mayne Kienzle, 259–94. Leiden: Brill, 2012.

Graf, Katrin. "Les portraits d'auteur de Hildegarde de Bingen." *Scriptorium* 55, no. 2 (2001): 179–96.

———. *Bildnisse schreibender Frauen im Mittelalter, 9. bis Anfang 13. Jahrhundert.* Basel: Schwabe, 2002.

Grisé, C. Annette. "Catherine of Siena in Middle English Manuscripts: Transmission, Translations, and Transformation." In *The Theory and Practice of Translation in the Middle Ages.* Edited by Rosalyn Voaden et al., 149–59. Turnhout: Brepols, 2003.

Hale, Rosemary. "*Imitatio Mariae*: Motherhood Motifs in Devotional Memoirs." *Mystics Quarterly* 16 (1990): 193–203.

Hamburger, Jeffrey F. and Gabriela Signori. "The Making of a Saint: Catherine of Siena, Tommaso Caffarini, and the Others." In *Catherine of Siena: The Creation of a Cult.* Edited by Jeffrey F. Hamburger and Gabriela Signori, 1–22. Turnhout: Brepols, 2013.

Harvey, Margaret. *The English in Rome, 1362–1420: Portrait of an Expatriate Community.* Cambridge: Cambridge University Press, 1999.

Hedlund, Monica. "Vadstenapredikanter om Birgitta." In *Heliga Birgitta – budskapet och förebilden. Föredrag vid jubileumssymposiet i Vadstena 3–7 oktober 1991.* Edited by Alf Härdelin and Mereth Lindgren, 311–27. Stockholm: KVHAA, 1993.

Helbling, Hanno. *Katharina von Siena. Mystik und Politik.* Munich: Beck, 2000.

Hergemöller, Bernd-Ulrich. *Magnus versus Birgitta. Der Kampf der heiligen Birgitta von Schweden gegen König Magnus Eriksson.* Hamburg: HHL Verlag, 2003.

Herzig, Tamar. *Savonarola's Women: Visions and Reform in Renaissance Italy.* Chicago, IL: The University of Chicago Press, 2008.

———. *Christ Transformed into a Virgin Woman. Lucia Brocadelli, Heinrich Institoris, and the Defense of the Faith.* Rome: Edizioni di Storia e Letteratura, 2013.

Heß, Cordelia. *Heilige machen im spätmittelalterlichen Ostseeraum. Die Kanonisierungsprozesse von Birgitta von Schweden, Nikolaus von Linköping und Dorothea von Montau.* Berlin: Akademieverlag, 2008.

Hobbins, Daniel. *Authorship and Publicity Before Print: Jean Gerson and the Transformation of Learning.* Philadelphia: University of Pennsylvania Press, 2009.

Hodgson, Phyllis. "The Orcherd of Syon and the English Mystical Tradition." in *Proceedings of the British Academy* 50 (1964): 229–49.

Hoffmann, Erich. "Politische Heilige in Skandinavien und die Entwicklung der drei nordischen Reiche und Völker." In *Politik und Heiligenverehrung im Hochmittelalter.* Edited by Jürgen Petersohn, 277–324. Sigmaringen: Thorbecke, 1994.

Hohlstein, Michael. "'Sacra lipsana': The Relics of Catherine of Siena in the Context of Propagation, Piety, and Community." In *Catherine of Siena: The Creation of a Cult.* Edited by Jeffrey F. Hamburger and Gabriela Signori, 47–68. Turnhout: Brepols, 2013.

Holloway, Julia Bolton. "Saint Birgitta of Sweden, Saint Catherine of Siena: Saints, Secretaries, Scribes, Supporters." *Birgittiana* 1 (1996): 29–45.

Hollywood, Amy. "Feminist Studies in Christian Spirituality." In *Acute Melancholia and Other Essays: Mysticism, History, and the Study of Religion,* 96–116. New York: Columbia University Press, 2016.

———. "On Gender, Agency, and the Divine in Religious Historiography." In *Acute Melancholia and Other Essays: Mysticism, History, and the Study of Religion,* 117–27. New York: Columbia University Press, 2016.

Housley, Norman. *The Later Crusades, 1274–1580. From Lyons to Alcazar.* Oxford: Oxford University Press, 1992.

Hutchinson, Ann M. "What the Nuns Read: Literary Evidence from the English Bridgettine House, Syon Abbey." *Mediaeval Studies* 57 (1995): 207–22.

Huter, Carl. "Cristoforo Cortese in the Bodleian Library." *Apollo* January (1980): 10–17.

Irwin, Robert. *The Middle East in the Middle Ages: The Early Mamluk Sultanate, 1250–1382.* London: Croom and Helm, 1986.

Jansen, Katherine Ludwig. "Maria Magdalen: Apostolorum Apostola." In *Women Preachers and Prophets.* Edited by Beverly Mayne Kienzle and Pamela J. Walker, 57–96. Berkeley: University of California Press, 1998.

———. *The Making of the Magdalen. Preaching and Popular Devotion in the Later Middle Ages.* Princeton, NJ: Princeton University Press, 2001.

Jensen, Kurt Villads. "Martyrs, Total War, and Heavenly Horses." In *Medieval Christianity in the North: New Studies.* Edited by Kirsi Salonen, Kurt Villads Jensen, and Torstein Jørgensen, 89–120. Turnhout: Brepols, 2013.

Jungmayr, Jörg. "Ekstase und politische Mission. Die Stigmata der Caterina von Siena (1347–1380)." In *Zwischen Himmel und Erde. Körperliche Zeichen der Heiligkeit.* Edited by Waltraud Pulz et al., 61–77. Stuttgart: Steiner 2012.

Juster, Susan. "Mystical Pregnancy and Holy Bleeding. Visionary Experience in Early Modern Britain and America." *William and Mary Quarterly*, 3rd series 57 (2000): 249–88.

Kedar, Benjamin Z. *Crusade and Mission: European Approaches Towards the Muslims*. Princeton, NJ: Princeton University Press, 1984.

Kendrick, Laura. *Animating the Letter: The Figurative Embodiment of Writing from Late Antiquity to the Renaissance*. Columbus: Ohio State University Press, 1999.

Klaniczay, Gábor. *Holy Rulers and Blessed Princesses: Dynastic Cults in Medieval Central Europe*. Cambridge: Cambridge University Press, 2002.

———."Le stigmate di santa Margherita d'Ungheria: immagini e testi." *Iconographica. Rivista di iconografia medievale e moderna* 1 (2002): 16–31.

———. "The Process of Trance: Heavenly and Diabolic Apparitions in Johannes Nider's *Formicarius*." In *Procession, Performance, Liturgy, and Ritual*. Edited by Nancy van Deusen, 203–58. Ottava: Institute of Medieval Music, 2007.

———. "On the Stigmatization of Saint Margaret of Hungary." In *Medieval Christianity in Practice*. Edited by Miri Rubin, 274–84. Princeton, NJ: Princeton University Press, 2009.

——— ed. *Discorsi sulle stimmate dal Medioevo all'età contemporanea – Discours sur les stigmates du Moyen Âge à l'époque contemporaine*. Rome: Edizioni di Storia e Letteratura= *Archivio italiano per la storia della pietà* 26 (2013): 7–385.

———. "Using Saints: Intercession, Healing, Sanctity." In *The Oxford Handbook of Medieval Christianity*. Edited by John Arnold, 217–37. Oxford: Oxford University Press, 2014.

Kleinberg, Aviad M. *Prophets in Their Own Country: Living Saints and the Making of Sainthood in the Later Middle Ages*. Chicago: The University of Chicago Press, 1992.

Koch, Barbara. "Margaret Ebner." In *Medieval Holy Women in the Christian Tradition, c.1100–c.1500*. Edited by Alastair Minnis and Rosalynn Voaden, 393–410. Turnhout: Brepols, 2010.

Krafft, Ottfried. "Many Strategies and One Goal: The Difficult Road to the Canonization of Catherine of Siena." In *Catherine of Siena: The Creation of Cult*. Edited by Jeffrey F. Hamburger and Gabriela Signori, 25–45. Turnhout: Brepols, 2013.

Kraus, Matthew A. *Jewish, Christian, and Classical Exegetical Traditions in Jerome's Translation of the Book of Exodus*. Leiden: Brill, 2017.

Ladner, Gerhart B. "Homo Viator: Mediaeval Ideas about Alienation and Order." *Speculum* 42, no. 2 (1967): 233–59.

Lancellotto. "De monasterio Quartano." *Id. Historiae Olivetanae* II, 15 (Venice: 1623).

Lazzi, Giovanna and Paolo Vitti, eds. *Immaginare l'autore. Il ritratto del letterato nella cultura umanistica*. Florence: Polistampa, 2000.

Legassie, Shayne. *The Medieval Invention of Travel*. Chicago, IL: The University of Chicago Press, 2017.

LeGoff, Jacques. *The Birth of Purgatory*. Translated by Arthur Goldhammer. Chicago, IL: The University of Chicago Press, 1984.

Lehtonen, Tuomas M. S., Kurt Villads Jensen, with Janne Malkki and Katja Ritari, eds. *Medieval History Writing and Crusading Ideology.* Helsinki: Finnish Literature Society, 2005.

Leonardi, Lino. "Il problema testuale dell'espistolario cateriniano." In *Dire l'ineffabile. Caterina da Siena e il linguaggio della mistica. Atti del Convegno (Siena, 13–14 novembre 2003).* Edited by Lino Leonardi and Pietro Trifone, 71–90. Florence: SISMEL, Edizioni del Galluzzo, 2006.

Leoncini, Giovanni. "Un certosino del tardo Medioevo: don Stefano Maconi." In *Die Ausbreitung kartäusischen Lebens und Geistes im Mittelalter.* Analecta Cartusiana 63. Salzburg, 1990, vol. 1, 54–107.

Leopold, Antony. *How to Recover the Holy Land: The Crusade Proposals of the Late Thirteenth and Early Fourteenth Centuries.* Aldershot: Ashgate, 2000.

Lerner, Robert E. "Alfonso Pecha on Discriminating Truth about the Great Schism." In *Autorität und Wahrheit. Kirchliche Vorstellungen, Normen und Verfahren.* Edited by Gian Luca Potestà, 127–46. Munich: De Gruyter, 2012.

Lind, John H. "Magnus Eriksson som Birgittinsk Konge i Lyset af Russiske Kilder." In *Birgitta, hendes værk og hendes klostre i Norden.* Edited by Tore Nyberg, 103–28. Odense: Universitetsforlag, 1991.

———. "The Russian Testament of King Magnus Eriksson – A Hagiographic Text?" In *Medieval Spirituality in Scandinavia and Europe. A Collection of Essays in Honour of Tore Nyberg.* Edited by Lars Bisgaard et al., 195–212. Odense: Odense University Press, 2001.

Lindkvist, Thomas. "Crusades and Crusading Ideology in the Political History of Sweden." In *Crusade and Conversion on the Baltic Frontier, 1150–1500.* Edited by Alan V. Murray, 119–30. Aldershot and Burlington: Ashgate, 2001.

Lock, Peter. *The Routledge Companion to the Crusades.* New York and London: Routledge, 2006.

Luongo, F. Thomas. *The Saintly Politics of Catherine of Siena.* Ithaca, NY: Cornell University Press, 2006.

———. "Saintly Authorship in the Italian Renaissance: The Quattrocento Reception of Catherine of Siena's Letters." In *Catherine of Siena: The Creation of a Cult.* Edited by Jeffrey F. Hamburger and Gabriela Signori, 135–67. Turnhout: Brepols, 2013.

———. "Inspiration and Imagination: Inspired Authorship in the Early Manuscripts of the *Revelations* of Birgitta of Sweden." *Speculum* 93 (2018): 1102–50.

———. "God's Words, or Birgitta's? Birgitta of Sweden as Author." In *A Companion to Birgitta of Sweden and Her Legacy in the Later Middle Ages.* Edited by Maria H. Oen, 25–52. Leiden: Brill, 2019.

———. "Catherine of Siena, *Auctor*." In *Women Leaders and Intellectuals of the Medieval World.* Edited by Katie Bugyis, Kathryn Kerby-Fulton, and John Van Engen. Woodbridge: Boydell & Brewer [forthcoming].

Maier, Christoph T. *Preaching the Crusades: Mendicant Friars and the Cross in the Thirteenth Century.* Cambridge: Cambridge University Press, 1995.

Maître, Jacques. *Anorexies religieuses, anorexie mentale. Essai de psychanalyse sociohistorique. De Marie de l'Incarnation à Simone Weil.* Paris: Le Cerf, 2000.

Malm, Mats. *The Soul of Poetry Redefined: Vacillations of Mimesis from Aristotle to Romanticism.* Copenhagen: Museum Tusculanum Press, University of Copenhagen, 2012.

Marchetti, Valerio. "Il re bambino. Cronologia e geografia di un culto monarchico." In *Infanzie. Funzioni di un gruppo liminale del mondo classico all'Età moderna*. Edited by Ottavia Niccoli, 287–97. Florence: Ponte alle Grazie, 1993.

Matter, E. Ann. "Prophetic Patronageas Repression: Lucia Brocadelli da Narni and Ercole d'Este." In *Christendom and its Discontents: Exclusion, Persecution, and Rebellion, 1000–1500*. Edited by Scott L. Waugh and Peter D. Diehl, 168–76. Cambridge: Cambridge University Press, 1995.

Mazeika, Rasa and Loïc Chollet. "Familiar Marvels? French and German Crusaders and Chroniclers Confront Baltic Pagan Religions." *Francia* 43 (2016): 42–43.

Mazzoni, Cristina. "Angela of Foligno." In *Medieval Holy Women in the Christian Tradition, c.1100–c.1500*. Edited by Alastair Minnis and Rosalynn Voaden, 581–600. Turnhout: Brepols, 2010.

Mazzotta, Giuseppe. *Dante, Poet of the Desert: History and Allegory in the Divine Comedy*. Princeton, NJ: Princeton University Press, 1979.

Meersseman, Giles Gérard "Spirituali romani, amici di Caterina da Siena." In *Ordo fraternitatis. Confraternite e pietà dei laici nel Medioevo*. Edited by Gilles Gérard Meersseman and Gian Piero Pacini, vol. 1, 535–73. 3 vols. Rome: Herder, 1977.

Menozzi, Daniele. "La critica alla autenticità della Donazione di Costantino in un manoscritto della fine del XIV secolo." *Cristianesimo nella Storia* I (1980): 123–54.

Messerini, E. "Lo *scriptorium* di Fra Tommaso Caffarini," *S. Caterina da Siena* 19, no. 1 (1968): 15–21.

Mews, Constant J. "Thomas Aquinas and Catherine of Siena: Emotion, Devotion and Mendicant Spiritualities in the Late Fourteenth Century." *Digital Philology: A Journal of Medieval Cultures* 1, no. 2 (2012): 235–52.

Millet, Hélène. "Un réseau international d'ermites et de réformateurs en quête d'une nouvelle spiritualité dans la seconde moitié du XIVᵉ siècle." In *La circulation des élites européennes*. Edited by Henri Bresc, Fabrice d'Almeida, and Jean-Michel Sallmann, 100–22. Paris: Seli Arslan, 2002.

———. "Le *Liber dialogorum hierarchie subcœlestis* (1388)." In *Vaticana et medievalia. Études en l'honneur de Louis Duval-Arnould*. Edited by Jean-Marie Martin, Bernadette Martin-Hisard and Agostino Paravicini Bagliani, 367–94. Florence: SISMEL, Edizioni del Galluzzo, 2008.

Minnis, Alastair. *Medieval Theory of Authorship: Scholastic Literary Attitudes in the Later Middle Ages*. 2nd edn. Philadelphia: University of Pennsylvania Press, 2009.

———. "Religious Roles: Public and Private." In *Medieval Holy Women in the Christian Tradition, c.1100–c.1500*. Edited by Alastair Minnis and Rosalynn Voaden, 47–81. Turnhout: Brepols, 2010.

Miriello, Rosanna. *I manoscritti del monastero del Paradiso di Firenze*. Florence: SISMEL, Edizioni del Galluzzo, 2007.

Mittelalterliche Handschriften der Universitätsbibliothek Uppsala. Katalog über die C-Sammlung. Edited by Margarete Andersson-Schmitt, Håkan Hallberg, and Monica Hedlund, 8 vols. Uppsala: Uppsala University, 1988–95.

Mixson, James David and Bert Roest, eds. *A Companion to Observant Reform in the Late Middle Ages and Beyond*. Leiden: Brill, 2015.

Moerer, Emily Ann. "The Visual Hagiography of a Stigmatic Saint: Drawings of Catherine of Siena in the 'Libellus de Supplemento'." *Gesta* 44 (2005): 89–102.

Mollat, Guillaume. *The Popes at Avignon (1305–1378)*. London: Thomas Nelson, 1963.

Mooney, Catherine M. "*Imitatio Christi* or *Imitatio Mariae*? Clare of Assisi and Her Interpreters." In *Gendered Voices: Medieval Saints and Their Interpreters*. Edited by Catherine M. Mooney, 52–77. Philadelphia: University of Pennsylvania Press, 1999.

———. "Wondrous Words: Catherine of Siena's Miraculous Reading and Writing According to the Early Sources." In *Catherine of Siena: The Creation of a Cult*. Edited by Jeffrey F. Hamburger and Gabriela Signori, 262–87. Turnhout: Brepols, 2013.

Morris, Bridget. "The Monk-on-the-Ladder in Book v of St. Birgitta's *Revelaciones*." *Kyrkohistorisk Årsskrift* (1982): 95–107.

———. "Swedish Foreign Policy of the 1340s in the Balance: An Interpretation of Book IV chapter 2 of St. Bridget's *Revelations*." *Studies in St. Birgitta and the Brigittine Order* 1 (1993): 180–91.

———. *St Birgitta of Sweden*. Woodbridge: Boydell Press, 1999.

———. "Birgitta of Sweden and Giovanna of Naples: An Unlikely Friendship?" In *Santa Brigida, Napoli, l'Italia*. Edited by Olle Ferm, Alessandra Perriccioli Saggese, and Marcello Rotili, 22–33. Naples: Arte Tipografica Editrice, 2009.

Mouchel, Christian. *Les femmes de douleur. Maladie et sainteté dans l'Italie de la Contre-Réforme*. Paris: PUF, 2007.

Movrin, David. "The Beloved Disciple: Stephen Maconi and St. Catherine of Siena." *Annual of Medieval Studies at Central European University* 10 (2004): 45–53.

Muessig, Carolyn. "Prophecy and Song. Teaching and Preaching by Medieval Women." In *Women Preachers and Prophets through Two Millennia of Christianity*. Edited by Beverly Mayne Kienzle and Pamela J. Walker, 146–58. Berkeley: University of California Press, 1998.

———. "Catherine of Siena in Late Medieval Sermons." In *A Companion to Catherine of Siena*. Edited by Carolyn Muessig, George Ferzoco, and Beverly Mayne Kienzle, 203–26. Leiden: Brill, 2012.

———. "The Stigmata Debate in Theology and Art in the Late Middle Ages." In *The Authority of the Word: Reflecting on Image and Text in Northern Europe, 1400–1700*. Edited by Celeste Brusati, Karl Enenkel, and Walter Melion, 481–504. Leiden: Brill, 2012.

———. "Signs of Salvation: The Evolution of Stigmatic Spirituality before Francis of Assisi." *Church History* 82 (2013): 40–68.

Muessig, Carolyn, George Ferzoco, and Beverly Mayne Kienzle, eds. *A Companion to Catherine of Siena*. Leiden: Brill, 2012.

Murray, Alan V. "The Saracens of the Baltic: Pagan and Christian Lithuanians in the Perception of English and French Crusaders to Late Medieval Prussia." *Journal of Baltic Studies* 41, no. 4 (2010): 413–29.

Murray, Alan V., ed. *Crusade and Conversion on the Baltic Frontier 1150–1500*. Aldershot: Ashgate, 2001.

Nagy, Piroska. "Sensations et émotions d'une femme de passion: Lukarde d'Oberweimar († 1309)." In *Le sujet de l'émotion au Moyen Age*. Edited by Damien Boquet and Piroska Nagy, 323–53. Paris: Beauchesne, 2009.

Newman, Barbara. *From Virile Woman to WomanChrist*. Philadelphia: University of Pennsylvania Press, 1995.

Nieuwland, Jeannette. "Motherhood and Sanctity in the Life of Saint Birgitta of Sweden: An Insoluble Conflict?" In *Sanctity and Motherhood: Essays on Holy Mothers in the Middle Ages*. Edited by Anneke B. Mulder-Bakker, 297–330. New York: Garland, 1995.

Nocentini, Silvia. "Lo'scriptorium' di Tommaso Caffarini a Venezia." *Hagiographica* 12 (2005): 79–144.

———. "'Fare per lettera': le traduzioni Latine del *Libro di divina dottrina* di Caterina da Siena." *Studi medievali* 56, no. 2 (2015): 639–680.

———. "Guillemus Flete." In *C.AL.M.A. (Compendium Auctorum Latinorum Medii Aevi)*, vol. V, 27–28. Florence: SISMEL, Edizioni del Galluzzo, 2015.

———. "Il problema testuale del *Libro di divina dottrina* di Caterina da Siena: questioni aperte." *Revue d'histoire des Textes* 11 (2016): 255–94.

———. "Un eremita, due confessori, tre redazioni: i primordi dell'agiografia brigidina in Italia," *Hagiographica* 26 (2019): 289–330

Noffke, Suzanne. "The Writings of Catherine of Siena." In *A Companion to Catherine of Siena*. Edited by Carolyn Muessig, George Ferzoco, and Beverly Mayne Kienzle, 295–337. Leiden: Brill, 2012.

Nordenfalk, Carl. "Saint Bridget of Sweden as Represented in Illuminated Manuscripts." In *De Artibus Opuscula XL. Essays in Honor of Erwin Panofsky*. Edited by Millard Meiss, vol. 1, 371–93. 2 vols. New York: New York University Press, 1961.

———. "Der Inspirierte Evangelist." *Wiener Jahrbuch für Kunstgeschichte* 36 (1983): 175–90.

Nyberg, Tore. *Birgittinische Klostergründungen des Mittelalters*. Leiden: CWK Gleerup, 1965.

———. "Paradiso." *Birgittiana* 1 (1993): 9–14.

———. "The Canonization Process of St. Birgitta of Sweden." In *Procès de canonisation au Moyen Âge. Aspects juridiques et religieux – Medieval Canonization Processes. Legal and Religious Aspects*. Edited by Gábor Klaniczay, 67–85. Rome: École française de Rome, 2004.

Oen, Maria H. *The Visions of St. Birgitta: A Study of the Making and Reception of Images in the Later Middle Ages*. PhD dissertation, University of Oslo, 2015.

———. "The Iconography of *Liber celestis revelacionum*." In *A Companion to Birgitta of Sweden and Her Legacy in the Later Middle Ages*. Edited by Maria H. Oen, 186–222. Leiden: Brill, 2019.

Oertel, Christian. *The Cult of St Erik in Medieval Sweden: Veneration of a Royal Saint, Twelfth–Sixteenth Centuries*. Turnhout: Brepols, 2016.

Oexle, Otto Gerhard. "Utopisches Denken im Mittelalter: Pierre Dubois." *Historische Zeitschrift* 224 (1977): 293–339.

Ourliac, Paul. "Les Lettres à Charles V." In *Atti del Simposio Internazionale Cateriniano-Bernardiniano, Siena 17–20 Aprile, 1980*. Edited by Domenico Maffei and Paolo Nardi, 173–80. Siena: Accademia Senese degli Intronati, 1982.

Palazzo, Eric. "Le portrait d'auteur dans les manuscrits du Moyen Âge." In *Portraits d'écrivains. La représentation de l'auteur dans les manuscrits et les imprimés du Moyen Âge et de la première Renaissance*, 21–34. Paris:

Fédération française pour la coopération des bibliothèques, des métiers du livre et de la documentation, 2002.

Parsons, Gerald. *The Cult of Catherine of Siena. A Study in Civil Religion.* Aldershot: Ashgate, 2008.

Paviot, Jacques. *Projets de croisade, v. 1290–1330.* Paris: Académie des inscriptions et Belles-Lettres, 2008.

Petkov, Kiril. "The Rotten Apple and the Good Apples: Orthodox, Catholics, and Turks in Philippe de Mézières' crusading propaganda." *Journal of Medieval History* 23, no. 3 (1997): 255–70.

Petrucci, Enzo. "Bohier Pietro." In *Dizionario Biografico degli Italiani* 11 (1969): 193–203.

———. "L'ecclesiologia alternativa alla vigilia e all'inizio del grande scisma: S. Caterina da Siena e Pietro Bohier vescovo di Orvieto." In *Atti del Simposio Internazionale Cateriniano–Bernardiniano, Siena 17–20 aprile 1980.* Edited by Domenico Maffei and Paolo Nardi, 181–253. Siena: Accademia Senese degli Intronati, 1982.

Pezzini, Domenico. *The Translation of Religious Texts in the Middle Ages: Tracts and Rules, Hymns and Saints' Lives.* Bern: P. Lang, 2008.

———. "Il primo volgarizzamento Italiano delle *Rivelazioni* e degli altri scritti di S. Brigida: il codice I.V.25/26 della Biblioteca degli Intronati di Siena (1399)." In *Santa Brigida, Napoli, L'Italia.* Edited by Olle Ferm, Alessandra Perriccioli Saggese, and Marcello Rotili, 61–73. Naples: Arte tipografica editrice, 2009.

Philibert, Paul. "Roman Catholic Prayer: The *Novem modi orandi sancti Dominici.*" In *Contemplative Literature: A Comparative Sourcebook on Meditation and Contemplative Prayer.* Edited by Louis Komjathi, 547–91. New York: SUNY Press, 2015.

Piltz, Anders. "Magister Mathias of Sweden in his Theological Context: A Preliminary Survey." In *The Editing of Theological and Philosophical Texts from the Middle Ages.* Edited by Monika Asztalos, 137–60. Stockholm: Almqvist and Wiksell, 1986.

———. "Nostram naturam sublimaverat. Den liturgiska och teologiska bakgrunden till det birgittinska mariaofficiet." In *Maria i Sverige under tusen år. Föredrag vid symposiet i Vadsena 6–10 oktober 1994.* Edited by Sven-Erik Brodd and Alf Härdelin, 255–88. Skellefteå: Artos, 1996.

———. "Revelation and the Human Agent: St. Birgitta and the Process of Inspiration." In *Tongues and Texts Unlimited. Studies in Honour of Tore Janson on the Occasion of His Sixtieth Anniversary.* Edited by Hans Aili and Peter af Trampe, 181–88. Stockholm: Stockholms Universitet, Institutionen för klassiska språk, 2000.

———. "Birgitta and the Bible." In *A Companion to Birgitta of Sweden and her Legacy in the Middle Ages.* Edited by Maria H. Oen, 52–79. Leiden: Brill, 2019.

Pou y Marti, José M. *Visionarios, beguinos y fraticelos catalanes (siglos Xii–Xv).* Madrid: Colegio "Cardenal Cisneros," 1992.

Puma, Giulia. "Brigitte de Suède et Alfonso de Jaén: une 'amitié spirituelle'à la fin du XIV⁰ siècle." *Arzanà* 10 (2013): 329–64.

Renouard, Yves. *The Avignon Papacy: The Popes in Exile 1305–1403.* New York: Barnes & Noble Books, 1994 [1954].

Roberts, Ann M. "Chiara Gambacorta as Patroness of the Arts." In *Creative Women in Medieval and Early Modern Italy: A Religious and Artistic Renaissance.* Edited by E. Ann Matter and John Coakley, 120–54. Philadelphia: University of Pennsylvania Press, 1994.

———. *Dominican Women and Renaissance Art: The Convent of San Domenico of Pisa.* London and New York: Routledge, 2016.

Rollo-Koster, Joëlle. *Avignon and its Papacy, 1309–1417: Popes, Institutions, and Society.* New York: Rowman & Littlefield, 2015.

Rollo-Koster, Joëlle and Thomas H. Izbicki, eds. *A Companion to the Great Western Schism (1378-1417).* Leiden: Brill 2009.

Rousset, Paul. "Cathérine de Sienne et le problème de la croisade." *Revue Suisse d'histoire* 25 (1975): 499–513.

Rouxpetel, Camille. "Subiaco à l'épreuve du Grand schisme d'Occident: la mainmise espagnole sur le Sacro Speco (1378–1401)." In *Gli spazi della vita comunitaria.* Edited by Letizia Panni Ermini, 419–39. Spoleto: Centro Italiano di studi sull'alto medioevo, 2016.

———. "D'or ou de pourriture, les pommes de Philippe de Mézières." In *Philippe de Mézières et l'Europe. Nouvelle Histoire, nouveaux espaces, nouveaux langages.* Edited by Joël Blanchard and Renate Blumenfeld-Kosinski, 227–46. Geneva: Droz, 2017.

———. "Philhellénisme et réforme pendant le Grand schisme: Guillaume Saignet et les Grecs." In *Humanisme et politique en France à la fin du Moyen Âge. Hommage à Nicole Pons.* Edited by Carla Bozzolo, Claude Gauvard, and Hélène Millet, 123–39. Paris: Éditions de la Sorbonne, 2018.

Rubin, Miri. *Mother of God: A History of the Virgin Mary.* New Haven, CT: Yale University Press, 2009.

Rychterová, Pavlína. *Die Offenbarungen der heiligen Birgitta von Schweden. Eine Untersuchung zur alttschechischen Übersetzung des Thomas von Štítné.* Cologne: Böhlau, 2004.

Sahlin, Claire L. "A Marvelous and Great Exultation of the Heart: Mystical Pregnancy and Marian Devotion in Bridget of Sweden's Revelations." In *Studies in Saint Birgitta and the Brigittine Order.* Edited by James Hogg, vol. 1, 108–28. New York: Edwin Mellen, 1993.

———. *Birgitta of Sweden and the Voice of Prophecy.* Woodbridge: Boydell Press, 2001.

Salmesvuori, Päivi. *Power and Sainthood: The Case of Birgitta of Sweden.* New York: Palgrave MacMillan, 2014.

Sander-Olsen, Ulla, Tore Nyberg, and Per Sloth Carlsen, eds. *Birgitta Atlas: Saint Birgitta's Monasteries. Die Klöster der Heiligen Birgitta.* Uden: Societas Birgitta Europa, 2013.

Schein, Sylvia. "Bridget of Sweden, Margery Kempe, and Women's Jerusalem Pilgrimages in the Middle Ages." *Mediterranean Historical Review* 14, no. 1 (1999): 44–58.

Schultze, Dirk. "Translating St Catherine of Siena in Fifteenth-Century England." In *Catherine of Siena: The Creation of a Cult.* Edited by Jeffrey F. Hamburger and Gabriela Signori, 185–212. Turnhout: Brepols, 2013.

Scott, Karen. "St. Catherine of Siena, 'Apostola.'" *Church History* 61, no. 1 (1992): 34–46.

Sensi, Mario. "Il beato Tomasuccio: biografi, biografe e culto." In *Il b. Tommasuccio da Foligno, terziario francescano ed i movimenti religiosi popolari Umbri nel Trecento. Ciclo di conferenze alla Biblioteca Jacobilli (Foligno, 13–18 novembre 1978)*. Edited by Raffaele Pazzelli, 11–48. Rome: Ed. Analecta TOR, 1979.

———. "La regola di Niccolò IV dalla Costituzione 'Periculoso' alla bolla 'Pastoralis officii' (1298)." In *La "Supra montem" di Niccolò IV (1289): genesi e diffusione di una regola. Atti del V convegno di studi francescani (Ascoli Piceno, 26–27 ottobre 1987)*. Edited by Raffaele Pazzelli and Lino Temperini, 147–98. Rome: Ed. Analecta TOR, 1988.

———. "Alfonso Pecha e l'eremitismo italiano di fine secolo XIV." *Rivista di Storia della Chiesa in Italia* XLVII (1993): 51–80.

———. "*Mulieres in ecclesia*." *Storie di monache e bizzoche*. 2 vols. Spoleto: Fondazione Centro Italiano di studi sull'Alto Medioevo CISAM, 2010.

Setton, Kenneth M. *The Papacy and the Levant (1204–1571)*. Philadelphia: American Philosophical Society, 1976.

Simons, Walter. "Reading a Saint's Body: Rapture and Bodily Movement in the *Vitae* of Thirteenth-Century Beguines." In *Framing Medieval Bodies*. Edited by Sarah Kay & Miri Rubin, 10–23. Manchester: Manchester University Press, 1994.

———. *Cities of Ladies: Beguine Communities in the Medieval Low Countries*. Philadelphia: University of Pennsylvania Press, 2001.

Simons, Walter and J. E. Ziegler. "Phenomenal Religion in the Thirteenth Century and Its Image: Elisabeth Spalbeek and the Passion Cult." In *Women in the Church*. Edited by W. J. Sheils and Diana Wood, 117–26. Oxford: Basil Blackwell, 1990.

Smith, Lesley. "*Scriba, Femina*: Medieval Depictions of Women Writing." In *Women and the Book: Assessing the Visual Evidence*. Edited by Lesley Smith and Jane H.M. Taylor, 21–44. London and Toronto: The British Library and University of Toronto Press, 1996.

Sorelli, Fernanda. "La production hagiographique du dominicain Tommaso Caffarini." In *Faire croire. Modalités de la diffusion et de la réception des messages religieux du XIIᵉ au XVᵉ siècle*. Edited by André Vauchez, 189–200. Rome: École française de Rome, 1981.

———. *La santità imitabile. "Leggenda di Maria da Venezia" di Tommaso da Siena*. Venice: Deputazione di storia patria per le Venezie, 1984.

Staley, Lynn. "The Trope of the Scribe and the Question of Literary Authority in the Works of Julian of Norwich and Margery Kempe." *Speculum* 66 (1991): 820–38.

Stock, Brian. *The Implications of Literacy: Written Language and Models of Interpretation in the Eleventh and Twelfth Centuries*. Princeton, NJ: Princeton University Press, 1983.

Summit, Jennifer. "Women and Authorship." In *The Cambridge Companion to Medieval Women's Writing*. Edited by Carolyn Dinshaw and David Wallace, 91–108. Cambridge: Cambridge University Press, 2003.

Thorold, Algar. *The Dialogue of the Seraphic Virgin Catherine of Siena*. London: Kegan Paul, Trench, Trubner & Co., 1907.

Trexler, Richard. "The Stigmatized Body of Francis of Assisi: Conceived, Processed, Disappeared." In *Frömmigkeit im Mittelalter. Politisch-soziale Kontexte, visuelle Praxis, körperliche Ausdrucksformen*. Edited by Klaus Schreiner and Marc Müntz, 463–97. Munich: Wilhelm Fink, 2002.

Tyerman, Christopher. *God's War: A New History of the Crusades*. Cambridge, MA: Harvard University Press, 2006.

Tylus, Jane. *Reclaiming Catherine of Siena: Literacy, Literature, and the Signs of Others*. Chicago, IL: The University of Chicago Press, 2009.

———. "Mystical Literacy: Writing and Religious Women in Late Medieval Italy." In *A Companion to Catherine of Siena*. Edited by Carolyn Muessig, George Ferzoco, and Beverly Mayne Keinzle, 155–84. Leiden: Brill, 2012.

———. "Writing versus Voice: Tommaso Caffarini and the Production of a Literate Catherine." In *Catherine of Siena: The Creation of a Cult*. Edited by Jeffrey F. Hamburger and Gabriela Signori, 291–312. Turnhout: Brepols, 2013.

———. "Parole pellegrine. L'ospitalità linguistica nel Rinascimento." In *L'ospite del libro: Sguardi sull'ospitalità*. Edited by Nicola Catelli and Giovanna Rizzarelli, 13–26. Lucca: Facci Editore, 2015.

Urban, William L. *The Baltic Crusades*. 2nd edn. Chicago, IL: Lithuanian Research and Studies Center, 1994.

Vailati Schonenburg Waldenburg, Grazia. "Le Rivelazioni di Santa Brigida MS. I V 25/26 della Biblioteca Comunale di Siena." In *La miniatura italiana in età romanica e gotica. Atti del I congresso di storia della miniatura italiana*. Edited by Grazia Vailati Schonenburg Waldenburg, 553–74. Florence: Olschki, 1979.

Vauchez, André. "Les stigmates de Saint François et leurs détracteurs dans les derniers siècles du moyen âge." *Mélanges de l'École française de Rome* 80 (1968): 595–625.

———. *La Sainteté en occident aux derniers siècles du Moyen Age, d'après les procès de canonisation et les documents hagiographiques*. Rome: École française de Rome, 1981.

———. "Sainte Brigitte de Suède et sainte Catherine de Sienne. La mystique et l'église aux dernier siècles du Moyen Age." In *Temi e problemi nella mistica trecentesca*, 227–48. Todi: Accademia Tudertina, 1983.

———. *The Laity in the Middle Ages: Religious Beliefs and Devotional Practices*. Edited by Daniel E. Bornstein. Translated by Margery J. Schneider. Notre Dame, IN: University of Notre Dame Press, 1993.

———. "The Reaction of the Church to Late Medieval Mysticism and Prophecy." In *The Laity in the Middle Ages: Religious Beliefs and Devotional Practices*. Edited by Daniel E. Bornstein, translated by Margery J. Schneider, 243–53. Notre Dame, IN: University of Notre Dame Press, 1993.

———. *Sainthood in the Later Middle Ages*. Translated by Jean Birrell. New York: Cambridge University Press, 1997.

———. *Francis of Assisi: The Life and Afterlife of a Medieval Saint*. New Haven, CT: Yale University Press, 2012.

———. *Catherine de Sienne. Vie et passions*. Paris: Cerf, 2015.

Voaden, Rosalynn. *God's Words, Women's Voices: The Discernment of Spirits in the Writing of Late-Medieval Women Visionaries*. York: York Medieval Press, 1999.

———. "Mysticism and the Body." In *The Oxford Handbook of Medieval Christianity*. Edited by John H. Arnold, 396–412. Oxford: Oxford University Press, 2014.

Warr, Cordelia. "Re-reading the Relationship between Devotional Images, Visions, and the Body: Clare of Montefalco and Margaret of Città di Castello." *Viator* 38 (2007): 217–49.

———. "Visualizing Stigmata: Stigmatic Saints and Crises of Representation in Late Medieval and Early Modern Italy." *Studies in Church History* 47 (2011): 228–47.

Williams-Krapp, Werner. *Die Deutschen und Niederländischen Legendare des Mittelalters. Studien zu Ihrer Überlieferungs-, Text- und Wirkungsgeschichte.* Tübingen: Niemeyer, 1986.

———. "Die Bedeutung der reformierten Klöster des Predigerordens für das literarische Leben in Nürnberg in 15. Jahrhunderts." In *Studien und Texte zur literarischen und materiellen Kultur der Frauenklöster im späten Mittelalter. Ergebnisse eines Arbeitsgesprächs in der Herzog August Bibliothek Wolfenbüttel, 24.-26. Febr. 1999.* Edited by Falk Eisermann, Eva Schlotheuber and Volker Honemann, 311–29. Leiden: Brill, 2004.

———. "*Wir lesent daz vil in sölichen sachen swerlich betrogen werdent.* Zur monastischen Rezeption von mystischer Literatur im 14. und 15. Jahrhundert." In *Nonnen, Kanonissen und Mystikerinnen. Religiöse Frauengemeinschaften in Süddeutschland. Beiträge zur interdisziplinären Tagung vom 21. bis 23. September 2005 in Frauenchimiensee.* Edited by Eva Schlotheuber, Helmut Flachenecker and Ingrid Gardill, 263–78. Göttingen: Vandenhoeck & Ruprecht, 2008.

Zancan, Marina. "Lettere di Caterina da Siena." In *Letteratura italiana. Le opere,* vol. 1, *Dalle origini al Cinquecento.* Edited by Alberto Asor Rosa, 593–633. Turin: Einaudi, 1992.

———. "Lettere di Caterina da Siena. Il testo, la tradizione, l'interpretazione." *Annali d'italianistica, Women Mystic Writers* 13 (1995): 151–61.

Zarri, Gabriella. *Le sante vive. Profezie di corte e devozione femminile tra '400 e '500.* Turin: Rosenberg & Sellier, 1990.

Index

Note: Page numbers followed by "n" denote endnotes.

For Product Safety Concerns and Information please contact our EU
representative GPSR@taylorandfrancis.com
Taylor & Francis Verlag GmbH, Kaufingerstraße 24, 80331 München, Germany